To God Alone Be Glory

TO GOD ALONE
BE GLORY

The Story and Sources of the
Book of Common Worship

Harold M. Daniels

Geneva Press
Louisville, Kentucky

Scripture quotations, unless otherwise indicated, are from the New Revised Standard Version of the Bible, copyright © 1989 by the Division of Christian Education of the National Council of the Churches of Christ in the U.S.A. and are used by permission.

Scripture quotations marked NEB are taken from *The New English Bible,* © The Delegates of the Oxford University Press and The Syndics of the Cambridge University Press, 1961, 1970. Used by permission.

Book design by Sharon Adams
Cover design by LMNOP/Eric Handel

First edition
Published by Geneva Press
Louisville, Kentucky

This book is printed on acid-free paper that meets the American National Standards Institute Z39.48 standard. ⊗

PRINTED IN THE UNITED STATES OF AMERICA

03 04 05 06 07 08 09 10 11 12 — 10 9 8 7 6 5 4 3 2 1

Library of Congress Cataloging-in-Publication Data

Daniels, Harold M., 1927-
    To God alone be glory : the story and sources of the Book of common worship / Harold M. Daniels.— 1st ed.
        p. cm.
    Includes bibliographical references.
    ISBN 0-664-50235-0 (alk. paper)
    1. Presbyterian Church (U.S.A.). Book of common worship (1993). 2. Presbyterian Church (U.S.A.)—Liturgy—Texts—History and criticism. 3. Cumberland Presbyterian Church—Liturgy—Texts—History and criticism. I. Title.

    BX8969.5 .D36 2003
    264'.05137—dc21

                                                                    2002073473

To all
who across one and a half centuries
have sought to restore
among American Presbyterians
a liturgy that is
truly reformed
and truly catholic

Contents

Preface   ix
Acknowledgments   xv

Part I. The Story of the *Book of Common Worship*   1
  1. Rebuilding the Church from the Ground Up   3
  2. A Book of Services Is Recovered   21
  3. Liturgical Reform in the Mid-Twentieth Century   34
  4. A New Book of Services Is Called For   48
  5. The *Book of Common Worship* Is Prepared   56
  6. The *Book of Common Worship:* What's New?   67
  7. Future Service Books   82
  8. Eucharistic Recovery, the Centerpiece of Liturgical Reform   92
  9. Four Primary Liturgical Reforms   107
 10. The Promise for Renewal   127

Part II. The Sources of the *Book of Common Worship*   141
  Introduction   143
  Abbreviations   147
  Glossary   152
  1. Commentary on Preparation for Worship   171
  2. Commentary on the Service for the Lord's Day   175
  3. Commentary on Resources for the Liturgical Year   190
  4. Commentary on Baptism and Reaffirmation of the Baptismal Covenant   213
  5. Commentary on Daily Prayer   219
  6. Commentary on the Psalms   232
  7. Commentary on Prayers for Various Occasions   240
  8. Commentary on Christian Marriage   247

 9. Commentary on The Funeral: A Service of Witness to
    the Resurrection   250
10. Commentary on Pastoral Liturgies   254
11. Commentary on Calendar and Lectionaries   258

Notes   261
For Further Reading   279
Index of Sources   283
Index of Subjects   296

Preface

Across the ages three books have nurtured the church's life—Bible, hymnbook, and service book—the church's Scripture, the church's song, the church's prayer.

But to speak of them simply as books is to miss what is important about them. They are not merely books. Unlike other books written to inform or entertain, these books occasion an *event* in the community of faith. Their use is the principal means by which the faith community encounters the living God. They nurture us in the faith. They loosen our tongues in praise. They kindle our hearts in prayer.

The church's Scripture is at the center of our life together. A book of wondrous richness, the Bible recounts the faith story from its dawning to the formation and early growth of the church. Here are stories of the acts of God, told and retold by ancient peoples—contained in scrolls unrolled and read in the assemblies of God's people, in illuminated manuscripts laboriously copied in monastery scriptoriums, in elaborately bound volumes printed on the earliest printing presses, in cherished family Bibles. Here are admonitions to keep God's law; the chronicles of the history of the people of God; the proclamations of prophets declaring God's justice and mercy; Gospels announcing the good news of God's coming to dwell among us in Jesus Christ; Jesus' miracles and teachings, his suffering, dying, and rising; pastoral letters to the earliest Christian churches.

The Bible bearing witness to the living Word, Jesus Christ, "in whom are hidden all the treasures of wisdom and knowledge" (Col. 2:3) is as it has been through the centuries, a living Word spoken to a living community, the fellowship of believers.

Gathered before this book, a diverse people of faith are made one. An Orthodox priest reading from a Gospel book covered with precious metal and adorned with jewels, processing into the midst of the people, surrounded by flickering torches, enveloped in the smoke of incense; an evangelist, shouting calls to repentance, Bible clutched in hand, strolling back and forth before a crowd enmassed in a public stadium; nuns embodying the compassion of Jesus bringing a healing touch to the fever ridden; advocates of justice for the poor, echoing the cries of the prophets before the centers of economic power; a monastic community praying the daily office silently contemplating a reading from Scripture; a faithful pastor guiding her flock into faithful discipleship in studying the Scripture. Although there are vast differences in understanding how the Bible was inspired and how it is to be interpreted, the Bible is for all Christians the source for shaping faith and life.

As the Scriptures are opened to be read, Eastern Orthodox Christians hear the proclamation, "Wisdom! Let us attend!" Attend to the wisdom of all Wisdom— Holy Wisdom that transforms sinners, humbles the powerful, lifts the lowly, and guides us in our daily walk as disciples. So, as we begin the reading of this book in our assemblies, we call the people to attend to that Wisdom, echoing the seer on the Isle of Patmos proclaiming a word from God to the ancient churches: "Hear what the Spirit is saying to the churches." We listen not simply to learn the contents of Scripture. We listen with mind and heart, opening our lives to the Word, that the ancient story may become our story, our judgment, assuring us of God's grace and forgiveness, giving direction and meaning to life. Through it the Holy Spirit speaks today, as in ages past. The words of Scripture, spoken in the midst of our assemblies is thus *an event, a living encounter* with the God who is the Alpha and the Omega, the beginning and the end.

The church's book of song is also essential to our life together. Music is one of God's greatest gifts to humankind. When deep feeling rises within, when emotions overwhelm, words burst into song. We sing when we are happy, for words alone cannot contain our joy. When life's burdens weigh upon us, our load is lightened when prayer is voiced in song.

In the worship of God, words alone are not enough. Sacred verse sung to melody lifts us above the ordinary into the presence of God. When we reach beyond the capacity of speech to express the emotional depths of our prayer, music alone can draw from the depths of our spirits that language which surpasses all spoken words. Transcending common discourse, sacred song gives fervency to the deepest yearnings of our hearts and intensity to our prayer; it enables our praise to soar. It reaches beyond the rational, touching reality that our minds cannot fully know this side of eternity. Philip H. Pfatteicher, a Lutheran liturgical scholar, expressed this when he wrote: "That which words and reason cannot reach is touched by music, for music can see the invisible and understand the incomprehensible."[1] Through music we encounter God in the deepest recesses of our being.

It may be a translation of a Latin or Greek hymn from the third or fourth century, a metrical psalm from the sixteenth-century Reformation, a seventeenth-century German chorale, an eighteenth-century hymn of Isaac Watts or Charles Wesley, a hymn of a contemporary writer, a Gloria, a Kyrie, a Sanctus, or other sung response integral to worship, repeated Sunday after Sunday. Sacred song from whatever time and place is a means by which we offer God our prayer in this time and place.

Sacred song, spanning the length of Christian history, embraces our deepest hunger, our highest praise, our most fervent prayer. It employs our voices in singing praise and offering prayer to the God who created us, who in Jesus Christ redeemed us, and whose Spirit guides us into the way of truth, peace, justice, and joy. When sung by the faithful gathered to worship God, the church's book of song, its hymns, psalms, and responses, become a living, transforming *event, a living encounter* with the God who is beyond all that we can imagine.

Across the centuries, the church has cherished another book—its book of prayer. We ordinarily refer to it as a service book, or book of services. It preserves the ordering of the liturgy that has been handed down to us from earliest times. It passes on to us prayers of the faithful, prayers that have survived the erosions of time. It gives us prayers that transcend the divisions of the church. It joins us in prayer with the faithful throughout the world of our time. We are thus united in prayer with the faithful in every place, in every time and in every circumstance. This book breathes with a sense of the communion of the saints.

Here is the church's prayer—in sacraments through which God acts in and for us now, in our baptism and in our communion in Christ's body and blood, when we celebrate the mighty acts of God in festivals and seasons, when we are married, when we are buried, in ministry with the sick and the dying, in every situation of life, in the stillness as we quietly wait before God in the morning, evening, or night.

This book of prayer is more than a book of words, for its prayers engage our hearts in prayer. They become our prayers. Through them we confess our sins, express adoration of God rising from our hearts, intercede for the church, the world and those in need, make our supplication for the abundance of God's grace, praise God for all that is true, good, and beautiful, and ask for strength to be faithful in God's service.

Joined in prayer with the long continuum of the faithful through the ages, and with all of the baptized, our prayer becomes *an event, a living encounter* that engages our whole being in the worship of God. While the prayers of the church's book of services do not replace the prayers rising from the heart in the immediacy of a moment, they provide depth and direction to all our praying.

The church's Scripture, song, and prayer—here are the sources that shape the defining moment of the church's life, its worship. Rooted in Scripture, combining movement and gesture, carefully crafted words, sacramental drama, and sacred music, the liturgy touches the deepest springs of the human spirit. Here at the life-giving center of the church's life is the promise of the renewal of our lives in loving and serving God.

The book of the church's prayer is the focus of this volume.

It is a surprise to some to learn that Presbyterians have a book of services and prayers. In matters of worship, we speak of American Presbyterians as a "directory church," rather than a "prayer book church." In the tradition established by the seventeenth-century Westminster Assembly, Presbyterians have maintained a directory for worship to guide them in shaping worship. A directory for worship forms a major part of the church's *Book of Order,* thereby having constitutional authority.

But American Presbyterians also have a book of services, the first edition of which appeared in 1906, the result of reforms beginning early in the nineteenth century. The General Assembly authorizes its revisions and endorses its use. Unlike the directory for worship, which has the force of church law, the book of services is provided for "voluntary use." However, the church's directory for worship and its service book are closely linked. In fact, it was the emergence of the service book in the twentieth century that rescued the use of a directory, which had long been neglected in the church's life.

The purpose of the directory is something other than providing orders and liturgical texts. It sets forth guidelines for ordering worship and provides theological underpinning for worship. Like a levee holding back a river from flooding its banks, it sets the bounds within which faithful worship shall take place. The book of services, on the other hand, gives body to the directory's guidelines by providing orders and liturgical texts. Directory and service book are interdependent. Together they provide the liturgical standards of the church.

Before the Westminster Assembly, service books were a valued part of the liturgical tradition of our spiritual ancestors in England and Scotland. This book tells the story of the recovery of a book of services by American Presbyterians, tracing it through its several incarnations, and most particularly the *Book of Common Worship* commended to the church by the 1993 General Assemblies of the Presbyterian Church (U.S.A.) and the Cumberland Presbyterian Church. (Unless the context makes it clear which edition is being referred to, wherever the title *Book of Common Worship* appears throughout this book, it refers to the 1993 edition. Ordinarily, earlier editions are distinguished from the 1993 edition by including the year of publication.)

This book also seeks to set forth the agenda for liturgical reform embodied in the *Book of Common Worship,* identifying those aspects of renewal most crucial to the renewal of the church's life. It provides information enabling those who use the *Book of Common Worship* to have a greater appreciation of the place of a book of services in the Reformed tradition, and how it can shape our discipleship.

Since my college and seminary years I have had a growing appreciation of the liturgy of the church catholic. However, it began to bloom most fully in 1957 with a gift. That gift was my first copy of *The Book of Common Worship* (1946 edition), given to me by a friend, Dr. G. Christie Swain, then pastor of First Presbyterian Church, Spokane, Washington. Taking a copy, he opened it and boldly inscribed it, "With Good Wishes, G. Christie Swain." I was a very new Presbyterian, the culmination of many years of wrestling as to what branch of Christ's church was where I truly belonged. As he gave me the book, he said, "You may never use this, but, still, you just might find it of value."

I did use it, and found it of great value. From the very beginning of my ministry as a Presbyterian pastor, I faithfully used *The Book of Common Worship* in preparing and leading worship. Academic studies in liturgics and in pastoral ministry followed. When it was published in 1970, the congregation I served quickly embraced *The Worshipbook*. Liturgical studies and continuing worshiping with the people of faith have given me an ever deepening love for the liturgy, and especially an appreciation of the evolution of Reformed liturgy, its patristic roots, its reform in the sixteenth century, and its continuing reform in our time. The story of that evolution and reform is the focus of this volume.

While much that follows in chapters 1 through 8 of part 1 has appeared in various articles in publications with limited circulation, this material has been thoroughly revised, updated, and organized to present in a single resource an overview of the development and objectives underlying the *Book of Common Worship*. There is also much new material, particularly reflections on the continuing liturgical reformation. The result is essentially a new work.

The second part of the book, titled "The Sources of the *Book of Common Worship*" provides commentary and information concerning texts in the *Book of Common Worship*. While the Acknowledgments section of the *Book of Common Worship* cites the immediate source of the texts by acknowledging permissions to reprint copyrighted material, it does not inform the user of the rich tradition lying behind many of the texts. This section seeks to provide background as to a text's original source, biblical allusions contained in the text, important aspects of the text, and occurrences of the text in some other English-language service books, particularly those within the Reformed tradition. Such information can contribute to a greater appreciation of the liturgy, adding depth and meaning.

I am grateful to my wife, Marie, who has with meticulous care proofread the manuscript in its various stages. I am grateful also to those who have encouraged me in the project, especially former staff who followed me in the Office of Worship, Gláucia Vasconcelos-Wilkey, Dennis Hughes, and Paul Detterman. I also gratefully appreciate the constructive suggestions given me by Hal and Martha Hopson, Robert and Patricia Fort, and Aurelia Fule, who reviewed the final draft of the last chapter of this book. I am indebted to Joseph D. Small III and Martha Moore-Keish of the Congregational Ministries Division, who have been advocates for me in facilitating its publication. And to all who have instilled within me the importance of faith and worship, past teachers, colleagues (both Reformed and ecumenical) with whom I have been joined in advocating liturgical reform, and parishioners in the congregations I have served as pastor who have taught me what was important to them in matters of faith. For their enrichment, I will forever be grateful.

H.M.D.

Advent, 2000

Acknowledgments

Grateful acknowledgment is made to the following for permission to reproduce copyrighted material.

Dr. Eva Fleischner, for "Native American Greeting."

Anglican Digest, for "Fantasy" by the Rt. Rev. Robert E. Terwilliger (vol. 32, no. 6).

Vanguard, for portions of the author's article "The Book of Common Worship" (vol. 30, no. 3 [July 1993]).

American Presbyterians: the Journal of Presbyterian History, for permission to incorporate into the text revisions of portions of the author's article "Service Books among American Presbyterians" (vol. 71, no. 3 [1993]).

Reformed Liturgy & Music, for permission to incorporate into the text revisions of portions of the following articles by the author: "Re-building the Church from the Ground Up" (vol. 30, no. 1 [1996]); "Presbyterian Worship: Directories and Service Books" (vol. 23, no. 4 [1989]); "The Story of the Process Leading to the New Service Book" (vol. 26., no. 3 [1992]); "General Assembly Commends Book of Common Worship (1993)" (vol. 27, no. 1 [1993]); "Book of Common Worship (1993): What's New?" (vol. 27, no. 1 [1993]); "The Norm of Christian Worship: Word and Eucharist" (vol. 29, no. 3 [1995]).

North American Academy of Liturgy, for permission to incorporate into the text revisions of portions of the author's response upon the occasion of his reception of the Academy's 1995 Berakah Award, published in *Proceedings of the North American Academy of Liturgy, Annual Meeting, Boston, Mass., 5–8 January 1995* (reprinted in *Reformed Liturgy & Music,* vol. 29, no. 1 [1995]).

Perspectives: A Journal of Reformed Thought for permission to quote from an article by Joan Zwagerman Curbow, "Honey in the Rock: Liturgy as Conversion" (August–September 1999) (reprinted in *Reformed Liturgy & Music,* vol. 33, no. 4 [1999]).

Abingdon Press for permission to quote from Stanley Hauerwas and William H. Willimon, *Resident Aliens: Life in the Christian Colony* (1989).

The Princeton Seminary Bulletin for permission to quote from an article by Lawrence Hull Stookey, "Baptism Rites in the *Book of Common Worship* (1993)" (vol. XVI, No. 2 New Series [1995]).

PART I
THE STORY OF THE
BOOK OF COMMON WORSHIP

Chapter 1

Rebuilding the Church from the Ground Up

I was speaking with a friend before a worship conference held shortly after the *Book of Common Worship* was published. My friend pointed to a copy of that book and said, "This is the blueprint for rebuilding the church from the ground up."

I've given a lot of thought to that comment. It brought to mind a little book I read over thirty years ago. The book was published before most church leaders acknowledged there was a crisis in the church, a concern finding urgency only after memberships and budgets persisted in decline. Writing from within the Reformed tradition, its author, Geddes MacGregor, presented a clear case that Protestantism in our time has lost the vision of the Reformers. He wrote:

> None of the sixteenth-century Reformers would find himself at home in any of the churches that claim the Reformation heritage. Nor would this be due merely to the passage of four centuries and the inevitable changes this must naturally bring about; the ethos of modern Protestantism would be in many ways more repugnant to the aims of the Reformers than were the abuses in the medieval Church against whose corruptions they so vigorously protested.[1]

He stated that the "heirs of the Reformation are guilty of nothing less than apostasy from the spirit of the Reformation and consequently from Christianity itself,"[2] because of the fact that the "essential, ontological reality of the Church" has largely been lost from church life. He declared that in spite of "the most splendid principles of reform, theological and practical," the church "has in practice all but lost the living reality of the Church."[3] He asserted:

> For all the noble achievements within the Reformation heritage, we are in some ways—ways they would have accounted essential—more remote from their ideals than ever was the Church whose corruptions evoked their protests.[4]
>
> No institution on earth can survive such a widespread loss of its own ideals of perfection. If it is a purely human institution, it will decay and die. If it is—as we believe the Church to be—the very handiwork of the living God, it may indeed decay through human sin; but He [sic] who created it will revive it, and for us this is only another way of saying that the next Reformation is coming.[5]

This was a hard hitting indictment. But it also expressed hope for the church that opened itself to the Holy Spirit's renewing power. He identified three basic elements that are crucial to the reformation of Protestantism:

First, a recovery of discipline in the church's life. To be Christ's disciples is to heed his invitation to "Take my yoke upon you, and learn from me" (Matt. 11:29). Discipleship shared in common involves a practice of daily living embracing serious theological reflection, and being so engaged in the faith that it shapes the way we think and act, what we do or do not do, how we live and how we die—a discipline shaped by Scripture, and the wisdom of the church.

Second, a recovery of the nurturing of the interior life. This is what our ancestors called piety, or sanctification, and what many Christians today mean when they speak of spirituality. It is the nurturing of our spirits through prayer, contemplation, and listening for the Spirit's speaking through the Scripture. It is seeking to live in harmony with God who is the ultimate source of meaning and purpose for all of life.

Third, a recovery of the church's liturgy, flowing out of the essential reality of what the church is. Only such a liturgy "will be rich enough to be, like the Church of God itself, ever old yet ever new."[6] Whenever the liturgy does not flow out of the essential nature of the church, it lacks integrity. This is particularly tragic, because it is in worship that the church's life is most clearly expressed. Without a strong sense of the church as the body of Christ, its worship will be distorted. The recovery of the church's liturgy is therefore crucial to the reforming of the church.

MacGregor furthermore reminded his readers that the heart of the liturgy is the Lord's Supper, "the Sacred Feast of His love." Recalling Calvin's great disappointment in failing to establish the Sacrament as the normal weekly liturgy, he observed,

> [W]hat is perhaps the most remarkable irony in the history of the Christian Church, the form of service that came to be adopted as the norm in the Reformed tradition, even at its best, was a liturgical derivation of a late medieval and somewhat debased form of the Mass technically called *missa sicca,* a "dry" Mass.[7]

In other words, "a supperless Supper."[8]

MacGregor underscored the recovery of discipline as foundational to both the recovery of the interior life and the recovery of the liturgy. Efforts to reform the church's worship will have superficial results, unless worship is accompanied by a disciplined church life. Regretfully he observed that "we are on the whole by no means disciplined in the Spirit of Christ," and that "many among us . . . openly mock every attempt to deepen personal spiritual life, every venture to recover the joyful splendor and solemnity of fully sacramental devotion, every effort to submit Christ's flock to Christ's yoke."[9]

MacGregor set forth the recovery of these three basic elements—discipline, the interior life, and the church's liturgy—as the conditions of the church's survival.

Published early in the work of the committee responsible for *The Worshipbook,* this book made a powerful impact on the committee's work. Upon reading the book, one of the committee members gasped, "My Presbyterian hide is hanging in great patches," and recommended that the committee give "serious, if critical" attention to MacGregor's book.[10] The central message of this prophetic book perhaps has even greater urgency today than when it was written four decades ago.

While the primary focus of this book is upon the recovery of the church's liturgy, the need for the church to recover both discipline and the interior life is never far from the surface.

REFORM AND RENEWAL

Many will agree that there is a problem with worship in most Protestant churches. Protestant worship has lost much of the integrity it once had. Such a loss is a serious matter, for whenever the liturgy fails to manifest Christ's living presence, discipleship is dwarfed and spirits shrivel. But the problem with the church's worship is symptomatic of a deeper problem, an erosion of an understanding of and commitment to the essential reality of what the church is.

It was in response to this that the *Book of Common Worship* was created. The underlying concern was a desire to produce a book of services that would contribute to the church's renewal. This was explicitly stated in 1980 when the Presbyterian General Assembly initiated the project. It expressed its hope that the book, and the process leading to its completion, "would provide a new instrument for the renewal of the church at its life-giving center."[11] This concern pervaded every step of the book's creation.

Upon publication of the *Book of Common Worship* in 1993, this hope was clearly stated in the preface (emphasis added):

> In an age dominated by individualism and secularism, it is particularly important to embrace forms of worship that are firmly rooted in the faith and foster a strong communal sense of being united with God, with the community of faith in every time and place, and with a broken world in need of God's healing touch. In other words, *the concern for the reform of worship is, above everything else, a concern for the renewal of the church.*[12]

Two important words thus describe the guiding light in the preparation of the *Book of Common Worship*: reform and renewal.

The focus of the word *reform* is embodied in the cherished motto *Ecclesia reformata semper reformanda* (The church reformed, always to be reformed). The essential meaning of the motto is that the church is reformed not simply because it emerged from the sixteenth-century Reformation; the church is reformed when it lives in the recognition that it is constantly under the judgment of God and therefore always needs reformation, needs to reform its life according to the Word of God.[13]

This is in sharp contrast to the chameleon-like relationship with the secular culture that the church sometimes takes, always changing to be in harmony with the dominant culture, letting it shape what the church is and does, and then, curiously, passing this off as reform. While we serve and witness within the culture, the church's relentless need for reform comes not from the culture, but from the persistent demands for faithful discipleship.

The ultimate focus of the word *renewal* is upon the Holy Spirit—the Giver of Life—giving new life to the church. From this perspective, reform and renewal are inseparably linked. Though the words are often used interchangeably, renewal is the promise of reform.

All of our efforts toward liturgical renewal, and elaboration of the theology that attends it, aim at re-centering the church's life so that its worship once again becomes the life-giving source of all that the church believes and does. Lutheran liturgical scholar Gordon Lathrop describes the efforts for liturgical renewal as the clearing out of a water spring to allow the water to flow more freely. He writes: "By 'Renewal' we can only mean that the spring that has poured out water for generations of Christians might, once again, for our time, be cleared out so that the water might flow."[14]

Reforming the church's life in faithfulness to the gospel of Jesus Christ is a constant need in every generation. Without diligence in *re*form, the church becomes *de*formed. The continuing need for reform and renewal is thus an agenda of great urgency.

COMMON WORSHIP

How then can the *Book of Common Worship* be "the blueprint for rebuilding the church from the ground up"? How can it be "an instrument for the renewal of the church"? A clue is in the title. While "common worship" designates an ordering of worship that is shared in common, the words have deeper levels of meaning. These dimensions of meaning make the *Book of Common Worship* culturally subversive wherever the culture surrounding us is dominated by a self-serving individualism and a secularism that finds no meaning beyond our human devices.

Common

The word *common* was restored to the title of the church's book of services because it underscores a fundamental aspect of the nature of the church and its worship. The word *common* is an important word. From that root word comes a whole host of words that express life together as a body, such as communal, commune, communion, community. The word is important because it speaks of a basic understanding of human life and the very nature of the church. The word is thus the antithesis of the radical individualism that dominates contemporary culture. Individualism tears at the very fabric of our society and gnaws at the foundations of the church, threatening its very essence. Much of popular religion today feeds on the individualism of our culture and so undermines the communal basis of the faith.

The recognition of the communal nature of the faith and its prayer in no way detracts from the uniqueness of the individual or the personal dimensions of faith. Just as a symphony orchestra blends the uniqueness of each instrument to create music of matchless beauty, so the communal understanding of the faith gives new importance to who I am, and directs what I do or do not do.

Furthermore, it is important to preserve the relationship between personal and communal prayer, for while Christian worship is communal, it is at the same time intensely personal. Personal prayer and prayer of the community are spiritually joined in a permanent union. They depend upon each other for their existence and are mutually supportive. Just as communal prayer inspires and directs private prayer, so private prayer gives depth and fervency to communal prayer.

The *Book of Common Worship* is a living expression of the worship of the whole church of Jesus Christ. In all essentials it embodies liturgical forms that are shared in common with Christians throughout the world, through the ages, as well as with those of our own family of faith.

Worship

Just as the word *common* stands over against individualism, the word *worship* stands over against secularism, which, like radical individualism, threatens the integrity of the church. The prayers in the *Book of Common Worship* engage us in prayer, and they elicit our praise and adoration of the One who created and redeemed us. A fundamental principle of Reformed worship is that it must be theocentric, focusing unwaveringly upon God, as when we sing in adoration the Glory to God (Gloria in Excelsis):

> . . . we worship you,
> we give you thanks,
> we praise you for your glory. . . .
> . . . you alone are the Holy One,
> you alone are the Lord,
> you alone are the Most High. . . .[15]

Secularism has had a subtle influence on much Protestant worship. In many popular forms of worship the focus on God has withered, replaced by a shallow preoccupation with human feelings and desires.

For those who care deeply about the integrity of the church, the theocentric focus of the church's book of services can help ensure that God will be the center of worship, thereby effectively strengthening the church's resolve to hold steady in times of testing. Such worship can help foster a discipleship that above all else seeks to be faithful to the will of God in all of life.

Since it is in its worship that the essential nature of the church is most clearly expressed, let us review what we believe about the church and how that is embodied in the *Book of Common Worship*.

CALLED BY GOD

We believe that God through the Holy Spirit has called the church into being, uniting us with Christ and with one another as the community of faith. Called by God, the church belongs to God, and not to us.

In the church's worship this is most tangible, as persons are joined to Christ in Baptism and incorporated into the church, the community of the baptized. When persons are baptized, we say what we believe about Baptism and the life the baptized are called to:

> Obeying the word of our Lord Jesus,
> and confident of his promises,
> we baptize those whom God has called.
>
> In baptism God claims us,
> and seals us to show that we belong to God.
> God frees us from sin and death,
> uniting us with Jesus Christ in his death and resurrection.
> By water and the Holy Spirit,
> we are made members of the church, the body of Christ,
> and joined to Christ's ministry of love, peace, and justice.[16]

Renunciation of evil, and profession of faith in the words of the Apostles' Creed, make it clear that the Christian life is one of dying and rising with Christ—dying to all that is destructive of life, and rising into newness of life.

The prayer over the water reminds us that we are baptized into the community that is shaped by the mighty acts of God throughout salvation history.

Through the waters of Baptism we are reborn into a new family. Reborn as children of God, we dwell as brothers and sisters in the same household and are made one with all, from every time and place, who have been washed in the waters of Baptism.

As hands are laid on the head of the newly baptized, which may include marking the forehead with the sign of the cross, the minister declares that in Baptism we belong to Christ:

> N., child of the covenant,
> you have been sealed by the Holy Spirit in baptism,
> and marked as Christ's own forever.[17]

When we live out of our baptism, all of life is informed and directed by this sacrament. It touches upon vocation, upon ethics, and all of life's decisions both large and small. Woven into the liturgical fabric throughout the *Book of Common Worship* is a recognition of the formative character of Baptism that shapes the ongoing life of the church and each of its members.

God's taking the initiative in Baptism, and claiming us as God's own, stands in sharp contrast to the sentimentality that so often shapes baptismal practice, and to the popular thinking that baptism of a youth or adult is little more than the marking of a decision to be a Christian. In the waters of Baptism, "we are buried with Christ in his death . . . raised to share in his resurrection . . . reborn by the power of the Holy Spirit."[18]

God has called the church into being, and Baptism is the moment of its birth.

KOINONIA—FELLOWSHIP OF BELIEVERS

The church is a koinonia, a fellowship of believers. As such the church tends to the maturing of the faith of its members that they may be rooted in the faith and grow in grace (Eph. 4:13). The liturgy is the primary means by which the fellowship of believers is nurtured.

Eucharist

For centuries, Protestants have relied on the reading of Scripture and preaching to nurture the people in the faith. To their detriment, Protestants have largely failed to recognize that the Eucharist is also fundamental to the liturgy, as indispensable as the reading and proclamation of Scripture. The Eucharist is a means of grace, given by Christ himself and essential to the nurturing of the fellowship of believers.

From the church's very beginning, the Eucharist has been at the heart of Christian worship on each Lord's Day. For nearly two thousand years it has been so for most Christians. However, in spite of the Reformers' efforts to preserve it, weekly Eucharist was a casualty of the Reformation. Only in our time is the Eucharist finally being restored to the center of the church's life together. This recovery is dramatic evidence of reformation in our time.

There is no place in the church's life where the church as a fellowship of believers comes more clearly into focus than in the Eucharist. Max Thurian of the Taizé Community once wrote, "The Church makes the Eucharist, but the Eucharist makes the Church."[19] The forming of the church by the Eucharist is the result of our participation in the body and blood of Christ in the Sacrament: "[T]he faithful are joined indissolubly together by communion in the Body of Christ."[20] Thurian asserts:

> The Eucharist unifies and joins together the members of the Body of Christ; those who have been baptized are joined together in unity and can but seek the deepening, extension and fulfillment of their unity. As the sacrament of unity, the Eucharist is the sacrament of charity which it supports and extends.[21]

And so we pray in the eucharistic prayer, the Great Thanksgiving:

> By your Spirit make us one with Christ,
> that we may be one with all who share this feast,
> united in ministry in every place.[22]

Each time we celebrate the Lord's Supper, as we pray the eucharistic prayer, we once again recall the story of our creation and redemption, and gratefully remember who we are. In this thankful remembering, in partaking of Christ's body and blood, we become participants in Christ's saving work.

The Service for the Lord's Day in the *Book of Common Worship* clearly sets forth the Eucharist as normative in worship on each Sunday and festival.

Word

The renewed emphasis upon the Eucharist does not come at the expense of the reading and proclamation of the Scripture. In fact, the contemporary liturgical renewal movement is responsible for restoring greater prominence to the place of Scripture in the liturgy.

Reclaiming the church's roots in the Scripture is essential to reforming the church. Since the Scripture is at the heart of the faith, and essential to the recovery of a Christian discipline firmly rooted in the faith, the reading and proclamation of Scripture stands with the Eucharist at the heart of the liturgy.

In a variety of ways, the liturgy in the *Book of Common Worship* restores the centrality of the Scripture in the liturgy. In its language, the feasts and seasons it calls us to celebrate, the lectionary it prescribes, the psalms it encourages us to sing, the *Book of Common Worship* reconnects us with the biblical story that shapes who we are. Its prayers are filled with biblical allusions and metaphoric language from the Scripture. Thus, with repeated use, the prayers and other texts of the *Book of Common Worship* become part of the faith language of the people.

The recovery of the use of a lectionary has played an important role in the recovery of the centrality of the Scripture in worship. While Presbyterians have had a lectionary longer than most realize, it was not until the advent of *The Worshipbook* in 1970 and the evolution of a common lectionary, that a lectionary has been taken seriously. The *Book of Common Worship* incorporates the *Revised Common Lectionary*, published in 1992, which is shared by an increasing number of churches throughout the world.

The Reformation placed a great deal of emphasis upon biblical preaching. In time, however, expository preaching declined as topical preaching became dominant. The result was a decline in biblical preaching. Use of the lectionary has resulted in congregations being more thoroughly grounded in the Scripture, as preaching has become less topical and more biblical, with worshipers fed a richer fare of the Bible's treasures.

Daily Prayer

The recovery of the discipline of daily prayer is also an important part of the nurture of the fellowship of believers and central in the cultivation of the interior life. Forms for daily prayer are a major part of the *Book of Common Worship.*

Following the natural cycle of the day, daily prayer engages us in praying the psalms, prayerful reflection on a reading from Scripture, silent contemplation, and prayers of thanksgiving, intercession, and supplication. From ancient times, it has been a discipline that has enriched the life of faith. In maintaining this discipline, we are enriched knowing that we are joined with others in prayer, our spiritual lives are deepened, and we are strengthened to persevere in the faith in the face of the invasive secularism that surrounds us. The preface to the *Daily Prayer* edition of the *Book of Common Worship* underscores the value of daily prayer:

> It helps deliver us from the inclination to divide life into separate compartments and opens our lives to allow the faith to permeate all we are and do. Daily prayer helps us engage our whole life—all our thoughts, words, and actions—as a vocation offered to God in humble service.[23]

Daily prayer enriches the life of faith whether one prays alone, with the family, or in small groups.

The church is a fellowship of believers seeking to mature in the faith and grow in God's grace.

LOCAL AND CATHOLIC

The church is both local and catholic. It is a body of believers in a particular place, where worship, nurture, and pastoral care regularly occur. But the church is more, for it transcends every local expression. Gathered for worship in a particular place and time, the church is one with the whole of Christ's church in every place and time.

In drawing from the liturgical richness of the wider tradition, a book of services effectively reinforces a sense of the catholicity of the church. In using forms shared by the church catholic, we discover the significance of prayer that is offered in common with the whole church.

Public prayers need to engage the people in prayer that is the prayer of the whole Christian community. Arising out of the collective wisdom and faith experience of the whole, a book of services expresses the piety and the affections at the heart of the whole church. It can engage leader and people alike in prayer that transcends all individual limitations and that roots us in the faith of the church.

This is in keeping with the "connectional" way we relate to other aspects of ecclesial life. In our polity, the collective wisdom shapes the way we govern ourselves. Statements of faith are drafted and agreed upon by the whole, and thereafter inform the response of faith of all parts of the church. So also a directory for worship and a book of services together embody the liturgical wisdom of the whole. They provide the shape of the liturgy that has evolved over time as an effective means to root the people in the faith and engage them in prayer. In embracing them, we submit ourselves in matters liturgical to the discipline of the church.

The bifocal (local/catholic) nature of liturgical prayer is clearly seen in the prayers of the people, or prayers of intercession. While our prayer will express the burdens and concerns of a particular people in a particular time and place, we also need to voice the broader concerns of the whole church, the whole world. Guidelines are given in the *Book of Common Worship* so that the prayers will avoid becoming parochial and will embrace concerns that are worldwide as well as local. Use of a service book, which enables both the local and catholic, identifies a congregation in one place as an expression of the church catholic.

Ecumenism

Since the church is truly catholic, it is appropriate that the church's book of services be strongly ecumenical in character, and not simply a sectarian expression. This is in keeping with what being Reformed is about, since the objective of the Reformation was one of *correction*, not *innovation*. The Reformers sought to purify and renew the one church of Jesus Christ, rather than form a separate church. They sought to reform the liturgy, not replace it. The historian James Hastings Nichols made this clear:

Like those in the twentieth-century liturgical movement, the Protestant Reformers preferred the ancient worship of the third to the sixth centuries to that of the Middle Ages. Calvin, for example, contended that Reformed worship was closer to that of the days of Gregory, Basil, Chrysostom, Augustine, Ambrose, and Cyprian than was the sixteenth-century Mass. The title of his service book was *The Form of Prayers According to the Custom of the Early Church*, and by "Early Church" he did not mean just that of the first century. From a literary standpoint, interested in the language of the texts, he was clearly wrong. From a liturgical standpoint, concerned with the functions of these services in the Christian life of congregations, Calvin was probably right.[24]

Centuries of living with multiplying numbers of denominations has eroded our sense of the catholicity of the church, leading to a growing sectarian perspective. Concerned for the church's integrity, we can ill afford to yield to the sectarian tendencies that prevail around us.

Faithfulness to the Reformed objective of reforming the church catholic propels us into the arena wherever the worship of the church catholic is being reformed, where ecumenical dialogue takes place. When the renewal of the whole church of Jesus Christ is central, we are joined with all those in the church catholic who share a common concern for the reform of the church in our time.

The result is that Christians from a variety of traditions are now joined together (especially since the Second Vatican Council) in seeking liturgical reform to the end that Christian worship in our time may more faithfully witness to the faith. The result is that as new service books are published, each bears the influence of liturgical work occurring in other traditions. The book that is the latest to appear has the advantage of all that has preceded in liturgical reform. This led James F. White, a Methodist liturgical scholar teaching at the University of Notre Dame, to write in a review of the *Book of Common Worship* for *Theology Today*:

> To those who have watched North American liturgy develop, there are no surprises here. But to the average Presbyterian pastor, unless he or she has kept up with the Directory for Worship and the Supplemental Liturgical Resources, there will be plenty of surprises. These are not just familiar services in new language. All the services are the results of careful rethinking of liturgical history, theology, and practice. Above all, they represent a new consensus as to what the church is and does. And for those not prepared for these shifts, they will prove indeed troubling. But then, Calvin had a similar problem with the magistrates in Geneva. Unfortunately, the magistrates won. Without a massive program of education, the same thing may happen again.
>
> At any rate, the liturgical texts are there. Presbyterians now have all the liturgical resources for parish use that Roman Catholics or anyone else has. And there are none better. These are truly state of the art liturgical resources for our time and continent. Let us hope that the seminaries and the institutions are equal to interpreting and teaching the use of these magnificent resources.[25]

Many see in this growing consensus the gradual emergence of a North American rite that is reformed, catholic, and evangelical. It is an exciting and prophetic issue to ponder.[26]

The church is both local and catholic. The *Book of Common Worship* is the best vehicle Presbyterians have for implanting this truth in the faith and life of its members.

MEMORY AND HOPE

The church is a community of memory and of hope, embracing both past and future. The church is therefore not simply a present reality but is in living continuity with the people of faith of times past and future. Unfortunately, most Christians see the church only in terms of the present.

Memory

The church as a community of memory is shaped by its past, joined with the people of God portrayed in the Scripture, with Israel, with the church of the New Testament, and with the church throughout history up to the present.

A book of services that draws deeply from the faith tradition can instill in a congregation a sense that it is joined with those from every time and place, a long procession of the faithful streaming across the centuries, who sought to live in faithful response to God's call.

We have cited how our memory is renewed in Baptism and the Lord's Supper. Our memory is also renewed in the way the church keeps time.

The church as a community of memory is clearly in focus as it observes the liturgical year. In celebrating the festivals and seasons as they are embodied in the *Book of Common Worship,* we remember the sacred story. And, in remembering, we encounter the living Christ. We are drawn into the mystery of Christ's saving work, to the end that it may permeate our very being and shape the way we live. Across the centuries the liturgical calendar has evolved as an effective instrument assisting the faithful to appropriate all the benefits of the saving events of salvation history.

Recent decades have seen a new appreciation of the liturgical calendar. Of particular importance is the recovery of the services that center upon the paschal mystery. The three great days (the Triduum)—Maundy Thursday, Good Friday, and the Easter Vigil—focusing upon Christ's death and resurrection, are at the core of who we are as the fellowship of believers. Here, the most treasured and richest of Christian festivals centers us in the redeeming work of Christ.

When we lose our memory, we no longer know who we really are. When we lose our rootedness in the faith, and our link with our ancestors in the faith, we suffer from ecclesiastical amnesia. Remembering gives us identity, and thus meaning and direction.

The *Book of Common Worship* embodies the church's memory and helps us to draw deeply from the faith tradition. As in the eucharistic prayer, we pray:

> Therefore we praise you,
> joining our voices with choirs of angels,
> with prophets, apostles, and martyrs,
> and with all the faithful of every time and place,
> who forever sing to the glory of your name:
>
> Holy, holy, holy Lord, . . .[27]

Hope

But the church is not only a community of memory, it is also a community of hope. Memory and hope are closely linked, in that the memory of God's promises makes the church a community of hope. The church lives in God's future, since the promised kingdom of God points us into the future. As citizens of that kingdom, the church is a foretaste, here in the present, of the coming reign of God when all shall dwell in love, peace, and righteousness. The church lives out of God's promised future; it engages in ministries of compassion and love, and works for peace and justice.

The liturgical year quickens memory and kindles hope as we remember the story of God's dealings with humankind, are reminded of God's promises, and anticipate Christ's coming again.

It is most especially in the Eucharist that memory and hope regularly come together. In the eucharistic prayer we remember God's mighty acts of creation and redemption in Christ, and anticipate the fullness of God's kingdom. Together we proclaim the mystery of faith in words that remember Christ's sacrificial death and resurrection, and anticipate with hope his coming again:

> Christ has died,
> Christ is risen,
> Christ will come again.

Or,

> We remember his death,
> we proclaim his resurrection,
> we await his coming in glory.[28]

In the Eucharist the church "gratefully anticipates the fulfillment of the Kingdom Christ proclaimed, and offers itself in obedient service to God's reign."[29] This holy meal is a foretaste of the messianic feast of the kingdom of God at the end of time. And so the eucharistic prayer ends with these words:

> Keep us faithful in your service
> until Christ comes in final victory,

and we shall feast with all your saints
in the joy of your eternal realm.[30]

There is no prayer in Christian liturgy of greater importance than the eucharistic prayer. Through it we remember the covenant God has extended to humankind, and in the light of that covenant we pray that, through the Holy Spirit, God will fulfill every promise and grant us communion in Christ. Just as a magnifying glass can focus the rays of the sun to burn a hole in a piece of paper, so the Eucharist focuses all of the mighty acts of God for us and burns them into our hearts.

In eating this bread and drinking this cup each Lord's Day and festival, we experience the saving work of Christ as a present reality and are renewed in the covenant. With the Eucharist at the heart of our faith, we come to experience the church as a community of memory and hope.

MISSION

As the firstfruits of the reign of God, the church does not exist just for its own sake, but for the sake of a broken and bleeding world. God has given the church a mission to perform. That thrust is a recurring theme throughout the *Book of Common Worship,* as expressed in its eucharistic prayers:

> Gracious God, . . .
> By your Spirit unite us with the living Christ
> and with all who are baptized in his name,
> that we may be one in ministry in every place.
> As this bread is Christ's body for us,
> send us out to be the body of Christ in the world. . . .
>
> Help us, O God, to love as Christ loved.
> Knowing our own weakness,
> may we stand with all who stumble.
> Sharing in his suffering,
> may we remember all who suffer.
> Held in his love,
> may we embrace all whom the world denies.
> Rejoicing in his forgiveness,
> may we forgive all who sin against us.[31]

The Eucharist reminds us that as Christ's body was given for us, we are to be the body of Christ given for the sake of the world. And so we pray (in reference to the bread and wine):

> Make them be for us the body and blood of Christ
> that we may be for the world
> the body of Christ, redeemed by his blood.[32]

OVERCOMING OBSTACLES

Although renewal was the church's objective in providing the *Book of Common Worship,* this book, no matter how excellent it may be, will not by itself ensure renewal. There are disciplines to learn and obstacles to overcome. Use of the service book must be accompanied by a desire to learn what the church's liturgy is all about, and by a diligent effort to overcome ignorance and indifference concerning liturgical matters.

The unfamiliar is too easily scorned, and liturgical traditions are too often spurned as elitist. MacGregor reminds us that a major obstacle to liturgical reform is the lack of a "humility that seeks to learn from others and does not scorn all it does not find immediately and easily comprehensible." He adds:

> Corporate worship that contains nothing I cannot easily understand has little to offer me. The liturgy ought to be a mine of living treasure endlessly surprising me with newly discovered joy. It ought to fill me with humble awe before its unfathomable riches. If I am already on my knees, it ought to make me want to bow my head to the ground, as even the Moslems do before the inscrutable mystery they find in Allah.[33]

Lacking adequate liturgical preparation in seminary, many pastors feel threatened by liturgical reform, not recognizing the need for it.[34] Fearing that changes in ordering worship may be unpopular, they remain indifferent to liturgical reform, feeling secure in familiar ways. But there is no security in ignorance and indifference, nor any promise for renewal.

Serious reflection in liturgical theology, including theology concerning the sacraments, is a prerequisite to the revitalization of our worship and thus to the church's renewal. When we understand that all we say and do in worship is fundamentally a theological expression, we are pressed to ensure that the words and actions of our worship adequately reflect the faith we proclaim. We can no longer give excuse for ignorance and indifference.

Other major obstacles include a suspicion of all "liturgical prayer" and a fear of a commitment to any discipline thought to infringe on individual liberties. Too often prayers from prayer books are dismissed as "canned prayers," in the belief that only "prayers from the heart" are true prayers. Certainly, from time to time, the offering of a prayer by one with a gift for praying out of the heart's promptings, effectively engages others in prayer. But prayers from prayer books can be just as fervent and "heartfelt." Common prayer does not preclude the use of free prayer. In fact, common prayer elicits free prayer in the expression of the burdens and concerns of a given time and place. But common prayer is more effective than free prayer in engaging us in the full breadth of the church's prayer.

Even when congregations accept prayers to be prayed in unison, there remains a widespread notion that such prayers should differ each Sunday. It is thought that prayer texts repeated again and again become threadbare. Such a notion actually hinders worshipers from engaging in prayer. Prayers that are not repeated often enough to become deeply embedded in minds and hearts simply become exercises in unison reading. Attention is so drawn to speaking words together that true prayer becomes next to impossible. Participation in worship is not simply vocalizing together, but engaging in prayer in the depths of one's being.[35]

The church's prayer is especially valuable in that it provides us with a reservoir of devotion that is readily available in the daily living out of our discipleship. Through repeated use, common prayer shapes the language of faith of the people. Like favorite hymns, prayers made familiar through repeated use are available to comfort in times of sorrow and to give voice to praise in times of joy.

Ours is an age when most people no longer know how to pray, except to cry out in despair in life's extreme moments. Prayer books can teach us to pray. Prayers from a prayer book can inspire our minds, awaken our hearts, and so guide us into prayer. A prayer book can help the faithful pray in every circumstance of life, quickening prayer within them to express thoughts and feelings which, if left to their own resources, would never rise within their minds and hearts.

Prayers from a prayer book can awaken our hearts for prayer, bringing forth prayer from the depths of the soul. Sometimes prayer book prayers inspire us to a kind of prayer that words are unable to express. Sometimes they prompt us to wait in silence, listening for the promptings of the Spirit. The words thus lead into prayer beyond words. Liturgical prayer teaches us how to pray, what to pray for, and how to be still before God.

Prayers from a prayer book can elicit our praise and adoration of the One who created and redeemed us. They can prompt us to bow humbly before God and admit our failings. They can engage us in prayer for the world, laying out before God the needs of humanity. They can quicken our caring for those who suffer, near and far. They can enable us to praise God who acted in history to make us whole. They can prompt us to pray for the grace of God that we may be faithful disciples. Such enrichment is available, but can only be discovered when prejudices toward liturgical prayer are set aside.

It is encouraging to note that an increasing number of congregations are finding renewal through a reform of the liturgy. However, the number is still relatively small in light of the fact that it has been nearly a century since American Presbyterians first adopted a service book. It is also cause for concern that congregations, having been led into use of the service book, frequently lose it with the coming of pastors who replace the church's liturgy with their own ideas of what worship is about.

Often the only choices Presbyterians have are between congregations that resist any reforms in their worship, and congregations that embrace modish and superficial styles of worship. The result is that Presbyterians who hunger to be nurtured in the church's liturgy are denied the opportunity. Unfulfilled by such meager fare, some quietly depart to other tables where the hunger of their souls is more fully satisfied.

This should be a major concern for presbyteries in their responsibility for the care and oversight of congregations. Presbyteries need to be challenged to take bold steps as they form new congregations, and redevelop existing congregations, to deliberately and carefully establish some congregations (perhaps as pilot congregations) in keeping with the model of the church set forth in the *Book of Common Worship*.

The obstacles to liturgical reform can be overcome through serious study on the nature and meaning of the church's worship, and through engagement in the church's prayer over time. All this calls for wise and pastorally sensitive leaders who will nurture the faithful in understanding how the liturgy roots them in the faith.

Also important in overcoming the obstacles is diligence in improving skills in liturgical leadership, and in training those laypersons who are invited to participate in the roles of reading Scripture and leading the prayers of the people. Doing worship well is important. Poorly led worship is an obstacle to engaging a congregation in prayer. Prayerful preparation of worship, giving careful attention to the words and actions of the liturgy, is crucial. The faithful will never know the power of the church's prayer if it is poorly led. Unfortunately, when the church's service book is used poorly, the blame for ineffective worship is usually laid on the book rather than the lack of a caring and prayerful leadership. The goal should be that the reality of the liturgy may so penetrate our being that leaders and people alike are engaged in the true spirit of prayer. It will be among such a people whose hearts have been changed that the Holy Spirit will come with renewal.

THE PROMISE OF REFORM

The *Book of Common Worship* challenges the church to rethink its basic understanding of worship. It invites us into liturgy as a discipline that holds promise of the discovery of riches beyond our imagination. It invites us to adopt a common order as the way we worship, and to allow common prayer to engage us in prayer. It asks us for humility that is willing to learn from others and set aside long-cherished prejudices. We are challenged to take the church's liturgy, its orders and texts, just as seriously as we have embraced the lectionary within the last thirty years. The surprising discovery will be that there is a liberating freedom to be found in the discipline of the church's ordered liturgical wisdom.

Use of the *Book of Common Worship* can root us more firmly in the faith, engage us in communal prayer that moves us beyond ourselves to center upon the grace and power of God, and help us to be participants in all the benefits of God's grace. Its orders, prayers, and other texts, along with its ceremonial suggestions, are not there simply to ensure that worship be "correctly done" or "aesthetically pleasing." Rather, the renewal of faith and a faithful response of discipleship is the goal of the *Book of Common Worship*.

In rebuilding the church from the ground up, the *Book of Common Worship* is a blueprint for worship that is foundational to all that the church is and does, for it sets forth a church that is "built upon the foundation of the apostles and prophets, with Christ Jesus himself as the cornerstone" (Eph. 2:20).

These are very difficult times in the church's life. Gone is the security of the past. The loss of members and shrinking budgets result in congregations being confronted with powerful temptations to seek out and adopt worship styles that are believed to be the most alluring. The result is that out of a concern for self-preservation, some churches accommodate themselves to the current popular culture in ways that threaten the integrity of the faith. Market driven, they refashion the church's worship in ways that erode the church's integrity. They end up yielding to a value system that conflicts with the church's ability to be Christ's faithful witness in contemporary culture.

Such alternatives hold no enduring promise. Like junk food's inability to develop healthy bodies, these superficial worship styles are incapable of bringing health to the body of Christ. Our worship can leave us spiritually malnourished just as easily as it can nourish. There is no healthy building of a strong body in a liturgical diet that entertains us with would-be superstars, and that simply gives us what we think we want. In such worship all sense of mystery evaporates and we are left where we were, having missed the transforming power that God gives.[36]

Gordon Lathrop, in commenting on the popular worship trends emerging in some congregations, wrote: "The liturgy itself is more engaging, more striking, more interesting than any of these common Christian deviations, if only it is allowed full sway."[37]

If only it is allowed full sway!

The church's liturgy centers us in community, points us to that which is time-less, engages us in the mystery of the One who is beyond all we could ever imagine. It raises us beyond ourselves, calling us to give voice, mind, and body in acts that unite us with God and each other. And we are transformed.

Only worship that springs out of the essential reality of the church can endure. Only worship that roots us in the faith and is filled with the metaphor and poetry of Scripture, engaging body and mind, can lead us into the mystery of the Eternal. It is such worship that—even in these times—will draw those who hunger for the bread that truly satisfies, and those who yearn for the water that quenches the deepest spiritual thirst.

Chapter 2

A Book of Services
Is Recovered

The story of the Presbyterian recovery of a book of services begins in 1855, with the publishing of a book bearing the title *Eutaxia, or the Presbyterian Liturgies: Historical Sketches*. Authorship was anonymous, simply stated as "by a minister of the Presbyterian Church."[1] It was later learned that the author was Charles Baird, a young minister who had been exposed to European Reformed life early in his ministry. He had come to appreciate the worship of Continental Protestants, which was more liturgical than the worship of American Presbyterians. The book contained liturgies from Calvin and Knox, as well as subsequent Reformed liturgies from England, the Netherlands, and Germany. These liturgies stood in sharp contrast to the way Presbyterians were worshiping in America in the mid-nineteenth century, a time of serious decay in the church's worship. In publishing the book, Baird sought to demonstrate that Presbyterians had a rich liturgical history that was worth recovering, and he called the church to embrace the liturgical heritage it had long forgotten.

In this call to liturgical reform, Baird was joining with others who were making similar calls. Within the Reformed family, the first call for liturgical reform came twenty years earlier from George Washington Bethune of the Dutch Reformed Church.

LITURGICAL REFORMS OF THE SIXTEENTH AND SEVENTEENTH CENTURIES

Recognizing that worship is a primary carrier of the faith, and the principal means by which the faith is reinforced in the lives of believers, the sixteenth-century Reformers sought to purge the liturgies inherited from the medieval church of all that was alien to the Reformed faith. Rather than creating new forms of worship, they accepted the liturgical patterns coming from patristic times and preserved in catholic tradition.

Contrary to popular belief, service books for the people to use in worship were not a creation of the Roman church. They were a product of the Reformation and were not possible before the invention of the printing press. While the pre-Reformation church had service books, they were in Latin and were for use by the clergy in leading worship. In the Reformation, service books were made available to the people in the vernacular language to enable them to participate in the liturgy, rather than simply be passive observers. Service books were not only for use in worship on Sunday but were also for use in private and family worship as well. Common worship was therefore a Protestant notion.

Reformed service books have their roots in the liturgical reforms of Strassburg, which began in 1524. Martin Bucer, the dominant influence in Strassburg, is thus the "chief architect of the Calvinist form of worship."[2] The Strassburg liturgy became the model for Calvin's liturgy in French and then John Knox's liturgy in English. Several characteristics of this lineage are important to our consideration. These liturgies adhered to the order of the liturgy inherited from catholic tradition. They embraced the norm of a balance between Word and Sacrament. Preaching had a dominant place. Although the norm of weekly Communion was imperfectly realized in practice, worship on each Lord's Day was ordered the same whether or not the Sacrament was celebrated. On those Sundays when the Sacrament was not celebrated, only those things pertaining to the Sacrament were omitted. Furthermore, in Strassburg and Geneva it was customary for the minister to stand at the holy table for all portions of the liturgy except for reading the Scripture and preaching. Worship on each Lord's Day thus anticipated the Lord's Supper.

The Reformation in England and Scotland, also strongly influenced by Strassburg, proceeded unabated during the reign of King Edward VI. Thomas Cranmer was archbishop, and was responsible for the early reforms of the English liturgy. But upon the king's death, Mary Tudor ascended the throne; Cranmer was executed, and the church of Rome was restored in England. The future course for the English Reformation was altered.

Upon Queen Mary's death, those who had gone into exile to escape persecution returned. Among them were John Knox and others who brought with them an English translation of the Genevan-Strassburg liturgy. In the decades that followed, two sharp party lines emerged within the English church. One was the royal and episcopal party aligned to the will of the monarchy. The other was the Puritan party, which sought reforms on the order of Geneva. This set the Puritans in direct conflict with the royal party, which had the power to legislate both content and use of a service book. While both parties agreed on the value of a service book, they disagreed over what the book should contain. Protesting that a service book not to their liking was being thrust upon them, the Puritans struggled against relentless pressures while seeking liberty to order their own life and worship.

After Presbyterian Puritans briefly gained control of parliament in 1640, the Westminster Assembly was convened (1643) with the intent of reforming the standards of the church. Though Presbyterian Puritans were in the majority, the Independents constituted a vigorous minority. In contrast to the mainstream of English Puritans at the time, Independents were opposed to liturgical forms and believed in the total autonomy of the local congregation. Five Scots commissioners were admitted, but without vote.

Among the tasks of the Assembly was that of preparing a new service book, and for this purpose a committee was appointed. The work of this committee resulted in a compromise measure in an attempt to please all three factions. But the views of the Independents overpowered Puritan views. What was to have been a new service book became The Directory for the Publique Worship of God, void of liturgical text. This directory, commonly called the Westminster Directory, was once described as the only liturgy in Christendom to consist of nothing but rubrics. Completed in 1644, it was officially adopted by Parliament in January of 1645. The Church of Scotland subsequently adopted it with reservations and revisions, stating that it was not to replace the present practice and order of the kirk. The Anglicans ridiculed it. Nor was it satisfactory to the Independents for it was still too precise. What had begun as a rejection of liturgical forms being forced on them, resulted in a rejection of all liturgical forms. In spite of its inadequacy, the Westminster Directory was destined to be the dominant influence upon Presbyterian worship for the next three hundred years.

WORSHIP IN AMERICA IN THE
SEVENTEENTH AND EIGHTEENTH CENTURIES

It was during this period following Westminster that the Puritans and the Scots settled in the New World, forming the nucleus that initially shaped American Presbyterianism. Thus Puritan views of the time dominated the way the church took root in American soil.

The Puritans were no longer engaged in a struggle for liberty; they were free to develop their own service books. However, they continued to oppose service books, apparently having forgotten why they opposed them. In keeping with the Westminster legacy, Presbyterians who settled the New World chose to be served by a directory for worship rather than a book of services. In 1788 the first Presbyterian General Assembly adopted a revised 1644 Westminster Directory for use in the United States.

Other influences contributed to liturgical decline. Rationalism's implict trust in human intellect and reason downplayed rites and sacraments rooted in tradition and nonverbal symbol. The past was forgotten in the predominant concern with the present. Thus, rites and sacraments, being rooted in tradition, symbol, and metaphor, were downplayed.

Revivalism was another factor contributing to liturgical decline. Revivalism was not compatible with the strong sense of tradition rooted in the history of the church's faith. "Saving souls" became the primary goal of worship, usurping the role of the sacraments. A communal understanding of the faith gave way to a focus on the individual. The objective character of worship yielded to subjective feelings and emotional manipulation. Gospel songs replaced metrical psalms. Revival sermons supplanted strongly biblical preaching. As revivalism faded, the church was thrust even further into a liturgical wasteland. James Hastings Nichols notes that "when the revivalistic fire cooled, little was left of the pattern of worship save a moralistic sermon with a few sentimental embellishments fore and aft."[3] Without the stability provided by liturgical forms from the faith tradition, the church's worship was vulnerable to whatever ideology would sweep across society and the church.

By the end of the eighteenth century, Reformed churches everywhere had struck their lowest level in liturgical practice. The liturgy had virtually disappeared, and what liturgies were still in use were heavily didactic. The celebration of the Lord's Supper was so infrequent as to be negligible.

A CALL TO LITURGICAL REFORM

It was in this arid landscape in the middle of the nineteenth century that Baird's *Eutaxia* appeared, seeking to awaken American Presbyterians to a tradition they had long forgotten. Baird argued that "the principles of Presbyterianism in no wise conflict with the discretionary use of written forms," and further that "the practice of Presbyterian churches abundantly warrants the adoption and the use of such forms."[4]

Baird set forth an agenda for liturgical reform and called for the preparation of a book of liturgical forms:

> And while we have little expectation that such a formulary, however perfect, will ever be adopted as a standard of the Church, we see not why at some

future period it may not be recognized and sanctioned as a lawful aid to those who may desire its use.[5]

Princeton theologian Charles Hodge, leader among Old School Presbyterians, reviewed *Eutaxia*. He gave a strong defense for the use of optional liturgical forms. Julius Melton summarizes Hodge's review:

> Princeton Seminary's Charles Hodge greeted with enthusiasm the rediscovery of a "wide and safe middle ground" between Puritan and Anglican practice—namely, "the optional use of a liturgy, or form of public service, having the sanction of the Church." Hodge spoke for those who had long sought some modification of the extempore system when he said that such an arrangement would be "a very great blessing." In a twenty-two-page article prompted by Baird's book, Hodge himself defended liturgies from the charge of being "an adjunct of episcopacy," analyzed historically why Reformed liturgies had fallen into disuse, and repeated many of Samuel Miller's suggestions for improving public prayer.
>
> Aside from throwing the weight of his influence behind young Baird's proposals, Hodge's most important contribution was his suggestion that the denomination produce an officially approved prayer book. He gave detailed suggestions for one, sharing the fears of some that such works might be produced which would be unworthy. Some Presbyterians feared that such a step would play into the hands of the Episcopalians, either by making a concession in favor of liturgies or by producing forms unable to compete in authority or content with the venerable *Book of Common Prayer*. As to the former fear, Hodge pointed out the vast difference between the theory which would undergird such a Presbyterian book and the Episcopal theory of compulsory liturgy. As for the latter fear, he would not admit that it was impossible to improve upon the *Book of Common Prayer*. Its age certainly was no argument against attempting to make a new liturgical compilation: "No man objects to founding a new college because it cannot at once be an Oxford or a Harvard." But Hodge's chief argument was "We cannot believe that anything which would really improve our public service, could operate unfavorably to the interests of our Church."[6]

Baird accepted Hodge's challenge and in 1857 produced such a compilation. However, his work was generally dismissed as "Romanism in disguise." Furthermore, while the orders of worship might have had some merit, most of the prayers, appropriate to the context of the sixteenth century, failed to engage nineteenth-century congregations in prayer.[7] In Baird and Hodge we see the middle ground Presbyterians would take between an obligatory liturgy like the Episcopalian *Book of Common Prayer* and complete freedom, which too often is chaotic. They did not envision a people's prayer book, but rather a manual for pastors to use in leading worship.

These challenges to the state of the liturgy among nineteenth-century Presbyterians made it clear that liturgical forms were part of the Reformed tradition. If the church had once used liturgical forms, might it not once again have forms appropriate for the times? Nichols states the emerging questions:

> [I]f sixteenth-century forms were no longer satisfactory as they stood, could one go behind them? After all, the Reformers had conceived themselves as Reformed *Catholics* and had appealed in some measure to patristic precedents in matters of worship as well as discipline and theology. Might there not be forms of service in the legacy of pre-Reformation Catholicism which the Reformers had not appropriated but which were compatible with Reformed theology and suitable for modern churches, wishing to affirm historical continuity?[8]

Such questions continued to guide the endeavor of reforming nineteenth-century worship among Presbyterians.

THE MERCERSBURG MOVEMENT (1840–1884)

The first notable reforming of the liturgy within a Reformed context in America took place in the German Reformed Church. It emerged in a small German Reformed seminary in Mercersburg, Pennsylvania, and came to be called the Mercersburg movement. It was as much a theological movement as it was a movement for liturgical reform, and it ultimately influenced liturgical reform in other churches. The primary leaders were the historian Philip Schaff and the theologian John Williamson Nevin.

Schaff and Nevin regarded themselves as fully catholic and fully Reformed. The theology of the movement was strongly ecclesiological and was characterized by a strong sacramental emphasis. From this perspective, leaders of the movement made a frontal attack on the excessive revivalism of the time.[9]

Reformed liturgy in Germany had suffered the ravages of pietism, just as Puritanism led to the loss of the liturgy among English-speaking Reformed. Lamenting the loss of its liturgy, the German Reformed Church in America unsuccessfully made attempts to recover it. In 1847, in response to a proposal to prepare a liturgy for the church, the synod appointed a commission for the task. Thus began the Mercersburg liturgical movement. The work led to the *Provisional Liturgy* in 1857, and to the *Order of Worship* in 1866.

Unlike the early Presbyterian proposals, the book was intended to be a people's book, which would have reversed the Puritan and evangelical tendency to place everything in the hands of the minister. But it found little use as a people's book. It was opposed as an attempt to "Romanize" the church. When it was finally approved in 1866, after a decade of trial use, it was accepted for optional use at the discretion of the minister. Nevertheless, it had significant influence on the future of liturgical reform, including the future development of Presbyterian service books. Nichols notes, "It was a landmark when a Reformed church authorized such a service book even for voluntary use."[10]

OTHER CALLS AMONG PRESBYTERIANS
FOR LITURGICAL REFORM

Among Presbyterians, private attempts at stimulating liturgical reform continued. Among those seeking reform was Charles W. Shields, a Presbyterian minister trained at Princeton Seminary and a professor at Princeton College. Shields attempted to demonstrate how the *Book of Common Prayer* might be amended for Presbyterian use. In 1864 he published a service book titled *The Book of Common Prayer and Administration of the Sacraments . . . as Amended by the Westminster Divines in the Royal Commission of 1661 and in Agreement with the Directory for Public Worship of the Presbyterian Church in the U.S.A.*[11]

The book was of course not a product of the Westminster Assembly, but was based upon the liturgical work of the 1661 Savoy Conference, where Presbyterians and Anglicans attempted unsuccessfully to reach consensus on a common liturgy. Shields laid claim to the fact that some of the former members of the Westminster Assembly were part of the Savoy Conference, and so, he reasoned, the Savoy Conference reflected the opinions of the Westminster divines.[12] Shields's book prompted some examination of Presbyterian worship, but was generally met with apathy.

While early attempts to bring about Presbyterian liturgical reform were of the old school, toward the end of the nineteenth century some new school ministers (e.g., T. Ralston Smith and Joel Parker) began to prepare manuals of prayer and advocated a uniform order of worship. However, these resources evidenced a tendency to spurn classical liturgies in favor of contemporary creations.

Toward the end of the century, demand for such resources prompted the publishing house of the northern Presbyterians (PCUSA) to produce collections of liturgical forms. In 1877 Princeton's Archibald Alexander Hodge produced a *Manual of Forms* with a second edition five years later. Widespread use of these books evidenced the growing need for worship aids.

Other manuals began to appear such as Herrick Johnson (of McCormick Seminary), *Forms for Special Occasions* (1889); Samuel M. Hopkins (of Auburn Seminary in New York), *General Liturgy and Book of Common Prayer* (1883); and Benjamin Bartis Comegys (a Philadelphia banker), *An Order of Worship with Forms of Prayer for Divine Worship* (1885), and *A Presbyterian Prayer Book for Public Worship* (1895). In 1898, at age eighty, Comegys edited and published an American version of the Scottish Church Service Society manual, *Euchologion: A Book of Common Order,* a predecessor of the Scottish *Book of Common Order.*

But the work of individuals needed the force of a group if there was to be lasting impact upon the church. To meet this need, the American Church Service Society was formed. Its foremost advocates for worship reform were its president, Louis Benson of Philadelphia, and Henry van Dyke, a New York pastor. In its work, the society made surveys to determine current worship practices. These surveys revealed a rather dismal situation in Presbyterian worship and thus fortified the society's assessment for the need of denominationally authorized worship forms.

It is important to recognize that these calls for liturgical reform within the Reformed tradition in the nineteenth century were simultaneous with comparable calls for liturgical recovery emerging in other traditions, especially Roman Catholic, Anglican, and Lutheran. These calls for liturgical reform brought about the modern liturgical movement.[13]

The fact that these stirrings for liturgical reform emerged simultaneously, supports the conviction that they evidence work of the Holy Spirit reforming the church in our time. Added support for this conviction lies in the fact that the emergence of the liturgical movement was concurrent with the emergence of other reforming movements in the church, such as the ecumenical movement, the biblical movement (especially for Roman Catholics), and the movement bringing about resurgence of the social dimensions of the gospel.

These movements are interdependent, each drawing from and influencing the other. But it is the liturgical movement that gathers together all aspects of renewal, bringing them to focus in the central act of the congregation's life together—its worship—and thus relating the church in a vital way to the source of its life.

Although liturgical reform intensified toward the end of the nineteenth century, it was not until the twentieth century that the reforms called for would come to fruition.

THE BOOK OF COMMON WORSHIP—1906

In 1894 a directory for worship was adopted by the General Assembly of the southern-based Presbyterian Church in the U.S. This directory contained liturgical formulas, in that liturgies for marriages and funerals were appended to it. The southern Presbyterians were thus the first to give official sanction to liturgical forms.

Nine years later, in 1903, in response to overtures from the Synod of New York and the Presbytery of Denver calling for the creation of a book of worship forms and services, the General Assembly of the Presbyterian Church in the U.S.A., by unanimous vote, authorized the preparation of "a book of simple forms and services, helpful and proper for voluntary use in Presbyterian churches." It then formed a special committee for the task, the Committee on Forms of Service. The General Assembly instructed the committee to avoid ritualism, to "embody sound doctrine in the language of orderly devotion," and to seek to foster worship in which all of the people might participate.

Henry van Dyke was appointed chairperson. Two other members of the Church Service Society, Louis Benson and Charles Cuthbert Hall, were among the eleven ministers and elders on the committee. Historical research played an important role in the committee's work, but the committee also sought to know how Presbyterians were currently worshiping. A detailed questionnaire was distributed. Nearly one third of the total number of ministers of the church responded. The results gave strong encouragement to the committee's work. In spite of the affirming response that was reflected, there were many throughout the church who were violently opposed to such a book. Educating the church would, therefore, be another important part of the committee's work.

In 1904 the committee reported back to the assembly. In its report, the committee laid careful groundwork giving evidence that liturgical forms are indeed in harmony with Presbyterian principles:

> Historically, we observe, what every intelligent Presbyterian knows, that the use of forms of service was practically universal among the early Calvinistic or Reformed Churches. In Switzerland, in Germany, in France, in Italy, in Holland, in Scotland, and in England service-books were prepared for the use of the various congregations by the leaders of the Reformation. In these books are found directions for the order and conduct of public worship and the administration of the Sacraments, and prayers expressing, in language drawn for the most part from the Holy Scriptures and the fathers of the primitive Church, the desires and petitions of an assembly of Christians holding the Reformed Faith. The Genevan Liturgy of John Calvin, the "Book of Common Order" of John Knox, the Calvinistic Liturgy of the Church of Strasburg, the Christian Ordinances of the Netherlands Congregations, the Liturgy of the Palatinate, the "Prayers on the Psalms," published in the Scottish Psalm-book of 1595, "Hermann's Consultation," compiled by Bucer and Melanchthon—these and many other books of like character afford ample proof that the use of orderly forms and services, not only for the conduct of public worship, but also for the guidance of families in their daily prayers, is historically in harmony with Presbyterian principles. It was with such a form that Calvin celebrated his last communion; the reading of such a prayer cheered John Knox in his dying hour; and Admiral Coligny was engaged in repeating the beautiful liturgy of the Reformed Church in France when he was murdered on the morning of St. Bartholomew's Day.
>
> In most of the Reformed Churches, holding the same faith and order with us, the use of these ancient service-books, modified to meet present needs, still continues. The chief reason why a Directory for Worship was substituted for "the Book of Common Order," at the Westminster Assembly, was "to meet the preferences of the English Puritan divines," which the Scotch Presbyterians were willing to do on all points not essential to the faith.
>
> The Directory for Worship, adopted by our Church in 1788, and amended in 1789 and in 1886, while it disapproves "of *confining* ministers to set or fixed forms of prayer," says nothing against their voluntary use, or the preparation of an order of service which shall be helpful to the congregation in public worship. On the contrary, it protests against "mean, irregular and extravagant effusions" (Chap. I, 4); it speaks of prayer and praise as "the more important duties" not to be interfered with by unduly long sermons (Chap. VII, 4); and it gives such careful directions for the conduct of public services in an orderly manner, as naturally to suggest that a collection of good and proper forms would be helpful in the carrying out of these directions.[14]

By the 1905 General Assembly, the book was nearly completed, and a draft was to be presented. Van Dyke went to the assembly to report. It was quickly apparent that vigorous opposition to the book was developing. Some made accusations that the church was "being insidiously led toward ritualism." The anticipated book was evidence of that trend and "an instrument to promote it." Was not the principle of "Presbyterian simplicity" opposed to any tendency to make worship more elaborate? Indifference to the proposed book had turned to violent reaction against it. A report of the assembly stated:

> Dr. van Dyke faced all this opposition quite conscious of its extent and vehemence, and set himself deliberately to reason it down. His manner was the essence of frank sincerity. From step to step he proceeded to attack the adverse arguments that he had heard, and one could almost see the barriers melting away before his transparent logic. It was an instructive exhibition of the power of candor over reasonable men, and perhaps beyond that, an interesting evidence of Dr. van Dyke's personal magnetism. Before he was half through speaking it was evident that he had won over the Assembly and would carry the report.[15]

In his report, van Dyke took great care in pointing out how various aspects of worship contained in the book were enjoined in the Scripture. He told how the committee called upon the "vast and precious store of forms" from the Reformed tradition and from Christian antiquity. The committee also had prepared appropriate materials to express contemporary concerns. There was to be neither compulsion nor restriction in its use, the title page reading "For Voluntary Use in Presbyterian Churches." While use of the book was voluntary, the committee hoped that it would inspire a more uniform liturgical practice throughout the church. The committee sought to set forth the ideal form of Presbyterian worship as "order without monotony; variety without confusion."[16]

Three hours of debate followed. But instead of rejecting the report, the assembly authorized publication as soon as the committee made minor changes the assembly requested, and completed the portions yet unfinished. The assembly then added five new members to the committee. Since some felt that it was too much the work of a few "experts," the committee was asked to obtain the counsel of pastors.

Drawing upon published reports of the assembly actions, Julius Melton writes:

> Advocates of liturgical reform in Presbyterianism greeted this news joyfully. One obstacle had been hurdled. Their opponents were disgusted. Some scoffed at calling the book "voluntary." "Ritualism has a hypnotic influence," muttered one; "familiar with its face, we first endure, then pity, then embrace." "The bad weed of formalism never asks for anything more than toleration," he went on; "you give it a start and it will do the rest."[17]

The Book of Common Worship[18] was published less than two weeks before the 1906 General Assembly. The completed book included orders with liturgical texts for Lord's Day worship for both morning and evening. It provided an order for Holy Communion, which included a noteworthy eucharistic prayer. Texts were provided for some festivals and seasons of the liturgical calendar. There were liturgies for Baptism and for Confirmation of Baptismal Vows. Also included were a treasury of prayer, family prayers, a selective Psalter, and a collection of ancient hymns and canticles. Its prayers were drawn from a wide range within the church catholic and from across many centuries. Responses and unison prayers made it clear that congregational participation was encouraged.

The service book was destined to be a controversial item on the assembly's agenda. Prior to the assembly, articles appeared in church publications, some supporting the book, others attacking it. Twenty presbyteries, principally presbyteries with New School sentiments, had sent overtures opposing the book.

On May 22, 1906, *The Book of Common Worship* came before the assembly. Remembering the reactions of the 1905 assembly, the committee, in reporting to the assembly, stressed that liberty was a tradition in American Presbyterianism. Liberty, the committee emphasized, was liberty not only from being forced to use liturgical forms, but also liberty from being forbidden to use them.

The "final ordeal" came when a commissioner, "holding a copy of the book gingerly in his fingers . . . flung it from him crying: 'Faugh! It smells of priestcraft.'" Another commissioner began to pound the table with his fists. "Henry van Dyke, who a little before had been greeted by a veritable hurricane of applause grinned pleasantly amid the uproar." He then spoke quietly to the assembly, assuring them that he did not want to see a fight. He said, "This is not van Dyke's prayer book. It belongs to every member of the committee you appointed." He continued, "It's not a liturgy. It's not a ritual. It does not contain 'canned' prayers. It contains great live prayers of our fathers. Are you going to tell the man who wants to use this book that he can't have it?"[19]

The assembly carefully avoided anything that might be interpreted as giving an "authoritative recommendation." The committee had suggested that the title page read, "Published by authority of the General Assembly of the Presbyterian Church in the U.S.A. for voluntary use." But this was too strong a statement for the assembly to agree to. Compromise was finally reached with the words, "Prepared by the Committee of the General Assembly of the Presbyterian Church in the United States of America for Voluntary Use."[20]

While the road to approval was tempestuous, and the resulting *Book of Common Worship* lacked any authoritative recommendation of the General Assembly, the action of the assembly did acknowledge the growing concern for the reform of worship, and gave legitimacy to liturgical orders and texts in shaping Presbyterian worship. The 1906 book was therefore a significant step in the reform of Presbyterian worship in America.

The 1906 *Book of Common Worship* clearly showed dependence upon the liturgical reforms in the Church of Scotland, and it incorporated much of the catholic liturgical tradition in its borrowing from the *Book of Common Prayer*. But in a church born in a reactive Puritanism, fixed prayer was too easily dismissed as "canned prayer." Nevertheless, this service book gave witness that behind Puritan and revivalistic worship was a form of worship that legitimately laid claim to being Presbyterian and Reformed.

THE BOOK OF COMMON WORSHIP—1932

Within two decades, the book began to appear dated. Prior to the meeting of the General Assembly in 1928, Henry van Dyke wrote to Lewis S. Mudge, stated clerk of the General Assembly, calling attention to the need of revising *The Book of Common Worship*. Van Dyke was given hearty support. Invited to the General Assembly as a former moderator, he addressed the assembly proposing the revision. The assembly promptly voted to consider such a revision and, if it was found desirable, to proceed with it. A committee was elected composed of the six surviving members of the first committee and eleven new members, with van Dyke again the chairperson.

At the General Assembly the following year, the committee reported that it had voted unanimously that a revision was desirable and had begun its work. Since the average age of the committee members was high, they recognized the need for the counsel of younger pastors. The report stated, "The wisdom of age may be salutary—but the generous impulse of youth is vital." Thirty ministers who worked closely with youth were made advisors to the committee.[21]

During the course of their work, the committee addressed some of the objections to the book. In one statement, van Dyke wrote:

> We can see no force in the thoughtless opposition to such a book which is represented by the rather irreverent phrase, "canned prayers." The Bible and the service books of Calvin, Knox, and the other reformers, all contain written forms of prayer. All our hymns are written. Yet no one is foolish and crude enough to protest against "canned praise." The effectual fervent prayer of a righteous man is acceptable though it be written.[22]

The committee presented a draft of the revised *Book of Common Worship* to the 1931 General Assembly. It was an expanded version of the 1906 book. Texts for additional festivals and seasons were added. A rudimentary lectionary was included.

In his report to the General Assembly, van Dyke expressed gratitude that he was able to share in the work which was "the last labor" of his life.[23] He asked the assembly for approval of the committee's work and for permission to complete the Psalter and responsive readings which were yet to be added.

Evidence of changed attitudes was apparent in the ease in which the assembly received the report. There were no speeches against "canned prayers." The vote was unanimous to approve the committee's work. The assembly rose with applause. This time, the title page read, "Approved by the General Assembly of the Presbyterian Church in the United States of America for Voluntary Use." The book was published the following year, 1932.[24] In 1933 Henry van Dyke died. The legacy he left in shaping American Presbyterian worship is immeasurable and of lasting significance.

The General Assembly of the southern-based Presbyterian Church in the U.S. subsequently approved this edition for use by its congregations. In that action, a common liturgy became available to the two major streams of American Presbyterianism.

Chapter 3

Liturgical Reform in the Mid-Twentieth Century

It was at this point in history that the ecumenical movement began to emerge with strength. This movement was destined to impact all future editions of the *Book of Common Worship.*

From the beginning of the ecumenical movement, some of its strongest leaders were churches that had emerged from the sixteenth-century Reformation—Lutheran, Anglican, and Reformed. It is important to underscore that the early Reformers had not sought to form a separate church. Their goal was to purify and renew the one, indivisible, catholic, and apostolic church.

Though they failed to achieve their aim, the Reformers did not lose sight of the oneness of the church. As an interim step toward the ultimate reformation of the church catholic, Calvin, Melanchthon, and Cranmer diligently sought to consolidate the Reformation efforts. In the spring of 1552 Archbishop Cranmer made a proposal for a consensus. Responding by letter to Cranmer's proposal, Calvin declared that the disunity of the church was one of the greatest evils of the time. He wrote that "the members of the Church being severed, the body lies bleeding. So much does this concern me, that, could I be of any service, I would not grudge to cross even ten seas, if need were, on account of it."[1]

The death of Melanchthon in 1560 did not discourage Calvin from continuing his efforts to unify the Reformation churches. Late that year he proposed "a universal council to end the divisions" and "reunite all Christianity." But efforts toward unification failed. Regrettably, the churches that followed acquiesced to separate coexistence. Given the Reformers' convictions on the unity of the church, they could not have imagined the increasing fragmentation into denominationalism that was to develop in the centuries that followed, most particularly in North America. They would have been bitterly disappointed.

Such failures of the past began at last to be redressed in the ecumenical movement, giving the twentieth century a label as the Ecumenical Century.

It was in the Faith and Order movement that a vision of a reunited church was reborn. In part, it grew out of the missionary movement, for on mission fields the evils of denominational competition were obvious. An important milestone in ecumenical relations was a world missionary conference held in 1920 in Edinburgh. A few years later, in 1927, the first World Conference on Faith and Order was held.

Unlike ecumenical endeavors where cooperation was the objective, the Faith and Order movement confronted theological differences. Where simply cooperation among churches was the objective, there was no need to face doctrinal issues. But Faith and Order recognized that doctrinal issues were responsible for the breakdown of sixteenth-century efforts to consolidate the Reformation churches, and reunion could only result by confronting those issues once again.

The Faith and Order movement understood from its inception that in the study of liturgy we penetrate into the very heart of theology, that "worship is the living form of faith," and that liturgical reform is a struggle for the very center of the church's life.[2] Gerardus van der Leeuw, a prominent Dutch Reformed leader in the formative period of the movement, captured the theological-liturgical link by giving a fresh twist to the classic maxim *Lex orandi lex credendi* (The law of prayer is the law of belief) when he said, "Whoever takes the little finger of liturgy soon discovers that he has grabbed the whole fist of theology."[3]

By the end of the Faith and Order Conference of 1937 many theological differences had been resolved or bridged, but in matters of ministry and the sacraments deep continuing differences were apparent. Much of the work of Faith and Order that followed this conference focused on these areas and influenced the preparation of future Presbyterian service books.

THE BOOK OF COMMON WORSHIP—1946

In 1941, nine years after the publication of the 1932 edition of *The Book of Common Worship,* the General Assembly of the Presbyterian Church in the U.S.A. established a permanent committee on the revision of *The Book of*

Common Worship to monitor the liturgical needs of the church and periodically to propose revisions. Hugh Thomson Kerr became chairperson. At the same time, the General Assembly took action recognizing *The Book of Common Worship* "as an official publication of the Presbyterian Church in the United States of America" with supervision lodged in the Office of the General Assembly.

Most members of the committee were catholic in their liturgical views, and involved in the ecumenical movement. They benefited from the increasing availability of ecumenical liturgical scholarship and from knowledge of the contemporary liturgical movement taking place in other churches. Their work resulted in a thoroughgoing revision of *The Book of Common Worship* and a new edition being published in 1946.[4]

The primary source for shaping *The Book of Common Worship* (1946) was the Church of Scotland's *The Book of Common Order* (1940), which was acclaimed at the time as the finest Reformed prayer book in the English language. The other principal source was, as was the case with its two predecessors, the Episcopal prayer book, *The Book of Common Prayer.* The result was that the book was both fully catholic and fully reformed in a recovery of much that the Puritan tradition had rejected.[5]

This edition provided for more congregational participation. It expanded resources for Sunday morning and Sunday evening worship. The liturgy for celebrating the Lord's Supper closely followed that of *The Book of Common Order* of the Church of Scotland. The inclusion of a two-year lectionary from *The Book of Common Order* gave greater emphasis to the reading of Scripture in worship. While the 1932 *Book of Common Worship* included a very rudimentary lectionary, this was the first complete lectionary to appear in an American Presbyterian book of services. The lectionary appointed Old Testament, Epistle, and Gospel readings, and a psalm, for each Sunday and festival.

The liturgical year had greater emphasis, with prayers from the service books of other churches. Services for children and youth evidenced the church's concern for the young. A more extensive "Treasury of Prayers" included many collects from *The Book of Common Prayer* and *The Book of Common Order.*[6]

A major influence on the preparation of the 1946 edition of *The Book of Common Worship* was official discussion then taking place between the Episcopal and Presbyterian churches that many hoped would lead to recognition of each other's sacraments and ministry, if not full union. Discussions spanned eleven years from 1937 until 1948. This resulted in several features being included in *The Book of Common Worship* (1946) that were not in previous editions, in keeping with the committee's desire to aid the anticipated union by bringing that book closer to *The Book of Common Prayer.* While the discussions failed to result in union, *The Book of Common Worship* (1946) reflected a greater influence of *The Book of Common Prayer* than its predecessors.

The Book of Common Worship (1946) never attained the place in the church hoped for by the committee. Evangelicals were unsparing in their criticism that it was more Episcopalian than Reformed. Noting that the committee member who had prepared the eucharistic rite had received his Th.D. from an Episcopal seminary, one evangelical remarked, "[He] is so enamored of high ritual that I think he wants to lead our Church further and faster than it is willing to go."[7]

THE ECUMENICAL CONTEXT
FOR THE NEXT BOOK OF SERVICES

With the end of World War II, the momentum of the ecumenical and liturgical movements accelerated, providing a wholly different context for preparing the next Presbyterian service book. American Presbyterians were able to have a greater involvement in the Faith and Order movement. As American Presbyterians served on Faith and Order's committee on worship, they became more fully aware of liturgical reform taking place around the world, including in churches in the Reformed family on the Continent. A variety of other influences would shape future revision.

In France, the Taizé Community took shape in the hills of Burgundy. Emerging as a Reformed monastic community, it became a bold experiment in ecumenism, bringing together the Reformed, Lutherans, Roman Catholics, Episcopalians, and others, fusing the ecumenical and liturgical movements in its life.

By this time, Presbyterians were aware of changes taking place in Roman Catholic worship. Two decades before Vatican II, Scott F. Brenner, in his book *Way of Worship: A Study in Ecumenical Recovery,* noted the reforms taking place in Roman Catholic worship and observed, "The Protestant branch of the Church is equally in need of liturgical and ecumenical recovery."[8] Brenner for a time served on Faith and Order's Committee on Ways of Worship. He subsequently became one of the most influential members of the committee that produced the next edition of the Presbyterian service book, and he served for a time as its chair. In the mid-1960s, while serving on the service book committee, he worked with the Roman Catholic Church's International Commission on English in the Liturgy, and participated in the Liturgical Conference, which was even then becoming increasingly ecumenical, moving beyond its Roman Catholic, Benedictine origins.

And so in 1955, in the spirited renewal of the time, the General Assembly of the Presbyterian Church in the U.S.A. again called for a revision of the service book and reconstituted the Committee on the Book of Common Worship. The work on this edition would span a remarkably revolutionary period in ecumenism and liturgical reform.

Joining in the project was the United Presbyterian Church in North America, which in 1947 had published a book titled *The Manual for Worship*, containing guidelines for worship and some orders and liturgical texts. Before the new service book was completed, these two churches merged, forming the United Presbyterian Church in the U.S.A.

The southern-based Presbyterian Church in the U.S. became another partner. The Cumberland Presbyterian Church joined in the project at a later date. The Reformed Church in America and the United Church of Christ were also involved in early phases of the work.

A NEW DIRECTORY FOR WORSHIP

As the committee appointed to revise *The Book of Common Worship* began its work, it was confronted with the great disparity between the Directory for Worship and contemporary liturgical renewal. The directory was virtually unchanged since it was adopted nearly one hundred and seventy years earlier in 1788, and it was based on the Directory of the Westminster Assembly, which predated it by nearly one and a half centuries. A directory reflecting the liturgical climate of the seventeenth century was clearly outmoded.

It had not been possible for any of the preceding service books, since the beginning of the century, to be coordinated with the Directory for Worship. This disparity needed to be addressed since the service book and directory should be in accord. Therefore in 1956, the year following its appointment, the committee reported back to the assembly that it could not proceed until the church adopted a new Directory for Worship; it recommended to the General Assembly that it be permitted to develop a new Directory for Worship. The General Assembly concurred.

In 1959 the committee finished its draft of a new Directory for Worship. The merger between the Presbyterian Church in the U.S.A. and the United Presbyterian Church in North America had taken place the year before, forming the United Presbyterian Church in the U.S.A. The 1960 General Assembly of the newly merged church received the proposed Directory. After making some amendments, the assembly by a narrow margin approved the new directory, and sent it to the presbyteries for their vote. The presbyteries overwhelmingly approved the directory, with the General Assembly of the United Presbyterian Church in the U.S.A. giving final approval in 1961.

The new directory evidenced strong influence from the liturgical and ecumenical movements. Its principal writer, Robert McAfee Brown, was a member of the service book committee. Later, he served as a Presbyterian delegate-observer to Vatican II, and was the keynote speaker at the Liturgical Conference's 1969 Liturgical Week.

The new directory embodied the insights of the liturgical heritage of the Reformed tradition and of the contemporary liturgical movement. It emphasized the communal nature of worship and participation by the people, and it sought to correct the imbalance in practice between Word and Sacrament. At the time of its adoption, Lewis A. Briner acclaimed it as "the most significant change in our basic constitutional standards since our American church came into being."

During its nearly thirty years of life, the 1961 directory had significant influence upon the worship practice of the United Presbyterian Church in the U.S.A. It brought about widespread reordering of worship, established the propriety of celebrating the Lord's Supper on each Lord's Day, and led to an increased frequency of eucharistic celebration. A renewed sense of the nature of worship brought an appreciation for the communal nature of worship and participation of the people. It also restored the place of the liturgical calendar in the church's life and prepared the way for use of a lectionary.

While continuing to be joined with the United Presbyterian Church in the U.S.A. in producing the new service book, the Presbyterian Church in the U.S. did not adopt the new directory but prepared its own. In 1963 it adopted its new directory: The Directory for the Worship and Work of the Church. A major contribution of this directory was to link the church's mission with its worship. The style of the directory of the Presbyterian Church in the U.S. differed greatly from its United Presbyterian counterpart and was more conservative in tone.

Unlike the directory of the United Presbyterian Church in the U.S.A., the directory of the Presbyterian Church in the U.S. included some liturgical texts for Baptism, confirmation, and the Lord's Supper. The United Presbyterian directory did not include any texts, providing only a theology of worship, and rubrical admonitions for ordering worship. A contributing factor to this difference is perhaps the wider use of the service book in the United Presbyterian Church U.S.A. than in the southern-based Presbyterian Church in the U.S., especially when celebrating the sacraments. Ordinarily, if a service book provides liturgical texts, they are not needed in a directory.

The inclusion of liturgical texts in the directory was therefore not as important to the United Presbyterian Church as it was in the south where the free church tradition had deeper roots and a service book was generally under suspicion. Furthermore, it should be noted that the initiative for preparing a book of services lies in actions taken by the "northern" church at the beginning of the twentieth century. It was not until the appearance of *The Book of Common Worship* of 1932 that the southern-based church endorsed the use of a book of services.

It is significant that it was the twentieth-century recovery of a service book that led to the revision and restoring of the Directory for Worship to use. Three editions of *The Book of Common Worship* had appeared, and more than fifty years had elapsed since the first edition appeared, before the General Assembly called for updating its directory. Not until the General Assembly called for the development of the fourth edition of *The Book of Common Worship* was it apparent that if a service book was to be developed that would be relevant to the day, a new and contemporary directory needed to be prepared. With adoption of the directories, work to revise *The Book of Common Worship* proceeded.

With both a new Directory and a new service book being developed, the Church Service Society was reconstituted in 1957; it would have a significant role in interpreting the liturgical reform that was taking shape. It published an occasional newsletter, *Sanctus,* which ultimately became *Reformed Liturgics,* and subsequently the quarterly journal *Reformed Liturgy & Music.*[9] In 2001, this journal was given a new format and a new name: *Call to Worship.*

ECUMENICAL IMPACT

The year 1960, five years into the committee's work, gave birth to renewed hopes for a united church. The key players were the United Presbyterian Stated Clerk, Eugene Carson Blake (who as clerk was a member of the committee to revise *The Book of Common Worship*), and Episcopal Bishop James Pike. In a sermon in Grace Cathedral in San Francisco, Blake challenged Presbyterians and Episcopalians to invite the Methodists to join with them in forming a church that would be truly reformed and truly catholic.[10] It became popularly known as the Blake-Pike proposal. Coming twelve years after failed talks between Presbyterians and Episcopalians, the proposal leads one to conclude that those desiring the union of Presbyterians and Episcopalians were seeking fulfillment of their goal in a wider union.

Thus the Consultation on Church Union (COCU) emerged, soon embracing nine churches in the consultation, and eventually involving Roman Catholics, Lutherans, and the Reformed Church in America as advisory participants.

The Commission on Worship of the Consultation on Church Union was destined to be the major context within which Presbyterians would develop their new service book. This was the case since Presbyterians on COCU's Commission on Worship were also on the Presbyterian's *Book of Common Worship* revision committee. During this period, the Commission on Worship completed liturgical studies, and in 1968 it published a service of Word and Eucharist as the norm of Christian worship.[11] Episcopal liturgical scholar Louis Weil wrote of this liturgy that it was "one of the most hopeful signs yet to appear in both the ecumenical and liturgical movements."[12]

Two years after COCU's birth, in 1962, the first of four series of Lutheran-Reformed dialogues began moving toward full communion and recognition of each other's ministry. The happy result of the twenty-five years of conversations was that the Formula of Agreement emerging from the fourth dialogue was approved in 1997.[13]

Also in 1962 the Church of South India, which fifteen years before had been formed out of a union of the Presbyterian, Anglican, and Methodist churches, authorized a liturgy, *The Book of Common Worship,* which caught the attention of the Christian world.

In the same year the Second Vatican Council was convened, with the Constitution on the Sacred Liturgy promulgated at the end of 1963. The new climate ushered in by the Second Vatican Council intensified the openness between Presbyterians and Roman Catholics that had emerged after World War II. In 1965, officially appointed members of the Roman Catholic Church and Reformed churches began a series of dialogues. Along with Robert McAfee Brown, Scott F. Brenner was a delegate-observer at the council. It was a time of unexpected growing together of Roman Catholics and Presbyterians.

Also in 1963, the Fourth World Conference on Faith and Order was held in Montreal. The report of its section, Worship and the Oneness of Christ's Church, evidenced "the interaction of the liturgical revival with the ecumenical movement" and affirmed that renewal of liturgy would greatly strengthen Christian unity.[14] Faith and Order work following this meeting would focus on "The Eucharist, A Sacrament of Unity."

When the international liturgical journal *Studia Liturgica* was formed in 1962 by Wiebe Vos of the Dutch Reformed Church, two members of the Presbyterian *Book of Common Worship* revision committee, Scott Brenner and Dwight Chalmers, along with the liaison from the United Church of Christ to the committee, were named as advisors in its publication. Five years later, Societas Liturgica, the international academy of liturgical scholars, was formed. Reformed liturgical scholars, including American Presbyterians, make up an important constituency of Societas Liturgica.

In the mid-1960s the Consultation on Common Texts was formed as an ecumenical forum for churches in the United States and Canada. It began work preparing English-language liturgical texts common to most service books, in anticipation of uniformity of texts among the churches. This work became part of the work of the International Consultation on English Texts and was published as *Prayers We Have in Common*.[15]

Such was the context for preparing the next Presbyterian service book, with some members of the revision committee also engaged in the ecumenical conversations.

For a time it was hoped that the service books of the United Church of Christ and the Presbyterians could be as much alike as possible, but this did not happen. When the Presbyterians' book was published, it bore the name of three Presbyterian churches.

The Committee on the Book of Common Worship distributed two trial-use resources in the course of its work: *Service for the Lord's Day and Lectionary for the Christian Year*,[16] and *The Book of Common Worship: Provisional Services and Lectionary for the Christian Year*.[17]

THE WORSHIPBOOK IS PUBLISHED

In 1970 the work of the committee was published as *The Worshipbook—Services*,[18] and two years later it was republished with a collection of hymns as *The Worshipbook—Services and Hymns,* commonly called *The Worshipbook*. In its report to the 1970 General Assembly, the committee reported that its work was completed and described the book. The only recommendations that were part of the report were (a) that the committee be discharged and (b) that the assembly note the formation of an editorial committee to provide for necessary editorial functions until the book's publication. The report was received and the recommendations adopted. *The Worshipbook* was therefore "authorized" in the sense that the General Assembly authorized the revision of *The Book of Common Worship* and appointed a special committee to accomplish the task. In receiving the report the assembly recognized that the task it had authorized was completed.

The contributions of *The Worshipbook* are noteworthy:

1. the ordering of the Service for the Lord's Day
2. inclusion of a lectionary for Sundays and festivals
3. the break from Elizabethan English to contemporary English
4. combining the church's liturgy with the music for the liturgy into one pew book
5. more resources for the liturgical year

This is a significant list. The committee that prepared *The Worshipbook* moved boldly into uncharted areas and, therefore, produced a book that was vulnerable to resistance. The weaknesses of *The Worshipbook* have often been pointed out, but whatever its shortcomings, its contributions need to be underscored.

THE SERVICE FOR THE LORD'S DAY

The way in which *The Worshipbook* ordered Sunday worship is perhaps its most significant contribution. Prior to its publication, the 1946 *Book of Common Worship* provided five orders of morning worship and five orders of evening worship. The purpose of five orders was to provide a variety of texts, since the order did not change. Only one full order for the celebration of the Lord's Supper was included. However, a eucharistic liturgy to be added to a service of the Word was included, as well as a liturgy for serving Communion to the sick. While the 1946 *Book of Common Worship* provided a rich variety of liturgical texts for Sunday worship, this book of services reflected a service of the Word as the norm for the Lord's Day, and the Lord's Supper as an occasional observance.

The Directory for Worship adopted by the United Presbyterian Church in 1961 played a dominant role in shaping *The Worshipbook*. This is particularly true with the Service for the Lord's Day. The Directory stated, "It is fitting that it [the Lord's Supper] be observed as frequently as on each Lord's Day."[19] The Directory thus opened the door for the book of services to provide a service of Word *and* Sacrament as normative for Lord's Day worship. Reflecting the Directory, the committee chose to include only one order of worship for use every Sunday, an order that included both Word and the Lord's Supper. This action, clearly linking worship on the Lord's Day with preaching of the Word and celebration of the Lord's Supper, was a bold step forward in the face of prevailing practice.

The manner in which the committee structured this Service for the Lord's Day was a unique and valuable contribution to the ordering of Christian worship. While the service is a full service of the Word and Eucharist, it is unique in that it includes an alternative ending in recognition that most congregations were not yet ready to celebrate the Lord's Supper each week. At the point of the offering, a rubric was inserted directing the congregation to an alternative ending of the service, for use when the Lord's Supper is not celebrated. The alternative ending includes a prayer of thanksgiving that parallels the eucharistic prayer. Thus the structure remains the same whether or not the sacrament is celebrated.

When the Lord's Supper is not celebrated, only those elements are deleted that pertain exclusively to the celebration of the Sacrament. The effect of this service is to *delete* the Sacrament if it is not celebrated, rather than to *add* the Sacrament if it is to be celebrated. This ordering of Lord's Day worship thereby clearly sets forth the Word *and* Eucharist as normative for worship on each Lord's Day, yet accommodates those congregations that as yet do not embrace this in practice. Use of this order is a constant reminder that a service of Word *and* Sacrament is the norm of Christian worship.

This marked a radical change for congregations accustomed to following a different order of service when the Eucharist was celebrated. Although the Service for the Lord's Day is not as yet universally embraced, the structure of the Service is now followed by most Presbyterian Church (U.S.A.) congregations and is widely recognized by Presbyterians as the norm for worship on the Lord's Day. Adoption of this order has been accompanied by a steady increase in the frequency of eucharistic celebration.

LECTIONARY

While the 1946 *Book of Common Worship* was the first American Presbyterian service book to include a complete lectionary, it was the lectionary published in *The Worshipbook* that gained the attention of the church. At the time the Directory for Worship was adopted and *The Worshipbook* was being prepared, Scott Brenner argued that use of a lectionary, with readings determined by the liturgical calendar, would provide

> a full course of scriptural instruction, a planned and balanced curriculum that sets forth the whole gospel of God. Here is a heritage that belongs to all of us and it is much to be preferred over the tyranny of a so-called free lectionary which may be based upon one man's [*sic*] indigestion and imposed by the dictation of one froward mind. The minister, whose ego itches to be pampered even in the reading of God's word and who justifies it upon the grounds of Protestant freedom, should pause at the words of John Williamson Nevin, a reformed divine, who asserted: "Of all sorts of

tyrannical rule indeed, the most slavish always is that which owns no law, and moves in no fixed orbit, but stands only in the arbitrary will and pleasure of the individual by whom it is exercised."[20]

In preparing a lectionary for *The Worshipbook,* the committee based its work on a lectionary developed by a Scottish liturgical scholar, A. Allan McArthur.[21] A proposed lectionary was circulated throughout the church with the trial-use liturgies.[22] Lewis A. Briner was the principal member of the service book committee responsible for developing the lectionary.

As the new service book neared completion, an Episcopal member of the Consultation on Church Union's Commission on Worship, Massey Shepherd Jr., shared a prepublication draft of the new Roman Catholic lectionary with the Presbyterian members of the commission. This lectionary, the product of reforms set in place by the Second Vatican Council, was developed for use in the Roman Catholic Church as part of its post–Vatican II liturgical reformation. In developing the lectionary the Catholic task force was assisted by an ecumenical group of thirty biblical scholars. The work spanned five years and was completed in 1969.

When the Presbyterian committee preparing the new service book studied the new lectionary, it became apparent that the Roman lectionary was superior to the lectionary the committee had introduced in 1964. They also envisioned the ecumenical possibilities of adopting this lectionary. Permission was received to revise the Roman lectionary for inclusion in the final publication of the book of services, thus setting aside any further preparation of an exclusively Presbyterian lectionary. Lewis Briner had the major responsibility of revising the Catholic lectionary for Presbyterian use. After making appropriate changes, the Catholic lectionary was incorporated into *The Worshipbook.* This adoption of the Roman lectionary evidenced a significant shift in attitude among Presbyterians brought about by dialogue with Roman Catholics. Other churches soon followed, adapting the Roman lectionary for their own use.

LANGUAGE

The *Worshipbook* committee also took a bold step in breaking away from Elizabethan English in an attempt to seek a contemporary language style suitable for worship in the twentieth century. During the years of its work, the committee that prepared *The Worshipbook* gradually came to the conclusion that a new service book needed to be in contemporary English, rather than a form of English no longer spoken. The first liturgical material circulated by the committee for trial use was in Elizabethan English.[23] The next material, although using the older form of English, also included a Service for the Lord's Day in contemporary English.[24] When *The Worshipbook—Services* was finally completed in 1970, only contemporary English was incorporated.

As the first service book to appear in contemporary English, *The Worshipbook* was vulnerable in many ways. There was little experience in preparing prayer books in contemporary English. The Roman Catholics were only beginning to translate the Latin liturgy into English. While the Roman liturgies served the purpose for which they were intended, much of the language was rather pedestrian. The language of the liturgy did not soar. Nor did the committee preparing *The Worshipbook* have available any experience from another Protestant church, for none had yet attempted to prepare a service book using contemporary English. It was therefore unclear what direction liturgical language would take.

The committee chose a language style that tended to be colloquial, although it did avoid the jargon of much so-called "contemporary worship" characteristic of the 1960s. Unfortunately, its inclination toward colloquial language inevitably dated much of the liturgy contained in *The Worshipbook*. The language was not durable. The committee furthermore set aside the rich classic liturgical texts of the past, rather than recast them in modern English.

When *The Worshipbook—Services and Hymns* was published in 1972, it received a damaging blow. This 1972 volume, and its earlier 1970 companion edition (*The Worshipbook—Services*), became available at the very time that the church's consciousness was beginning to be raised concerning gender inclusive language. Thus, during the 1973 General Assembly, the Interim Task Force on Women pointed out that the 1971 General Assembly had mandated that the church revise all present church documents within three years (by 1974) in accordance with the principle of eliminating so-called generic usages of masculine language. This clear directive of 1971 and its three-year timeline, therefore, resulted in the 1973 General Assembly requesting that *The Worshipbook—Services and Hymns* be examined and that recommendations for its revision be made.[25]

At the assembly the following year (1974), the report was given, identifying five options for revising the text to make it more inclusive. Costs ranged from a low of $37,750 to a high of $1,070,000, with the Special Committee recommending a judicious $110,000 option. The 1974 Assembly, however, was also facing budget concerns. Therefore, upon hearing how much it would cost to reprint *The Worshipbook,* the assembly amended the committee's report by deleting all of the options to revise and reprint, and authorized "continued publication and distribution of current editions of *The Worshipbook.*" This action by the 1974 assembly left the 1971 assembly's commitment to inclusive language in limbo, if not undermined, and therefore prompted a number of commissioners to record their dissent. Although the recommended changes were not made in *The Worshipbook*, the report was a valuable aid in preparing the 1993 edition of the *Book of Common Worship* that was to follow.

A BOOK FOR THE PEW

One of the distinct achievements of *The Worshipbook* was that it combined the liturgy of the church with music for the liturgy. While the 1946 *Book of Common*

Worship was prepared for placement in the pews, it was not until *The Worship-book* was published along with the music for the liturgy, that a significant number of congregations had the service book in the pews, and thus readily accessible to the people. Not since the demise of the *Book of Common Order* after the Westminster Assembly, over three hundred years earlier, did Presbyterian worshipers have the liturgy in their hands. The services in *The Worshipbook* provided a liturgy in which the people were to participate, making it the worship of the people. To be most effective, therefore, the liturgies needed to be accessible to the people.[26]

Furthermore, by including both music and orders of service in a single volume, the church was given a book of worship that made it clear that music was integral to the worship of God. The 1946 edition of *The Book of Common Worship* had cited the propriety of singing liturgical music, and preceding hymnals had provided musical settings for liturgical music in a special section appended to the collections of hymns. The placement and separate numeration of this section implied a token recognition of its importance. *The Worshipbook—Services and Hymns,* however, was designed so that it was clear that music is integral to the liturgy, and that liturgical music has great importance to enabling worship to soar. Rather than being placed at the back of the hymnal, three musical settings for the Service for the Lord's Day were placed immediately following the orders of service and preceding the collection of hymns.[27]

OTHER CONTRIBUTIONS

The Worshipbook furthermore contributed to the growing appreciation of the liturgical calendar. It incorporated a clear description of the calendar in the lectionary and provided a collect for each Sunday and festival in the liturgical calendar. Though the collects were principally based on readings in cycle A of the lectionary, they were provided for use during all three cycles.

The development of *The Worshipbook* was undertaken during a time when the recovery of a biblical theology had great influence in reshaping the church. The church, helped by the theological movements of the time, reflected theologically upon the nature of the church and its ministry, particularly the ministry of the laity. The boards of education provided outstanding curriculum materials that helped the church recover a knowledge of the church's history and of the saving acts of God in human history. Norman Langford Jr. of the United Presbyterian Board of Christian Education was named to the committee preparing *The Worshipbook.* This provided a vital link between the board and the service book committee. Langford was editor-in-chief of the *Christian Faith and Life* curriculum, a curriculum with a solid biblical base and a strong sense of history and historical continuity. Langford also prepared a study guide to the Directory for Worship (1961). Church officer training resources centered upon the nature of the church, its worship, and purpose. Adult educational resources engaged the people in substantive theological reflection. The church's educational endeavor and the preparation of the book of services were closely linked. The result was that this strong biblical, theological, and historical emphasis helped shape *The Worshipbook* and the way it was introduced to the church.

While *The Worshipbook* had its critics, its contributions were major. It was a significant milestone in American Presbyterian worship.

Chapter 4

A New Book of Services Is Called For

The Second Vatican Council set off a great resurgence of liturgical reform in virtually every branch of the church. *The Worshipbook* was first in the wave of revised service books that were to appear among North American churches in the two decades following the Council. As the first of a new breed of service books, its long-term usefulness was vulnerable as liturgical reform spread. Presbyterians who cared a great deal about worship soon recognized the need to go beyond *The Worshipbook*. It was therefore no surprise that a new service book was soon called for.

AN OVERTURE FROM THE PRESBYTERY OF THE CASCADES

This part of the story begins in 1979. The place is the small county-seat town of Lakeview, Oregon, in a sparsely populated area of south central Oregon. The key player is Duncan Hanson, who at the time was pastor of the Presbyterian congregation in Lakeview. Hanson took great care in nurturing the congregation to understand that the liturgy is crucial in forming the faith and life of the church, and that it is at the very heart of the church's renewal. The Lord's Supper was increasingly important for the Lakeview church.

On March 27, 1979, Duncan Hanson guided the session of the Lakeview church in proposing that their presbytery send an overture to the General Assembly to prepare a new book of services. An overture to the presbytery was adopted, in which the session described the need for a new service book and identified specific concerns that the new book should address.

The overture was then sent to the stated clerk of the Presbytery of the Cascades. In the cover letter, it was apparent that the congregation was frustrated with the limitations of *The Worshipbook*. Hanson wrote:

> [W]e have discussed worship at length quite a number of times and practically every time the Session has felt that the *Worshipbook* has proven to be an inadequate guide for our parish worship. Our Session feels strongly that the time has come to prepare a new book, that this must be done at the General Assembly level, and that there is nothing we can do at a Presbytery level that can ameliorate the situation other than overture the General Assembly.[1]

At its October meeting, the Presbytery of the Cascades acted in support of the Lakeview motion. The presbytery fine-tuned the text of the Lakeview petition and adopted it as an overture to be sent to the 192nd General Assembly of the United Presbyterian Church in the U.S.A. (1980). The overture embraced each concern raised by the Lakeview session. While giving overwhelming support, many in the presbytery were not optimistic that the General Assembly would adopt the overture. It became Overture 10 to the assembly, and read as follows.

An Overture from the Presbytery of the Cascades to the 192nd General Assembly, Concerning a New Worship Book

> WHEREAS, a worship book is needed that lends itself naturally to the people's use in worship;
> WHEREAS, Presbyterian worship should reflect as fully as possible the richness of our apostolic and reformed heritage;
> WHEREAS, a worship book is needed whose felicity of language will bear the strains of repeated use;
> WHEREAS, a worship book is needed that witnesses to the oneness of male and female in the gospel;
> WHEREAS, the Psalter should be included in the worship book for the convenient use of God's people;
> WHEREAS, a worship book is needed which includes special services for Christmas, Ash Wednesday, Palm Sunday, Maundy Thursday, Good Friday, the Vigil of Easter, Pentecost, and other occasions;
> WHEREAS, a worship book is needed whose theology of confirmation/commissioning fully recognizes the meaning and place of Baptism as the sacrament of entry into Christ's Church and as a sign of the gift of the Spirit empowering the saints for ministry;
> WHEREAS, marriage and funeral services are needed which will be practical for varieties of use;

WHEREAS, the present ordination service needs to be clarified to reflect more clearly that ordination is to different tasks;

WHEREAS, the "Other Prayers for Christian Worship" and the "Prayers for Use at Home" included in the present *Worshipbook* should be supplemented by further new prayers and organized in a more usable fashion;

WHEREAS, both *The Worshipbook* and *The Book of Common Worship* have strengths that must be preserved; and whereas a people's worship book can result only from a general dialogue in the church; and whereas, above all, the renewal of worship is of great urgency at this particular moment;

THEREFORE, the Presbytery of the Cascades overtures the 192nd General Assembly, meeting in 1980, to cause to be prepared a new book of services for corporate worship, including a psalter and other worship aids, to be completed by the time of the 200th General Assembly in 1988.

ADOPTED—October 27, 1979

In the meantime another part of the story was beginning two thousand miles away at Montreat, North Carolina, where another spring began to flow, one that would form a tributary to join the stream from Oregon at the General Assembly.

In September 1978, after serving as a Presbyterian pastor for the previous twenty-one years in Montana and New Mexico, I accepted the position of director of the Joint Office of Worship of the United Presbyterian Church in the U.S.A. and the Presbyterian Church in the U.S. The following June (1979), I participated in the Worship and Music Conference at Montreat, North Carolina. This annual conference is sponsored by the Presbyterian Association of Musicians, and at that time the Joint Office of Worship was underwriting the cost of the worship component of the conference.

James F. White, then at Perkins School of Theology at Southern Methodist University (Dallas, Texas), led one of the seminars on worship. The other worship seminar was led by Arlo D. Duba, then Dean of the Chapel and Instructor in Worship at Princeton Theological Seminary (Princeton, New Jersey). I participated in the seminars and engaged in lengthy discussions with them about the direction the Joint Office of Worship might take to guide the future of worship in the Presbyterian Church.

In these conversations it became clear that, even though it had been only nine years since *The Worshipbook* was published, it was time to begin a long range plan to develop the successor to that book. White shared with me the process the United Methodists were using to lead them to a new book of worship.

Following the conference my wife, Marie, and I left for a vacation with some of our children in Albuquerque, New Mexico. Marie did most of the driving. I wrote on a legal pad virtually nonstop, thinking, planning, rewriting. Two days later, when we reached Albuquerque, I had in my hands a substantive beginning of a proposal for developing a new Presbyterian book of services, adapting a process used by the United Methodist Church.

When the Administrative Committee of the Joint Office of Worship met in the fall of 1979, I shared the proposal with the committee. James Kirk, Discipleship and Worship staff person in the Program Agency of the United Presbyterian Church in the U.S.A., asked, "Have you heard about the proposal for a new worship book coming from the Presbytery of the Cascades?" I had not. He then sent me a copy of the overture quoted above.

It was quickly apparent to the Joint Administrative Committee that the work that I had done in outlining a process that could lead to a new service book was complementary to the Presbytery of the Cascades overture. The Joint Administrative Committee encouraged me to further refine the proposal for its review at the March 1980 meeting of the committee.

In March, a revised proposal was presented to the committee. The Joint Administrative Committee received the proposal, approved it "in principle," supporting the position "that such a project be pursued through the Joint Office of Worship."[2] It was to be made available to the committee of the General Assembly that would consider the Presbytery of the Cascades overture. It would be offered as a staff document for use, if requested, in relation to the possible development of a new book of services. The proposal recommended

> That the Joint Office of Worship, in consultation with The Advisory Council on Discipleship and Worship,
> a.   proceed with a process of developing a new book of services and hymns for corporate worship, as a successor to *The Worshipbook;*
> b.   publish a series of supplementary liturgical resources for interim trial usage as an integral part of the developmental process; and
> c.   develop the book, as much as may be possible, in cooperation with other Presbyterian and Reformed churches.[3]

The proposal elaborated upon the place service books and hymnals fill in the church's life. It noted that the church has produced a new service book about every twenty-one years and a new hymnal about every nineteen years. It called attention to the vigor with which liturgical forms and liturgical theology had progressed in the decade following the publication of *The Worshipbook.* It cited strengths and weaknesses of *The Worshipbook,* and it noted the growing number of voices calling for a new book of services, and for orders, texts, and resources not presently available in that volume. It noted, in particular, Overture 10 going to the 192nd General Assembly.

The proposal set forth a very different process for developing the new worship resource from that followed with previous service books. Each of the previous service books had been developed by a committee appointed by the General Assembly. The work of these committees was funded out of the per capita apportionment that funds operations of the Office of the General Assembly. The Office of the Stated Clerk staffed the committee. For thirty of the sixty-seven years between 1903 and 1970, the General Assembly maintained a committee responsible for the church's service book, proposing revisions, and working on revision.

The church in 1980 was in a different place in providing, at the General Assembly level, assistance in worship concerns. In the restructuring of the national church in the previous decade, the United Presbyterian Church in the U.S.A. had formed an Advisory Council on Discipleship and Worship related to the General Assembly Mission Council. Among its responsibilities were theological and constitutional concerns regarding worship. Worship program was designated as the responsibility of the Discipleship and Worship Program in the Program Agency. James G. Kirk staffed both of these functions.

Furthermore, in 1970, the year that *The Worshipbook* was published, an Office of Worship and Music was formed to serve the United Presbyterian Church in the U.S.A. and the Presbyterian Church in the U.S.; Horace T. Allen Jr. was employed to staff this office. Three years later, this office evolved into the Joint Office of Worship. In its relationship with the United Presbyterian Church, the Joint Office of Worship was an integral part of the Discipleship and Worship Program of the Program Agency. In its relationship with the Presbyterian Church in the U.S., the Joint Office of Worship was part of the Division of National Mission. It was the first joint office serving the two churches, an early harbinger of the reunion of these two churches consummated in 1983.

Therefore, unlike the structure in place when the General Assembly called for the preparation of each of the previous service books, the church now had a worship program entity that could assume the responsibility of overseeing the development of a new service book. The proposal therefore stated:

> The Joint Office of Worship presently bears the responsibility for the development of worship resources for both The United Presbyterian Church in the USA, and The Presbyterian Church in the US. It is an integral part of the Discipleship and Worship Program (Program Agency) of The United Presbyterian Church in the USA, and is the worship locus of The Presbyterian Church in the US (through the Division of National Mission). Since it presently has this responsibility and will have the task of implementing use of the new liturgical materials upon their completion, The Joint Office of Worship will properly be responsible for their development.[4]

Fifteen subjects were proposed for possible development as trial use resources: (1) Service for the Lord's Day—Word and Eucharist; (2) Baptism; (3) Psalter; (4) Daily Prayer; (5) Christian Wedding; (6) Christian Funeral; (7) Commissioning/Confirmation; (8) Ordination; (9) Liturgical Year—Christmas Cycle and Lesser Festivals; (10) Liturgical Year—Paschal Cycle; (11) Hymns; (12) Musical Settings for the Liturgy; (13) Lectionary; (14) Ministry to the Sick and Dying; (15) Occasional Services (such as Dedications).

The proposal called for the establishment of a series of task forces across the following ten years, each with a task, defined by the Joint Administrative Committee, to prepare a particular component of the future service book.

Each component was to include "liturgical text, together with a brief theological, historical, pastoral rationale and practical suggestions for use." Care was to be taken that the language be gender inclusive and that the diversity of the church be given attention.

The director of the Joint Office of Worship would staff each of the task forces, and the work of each task force would be carefully monitored by the Administrative Committee of the Joint Office of Worship. Each task force was to propose a draft of the resource, which would then be tested. Evaluation of this draft would be sought from a wide range of testers. Counsel and advice of the Advisory Council on Discipleship and Worship were to be sought regarding the contents of the testing manuscript. The results would then inform the final revision of the manuscript.

It was hoped that this process would ensure that the service book would be "a liturgy of the church as a whole, eminently usable and widely supported." The proposal envisioned the final book of services, based on the trial-use resources, being available in May 1991.[5]

THE GENERAL ASSEMBLY ACTS

The 1980 General Assembly met in Detroit, Michigan. The opening celebration of the Eucharist at that assembly was carefully planned, thanks to the outgoing moderator, Howard Rice, professor of worship at San Francisco Theological Seminary. It was a fitting beginning to the assembly that was to give approval to the development of a new service book.

Overture 10 was assigned to the Assembly Committee on Liturgy and Worship, chaired by August J. Kling. Donald Wilson Stake, prominent in the promotion of liturgical renewal in the church, was the assistant to the committee, appointed by the Office of the Stated Clerk. Stake had recently chaired the "Special Committee of the General Assembly to Study the Theology, Nature and Practice of the Lord's Supper."

In providing resources to the assembly committee, I met and talked with Duncan Hanson for the first time. Each of us was available to the committee during its deliberations.

The assembly committee welcomed the proposal, which helped shape their deliberations and subsequent action to approve the overture. It made some minor changes, and gave greater specificity to the recommendations reflecting the proposal. The committee left open the possibility that the proposed worship resource might not be a single volume like *The Worshipbook,* so it inserted "(or books)" wherever "a worship book" appeared, so that it read: "a worship book (or books)." It expanded the overture to include a hymnal as a part of the projection. It recognized that the process would take longer than eight years and, therefore, deleted the 200th General Assembly (1988) as the projected date of publication. Otherwise the body of the overture remained as it had been received from the Presbytery of the Cascades.[6]

The Assembly Committee on Liturgy and Worship recommended the following action:

1. That the Program Agency, Discipleship and Worship Program, and the Joint Office of Worship, in consultation with the Advisory Council on Discipleship and Worship, proceed immediately with the development of materials for service book, Psalter, and hymnal, using inclusive language and being sensitive to the diverse nature of The United Presbyterian Church in the United States of America;

2. That over the next several years a variety of worship resources be made available in paperback for trial use throughout the church before any publication is finalized; and

3. That the initial cost for 1981 of such development be borne within the program budget of the Joint Office of Worship, with continuing cost to be displayed and reviewed by the Program Agency prior to the further development of resources and reported to the 193rd General Assembly (1981).[7]

With these friendly alterations to Overture 10, the committee recommended to the Assembly that the overture, with the committee's revisions, be adopted.

Three committee members from among those who opposed the preparation of a new book of services prepared and filed a minority report calling for the Assembly not to concur with the overture. The minority report cited worthy aspects of *The Worshipbook,* pointed out "that no service book can be entirely adequate," claimed that the cost of such a project would be "poor stewardship of the Church's resources and priorities," and that time needed to be given for the church fully to appropriate *The Worshipbook.*[8]

Wesley D. Lackey, a minister commissioner from Grace Presbytery (Texas), active in worship renewal in his presbytery, was selected by the committee to give the supporting speech on the assembly floor.

In the meantime, the General Assembly Mission Council asked for information as it dealt with the financial implications of the project. The chairperson of the Joint Administrative Committee of the Joint Office of Worship (and member of the General Assembly Mission Council), Dorothea Snyder, asked me to prepare a statement that would be useful to the Council.

I prepared a statement emphasizing why such a project is important. The statement cited worship concerns that had come before the General Assembly since publication of *The Worshipbook,* such as inclusive language, theology and practice of the Sacraments, personal and communal prayer. The statement also included an overview of the process set forth in the proposal, seeing the process as providing for the church "a long term program of worship nurture."

The statement underscored the centrality of worship in the church's life: "Worship is the living center in the life of the church both in its life together in relationship with its Lord, and in its commitment to God's mission." And: "The recommended program would provide a new instrument for the renewal of the church at its life-giving center."

When the General Assembly Council reported, the statement I had prepared constituted its advice and counsel to the General Assembly in relation to the action recommended by the Assembly Committee on Liturgy and Worship.[9]

In the evening, when the Committee on Liturgy and Worship was to report, its place in the agenda was repeatedly delayed by the press of other business. Marion Liebert, the Administrative Assistant for the Joint Office of Worship, and I sat high on the side watching and listening to the assembly's deliberations. Well past midnight the report of the committee was called for. The committee's recommendations were set forth. Wesley Lackey spoke to the recommendations. Those supporting the minority report spoke. The assembly debated. The vote was taken. We held our breath. The direction of the future work of the Joint Office of Worship would be determined in that vote. The vote of the assembly was overwhelmingly in favor of the committee's recommendation.

As momentous as the action seemed to those of us who believe that the church's service book is important in the church's life, the action received only a slight mention in the assembly newspaper. Nevertheless, the effect of that action in the years that followed continues to be felt in every part of the church.

The Presbyterian Church in the U.S.—which before the task was completed would reunite with the United Presbyterian Church in the U.S.A. to form the Presbyterian Church (U.S.A.)—became a partner in the project through its Division of National Mission's involvement in the Joint Office of Worship. The Cumberland Presbyterian Church became a partner in the project through action of its Board of Christian Education to participate. Thus the same partners that produced *The Worshipbook* were engaged in developing the new service book.

Substantial funding of the Joint Office of Worship for the project was required by the assembly action. In the years that followed, that funding was faithfully provided by the three churches engaged in the project.

Chapter 5

The *Book of Common Worship* Is Prepared

Following the 1980 General Assembly, James F. White and Hoyt Hickman of the Section on Worship of The General Board of Discipleship, United Methodist Church, were invited to a meeting of the Administrative Committee of the Joint Office of Worship to describe the process the Methodists were utilizing in developing trial-use resources. From these conversations it was clear that the process portrayed in the proposal to the General Assembly was on target, and the work would proceed.

SUPPLEMENTAL LITURGICAL RESOURCES

Between 1984 and 1992, seven trial-use resources were published, each including proposed text for a portion of the service book. The trial-use volumes were published under the series title Supplemental Liturgical Resources (SLR). Each volume was prepared by a task force chosen for the task, and was thoroughly tested prior to publication. Evaluations received from use of these resources greatly aided the preparation of the service book resulting from the process.

The projection of anticipated components in the series remained close to what was initially envisioned. Some of the projected resources were merged, and the hymnal was separated from the development of the service book. In 1986 the General Assembly launched an extended study of the theology and practice of ordination within the Reformed tradition. A decision was made that, instead of delaying the publishing of the service book until the study was completed and the church had a chance to act on any recommendations coming out of the study, the projected ordination rites would be incorporated into a separate book of occasional services, modeled after the ordinal of the Church of Scotland.

The series of trial-use resources was published by The Westminster Press, and following restructuring after reunion, by Westminster/John Knox Press. Each was published with a soft cover, and appeared as follows:

SLR-1   *The Service for the Lord's Day* (task force appointed in 1980, work published in 1984)

SLR-2   *Holy Baptism and Services for the Renewal of Baptism* (task force appointed in 1980, work published in 1985)

SLR-3   *Christian Marriage* (task force appointed in 1982, work published in 1986)

SLR-4   *The Funeral: A Service of Witness to the Resurrection* (task force appointed in 1982, work published in 1986)

SLR-5   *Daily Prayer* (task force appointed in 1981, work published in 1987)

SLR-6   *Services for Occasions of Pastoral Care* (task force appointed in 1986, work published in 1990)

SLR-7   *The Liturgical Year* (task force appointed in 1984, work published in 1992)

The Psalter that was envisioned in 1980 ultimately appeared in three forms: (1) *The Presbyterian Hymnal* (1990), containing a significant section of psalmody, most of which is metrical psalmody. (2) A new Psalter: *The Psalter—Psalms and Canticles for Singing* (1993), the work of a task force appointed in 1981, embodying nearly two hundred responsorial settings of psalms and canticles. (3) The text of an inclusive-language Psalter in the *Book of Common Worship,* pointed for singing to simple chant tones, and formatted for responsive reading in churches where such is needed.

The early vision of involving many people in the project was achieved. Whereas the development of each of the previous service books engaged a single committee, seven task forces were involved in developing the trial-use resources, along with a Psalter task force and the hymnal committee. Sixty-five persons were involved in the development of the various components of the action taken by the 1980 General Assembly by serving on one of the task forces or the hymnal committee.

Many others served in a review capacity, going over the work of the task groups. The Administrative Committee of the Joint Office of Worship (the Office of Worship after reunion), and then the Theology and Worship Ministry Unit following restructuring, were responsible for monitoring the work of each task force, then authorizing the publication of each resource upon its completion.[1]

Another important contribution to the project came in relation to the testing drafts. The evaluation and guidance provided by the Advisory Council on Discipleship and Worship, through its Worship Committee, was invaluable, until the Council was dissolved at the time of restructuring following reunion. The report of the Advisory Council was transmitted directly to the Administrative Committee and to the task force preparing the manuscript to inform its final draft. Since membership on these agencies was by elected classes, many additional persons were involved at some phase of the project.

The engagement of many people in the process is further evidenced in the number that were involved in testing the material. This number varied with each resource and ranged from fifty to nearly one hundred churches or individuals who were asked to evaluate each of the manuscripts. This testing was exceedingly helpful in final revision of the manuscripts.

Through various means, all who were using the trial-use resources were invited to submit evaluations. Many wrote or otherwise communicated their comments.

The development of the Supplemental Liturgical Resources spanned the reunion of the two churches that were involved in the Joint Office of Worship. This had a significant effect on the project. For example, a Directory for Worship normally precedes development of a service book. Reunion meant that the process would not be so tidy. A new Directory for Worship was needed to replace the provisional directory in the Plan for Reunion. The result was that five of the Supplemental Liturgical Resources were developed prior to or during the life of the committee that prepared the new Directory adopted in 1989.[2] The effect, however, was positive, in that there was a closer affinity between the theological and directive roles of a directory and the practice of worship reflected in a service book. The cross-fertilization produced a stronger directory and greater consistency in the liturgical resources. Thus, the *Book of Common Worship* fully reflects the Directory for Worship adopted in 1989.

The project also survived the restructuring of the church following reunion. The first volume in the series was published under the name of the Joint Office of Worship, volumes 2 through 5 appeared after reunion, and were published under the name of the Office of Worship. Volumes 6 and 7 were published after the restructuring and therefore were part of the work of the Theology and Worship Ministry Unit. In October 1989 the Unit approved the final phase of the project, opening the way to the preparation of the final manuscript of the service book itself.

ECUMENICAL IMPACT

Throughout the preparation and publishing of the Supplemental Liturgical Resources, the work previously done by other denominations proved invaluable. Since *The Worshipbook* was the first of a new wave of liturgical resources, it did not have this advantage. That disadvantage contributed to the brevity of its effective usefulness. In contrast, the *Book of Common Worship* came late in the cycle of churches preparing new service books. It had the advantage of building on the extensive liturgical reforms that followed the Second Vatican Council. As one church went about the task of liturgical revision, it stood on the shoulders of the work that had preceded in other churches. This would give the new book an extraordinary ecumenical breadth. James F. White noted this in comments on the Supplemental Liturgical Resources:

> They represent not only current concerns among Presbyterians but the liturgical state of the art of most North American liturgies. The later one commits oneself to print, the more up-to-date the materials produced are since no church acts unilaterally any longer.[3]

During the course of development of the *Book of Common Worship*, Faith and Order continued to influence the work, as it had done in Presbyterian service books that preceded it. In 1982, as work on the new book of services began, the Faith and Order paper *Baptism, Eucharist and Ministry* was published. Its preface reaffirmed the convictions of fifty years of Faith and Order work: "If the divided churches are to achieve the visible unity they seek, one of the essential prerequisites is that they should be in basic agreement on baptism, eucharist and ministry."[4] Work toward the *Book of Common Worship* reflected the ecumenical convergence that is embodied in *Baptism, Eucharist and Ministry.*

As with the committees that produced the 1946 *Book of Common Worship* and *The Worshipbook,* members of the task forces were active in ecumenical liturgical bodies. Some were Presbyterian representatives to the Consultation on Church Union. Discussions within the Consultation's Commission on Worship, and the resulting liturgical materials, thus helped shape the *Book of Common Worship,* as it had *The Worshipbook.*

During the thirteen years leading to the *Book of Common Worship,* manuscripts for the seven trial-use resources were reviewed not only by Presbyterian pastors and liturgical scholars, but by those in other traditions as well, including Methodists, Disciples of Christ, and Lutherans. Two Roman Catholic scholars in particular gave invaluable assistance. Through the years of preparing the trial-use resources, Patrick Byrne, then on the staff of the National Liturgical Office of the Canadian Conference of Catholic Bishops, carefully assisted in the editing and revising of each of the Supplemental Liturgical Resource manuscripts, particularly in formatting, sense-lining the prayers, and offering guidance in liturgical writing. It was at the Societas Liturgica meeting in Austria in 1983 that this relationship began. During the final phase of completing the *Book of Common*

Worship, Monsignor Alan Detscher of the National Conference of Catholic Bishops, Secretariat for the Liturgy, gave invaluable assistance in formatting the book, editing rubrics, and suggesting ways the book could be made more usable. The generous amount of time these two liturgical scholars devoted to the project was invaluable and contributed immeasurably to the high quality of the book.

Also, in the years following publication of *The Worshipbook,* Presbyterians were well represented in ecumenical liturgical bodies such as Societas Liturgica, formed in 1968, just as work on *The Worshipbook—Services* was being completed,[5] and the North American Academy of Liturgy, formed in 1974, four years after that book was published.[6]

Involvement in these professional academies provided an arena for ecumenical review of Presbyterian liturgical work. One example was a review of the first draft of the initial eucharistic prayers by members of the North American Academy of Liturgy's working group on Eucharistic Prayer and Theology. Also, the Academy's Liturgical Theology working group reviewed the draft of the Directory for Worship that Presbyterians adopted in 1989.

Similar interaction resulted from participation in the Consultation on Common Texts. The major example is, of course, the lectionary. Another concerns a baptismal rite. The Presbyterian task force, in the course of preparing its baptismal rite, concluded that an ecumenically prepared baptismal rite was a possibility. The Joint Office of Worship therefore petitioned the Consultation on Common Texts (in 1983) to consider such a project. Although some of the members doubted that agreement between the churches could be reached, the consultation accepted the challenge, succeeded in preparing a rite, and published it in 1988.[7] This rite was included in the *Book of Common Worship* for optional use as an alternative to the one prepared for that book, as a witness to the one Baptism through which we are joined to the one holy catholic and apostolic church.

English Language Liturgical Consultation revisions of texts previously made available in *Prayers We Have in Common* (International Consultation on English Texts), and published as *Praying Together,*[8] and *The Revised Common Lectionary* of the Consultation on Common Texts[9] were completed in time for inclusion in the *Book of Common Worship,* giving ecumenical strength to the book.

A wonderful example of ecumenism lies behind the Psalter text that ultimately was included in the *Book of Common Worship.* One of the guidelines for preparing the book was that its language be gender inclusive. There seemed to be no satisfactory inclusive-language Psalter text available that met the criteria until we discovered the Psalter of the Church of the Province of New Zealand (Anglican), released in 1989. So, this Psalter was included in the final draft of the service book.

At the fall 1992 meeting of the Consultation on Common Texts, I shared our decision. David Holton of the Anglican Church of Canada quietly responded, "Are you prepared to handle the charges that the New Zealand Psalter is anti-Semitic?" What a bombshell! He later told me of the controversy surrounding the Psalter and agreed to obtain information for me. This was discouraging, for by this date the publishers were engaged in copyediting the completed service book manuscript.

At the January 1993 meeting of the North American Academy of Liturgy in Albuquerque, New Mexico, Msgr. Alan Detscher approached me and said that he might have the solution. Lutheran liturgical scholars Gail Ramshaw and Gordon Lathrop had just completed a gender-inclusive revision of the *Book of Common Prayer* Psalter and were even then making final publishing arrangements with Fr. Michael Naughton of Liturgical Press (at the Benedictine Abbey in Collegeville, Minnesota). I immediately talked with Lathrop, Ramshaw, and Naughton. After the Academy meeting, I was sent a copy of the Psalter on a computer diskette. By then I had copies of articles from David Holton giving both sides of the New Zealand debate. This led to a decision that, if it was not too late in the publishing schedule, we would not use the New Zealand Psalter but would use the text prepared by Ramshaw and Lathrop.

Fortunately, Westminster/John Knox Press had not yet begun copyediting the Psalter section of the *Book of Common Worship* manuscript and was willing to permit us to substitute the new text. Permission was obtained from Liturgical Press. In two weeks, the text was pointed, the psalm prayers were moved into place, and three hundred fifty substitute manuscript pages were given to the publisher. Four months later the book was in print.

This is ecumenism. A Canadian Anglican alerted us to a problem. A Roman Catholic pointed us to the solution—an Episcopalian text, revised by Lutherans, destined for publication by Roman Catholic Benedictines, and first incorporated into a service book by Presbyterians. It is an example of the way service book revision should work in an ecumenical time.[10]

THE FINAL PHASE

The research department of the Presbyterian Church (U.S.A.) documented remarkable support and use of the Supplemental Liturgical Resources throughout the church, despite the fears voiced by a few. Detractors viewed the resources as an "Episcopalization" of the church, and as a departure from "Reformed" worship. On the other hand, those involved in developing the resources, and those who find them useful, recognize them as solidly preserving the values of the previous service books and providing a fuller resourcing of worship. All of the evaluations, suggestions, and critiques that were received, whether supportive or critical, were carefully reviewed in the preparation of the final draft of the *Book of Common Worship*.

Since no insurmountable problems emerged in relation to the Supplemental Liturgical Resources, the final phase leading to publication consisted primarily in editing existing material. Having served as editor of all of the Supplemental Liturgical Resources, it was my privilege to edit them for inclusion in the *Book of Common Worship*.

The time line for completing the final draft of the service book was exceedingly tight. Due to a shrinking budget, the church was faced with a major downsizing of the national structure. Fall 1992 was tentatively set for completion of the final draft of the service book.

The worship committee of the Theology and Worship Ministry Unit, augmented by four liturgical consultants, was responsible for the oversight of revision and for submitting the final draft to the unit for approval.

A network of editorial advisors was formed to assist the editor in refining the texts during an intensive final six months of preparing the final manuscript. The advisors communicated their suggestions via PresbyNet, an early network for communication via computer. About forty-five people served in this capacity.

With the great number involved in preparing the resources, in testing, and in revision, one can rightly say that the whole church shared in the preparation of the "book."

The final draft was unanimously approved by the Theology and Worship Ministry Unit on September 19, 1992, and in that vote, the title, *Book of Common Worship,* was restored (see chapter 6). In approving the book for publication, the unit brought to completion the twelve-year process by which the book had been developed, fulfilling the request of the General Assembly in 1980. That meeting would be the unit's final meeting, as the Theology and Worship Ministry Unit was being dissolved, a victim of downsizing.

At the meeting, after the unit had approved the manuscript for publication, it was reminded of the action of the General Assembly in 1980. The assembly had expressed its hope that the book "would provide a new instrument for the renewal of the church at its life-giving center." It was then emphasized that "the hope of the 1980 Assembly remains our hope in 1992 now as the book moves to publication. The basic concern in reforming worship is above all else a concern for the renewal of the church's life and ministry."

Melva W. Costen, chairperson of the Theology and Worship Ministry Unit, expressed her belief that the *Book of Common Worship* can help root worshipers more firmly in the gospel. However, she was quick to say, "A book is not enough. For this book to be an effective instrument for renewal, it will require careful planning of worship week by week, pastoral sensitivity to the people's needs, and taking adequate time to help people understand the significance of changes that may be introduced in worship." She added, "But all of our continuing efforts in reforming worship must be inflamed by the Holy Spirit if we are to be truly renewed."

GENERAL ASSEMBLY COMMENDS
THE *BOOK OF COMMON WORSHIP*

In order to have the *Book of Common Worship* available at the 1993 General Assembly, Westminster/John Knox Press placed the book on a fast track. The

Press was also the object of downsizing, to take effect at the conclusion of the General Assembly. It was an exceedingly tight schedule. Design and composition were done in-house to expedite the schedule. As editor of the *Book of Common Worship* I had the privilege of working with the very dedicated and competent staff who devoted long hours to producing a book of quality and beauty that could be used with ease. In order to make the deadline, it meant that Maureen O'Connor and her staff often had to work till late in the night and on weekends to keep the project on schedule.

Many decisions had to be made, including choice of cover stock and design, typeface, paper, color of ink for rubrics, art to accent particular pages throughout the book, ribbons, and so on. In working with the Westminster/John Knox staff in every phase of the production, I found them highly dedicated to this project, accepting the task with a sense of Christian vocation to offer the church the best they could give in order that the church's worship might be strengthened.

All of the deadlines were met and the book was published on schedule. The printer was scheduled to ship five hundred advance copies directly to the General Assembly. Arrangements were made for me to pick up from the printer in Crawfordsville, Indiana, on May 28, two boxes of books for a celebration to be held that evening in Louisville marking the first day of the availability of the *Book of Common Worship.*

My wife and I drove to Crawfordsville, picked up the two boxes, wrapped them in blue paper and gold streamers and carried them into the party waiting for the unveiling. Gathered for a dinner together were staff members of both the Theology and Worship Ministry Unit and Westminster/John Knox Press. None of us had seen the books before the boxes were opened and we looked at them together. Some began to sense the significance of the moment as we shared in delight at such a beautiful book. It was suggested that we offer a prayer from the book, and then we agreed to celebrate together Prayer at the Close of Day. As we began to realize that this was the first occasion of use of the new *Book of Common Worship,* it became a time of special significance.

That same weekend (the last weekend of May), immediately preceding the General Assembly, an Associated Press article telling of the new *Book of Common Worship* appeared in newspapers across the country. The article elaborated on the ecumenical significance of the book.

A great deal of interest and excitement accompanied the availability of the new *Book of Common Worship* at the General Assembly, June 2–9, 1993, in Orlando, Florida. The book was the special feature at the Westminster/John Knox Press exhibit booth. The publishing house had prepared coffee mugs as gifts to the commissioners in celebration of the book's publication. It also had printed placards with selected prayers from the *Book of Common Worship,* which were placed on the tables in the hall where the commissioners ate their meals. Shopping bags featuring the *Book of Common Worship* were given to the assembly's bookstore customers. The bookstore was sold out of the book well before the end of the assembly.

Two commissioners, upon learning that no recommendation for commending the book to the church was on the agenda of the assembly, decided to prepare a commissioners' resolution. The two commissioners were Duncan Hanson (Presbytery of San Jose) and Donald Wilson Stake (Presbytery of Albany). The fact that these two ministers had been elected commissioners by their presbyteries presented a unique set of circumstances. As noted above, both had played major roles thirteen years earlier, in the 1980 General Assembly in launching the service book project.[11] Furthermore, between 1981 and 1986 Stake chaired the task force that prepared *Daily Prayer* (Supplemental Liturgical Resource 5).

Though each had played important roles in the service book project, Stake and Hanson had never met prior to a General Assembly committee leadership training meeting before the 1993 General Assembly. At that meeting, their common interest in the *Book of Common Worship* drew them together and led to their collaborating on a commissioners' resolution to commend the book to the church.

The commissioners' resolution—93-14 of the 205th General Assembly of the Presbyterian Church (U.S.A.) (1993)—read as follows:

> On Commending the 1993 *Book of CommonWorship* for the Worship of Presbyterians
>
> Whereas, the 192nd General Assembly (1980) acting in response to an overture from the Presbytery of the Cascades, mandated the preparation of a new book of services in the hope that it would be "an instrument for the renewal of the Church at its life-giving Center"; and
>
> Whereas, after thirteen years of prayerful work, the 1993 *Book of Common Worship* represents a significant ecumenical contribution to Christian worship and provides a rich and faithful resource for members and worship leaders of the Presbyterian Church (U.S.A.); and
>
> Whereas, previous General Assemblies commended predecessor Books of Common Worship for worship throughout the broader church; therefore, be it
>
> Resolved, That the 205th General Assembly (1993):
> 1. commend the 1993 *Book of Common Worship* to the congregations for their use;
> 2. commend the 1993 *Book of Common Worship* to subsequent General Assemblies for use in Assembly worship;
> 3. commend the 1993 *Book of Common Worship* to presbyteries, synods, and sessions for use in worship in their meetings;
> 4. commend the 1993 *Book of Common Worship* to General Assembly Council and its divisions and committees for use in their worship;
> 5. commend the 1993 *Book of Common Worship* to individual church members and pastors for use in daily prayer;
> 6. request the publishing concerns of the Presbyterian Church (U.S.A.) to consider offering volume discounts to allow congregations to buy the 1993 *Book of Common Worship* for every worshiper; and

7. express its appreciation to Harold M. Daniels for his invaluable service as editor of the 1993 *Book of Common Worship*.

(signed)	(signed)
Duncan Hanson	Donald W. Stake
Presbytery of San Jose	Presbytery of Albany

The commissioners' resolution was part of the report of the Assembly Committee on Worship and Sacraments. Hanson and Stake spoke to the resolution. A vote by show of hands was taken. It was virtually unanimous. With the chair of the committee, George Espy, Donald Stake and Duncan Hanson took part in giving presentation copies of the *Book of Common Worship* to selected persons whose names had been inscribed on the cover. In the computer network report from the assembly summarizing the actions of the day (June 8, 1993), the following was released by Merrill Cook:

> Duncan Hanson presented copies of the new Book of Common Worship to David Dobler, John Fife, Melva Costen, James Andrews, James D. Brown, and finally to Harold Daniels, who received a standing ovation for his work of the last fifteen years. [3:45 p.m. 06/08/93 at the 205th GA in Orlando]

A few weeks later the General Assembly of the Cumberland Presbyterian Church met. The assembly received the *Book of Common Worship* with enthusiasm and adopted a recommendation of the Christian Education Committee:

> that the 163rd General Assembly commend the *Book of Common Worship* (1993) for use in worship of Cumberland Presbyterian congregations and judicatories.

In the months following the General Assembly, festivals of worship, organized by Deborah McKinley of the Office of Worship staff, introduced the *Book of Common Worship* in Evanston, Illinois; Philadelphia, Pennsylvania; Denver, Colorado; Charlotte, North Carolina; Portand, Oregon; and Dallas, Texas.[12] The Worship and Music Conferences sponsored by the Presbyterian Association of Musicians also gave strong advocacy for the *Book of Common Worship*.

Thus were completed thirteen years of intense work on the service book. A couple of weeks later, I retired as part of the downsizing of national staff. Tasks that remained were the completion of the software edition of the service book, and a book of occasional services that would include ordination liturgies. The software edition was released in 1995.[13] The *Book of Occasional Services* was published in 1999, in a format matching the *Pastoral Care* and *Daily Prayer* editions of the *Book of Common Worship*.[14]

In the years following its publication the *Book of Common Worship* has received international ecumenical acclaim. One Anglican liturgical scholar declared, "Indeed, BCW is in my estimation the finest modern English language liturgy hitherto available, and one which makes the 1979 *Book of Common Prayer* of the Episcopal Church appear anaemic."[15]

AN UNFINISHED TASK

An English archbishop once said with great wisdom and insight that we can change the rubrics and produce liturgical reform, but it takes a change of heart to produce liturgical renewal.[16] Liturgical resources can be instruments of renewal but more is needed for renewal to occur. The church must be diligent in providing the instruments for renewal by carefully preparing resources for worship. But it also needs to be constant in nurturing the people in the faith proclaimed in the liturgy, and it must provide leadership to help pastors carefully prepare and effectively lead worship with vitality. Perhaps through these efforts the liturgy will come to life.

Chapter 6

The *Book of Common Worship:* What's New?

The *Book of Common Worship* came twenty-three years after the publication of its most recent predecessor, *The Worshipbook—Services* (1970). The *Book of Common Worship* preserves most of its major contributions, while differing from it in important ways.

THE TITLE *BOOK OF COMMON WORSHIP*

The first difference one notes is the recovery of the title *Book of Common Worship*. This title has a long and venerable history.

In the years leading to its publication there was widespread sentiment in favor of restoring the title *Book of Common Worship* (rather than continuing to use the title *The Worshipbook*). The desire to restore the older title was prompted by an appreciation of the words "common worship." A good service book embodies prayer shared in common with the whole church, and it shares the prayer in common with the faithful through the ages. In an age dominated by a pervasive individualism, the communal nature of the church and its worship needs to be underscored.

The first service book used by the Church of Scotland following its reformation was the Church of England's *Book of Common Prayer* of 1552, to which John Knox and some continental reformers, both Lutheran and Reformed, contributed. The Scots later supplanted it with John Knox's service book, the *Forme of Prayers . . . ,*[1] which was later to be titled: *The Book of Common Order.*

The title *Forme of Prayers* is comparable to that of Calvin's 1542 Genevan liturgy, *The Form of Church Prayers . . .* prayer best describes what a book of services is. Prayer is of the very essence of worship. It is appropriate that service books are also called prayer books. Later, in choosing the title *The Book of Common Order*, the Scots chose a title similar to, but distinguished from, the Anglican prayer book. While relinquishing the word "prayers" from the title, the use of "order" has merit, when one understands that the liturgy is called the *ordo,* that is, the order, the shape of the liturgy that has come down to us since earliest Christian times. Furthermore it tends to shift the focus from text to shape.

The result of the Scottish choice is that throughout the English speaking world, the Reformed have called their service books *Book of Common Order* or as American Presbyterians have chosen beginning with their first service book, published nearly a century ago, *Book of Common Worship*. The title *The Worshipbook* was the exception.[2]

It is fitting that the *Book of Common Worship* does not include the name "Presbyterian" in its title. While the book expresses worship that is in keeping with the Presbyterian Directory for Worship, it is a living expression of the worship of the whole church of Jesus Christ. In a variety of ways the liturgy is shared in common with the church throughout the ages, the church throughout the world, as well as within our own family of faith. It is therefore appropriate that the book embodies prayer from the church in every place, as the list of acknowledgments will evidence.

Upon examining the *Book of Common Worship,* one will find that the contributions of *The Worshipbook* are preserved. One will also find that the extensive liturgical texts of the *Book of Common Worship* make it a richer liturgical treasury than any previous Presbyterian service book.

SERVICE FOR THE LORD'S DAY

While there are some minor variations and options in the order for Lord's Day worship, the *Book of Common Worship* maintains the basic structure introduced in *The Worshipbook,* consistently reinforcing Word *and* Eucharist as the norm of Christian worship. But while *The Worshipbook* provided a limited number of liturgical texts for the Service for the Lord's Day, the *Book of Common Worship* has a rich variety of texts.

Two sections of alternative texts in the *Book of Common Worship* are particularly significant: the prayers of the people,[3] and the great thanksgivings.[4]

Prayers of intercession are often a neglected part of a congregation's worship.

The Worshipbook provided a single bidding prayer, and a litany of intercession.[5] A revision of the bidding prayer is included in the *Book of Common Worship*,[6] along with six other forms. Each form is uniquely different.

As Presbyterians move toward weekly Eucharist, congregations experience a need for a variety of eucharistic prayers (called great thanksgivings in the *Book of Common Worship*). *The Worshipbook* included a single great thanksgiving.[7] The *Book of Common Worship* provides twenty-four great thanksgivings. The great thanksgiving included in the Service for the Lord's Day liturgy in the *Book of Common Worship* (pp. 69–73) is the prototype for thirteen great thanksgivings in the liturgical year section of the book.[8] Eight great thanksgivings are included in the section of "Additional Texts." These great thanksgivings are of a general nature, two (F and G) are taken from ancient sources, two (B and C) provide seasonal prefaces. Great Thanksgiving I combines a set text for important segments of the prayer with rubrics to guide the one presiding at the holy table in offering prayer in her or his own words. Great Thanksgiving J consists of only rubrics to guide presiders in congregations where free prayer is customary. There is a great thanksgiving for use in a wedding, and another for use in a funeral.

THE COMMON LECTIONARY

In the decade following adaptation of the Roman Catholic lectionary for inclusion in *The Worshipbook*, a remarkable and revolutionary development occurred. The Episcopalians and Lutherans toward the end of the decade followed the Presbyterian lead, making appropriate alterations to the Roman lectionary for their own use. The Consultation on Church Union's Commission on Worship made another revision, which the Methodists adopted. The United Church of Christ, the Disciples of Christ, other Reformed churches, and the Armed Forces Chaplains Board adopted the Presbyterian version. The result was that there were five versions of the lectionary. While most of the readings were the same in all versions, many users were frustrated when they used helps based on a version of the lectionary that was different from the one their denomination adopted.

Another frustration resulted from the different ways the readings were assigned during the time after Pentecost. This resulted in Lutherans and Presbyterians (and those who adopted the Presbyterian version), usually being at a different point in the sequence than Catholics, Episcopalians, and Methodists. This was particularly frustrating to ecumenical study groups who met weekly to discuss the readings for a given Sunday.

To resolve the differences between the versions of the lectionary, the Consultation on Common Texts set out to provide a lectionary that would reflect a consensus. It formed a committee, The North American Committee on Calendar and Lectionary, to prepare a consensus lectionary to recommend to the churches. The committee was representative of denominations (Catholic and Protestant) that were then using versions of the lectionary. Ultimately, this work took on international breadth with Catholic and Anglican representation from England. Lewis A. Briner, who was responsible for the adaptation of the Roman lectionary included in *The Worshipbook,* served as chairperson. Horace T. Allen Jr. (who was a member of the Consultation on Common Texts, and for a time its chairperson) also had a major role on the committee in developing the consensus lectionary. He continues to be one of the strongest advocates of the common lectionary, having contributed to its spreading acceptance throughout the world, and to its having gained the attention of the Vatican.

So in 1982 an ecumenical common lectionary appeared for trial use. After a long period of trial, the work was revised and published in 1992 as *The Revised Common Lectionary.* Included in the *Book of Common Worship,* this lectionary is now embraced by about half of Presbyterian Church (U.S.A.) congregations.

The Roman lectionary is thus one of the great gifts to the ecumenical church coming out of the reforms set in motion by the Second Vatican Council. The common lectionary is a living expression of the unity of the church gathered around the Word.

LITURGICAL CALENDAR

A clear example of the biblical, theological, and historical foundations of the liturgy in the *Book of Common Worship* is evidenced in the way in which the liturgical calendar is more fully developed than in *The Worshipbook.* An examination of the *Book of Common Worship* will reveal that the very center of the way in which Christians celebrate time and its sacred story focuses on the death and resurrection of Jesus Christ.

Because the dying and rising of Jesus is so central to the faith (and because the structure of some of the services varies from that of the Service for the Lord's Day), complete services are provided for important days in the paschal cycle: Ash Wednesday, Passion/Palm Sunday, and the great Three Days (the *Triduum*— Maundy Thursday, Good Friday, and the Easter Vigil). In contrast, *The Worshipbook* provided only a limited number of prayer texts for these days and did not include the Easter Vigil.

The *Book of Common Worship* furthermore provides Scripture sentences for use in a call to worship, and a variety of prayers for every Sunday and festival in the calendar. These are ordinarily linked with the Sundays and festivals in each of the three years of the Revised Common Lectionary. The provision of texts in *The Worshipbook* was more limited, with a prayer of confession and a prayer of thanksgiving for each season and festival, and the collects (called "prayers of the day" in the *Book of Common Worship*).

A significant contribution of the *Book of Common Worship* is the recovery of the centrality of the paschal mystery, expressed in the Three Days. These are the holiest days of the year for Christians. Celebrating the paschal mystery helps us to reaffirm the covenant into which we were baptized, and to experience the renewing grace of dying and rising with Christ.

PSALMS

An important feature in the *Book of Common Worship* is the inclusion of a selective Psalter in inclusive language.[9] While hymnals have included some psalms for responsive reading, no Psalter has been included in the service book since the 1932 *Book of Common Worship. The Worshipbook* marked the low point in the decline of use of the Psalms. Not only were texts of the Psalms not included, few metrical psalms were included. Nor did the lectionary in *The Worshipbook* include psalms for use on Sundays and festivals, since the draft of the lectionary available to the committee did not as yet embody the list of psalms. *The Worshipbook* cited only a few psalms for use throughout a season or on a festival.

The full recognition of the Psalms in the lectionary for use on Sundays and festivals, and in daily prayer, is a significant contribution of the *Book of Common Worship.* The psalm texts are pointed so that they may be sung to common tones and refrains such as those provided in the book, or others readily available.[10] They are also arranged so that they may be read responsively or antiphonally. When used in relation to *The Presbyterian Hymnal* and *The Psalter—Psalms and Canticles for Singing,* Presbyterians once again have a rich fare in psalmody, which for centuries played a dominant role in shaping Reformed piety. All of the psalms included in the lectionary for Sundays and festivals, as well as the daily lectionary, are included. Psalm prayers appear at the end of each psalm for use in daily prayer.

BAPTISM

The baptismal rite in the *Book of Common Worship* is quite different from the baptismal rite in *The Worshipbook.* The new rite recovers the shape of Baptism of the church catholic. Since Baptism is into the church catholic, and not into a branch of the church, it is appropriate that the act of baptism bear resemblance to the way Christians have baptized throughout time.

The rite restores a profession of faith that includes both the renunciation of evil and a profession in the words of the Apostles' Creed. While *The Worshipbook* made it clear that the Apostles' Creed was to be said in relation to the act of baptism, the rite in the *Book of Common Worship* includes the Apostles' Creed in the rite itself. The new rite includes a prayer over the water that recounts the waters of salvation history—creation, flood, exodus, Jesus' baptism. It also suggests that water be used liberally, with immersion or pouring being especially appropriate. The laying on of hands follows the baptism with water, with an optional anointing with oil. Both in theology and in liturgical practice, the rite reflects the ecumenical convergence that is evidenced in the World Council of Churches study *Baptism, Eucharist and Ministry*.[11]

While the Service for the Lord's Day may be the most significant contribution of *The Worshipbook,* one of the most significant contributions of the *Book of Common Worship* may be its baptismal rite.[12]

The commissioning/confirmation rite in *The Worshipbook,* becomes in the *Book of Common Worship* a rite for the reaffirmation of the baptismal covenant upon public profession of faith, and exhibits close connection with Baptism. Other services for the reaffirmation of the baptismal covenant are provided for other occasions, also incorporating elements from the baptismal rite. This is a unique contribution of the *Book of Common Worship,* and will be an instrument in helping the faithful to live out their baptism.

In the *Book of Common Worship,* Baptism is clearly seen as the very core of our life as the people of God. Linkages with Baptism run like a thread throughout all of the services and are a recurring note in the prayers.

DAILY PRAYER

Unquestionably, the recovery of the daily office will be another major contribution of the *Book of Common Worship.* Whereas *The Worshipbook* provided minimal liturgies for morning and evening prayer, the *Book of Common Worship* now provides all that is needed for churches, families, or individuals to engage in the discipline of daily prayer. Complete services for morning prayer and evening prayer are provided with a variety of prayer texts and canticles. Additional texts are provided for use throughout the liturgical year. A brief midday service and a service of prayer at the close of day are also provided. A vigil of the resurrection can be an effective service for Saturday evening at a weekend retreat to mark the beginning of the Lord's Day.

For the first time, a daily lectionary is included in an American Presbyterian service book. This lectionary is from the *Book of Common Prayer,* with modifications made to it for inclusion in the *Lutheran Book of Worship.* It is thus an ecumenical lectionary shared with Episcopalians and Lutherans. It has been used for nearly thirty years in the Presbyterian *Mission Yearbook for Prayer and Study,* and is now more readily accessible in the *Book of Common Worship.* When all of the readings are used, this lectionary will lead one through the Old Testament every two years, and through the New Testament each year.[13]

PASTORAL OFFICES

The marriage service in *The Worshipbook* was never widely used and so did not replace the greatly loved service in the 1946 *Book of Common Worship.* However, *The Worshipbook* order anticipated the ordering of future marriage services.

Christian Marriage (Supplemental Liturgical Resource 3) provided marriage liturgies that readily found a firm place in the life of the church; these were incorporated into the *Book of Common Worship.*

While the funeral in *The Worshipbook* was generally well received, the *Book of Common Worship* provides a richer treasure of liturgical texts for use in the funeral.

The *Book of Common Worship* also adds a service for use prior to the funeral where family and close friends may gather and thankfully share memories of their loved one. While initially provided for use in communities where a wake is part of the culture, this service helps bring healing in the midst of grief among those closest to the deceased.

The *Book of Common Worship,* like *The Worshipbook* and earlier service books, provides an order for celebrating Holy Communion with those unable to attend public worship. A service for wholeness, and a liturgy of repentance and forgiveness for use with a penitent individual, are now included in the church's book of services for the first time.

PRAYERS FOR VARIOUS OCCASIONS

Each of the prior service books included a treasury of prayers for use in a variety of situations. The *Book of Common Worship* is no exception. This rich collection of prayers is drawn from *The Worshipbook,* the *Lutheran Book of Worship, The Book of Common Prayer,* and other sources. Many were newly written for the *Book of Common Worship.*

LANGUAGE

A great deal of attention was given to the need for gender-inclusive language during the years that followed the publication of *The Worshipbook.* The General Assembly periodically received papers expressing the need for gender-inclusive language both in reference to human relations and in language about God. In 1985 the 197th General Assembly adopted an important paper on gender-inclusive language, "Inclusive Language—Definition and Guidelines." This statement along with papers that preceded it,[14] were carefully followed in preparing the *Book of Common Worship.* In language touching upon human relations, the *Book of Common Worship* is fastidiously gender inclusive. In language about God, language is used that expands our consciousness to include a wide spectrum of images of God.

The first task force established what would become a guiding principle throughout the work, stating their intention

> to use "Father" so sparingly and deliberately as to suggest that we are defining the human relationship in terms of the divine reality and inner trinitarian

relationships rather than using the term so extensively and indiscriminately as to permit the human relationship to define [the] divine reality.[15]

As with *The Worshipbook* preceding it, the style of language was also an important consideration in preparing the *Book of Common Worship.* The task forces preparing portions of the *Book of Common Worship* had the benefit of the work completed since the publication of *The Worshipbook* by other denominations who had struggled to find a style of English appropriate for the worship of God in our time. In preparing the *Book of Common Worship,* care was taken to avoid colloquial language. Care was also taken to avoid archaic language. The liturgies furthermore make generous use of biblical images and metaphors.[16] While the *Book of Common Worship* distances itself from the more colloquial style of *The Worshipbook,* it includes over one hundred prayers from *The Worshipbook.* Most of these prayer texts are altered to avoid some of the colloquialisms, and to make them gender inclusive. The report to the 1974 General Assembly recommending changes in the language of *The Worshipbook* was of great value in revising *Worshipbook* texts for inclusion in the *Book of Common Worship.* While the language in the *Book of Common Worship* is contemporary, its avoidance of the colloquial may give it a more lasting usage than its predecessor.

The language of liturgy is important, for it shapes the faith within us. Trivial language, jargon, and shoddy prose tend to trivialize the faith. The worship of God demands the best we can offer. During the final year of preparing the *Book of Common Worship,* as its editor, I kept a quotation on the wall in front of my desk to remind me that a book designed for use in worship merits the best prose of which we are capable. It was written by Walter Wangerin Jr., a Lutheran pastor and author:

No matter how true the truth,
it is shaped by the form in which it is presented.
Cheap language will make the message seem cheap,
as cheap clothes cheapens a messenger.
Shoddy prose presents a slipshod truth.
Jargon dies before we do
and offends the very truth we had intended to express.
This judgment applies to any form
in which we communicate the truths of a merciful God:
Christian, learn thy craft!
Be the best you can be,
to honor that God who is better than all.[17]

A PEW BOOK IS LOST

As has been noted, one of the distinct achievements of *The Worshipbook* was that it combined in a single volume liturgical orders and texts with the music for the services. For congregations using *The Worshipbook,* the service book was in the pew for the first time, and thereby readily accessible to the people. Unfortunately, this is no longer the case with the *Book of Common Worship.*

In the 1980 General Assembly action, setting in motion the development of a service book, hymnal, and Psalter, it was envisioned that the projects would be coordinated, and at least the people's portion of the liturgy would be in the hymnal. Following reunion in 1983, a move to hasten the preparation of the hymnal resulted in its development independently from the preparation of the book of services. The committee appointed to prepare the hymnal zealously guarded its independence, insulating the preparation of the hymnal from that of the book of services. When attempts were made to encourage the hymnal committee to include the people's portions of the basic liturgies, the committee indicated that it had been asked to create a hymnal and wanted the entire book to be composed of hymns.

At the time the committee was being formed to prepare the new hymnal, the Executive Committee of the Presbyterian Association of Musicians acted to send a letter communicating its concerns to those responsible for forming the committee that would develop the new hymnal. Reflecting the action of the Executive Committee, the letter stressed the importance of including in the hymnal the basic liturgies of the church: the Service for the Lord's Day, Baptism, the service for marriage, the funeral, and a selective psalter along with other readings from Scripture.[18] Staff of the Office of Worship also made an appeal to the hymnal committee to include at least the people's portions of these liturgies. The hymnal committee did agree to include the order of the Service for the Lord's Day, and the order of the Great Thanksgiving with the text of the congregation's portions, and the minister's portions rubricized. Both of these are valuable inclusions. Texts of the creeds and Lord's Prayer were also included. However, the committee chose not to include more.

In *The Presbyterian Hymnal,* the committee gave the church an excellent resource, providing the finest of sacred song from the great surge of hymnody of the middle of the twentieth century, as well as the best of the past. It is a rich treasury, and its focus on psalmody is another important contribution. However, Presbyterians no longer have a book that combines the people's portion of the service book with the church's hymnody and service music as other churches do, such as the Methodists and Lutherans. In this respect, no longer having, as in *The Worshipbook,* a single pew book embodying both liturgical text and song is an unfortunate loss.

Thus, congregations desiring the texts to be available to the people must purchase the *Book of Common Worship* for placement in the pews alongside the hymnal. It is highly unlikely that many congregations will do so.

With the failure to include an abbreviated liturgy in the hymnal, for a time it was anticipated that a smaller edition of the service book (to include only those portions of the service book essential for the people's participation) could be made available. More congregations might have seen the value of a pew edition if this had resulted, but even this would have meant that worshipers would have to fumble with two books.

Lacking a pew edition of the *Book of Common Worship,* some congregations have prepared their own service book for the pew, customizing it for their local situation. These projects of course entail extensive and cumbersome copyright clearances, not covered by the permissions granted in using texts from the *Book of Common Worship* for single occasions, such as in the Sunday's worship folder.

Without a pew edition of the *Book of Common Worship,* the people's portions of the liturgy need to be placed in the church's worship folder. Regrettably, worship folders, or church bulletins, are often unattractive and cumbersome to use. Congregations need basic guidance in composing and producing church bulletins. With such training, use of the software edition of the *Book of Common Worship,* the LabOra software, or the CD-ROM *Presbyterian Worship Planner,* can be a valuable tool in preparing visually attractive and user-friendly orders of service. To be effective in engaging people in worship, the folder needs to be inviting to use. Furthermore, such a folder can help persons unfamiliar with the way the congregation worships, to be at ease, and less self-conscious.

As valuable as a pew edition might have been, Presbyterians are more comfortable with a worship folder prepared for the day that includes all that is needed for congregational participation. Furthermore, the richness and variety embodied in the *Book of Common Worship* may be more effectively incorporated into a congregation's life through the use a worship folder prepared for the occasion rather than expecting worshipers to find their way in a book. Still further, the flexibility of a worship folder honors the diversity among congregations, in the way they seek to be faithful to the Directory for Worship in the *Book of Order* and in the manner in which they incorporate into their life the orders and texts from the *Book of Common Worship.*[19]

SINGING THE LITURGY

While the *Book of Common Worship* is not a musical resource, throughout the book its rubrics underscore the importance of music in the liturgy. It seeks to make clear that music is integral to the liturgy. The 1906 and 1932 service books suggested little more than the inclusion of hymns and anthems and the chanting (or reading) of a psalm. In addition to hymns, anthems, and psalms, the 1946 *Book of Common Worship* Holy Communion liturgy suggested singing particular liturgical texts, e.g., Kyrie, Gloria in Excelsis, Te Deum, other canticles, and responses at the reading of the Gospel.

A sung liturgy did not begin to take shape with any significance until the appearance of *The Worshipbook.* This is the result of a clear recognition, by the Joint Committee on Worship that prepared *The Worshipbook,* of the inseparable relationship between music and text in the liturgy. In the Service for the Lord's Day, the rubrics called for the singing of psalms, canticles, hymns, a doxology, and anthems. The rubrics also invited the singing of particular liturgical texts. The inclusion of the three settings for singing the Service for the Lord's Day liturgy made this abundantly clear. This proved to be a valuable resource and was widely used throughout the church, with a greater number of congregations embracing a sung liturgy.

When one recognizes this great contribution of *The Worshipbook* we begin to fathom the great loss to congregations in the failure to provide a book of worship that combines both sacred song and liturgical text.

Even though a combined service book and hymnal failed to materialize with the *Book of Common Worship,* the rubrics throughout the service book nudge congregations further in singing the liturgy. Underlying the *Book of Common Worship* is a conviction that music is of the very fabric of the liturgy. Music is not something added to the liturgy to give it greater appeal, or simply to serve some utilitarian end. Nor is its purpose to embellish a service of worship, or to emotionally warm up the people, preparing them to receive the sermon. The worship of God calls for a language that engages the soul, the language of music. The highest moments of the worship of God move us to song.

Singing the liturgy can transform the worship of a congregation and take it to deeper levels of communal prayer and praise. Responses that become familiar through frequent singing add spontaneity to the liturgy and engage the people in prayer at the deepest level of their being. Those portions of the liturgy sung by the choir alone are not primarily sung *to* the congregation; they are sung *for* the congregation in their worship of God. As part of the congregation, and singing on its behalf, the choir with its special gifts and training is able to lift the liturgy with beauty, and the congregation is quickened to participate vicariously, spirit joined with spirit in the worship of God. The purpose of sacred music is thus not to entertain, but to engage the people in prayer. Music borrowed from the pop culture, entertaining and titillating, cannot convey the creative beauty of the God who is the source of all that is truly beautiful. The music of the liturgy needs to touch us with wonder, engaging us with the splendor of God, with the Divine Mystery—the *mysterium tremendum*—at the center of the universe.

Rabbi Abraham J. Heschel once noted how words alone are inadequate to express the deepest yearnings of the human spirit, often failing to convey the fervency of our prayer:

> The inadequacy of the means at our disposal appears so tangible, so tragic, that one feels it a grace to be able to give oneself up to music, to a tone, to a song, to a chant. The wave of a song carries the soul to heights which utterable meanings can never reach. Such abandonment is no escape nor an act of being unfaithful to the mind. For the world of unutterable meanings is the nursery of the soul, the cradle of all our ideas. It is not an escape but a return to one's origins.[20]

While the *Book of Common Worship* does not include any music other than some psalm tones, it invites a liturgy in which song plays a dominant role. The "Gathering" in the Service for the Lord's Day suggests the singing of such elements as the "Lord, Have Mercy," "Holy God, Holy and Mighty," "Lamb of

God," "Glory to God," or "Worthy Is Christ, the Lamb." In the Great Thanksgiving, congregations are invited to sing the "Holy, holy, holy Lord" and the acclamation. The rubrics also invite the singing of the psalm appointed in the lectionary (following the first reading), the singing of Ps. 103:1–2 after Communion, and the singing of the Canticle of Simeon before the charge and blessing. Care is taken to cross-reference musical settings that are available in *The Presbyterian Hymnal* and *The Psalter—Psalms & Canticles for Singing.* There are abundant rubrics inviting song and singling out texts that may be sung. While *The Presbyterian Hymnal* includes a section of service music, an additional and richer resource is *Holy Is the Lord* (Louisville: Geneva Press, 2002).

ENGAGING OUR BODIES IN WORSHIP

Throughout the *Book of Common Worship,* unlike previous Presbyterian service books, a number of appropriate ceremonial acts are suggested in recognition that we bring our bodies as well as our minds to worship. Ceremonial acts serve to reinforce aspects of the faith in our lives. Thus a more sensory approach is suggested.

A generous use of water in Baptism is an example. The option of anointing with oil is another. The use of ashes is suggested on Ash Wednesday. Footwashing is suggested on Maundy Thursday. Use of the sign of the cross is suggested in services that link with Baptism. Fire and water are primary signs in the Easter Vigil. Evening prayer includes the lighting of a candle, and incense is suggested for use during the singing of Psalm 141 at evening prayer. Through these and other ceremonial acts we are invited to engage our "'other ears' (sight, smell, taste, touch)."[21] We will find that God speaks to us through all of our senses.

Thus, those who use the *Book of Common Worship* are invited to a fuller participation in worship than has previously characterized Reformed service books. Furthermore, since children readily respond to movement and color, a more sensory approach to worship will more effectively engage children in worship than simply resorting to a "children's sermon."

Like the service books preceding it, the *Book of Common Worship* takes care to suggest appropriate posture for various acts of worship. While kneeling is suggested for confession on Ash Wednesday, standing is ordinarily suggested for prayer, for singing most hymns, for saying the creeds, and for the Great Thanksgiving. There is a long tradition of standing for prayer. It is an active position engaging the person. It is thus the posture of participation. Sitting is not encouraged as a proper posture for prayer. Sitting is the proper posture for listening to the Word read and preached. There is widespread disregard of the way in which kneeling-standing-sitting both shape and express the attitude we bring to worship.

George F. MacLeod, through whose leadership the Iona Community was founded, once humorously noted the gradual erosion of the language of posture, and of the discipline of devotion linked with it:

> I have heard it often claimed the "Presbyterians" sit to pray. It is well to remember that for a long period they knelt and for a longer period they stood. It was less than a hundred years ago that Presbyterians first thought to be seated while in corporate prayer: having neither the church furniture that allowed of kneeling nor the old stamina that assisted them to stand.[22]

As we have become increasingly sensitive to the concern for hospitality for those with handicapping conditions, attention has come to center on how we invite persons to stand for some acts of worship. In the *Book of Common Worship,* rubrics suggesting posture use "may" language, such as: "The people may stand." Prior to the publication of the *Book of Common Worship* there were conversations with those who minister with persons having handicapping conditions, concerning the inclusion of persons unable to stand. It became clear that such phrases as "all who are able may stand" unfortunately draw attention to those who cannot stand, and are often resented by them. It became clear that the simple rubric "The people may stand" was the more inclusive.

CATHOLIC, REFORMED, AND EVANGELICAL

Presbyterian service books can be described as being catholic, reformed, and evangelical.

The *Book of Common Worship* is truly *catholic.* As Presbyterian service books have evolved, they have appropriated, to an increasing degree, catholic (universal) elements of the liturgy. As we have noted, the Reformers sought to reform the one church, not start a new church. They rooted their reforms in the traditions emanating from the earliest centuries of the church. These include the centrality of sacraments, the liturgical calendar, the daily office, as well as prayer texts that are the heritage of the whole church.

The *Book of Common Worship* is truly *Reformed.* Presbyterian service books have always endeavored to preserve their Reformed character. Scripture and preaching have a central role. Furthermore, the unwavering focus upon God rather than upon ourselves and our feelings is an important characteristic of Reformed worship. The motto, often cited within the Reformed tradition, *Ecclesia reformata semper reformanda* (The church reformed, always to be reformed) will always link us with those within the church catholic who seek reform in accordance with the demands of the gospel in the age in which we live. While the motto is an emblem under which the Reformed operate when at their best, it is at the same time a banner of unity with every other part of the church that is open to the reforming winds of the Spirit. Liturgically, this means that there is a unifying character as Presbyterians and other parts of the whole church discover the renewing power in a liturgical reform that is finding common roots in the Scripture and the early life of the church.

To be Reformed is far from being sectarian; it is to have a kinship with every part of the church catholic where the Spirit of God is effecting reform in our time. The *Book of Common Worship* is, therefore, an expression of Christian worship that, while being Reformed, is shaped by the ecumenical convergence that has emerged in the late twentieth century.

The *Book of Common Worship* is truly *evangelical*. The church evangelical is the church seeking to be faithful to the good news declared to humankind in Jesus Christ. To be evangelical underscores the need for a personal engagement with the gospel. The *Book of Common Worship* unwaveringly centers us on a faithful response to the gospel.

The Worshipbook evidenced sensitivity to evangelical concerns within the Presbyterian church by incorporating a variety of options, including the option of an invitation following the sermon and an invitation for leaders of worship to insert their own prayers if desired. The *Book of Common Worship* retains these elements and also introduces guidelines for use by leaders of worship in preparing their own prayers.

ECUMENICAL CONVERGENCE

Over the past century, Presbyterians, like other churches, have drawn liberally from the *Book of Common Prayer* in the preparation of their service books. In recent decades the Anglican tradition has moved to embrace a wider range of texts than in the past, affording a rich treasury upon which to draw. Consequently Anglican prayer books in the United States, New Zealand, Australia, Canada, and England have all contributed to the richness of the *Book of Common Worship*. Prayer texts were also borrowed from the Roman tradition, since some of the best liturgical texts are now being prepared by the Roman Catholic Church, resulting from reforms issuing from the Second Vatican Council. A significant number of texts were also incorporated from the *Lutheran Book of Worship*. Reformed service books from Canada, the United States, Australia, England, and Scotland were also sources of liturgical texts. Drawing heavily from ecumenical sources is not prompted by a desire to make the task of preparing a book of services easier, but is based on the firm conviction that the church's service book should be a living expression of the whole church at worship.

An examination of the acknowledgments will reveal the ecumenical breadth of the *Book of Common Worship*. There are over 870 prayers in the book. About half of the prayers in the *Book of Common Worship* either were newly written in the process of developing that book or originated in one of the four Presbyterian service books that preceded it. The tradition of borrowing from the *Book of Common Prayer* continued, about one fourth of the prayers being from the Anglican tradition, mostly from the American prayer book, but a large number from the Anglican Church in Canada's *Book of Alternative Services* and the New Zealand *Prayer Book,* with a few from the Church of England and Australian Anglicans. Prayer texts from Roman Catholic sources constitute about one-tenth of the prayers, and those from the *Lutheran Book of Worship* another tenth.

Four members of the committee responsible for overseeing the final preparation of the manuscript, and submitting it for approval, had liturgical training in an ecumenical setting, having earned either a doctorate or a master's degree in the liturgical studies program at the University of Notre Dame. The chairperson of the committee subsequently served for several years as COCU's executive secretary.

The *Book of Common Worship* gives ample evidence that the past one hundred and fifty years have brought about a remarkable recovery in Presbyterian worship. Presbyterians are discovering that a book of services expresses the communal nature of the church and its worship as no other vehicle can. They are coming to appreciate forms of worship that are rooted in the longer tradition, thereby keeping the church today in communion with the church of all the ages. They are beginning to recognize that a book of services can help root the people in the faith. The task of continuing reform in the light of Scripture and the tradition of faith includes the church's liturgical forms no less than any other aspect of the church's life.

Chapter 7

Future Service Books

As the Age of Constantinian Christendom has waned, movements of reform have evolved promising renewal, signs of the Holy Spirit's work among us. The emergence of these movements leads us to believe that a new Reformation is unfolding in our midst.

Of the movements that have become prominent in the past century, two are in focus in this volume. Since our subject is a book of services, the liturgical movement is the primary focus. The other movement important to this study is the ecumenical movement.

LITURGICAL CONVERGENCE AND ECUMENISM

We have noted that the liturgical movement had its beginning in the nineteenth century.[1] As it matured, it brought all aspects of renewal into focus in the central act of the congregation's life together—its worship—relating the church in a vital way to the source of its life.

The liturgical movement is misunderstood when it is viewed as simply a movement to restore ancient rites or to make worship beautiful. The concern of the liturgical movement is not only with rites and ceremonies, but also with who we are as the people of God, with the nature of the church and its faith. Its concerns are therefore ecclesiological concerns. The movement seeks reform at the very place where the church is most visible and where its life is most directly shaped, its worship. Worship flowing out of the essential nature of the church is transforming. The liturgical movement therefore focuses on how our rites and ceremonies lead the church into an encounter with the living God, shape its faith, and direct its ministries of compassion and witness for peace and justice. Its overarching concern is, therefore, with the reformation and renewal of the whole life of the church. As such, the liturgical movement has been described as "at once a theological movement, a biblical revival, and a prophetic outburst."[2] The fact that the liturgical movement is ecumenical in scope gives strength to the conviction that we are involved in a far-reaching reformation in the whole of Christ's church.

The last half of the twentieth century saw a remarkable convergence between the liturgical movement and the ecumenical movement in consultations and academies we have already cited in this work.[3] By mid-century the Faith and Order movement had examined the various ways Christians worship and was addressing sacramental issues that have long divided. The continuing work of Faith and Order evidences the greatest level of theological convergence since the Reformation.

The Liturgical Conference began in mid-century among Roman Catholic Benedictines seeking liturgical reform. Following Vatican II, which adopted vast liturgical reforms advocated by the Liturgical Conference, the conference increasingly became an ecumenical agency directed toward the revitalization of worship in congregations.[4]

The Second Vatican Council (1962-1965), which brought about sweeping changes in Catholic worship, broadened the span of ecumenism. Indeed, in Vatican II much of the liturgical reform sought in the sixteenth-century Reformation was embraced. The council set forth a powerful ripple effect that has affected liturgical reform throughout Protestantism as well as giving a new face to ecumenism. The openness of the Roman Catholic church as a result of the council's embrace of all Christians, hastened the convergence of ecumenism and liturgical reform, launching an ecumenical liturgical movement, the dimensions of which are yet to be fully experienced.

As we have noted, the period from the mid-1960s to the mid-1970s was a remarkable time of forming ecumenical liturgical agencies: the Consultation on Common Texts, the International Consultation on English Texts, Societas Liturgica, and the North American Academy of Liturgy. Shortly thereafter, the Liturgical Conference became ecumenical in scope, and in the 1980s the English Language Liturgical Consultation was formed to carry forward the work of the International Consultation on English Texts. These ecumenical-liturgical agencies continue to influence the worship life of a variety of traditions. They will continue to play a major role in birthing an American liturgy transcending any single tradition, rooted in a common heritage, thereby giving greater visibility to the unity of the church.

Methodist liturgical scholar Paul Waitman Hoon, noting the convergence of the liturgical movement and ecumenism, wrote in 1971:

> [O]ur ecumenical time is perforce a liturgical time. . . . Certainly it is arguable—if it is not already demonstrable—that the road to reunion starts more truly from altar, pew, pulpit, and font than from headquarters in Geneva or Rome, or from the telephone number of the local commission on ecumenical relations.[5]

This convergence was described in an address given thirteen years later by Eugene L. Brand, one of the architects of the *Lutheran Book of Worship* and formerly Assistant General Secretary for Ecumenical Affairs, Lutheran World Federation. Brand spoke on "Ecumenism and Liturgy" in his response to the North American Academy of Liturgy upon the Academy's granting him the coveted Berakah Award. In his address he noted how liturgy is playing a more conspicuous role in the ecumenical movement. He called attention to evidence of a grassroots ecumenism resulting from the use of common liturgies and texts. This has great significance when one recognizes that our worship—the principal mark of the church—defines the church. He said:

> What has been called a growing liturgical convergence (especially obvious in the USA) has had an impact on the climate of ecumenical relationships which can only gain momentum with the passing of time. Separateness because of classic dogmatic differences in the *understanding* of the sacraments and the ordained ministry is being challenged by the pragmatic impact of the celebrated liturgy. Either remaining differences in doctrine and polity will be resolved—or forgotten—or new, common understandings will quietly replace them. I think worship in common will forge relationships which, in the end, will prove irresistible.[6]

He further emphasized the centrality of liturgy in ecumenical discussions when he said:

> It is true, as several of our churches hold, that the eucharist *celebrates* unity in Christ, and such unity has unavoidable structural aspects. But I am not sure that such an affirmation precludes seeing in the eucharist and in common worship in general *also* a force *creative* of unity. I am even less sure that the unity we are speaking about has to do *primarily* with dogmatic agreement.[7]

It is not surprising then that Brand would recently ask, "If our celebrations of the Eucharist are so similar and if our Baptisms create a common bond, what is it that still requires us to be separated?"[8]

No dialogue between churches, nor any move toward the reunion of the church, can take place without engaging liturgical issues. Our brokenness has been most apparent in our worship, and the road to healing leads us in a search for unity at the font, pulpit, and holy table. We need to keep working to tear down the barriers that divide us. In a world where secularism rules and in a culture where individualism is all-pervasive, where the church is increasingly ignored or regarded as irrelevant, unity in the body of Christ has never been so crucial. In such a crisis, a divided house cannot prevail.

Each tradition within the Christian faith has something of unique value to contribute to the whole of Christ's church. The church will be impoverished if it ignores the ways the gifts of each can enrich the whole. In this regard I have found delight in a fantasy of Robert E. Terwilliger, who was bishop suffragan in the Diocese of Dallas (Episcopalian) from 1975–1986:

> If I may have a fantasy of a year of Christian re-integration for myself, I would spend Advent with Scottish Presbyterians because of their sense of sovereignty of God and judgment; Christmas in an English cathedral because of the Anglican feeling for the Incarnation; Epiphany with the Greek Orthodox because of the awareness of glory and transfiguration; Lent in the Benedictine or Cistercian Abbey because of the practice of austerity; Holy Week in a German Lutheran congregation because of the great devotion to the sacrifice of the cross; Easter with the Russian Orthodox because of their joy in the resurrection, and Pentecost in a charismatic Roman Catholic parish because of its new feeling for the Holy Spirit. This would be an experience of catholicity which would be a revelation in faith.[9]

While the contribution of the parts to the whole is reason enough to draw together, the unity that is ours in Christ judges all our divisions. The fact that there is but "one Lord, one faith, one baptism" (Eph. 4:5) means that the search for unity has no alternative.

NEW DIRECTIONS IN ECUMENISM

The past millennium was marred by an ever-increasing number of fractures in the body of Christ, the major schisms being the separation of Eastern and Western Christianity in 1054 and the sixteenth-century Protestant break from Rome. The rest of the millennium saw a continual splintering of the body of Christ, until to confess, "We believe in one holy catholic and apostolic church," seemed the greatest of hypocrisies. Only as the millennium drew to a close did a vision of the unity of the church begin to take shape. We pray that early in this new millennium these visions of the church's healing will find fulfillment, and the church's essential unity will be fully experienced.

As the new millennium dawns, we are discovering new ways of expressing our unity as Christians. The emerging focus of ecumenism is not so much upon the merging of churches into new and larger churches. The energy of ecumenism is now being directed toward reconciliation and mutual recognition among traditions. Dialogue is not directed toward finding final conclusive agreements, but rather, to finding agreements that profoundly accept legitimate differences in understanding the faith.

John F. Hotchkin, Executive Director of the Secretariat for Ecumenical and Interreligious Affairs of the National Conference of Catholic Bishops, believes that such agreements embrace the promise of a vital unity, without merging, and envision an ecumenism as revolutionary as any other form of ecumenism in the twentieth century.

In 1995, in addressing the Annual Conference of the North American Academy of Ecumenists, Hotchkin described how we have moved into a third stage of the ecumenical movement, the most developed to date.[10] He was careful to point out that while ecumenism has passed through three stages, each of the stages continue at the same time to "interpenetrate and overlap."

The first stage, "the pioneering and organizational" stage, began in 1910. This phase of ecumenism saw, for example, the early work of Faith and Order and the formation of the World Council of Churches. Local councils of churches were formed. This organizational work continues and gradually broadens to include other traditions.

The second stage, the "Dialogue" stage began at the time of the fourth World Conference on Faith and Order in Montreal in 1963. While early work centered on comparing Christian traditions in an effort to find a common ground, the second stage directly addressed the issues that divide. As churches talked with each other they found no disagreements so profound as to be church dividing. On the contrary they discovered that what is shared in common runs deeper than issues that differentiate them. Many of the dialogues resulted in convergence. *Baptism, Eucharist and Ministry* is one such convergence, as are the dialogues in which the Lutherans were engaged with the Reformed, Episcopalians, and Catholics. Hotchkin asserted: "It is no longer a matter of salvaging treasured elements of agreement from a turbulent sea of disputes, but rather of facing our disagreements within the context of our more profound accord."[11] Such dialogue, he affirms, must continue and be "a permanent feature of our life together, one not less necessary because we are becoming more united than in the past. Dialogue is not a stage of development one enters only eventually to leave."[12]

The third stage, "phased reconciliation," is the most developed, and the fruit of dialogue. He describes it:

> In this stage the churches have more to do than to create ecumenical agencies, convoke assemblies, conduct dialogues, and respond to their findings. In this stage the churches have coming before them proposals to redefine their relationships by decisive mutual action leading in the end to increased direct participation in one another's ecclesial lives, though without corporately merging. These proposals characterize the ecumenical movement today and indicate its overall direction. The most notable difference between these proposals and corporate union or merger plans is that none of these new proposals envisages the disappearance of the present churches as we know them or the emergence of newly identified churches, successor bodies different from and replacing them.[13]

While organic unions between churches within a tradition sharing a common heritage have marked the twentieth century, the way becomes more difficult when attempts are made to embrace a broader spectrum. This has been the experience of the forty years of efforts to realize the union initially envisioned in the Consultation on Church Union. The Church of Christ Uniting (now renamed Churches of Christ Uniting), proposed by the consultation, with churches bound together in "covenant communion," is an example of unity envisioned in the third stage of ecumenism. Other examples include the Lutheran-Reformed Declaration of Agreement and the Lutheran-Episcopal Concordat.

Quoting Robert McAfee Brown, who called the early pioneering period of the ecumenical movement an "ecumenical revolution," Hotchkin says, "I think this third stage could end up being much more revolutionary."[14] He concludes:

> What is developing among us is so far reaching and loaded with implications that it is hard to think it all through and see it whole. Indeed, from a strictly human point of view it all seems quite plainly impossible. In the closing words of Vatican II's Decree on Ecumenism, it "transcends human energies." So perhaps after all another Energy is indeed at work, leading and directing our efforts, blocking our attempted short cuts, unsettling our unexamined certainties, drawing us along pathways we did not anticipate, taking us farther than we expected to go.[15]

The reconciliations marking the final half of the decade following his address, provide an exciting chapter in the story of ecumenism. The main players in the Reformation are actors in the drama: The Formula of Agreement between Lutherans (ELCA) and Reformed churches, the Concordat between the Episcopalians and the Lutherans (ELCA), the Joint Declaration on the Doctrine of Justification by Lutherans and Roman Catholics.

The latter is particularly significant. Signed by the Lutheran World Federation and the Vatican on October 31, 1999, in Augsburg, Germany, the declaration bridges a theological divide that has separated Protestants and Catholics since Luther nailed his Ninety-five Theses to the church door in Wittenberg nearly five centuries ago. No future recognition of Reformation Day can ever be the same after Reformation Day 1999. After a millennium of schism, it is a hope-filled way to enter a new millennium.

As churches are reconciled, we are beginning to experience the healing of the fractures of the sixteenth century. This holds great promise and opportunities for the future. Upon reading the announcement of the agreement on the wording of the Joint Declaration on the Doctrine of Justification, I thought of efforts of Calvin, Melanchthon, and Cranmer. Having failed to reform the whole church, they sought without success to consolidate the Reformation efforts into a single body. Surely they would rejoice in the reconciliations we are witnessing.[16]

Given the realities of our time, Christ's church can no longer afford its divisions. There is no future in a renewed sectarianism. The witness and ministry of the church will be effective in confronting the secularism and individualism that dominate today's world to the extent that the church lives out its God-given unity. A broken church is ill equipped to bring hope to a broken world. Because the church is one, the church needs to give living expression to that unity, a foretaste of the unity God wills for all humankind. For this Jesus prayed, "Father, may they be one as we are one . . . *so that the world may believe . . .*" (John 17:21, emphasis added).

FUTURE SERVICE BOOK REVISION

With the convergence of the ecumenical and liturgical movements following World War II, one can begin to envision the possibility of an ecumenically prepared book of services. Except for churches within a particular church family, joint efforts of churches to produce service books are thus far rare.[17] But what we presently have are service books prepared by particular churches, books that bear a striking commonality, while still reflecting the uniqueness of a given tradition. This should not be a surprise, since no recently published service book has been prepared in isolation, and each tradition draws from the same sources—the riches of the longer tradition reaching back to the earliest Christian era. The result is that recent service books evidence a remarkable ecumenical convergence,[18] making a bit more tangible the unity that we profess when we confess that we believe in "one holy catholic and apostolic church," a unity that is inherent in the baptism we share in Jesus Christ.

In a time of changing technology, we may not yet envision the physical shape the church's liturgical "book" may take in passing along the liturgical tradition and wisdom of faith from one generation to another. Nevertheless, how it might be developed presents some exciting challenges. When Presbyterians begin to think about preparing the next book of services, the possibilities of a more intentional ecumenical involvement should be explored. The direction it might take depends on the state of ecumenism as we move further into the new millennium. With the convergence of our liturgical forms, the possibility of preparing the next service book jointly seems to be a viable and worthwhile endeavor.

One alternative would engage churches in the Reformed family. We seem to be near the time when member churches of the North American area of the World Alliance of Reformed Churches will be ready to join together in producing a single book of services for use by North American churches within the Presbyterian and Reformed family. In the early years of the development of *The Worshipbook,* the Reformed Church of America and the United Church of Christ were involved with the three churches that completed *The Worshipbook.* In the process leading to the *Book of Common Worship* a representative from The Presbyterian Church in Canada participated in the task force meetings during the development of the last of the Supplemental Liturgical Resources. Late in the process, the Reformed Church in America expressed interest in a closer relationship in developing liturgical resources.

A second alternative would include churches in the newly formed Churches Uniting in Christ, a loose federation of denominations covenanted together. It would seem logical that a service book would be developed in this new ecclesiastical relationship, for elective use by constituent churches, thereby continuing work like that of the Consultation on Church Union's Commission on Worship.

A third alternative would formally recognize those with whom Presbyterians have engaged in theological dialogue in recent years. With the adoption of the Formula of Agreement between the Lutherans (ELCA) and Reformed churches, it would be fitting for Lutheran representation to be included in the committee producing the next Presbyterian or pan-Reformed service book.[19] If in the meantime additional dialogues are begun and concords reached, it would be fitting to include such other representation as may seem appropriate.

If jointly producing a book is not possible, collaboration is certainly an alternative. In collaboration, two or more churches, through a collaborative process, might determine to develop their service books to be as similar as possible. This of course would mean an identical timetable.

However the next service book is developed, one can foresee greater influence upon the work coming from ecumenical bodies that address liturgical issues. The continued participation of Presbyterian liturgical scholars in the North American Academy of Liturgy, Societas Liturgica, the Consultation on Common Texts and its close ally the English Language Liturgical Consultation, and the Liturgical Conference will certainly continue to influence Presbyterian liturgical formation.[20]

Given a new level of ecumenical involvement, the next cycle of service books could do much to heal the church's brokenness, and unite us at the font, pulpit, and holy table. Such ecumenical developments give a deeper meaning to the word common, which is, as we have said above, the antithesis of the individualism of our time.

UNITY IN DIVERSITY

As we move together ecumenically, we are coming to appreciate a unity in things essential while welcoming diverse forms of expression within that unity. Ecumenism both advocates and facilitates a unity in diversity. Not only are we discovering the richness various traditions bring to the growing sense of unity bonding Christians together; greater diversity is increasingly embraced within particular traditions, even traditions long cherishing uniform liturgical practice based on prescribed prayer book texts. A liturgical refocusing is thus emerging, in which unity is found in a common sharing of the shape of the liturgy, though it may be expressed in a variety of ways.

Technological changes feed this shift. Fifteenth-century technology gave us the printing press with movable type, enabling sixteenth-century prayer books to be in the hands of the people. So now, the technological revolution is unfolding a wider range of options. Service book texts are increasingly becoming available online. A computer printer enables, with ease and economy, the preparing of quality worship folders utilizing a richer variety of liturgical text. The software edition of the *Book of Common Worship* was one of the first service books to be made accessible with a computer, and it was the first computer software designed to enable congregations to easily prepare worship folders using orders and texts from a book of services.[21]

The Church of England has taken the lead in another technological change in relation to service books. Introduced in Advent 2000, the full text of the Church of England's new prayer book, *Common Worship*,[22] is available on the church's website (http://cofe.anglican.org/commonworship). Readily accessible, texts and orders may be downloaded for inclusion in worship folders to be placed in the hands of the worshipers.

The richness and variety of liturgical text in *Common Worship* is without parallel in earlier prayer books of the Church of England. It thus marks a significant shift, and not only in Anglican worship; it gives further evidence of the direction in which service books in other traditions is moving.[23] *Common Worship* marks a shift from uniformity—in which common prayer is understood as sharing a common text—to sharing a common order.

Emphasis is placed upon unity in the ordering, or shape of the liturgy, and an embracing of variety in the way in which that shape takes root among congregations. The shape of the liturgy thus becomes more important than the precise wording of the liturgy, and it welcomes prayer that is ancient as well as modern, both prayer from a prayer book and free prayer. A common shape of the liturgy can be expressed in diverse ways and still remain faithful to the liturgical tradition.

This shift is reflected in the Church of England's choice of the title *Common Worship*, which replaces *The Book of Common Prayer*, a title greatly cherished for over four and one-half centuries. This seems to reflect what the Panel on Worship of the Church of Scotland may have been thinking when it published the 1994 edition of the Church of Scotland's book of services. Long known as *The Book of Common Order*, the 1994 edition displays the full title on the title page, but not on the volume's cover, which bears the simple title *Common Order*. The result is that this Presbyterian book of services is generally referred to as *Common Order*. The removal of the words "The Book of" from the title of their service books, by both the Church of Scotland and the Church of England, seems to mark the shift away from implying uniformity in use of particular liturgical texts as being the essence of common worship (or common prayer, or common order), to a focus on a *shared shape* of the liturgy, a *common ordering* of worship, as expressing true commonality.

In the process, the focus is more clearly on worship as event. While liturgical texts remain important, attention is drawn to the act of worship that the words attend. Had the implications of this simple change in title been foreseen by those responsible for the *Book of Common Worship*, might not the title of the Presbyterian book of services, on this side of the Atlantic, yielded to simply "Common

Worship"? Such titles may better reflect a refocusing toward worship as an event that finds varied expression within the unity of the liturgy's shape.

A shape of the liturgy shared in common ecumenically, and based on ancient tradition is one of the strengths of the *Book of Common Worship*. Another strength is that this book embodies a rich variety of texts (the basis for its 1,108 pages!), and includes guidelines for free prayer. Thus one may look upon the *Book of Common Worship* as somewhat avant-garde, marking the direction service books are moving, though it embodies a long-cherished Presbyterian liturgical principle of freedom within form. Presbyterian worship at its best welcomes diversity, but within the unity of the discipline and wisdom of the wider church. The greatest challenge for Presbyterians remains, on the one hand, to fully embrace a shape of the liturgy that is truly catholic as well as reformed and evangelical, and on the other hand, to steer clear of an undisciplined freedom that can border on license. All of which requires pastors and congregations to exercise greater discernment in determining what is and what is not appropriate in the worship of God.

Chapter 8

Eucharistic Recovery, the Centerpiece of Liturgical Reform

From the very inception of the Christian community, the Eucharist has been at the core of its life. Instituted by Christ, the Eucharist was received by the early Christians as an essential and indispensable part of their worship on the Lord's Day. We have glimpses in the New Testament of worship in the first century, such as the description in Acts 2:42: "They devoted themselves to the apostles' teaching and fellowship, to the breaking of bread and the prayers."[1] Many biblical scholars believe that the Gospel of John presents us with theological reflections of the first-century Christians on the sacraments.[2] Other biblical scholars recognize in the Emmaus story (Luke 24:13–32) the basic word/meal pattern of Christian liturgy, probably reflecting the meaning of the liturgical pattern of the first-century Lukan churches.

From the second and third centuries we have descriptions of Christian worship by Justin Martyr and Hippolytus. Though fragmentary, they give a picture of the way the early Christians ordered their liturgical life. At the center was the Eucharist.

In his defense of Christianity to the Roman emperor, Justin provides the earliest full description of Christian worship on the Lord's Day. Written in the middle of the second century (about A.D. 155), a portion reads:

And on the day called Sunday there is a meeting in one place of those who live in cities or the country, and the memoirs of the apostles or the writings of the prophets are read as long as time permits. When the reader has finished, the president in a discourse urges and invites [us] to the imitation of these noble things. Then we all stand up together and offer prayers. And . . . when we have finished the prayer, bread is brought, and wine and water, and the president similarly sends up prayers and thanksgivings to the best of his ability, and the congregation assents, saying the Amen; the distribution, and reception of the consecrated [elements] by each one, takes place and they are sent to the absent by the deacons. Those who prosper, and who so wish, contribute each one as much as he chooses to. What is collected is deposited with the president, and he takes care of orphans and widows, and those who are in want on account of sickness or any other cause, and those who are in bonds, and the strangers who are sojourners among [us], and, briefly, he is the protector of all those in need. We all hold this common gathering on Sunday.[3]

There is, therefore, nothing older in the church's tradition than the Eucharist. The *Book of Common Worship* reminds us:

Before church governments were devised, before creeds were formalized, even before the first word of the New Testament was written, the Lord's Supper was firmly fixed at the heart of Christian faith and life. From the church's inception, the Lord's Day and the Lord's Supper were joined.[4]

Across the centuries, the Eucharist, which has always included the reading and proclamation of Scripture, has given Christian worship its distinctive shape. It has been the invariable and universal mark constituting Christian liturgy. Or, rather, it was until the sixteenth century!

THE LOSS OF THE CENTRALITY OF THE EUCHARIST

In the late medieval church, practices and beliefs concerning the Eucharist emerged that were in sharp contrast to the faith of the first centuries of the church's life. These distortions of the faith helped kindle the flame of the Reformation in the sixteenth century. The doctrine of transubstantiation, the sacrifice of the Mass, the withholding of the cup from the people, the liturgy in Latin rather than the vernacular language, and the neglect of the preaching of the Word, all received vitriolic denunciations by the Reformers. The understanding of the Sacrament as a holy meal, in which the faithful communed in the body and blood of Christ and with each other, was virtually eclipsed by the concept of the meal as a sacrificial act in which the sacrifice of Christ was offered once again. Popular piety of the time regarded the adoration of the elements as more important than eating and drinking the elements. Indeed, communing was incidental. While the priests communed at each eucharistic celebration, the people communed but once a year at Easter and that with the bread alone.

While the Reformers successfully eradicated from among their followers the corruptions they saw in eucharistic thought and practice, they were not as successful in restoring the Sacrament to the center of the life of the church.

This was due in large measure to the influence of Ulrich Zwingli. Zwingli was a first-generation reformer and contemporary of Martin Luther. He was more radical in his reforms than either Martin Luther or John Calvin. His eucharistic practice was destined to influence Protestant worship for centuries.

Zwingli maintained that faith is nourished by the Holy Spirit alone apart from anything physical, such as eating bread and drinking wine in the Eucharist. For Zwingli, the Lord's Supper was no more than a spiritual exercise in which we are given a vivid reminder, engaging heart and mind to dwell in thanksgiving upon the goodness of God revealed to us in the redemption Christ won for us on Calvary. Since the Sacrament was a spiritual exercise on the worshiper's part, rather than a gift of God's self in the Sacrament, Zwingli did not regard the Lord's Supper as a means of grace.[5] The bread and the wine signified the body and blood of Christ, but did not embrace the thing signified.

Nothing in such an understanding of the Sacrament cried out for frequent celebration. It is not surprising then that Zwingli chose to provide the Lord's Supper only four times each year, Christmas, Easter, Pentecost, and once in the autumn. Tragically, the Eucharist was thus no longer recognized as normative to worship on the Lord's Day. Stripped of the Eucharist, liturgical practice was reduced to a service of the Word alone.

Therefore, only a fragment of how the church had ordered its worship since New Testament times and for the following one and a half millennia remained. On the infrequent occasions when the Lord's Supper was observed, it was merely an add-on to the service of the Word. Even to this day, little regard is given the Eucharist among Protestants in Zurich, the locus of Zwingli's reforms.[6]

Other centers of the Reformed faith did not suffer so badly. In the Strassburg reforms, the liturgy was a vernacular derivation of the Roman Mass, with the Eucharist celebrated each Sunday in the cathedral, and in the other churches of the city once each month. At first the eucharistic views of Martin Bucer, whose reforms centered in Strassburg, were influenced by Zwingli, but in time he moved to a eucharistic theology close to that of Calvin and Melanchthon.

THE EUCHARISTIC LEGACY OF JOHN CALVIN

While Zwingli influenced eucharistic practice, eucharistic theology for the Reformed in the English-speaking world has been shaped by John Calvin. This can be traced through John Knox, who studied with Calvin in Geneva when exiled from England from the wrath of Queen Mary I. For Calvin, Zwinglian eucharistic theology was nearly as problematic as that of Rome. Calvin's understanding of the Eucharist was much nearer that of Luther than that of Zwingli.

Calvin was a second-generation reformer. He was an eight-year-old boy when

Luther posted his Ninety-five Theses on the church door in Wittenberg. When he began his ministry in Geneva in 1536, at the age of twenty-seven, the Reformation was already moving into adolescence. The celebration of the first vernacular Mass (German) in the cathedral at Strassburg had occurred twelve years earlier (1524). A decade had already passed since Zwingli began his radical reforms in Zurich, and John Oecolampadius and Guillaume Farel began their reforms of the Basel liturgy following Zwingli's model. Calvin arrived in Geneva seven years after the Marburg Colloquy of 1529 in which Luther and Zwingli came to an impasse in eucharistic understanding, precipitating a breech in understanding between the Reformed and the Lutherans that persists to this day. Zwingli was killed in battle two years after Marburg (five years before Calvin began his ministry in Geneva), in a war between Protestants and Catholics. Zwingli's influence was perhaps more zealously preserved because his followers regarded him as a martyr of the faith.

Unlike Zwingli, Calvin maintained that the Eucharist was an "effective sign." That is, what "the sacraments depict is truly offered to us." In the Lord's Supper, by the power of the Holy Spirit, people of faith truly become "partakers of the body and blood of Christ." Since the Sacrament presents the reality it signifies, it is a means of grace.

The problem Calvin had with the Roman church's doctrine of transubstantiation was that the sign is transformed into the thing signified. Thus the distinction between the sign and that which is signified is not maintained. The problem Calvin had with Zwingli was the separation of the sign from that which was signified. What was signified was not joined to the sign. Zwingli's view thus marked more the absence of Christ than Christ's presence. In Calvin's arguments against Rome and against Zwingli, the concern of the real presence was a matter of "distinction without separation."[7]

Though Calvin did not resist attempts to explain how the Sacrament was an instrument of sacramental communion in the body and blood of Christ, he insisted that it was a mystery beyond comprehension. In the *Institutes* he wrote:

> Now, if anyone should ask me how this takes place, I shall not be ashamed to confess that it is a secret too lofty for either my mind to comprehend or my words to declare. And, to speak more plainly, I rather experience than understand it. Therefore, I here embrace without controversy the truth of God in which I may safely rest. He declares his flesh the food of my soul, his blood its drink [John 6:53ff.]. I offer my soul to him to be fed with such food. In his Sacred Supper he bids me take, eat, and drink his body and blood under the symbols of bread and wine. I do not doubt that he himself truly presents them, and that I receive them.[8]

When Calvin commenced his ministry in Geneva, Zwinglian reforms were already firmly rooted there. In Calvin's efforts to achieve what he regarded as the true church, Zwingli's sacramental views were destined to be a persistent frustration to him. For Calvin, the sacraments were of the very essence of the church. He taught that the marks of the church are "the Word of God . . . purely preached and heard, and the sacraments administered according to Christ's institution." Where these marks are found, "a true church of God exists."[9] Since, unlike Zwingli, he held that the Eucharist is a means of grace, it was to be celebrated every Sunday. For Calvin, failure to celebrate the Lord's Supper with the frequency of the ancient church was a fault that threatened the very foundations of the church.

Even though Calvin taught a high theology of the Eucharist, he was unable to overcome the Zwinglian influence of infrequent celebration of the Sacrament. This remains true also for the churches in the tradition of Calvin. While Calvin's eucharistic theology is reflected in Reformed confessions, his hopes for eucharistic practice have not been fully realized, impeded by the Zwinglian legacy of the infrequency of quarterly Communion. Where there has been erosion of the tradition of Calvin's eucharistic theology, it has most likely been due more directly to rationalism, revivalism, and pietism than to Zwingli.

CALVIN'S OBJECTIVE: LORD'S SUPPER EACH LORD'S DAY

Within months after Calvin's arrival in Geneva, Calvin and Farel presented "Articles Concerning the Organization of the Church and Worship at Geneva." Edification of the community was proposed by two means: frequent celebration of the Lord's Supper, and discipline. The proposal stated (emphasis added):

> When the Church assembles together for the great consolation which the faithful receive and the profit which proceeds from it, in every respect according to the promises which are there presented to our faith, then *we are really made participants of the body and the blood of Jesus, of his death, of his life, of his Spirit and of all his benefits.*[10]

On this basis, the proposal stated clearly that the Sacrament was

> not instituted by Jesus for making a commemoration two or three times a year, but for a frequent exercise of our faith and charity, of which the congregation of Christians should make use as often as they be assembled, as we find written in Acts ch. 2, that the disciples of our Lord continued in the breaking of bread, which is the ordinance of the Supper. Such also was always the practice of the ancient Church, until the abomination of the mass was introduced. . . .[11]

It is apparent in this document that Farel, whose reformation ideas initially had been shaped by Zwingli, had come finally to subscribe to this view of Calvin.

We need to recognize that restoration of communing by the people each Lord's Day (i.e., actual *reception* of the eucharistic elements by the communicants) was an essential part of the changes the Reformers sought in sacramental practice. Even though weekly *celebration* of the Mass was part of the medieval church, *communing* at each celebration (except by the priest) had long been lost, the result of the particular doctrines upon which the medieval Mass was built. In the medieval church the people were required to commune only once a year. For the Reformers, communing each Lord's Day was no less important than those reforms they were able to achieve, namely, restoration of the cup, use of the vernacular, and setting aside particular doctrines associated with the medieval Mass.

Even though it was firmly rooted in the ancient church, the idea of a weekly Eucharist was something the magistrates of Geneva would not accept. The Zwinglian pattern of Communion once every three months was already established before Calvin arrived. To those who had never been expected to commune more than once each year, the idea of communing each week was simply more than they could accept. Communing quarterly was quite enough.

Calvin and Farel therefore acquiesced to the magistrates' wishes, conceding that because "the frailty of the people" was "still so great," there was "danger that this sacred and so excellent mystery be misunderstood" if weekly Communion were to be required. So, a compromise was reached. That the people may be strengthened, the Sacrament was celebrated in each parish church in Geneva once each month, with the schedule arranged so that on each Lord's Day the Sacrament was celebrated in at least one of the churches. Furthermore, on a given Sunday the celebration was not just for that particular part of the city, but for "all of the Church." It was to be at a convenient hour so that persons from every quarter of the city could attend. The location of the celebration was to be announced in each church on the Sunday prior.[12] This meant that anyone desiring to commune weekly could do so, but would have to rotate attendance between the churches of the city.

Frequency continued to be a major issue. When ecclesiastical ordinances were drawn up in September 1541, the issue of frequency was a source of contention. In the section on the Lord's Supper, after declaring the importance of frequent celebration, the following compromise sentence was inserted (emphasis added), "*For the present,* let it be advised and ordained that it always be administered four times in the year."[13] The proposal evidences the inability to set in place the proposals of 1537, since the articles state that frequency of celebrating the Sacrament would be once a quarter in a given parish, but so scheduled in the parishes so that it would be once each month in the city. Furthermore, it was to be celebrated at Easter, Pentecost, and Christmas (but not again in the month in which these festivals occurred).

Calvin was not at ease with this concession. He once noted, "I have taken care to record publicly that our custom is defective, so that those who come after me may be able to correct it the more freely and easily."[14] To his death Calvin insisted that the Lord's Supper was to be celebrated each Lord's Day and that the faithful were expected to commune.

A TOO EASY COMFORT WITH INFREQUENT COMMUNION

It is to the discredit of those who followed Calvin that the Reformed tradition so easily accommodated itself to being satisfied with a fragment of Christian liturgy, rather than recovering the whole. Even though the confessional standards consistently portray a high view of the Eucharist, the persistence of infrequency in its celebration too clearly evidences a low regard for its importance. In this respect, the Reformed tradition cannot rightly claim for itself the distinction of being "reformed." The compromise "for the present" denoting a temporary measure of quarterly communion in the parish has stretched to four and one-half centuries! The "defective custom" is still not fully corrected.

A century after the Reformation, the Westminster Assembly's Directory for the Publique Worship of God (1644) stated that the Sacrament was to be celebrated frequently, with frequency to be determined by what is "most convenient for the comfort and edification of the people."[15] There is not the slightest hint of the norm of weekly celebration that was central to the reforms sought by the Genevan reformers. In Scotland, the observance of the Lord's Supper declined to once a year (in part due to the lack of clergy), though the occasion was one of great solemnity.

Similarly the Directory for the Worship of God adopted by American Presbyterians in 1788, nearly a century and a half after Westminster, stated: "The Communion, or Supper of the Lord, is to be celebrated frequently; but how often, may be determined by the minister and eldership of each congregation, as they may judge most for edification."[16]

It is clear that the Lord's Supper was looked upon as *something to add* to a preaching service, to be observed often enough to "edify the people." While no mention is made of even a minimum number of occasions to celebrate the Sacrament, it was customary for American Presbyterians to celebrate it in the Zwinglian practice of once each quarter, and often less frequently.

When the first stirring for liturgical reform emerged in the middle of the nineteenth century, weekly celebration was not among the reforms sought. An example is the remarkable work of Charles W. Shields in proposing his Presbyterian *Book of Common Prayer,* published in 1864.[17] While his work was visionary, appearing long before its time, he failed to recognize the need to recover the norm of weekly celebration of the Eucharist. He acknowledged the practice of weekly celebration in the primitive church, and recognized that the Eucharist was the norm in all of the ancient liturgies, but observed that "modern habits of worship have rendered the practice obsolete."[18] Yet he would also say in the same work that the Communion service was

> the most sacred portion of the office, or indeed of the whole book, and that for which the other services are but a preliminary training, leading to it as to the very crown and complement of all Christian worship, the "holy of holies" in the Church-service.[19]

In the liturgy itself, the "Divine Service for the Lord's Day," a rubric was inserted after the sermon indicating where the order for the Lord's Supper was to be placed. In the liturgical text for the Sacrament, a rubric concerning frequency was included, in keeping with the Directory for Worship as noted above. "The Holy Communion, or Supper of the Lord, is frequently to be celebrated; but how often, may be determined by the Pastor and Elders of each congregation, as they shall judge most for edification."[20]

So, when in 1906 the first American Presbyterian service book was approved by a General Assembly for voluntary use, it is not surprising that the Lord's Supper was included as an add-on to the Sunday liturgy of the Word. There was one order for a morning service and a similar order for an evening service. But neither service included a rubric noting where the Lord's Supper was to be inserted.

A separate liturgy was included for "The Celebration of the Communion or Sacrament of the Lord's Supper."[21] A rubric quoted the Directory for Worship concerning frequency (cited above).

A revision of *The Book of Common Worship* published in 1932 again included services for use on the Lord's Day (one for morning and one for evening), with no reference to the Lord's Supper. An add-on liturgy for celebrating the Lord's Supper appeared later in the book. Again, no rubric appeared in the liturgies for the inclusion of the Lord's Supper. The rubric concerning frequency had disappeared.

The Book of Common Worship published in 1946 included a revision of the 1906/1932 add-on eucharistic liturgy but also included a full service of Word and Eucharist for the first time.

While a full service of Word and Sacrament appears, the fact that the single services for morning and for evening of the 1906 and 1932 books were replaced with five orders each for morning and evening, clearly reveals that there was little change in the basic understanding of what was normative for each Lord's Day. It was not until 1961–1970 that a change began to take place.

SIGNS OF RECOVERY

The Directory for Worship adopted by the United Presbyterian Church in 1961 set the church in a new direction in frequency of celebration. The directory stated (emphasis added):

> The session shall determine how often the opportunity to partake of this sacrament may be provided in each church. *It is fitting that it be observed as frequently as on each Lord's Day,* and it ought to be observed frequently and regularly enough that it is seen as a proper part of, and not an addition to, the worship of God by his people.[22]

When two years later the Presbyterian Church in the U.S. adopted a new Directory, little movement from the Westminster-based directory was evident. A minimum of quarterly celebration was required. "The Sacrament of the Lord's Supper is to be celebrated frequently, but at least quarterly. The stated times are to be determined by the Session for each congregation."[23] It was with these constitutional provisions that the committee appointed to revise *The Book of Common Worship* undertook its work, which led to *The Worshipbook.*

In 1964 the trial-use draft of the Sunday liturgy distributed by the service book revision committee set the course for a dramatic change in Presbyterian worship on the Lord's Day.[24] No longer was there a service of the Word, with the Eucharist as a separate service or an add-on to a preaching service. A single service was proposed, titled: Service for the Lord's Day. This service clearly set forth the norm for worship on the Lord's Day as a service embracing both the reading and proclamation of the Word and the celebration of the Eucharist. It provided a rubric clearly setting forth the norm of Word/Supper on each Lord's Day, but described how the service was to be concluded if the Eucharist was not to be included. The rubric read:

> Properly, the Lord's Supper is to be celebrated every Lord's Day. Otherwise, the prayers shall conclude with the prayer for the COMMUNION OF SAINTS on page 23, and the LORD'S PRAYER; followed by the OFFERING, a HYMN, a PRAYER OF THANKSGIVING, and the BENEDICTION.[25]

No further order or texts were provided for non-eucharistic occasions. In using this liturgy, one had to *delete* the eucharistic portions when the Sacrament was not included.

In the testing of this liturgy it was evident that the committee had gotten too far ahead of the church. The church was not yet ready to acknowledge on a wide scale that the Eucharist is properly to be celebrated each Lord's Day. Critics were careful to note that the rubric went beyond the directories. When the committee released the next trial-use service in 1966,[26] the single service, the Service for the Lord's Day, remained solidly in place.[27] However, the rubric regarding the Lord's Supper was more in harmony with the United Presbyterian Directory for the Worship of God. Instead of stating, "Properly, the Lord's Supper is to be celebrated every Lord's Day," the rubric was softened to read, "It is fitting that the Lord's Supper be celebrated as often as each Lord's Day. If the Lord's Supper is not celebrated, let the service continue on p. 34."[28] Rather than simply listing elements to include when "the Lord's Supper is omitted" an order with texts was provided.[29] This then became part of the Service for the Lord's Day in *The Worshipbook—Services* when it was published in 1970.[30]

The committee's bold step taken in 1964 toward making the Eucharist normative was thus muted. Nevertheless, the resulting liturgy marked a very significant departure from centuries of Reformed liturgical norms. No longer was the Eucharist something to be *added to* the normal service. Now, if it was not being celebrated, it was something to be *omitted from* the normal service. This was the most important contribution of *The Worshipbook*.

THE *BOOK OF COMMON WORSHIP*

The *Book of Common Worship* not only preserved this achievement of *The Worshipbook* but it sought to reinforce further the Word and Eucharist as normative for each Lord's Day. The ordering of the service in the first trial-use resource remained essentially that included in *The Worshipbook*. However, the priority of the inclusion of the Eucharist was reinforced through diagramming the order in a manner that made it clear that the norm is to include both the Word and the Sacrament. The rubric in the liturgy remained essentially that of *The Worshipbook:* "It is fitting that the Lord's Supper be celebrated as often as each Lord's Day. When it is celebrated, the service proceeds as follows." In diagramming the order a rubric was placed in a parallel column: When the Lord's Supper is not celebrated, the service continues with a Prayer of Thanksgiving.[31]

Testing of the trial-use resources led to some changes in the outline to appear in the *Book of Common Worship,* since it had become apparent that the headings in the earlier trial-use resources were not adequate:

> Assemble in God's Name
>
> Proclaim God's Word
>
> Give Thanks to God
>
> Go in God's Name

The headings did not adequately encompass the elements of the service they were intended to identify, most particularly the central two sections. New headings were substituted in the *Book of Common Worship*:

> Gathering
>
> The Word
>
> The Eucharist
>
> Sending

These headings more adequately encompass the elements included in the various sections.

A second major change pertains to the third section. In the earliest trial-use resources, this portion of the liturgy, headed "Give Thanks to God" (diagram 1), identified the third part of the liturgy whether or not the Eucharist was celebrated. It was correctly based on the understanding that "eucharist" means "giving thanks," but was too easily misunderstood. The heading failed to give sufficient clarity to the norm of a Word/Eucharist liturgy. Testing revealed that many who used the resources misinterpreted the intent.

The outline did succeed in portraying the parallel structure between a service that included the Eucharist and a service that did not. Also, one could readily recognize that when the Eucharist was not included, only those elements pertaining specifically to the Sacrament were deleted. However, the two parallel tracks were too easily regarded as equal options in fulfilling the promise of the heading to give thanks to God. But they are not equals. Historically, biblically, theologically, and in ability to form the spiritual life of the faithful, a liturgy of Word and Eucharist remains the norm. A service in which the Eucharist has been deleted remains but a fragment of Christian liturgy. The outline of the service was therefore revised to make it clear that the norm of the service includes the Eucharist each Lord's Day and festival (diagram 2).[32]

The more precise heading of "The Eucharist" therefore heads the third section of the outline. Furthermore, although parallel elements are included when the Sacrament is not celebrated, these elements are not to be viewed as a substitute of equal merit to the Sacrament. Rather, they remind us that the norm is to include the Eucharist, of which these elements are but the shadow. For this reason no heading appears in the right-hand column. The result is that without the Sacrament it is clearly a Service of the Word, with three parts, not four.

Another change pertains to the rubric that was included in *The Worshipbook* and *Service for the Lord's Day* (Supplemental Liturgical Resource 1). The rubric in the *Book of Common Worship* now reads: "IF THE LORD'S SUPPER IS NOT TO BE CELEBRATED, THE SERVICE CONTINUES ON PAGE 79."[33] Gone is the interpretation, "It is fitting that the Lord's Supper be celebrated as often as each Lord's Day."

The reason is simple. Rubrics are to give clear instructions for the liturgical action, and are not to interpret the actions. Such interpretations belong elsewhere. Therefore, in the introductory essay of the *Book of Common Worship*, the norm of the Lord's Day service as one of Word and Eucharist is clearly set forth.[34] The essay quotes from the text of the Directory for Worship adopted in 1987, which reflects the directory of the former United Presbyterian Church in the U.S.A.[35] The *Book of Common Worship* thus continues to challenge the church to recover the centrality of the Eucharist. This reform can do much to further the renewal of the church's life in our time.

In both their Constitution and in their book of services, Presbyterians unequivocally have set before them a liturgy of Word and Eucharist as normative for worship on each Lord's Day and festival. This has resulted in the frequency of celebration dramatically increasing among Presbyterians in the years since the United Presbyterians adopted the 1961 Directory and since *The Worshipbook—Services* was published in 1970. While some congregations continue to celebrate the Sacrament four times each year, most churches now celebrate it more frequently.

In recent years there has been a steady increase in the number of churches celebrating the Eucharist on each Lord's Day. In 1989 a little over one percent of the congregations reported that they celebrated the Eucharist each Sunday. Two-thirds of the churches had moved beyond quarterly celebration of the Eucharist, with nearly one-half of the churches celebrating it monthly. Nearly all of the seven Presbyterian theological institutions now include a celebration of the Eucharist each week of the school term. With an increasing number of seminary graduates having embraced the pattern of weekly Eucharist, the congregations they serve will surely be led to that end.[36] One continuously hears of other congregations that have since established a celebration of the Eucharist each Lord's Day and festival.

But it is important to understand that the objective is not simply to increase the frequency of celebrating the Eucharist. Too many congregations feel they have arrived at the goal when they celebrate monthly. *The objective is not increased frequency, but recovering the full unity of Word and Lord's Supper on each Lord's Day and festival.* Anything short of full union of Lord's Supper and Lord's Day is inadequate and should be regarded as a temporary practice, while the goal remains that of full weekly Eucharist.

FULFILLING AN UNFULFILLED REFORM

Making constitutional changes, and preparing liturgies that set forth the norm of celebrating the Eucharist each Lord's Day, will not by themselves effect this needed liturgical reform. More is needed than simply acknowledging that the norm for Christian worship is celebrating the Eucharist on each Lord's Day, and agreeing that we ought to recover the practice. Bolder steps to correct this failure are required.

The biblical evidence is clear. The historical evidence of the church's earliest tradition cannot be disputed. The liturgical admonitions are in place in directory and *Book of Common Worship.* So, why are we so slow in recovering Word and Eucharist as the norm of Christian worship on the Lord's Day? Is not four and a half centuries far too long a span of time to have continued the "defective custom" Calvin called future generations to correct? If we believe in the validity of the coveted motto of the Reformed tradition, *Ecclesia reformata, semper reformanda,* why are we not more concerned to complete this unfinished task of reform? The failure to restore the Eucharist, the very heart of Christian liturgy, denies the intent of the Reformers and undermines any claim of following in the tradition of the primitive church.

The reasons for our failure are undoubtedly several. An inadequate theological understanding of the Sacrament prevails in most congregations. Too many fail to appreciate the formative role of ritual, and consequently do not recognize how the Eucharist forms us in the faith. A common reaction to the proposal for weekly Communion is a fear that the Sacrament will lose its significance and become commonplace. Experience proves this fear to have no basis in fact. Frequency, moreover, increases a sense of the Sacrament's significance. Some congregations fear being overwhelmed with the logistics of celebrating the Sacrament each Lord's Day and festival. Yet the experience of congregations that celebrate the Sacrament each Lord's Day proves otherwise.

I am convinced that the dominant reason is an inadequate theological understanding of the Sacrament. We shall never overcome the failure of the Reformation to maintain the Eucharist as the norm of Christian worship, until we are able to restore a theology of the Sacrament that will set it where it belongs: in the center of our life together. A good place to begin in filling this need is to explore the theological dimensions of the eucharistic liturgy in the *Book of Common Worship* and the Directory for Worship, and to carefully reflect on how the theology expressed in the liturgy and directory shapes the faith and life of the church. The common fears and the logistical challenges retreat from the center of attention as the meaning and power of the Eucharist come into focus.

The Eucharist is crucial to the maturing of our faith. We have long accepted the principle that the Supper is not to be celebrated without the exposition of Scripture, for the Eucharist seals the promises proclaimed in preaching. We have been taught that the Eucharist without the Word can lead to superstition. But we have not given sufficient attention to what results when the Eucharist does not accompany preaching.

Could it be that the divisiveness that has so troubled Protestantism has resulted in some measure from the loss of the unifying power of the Eucharist? Could it be that the reason Protestantism is often reduced to propositions for the mind to agree on is the result of our failure to sustain our entire being with the food of the living presence of Christ in the Sacrament? Could it be that the reason popular Christianity is so gripped by individualism is that we have failed in breaking bread together? Could it be that the preoccupation with concerns that center on the self, a preoccupation that characterizes much of contemporary church life, is due in part to the failure of remembering who we are in the Supper? Could it be that the erosion of God-centered worship may be traced to the loss of the renewing of our union with Christ that is ours in the Eucharist? There is no way we can fathom the extent to which the church has been impoverished as a result of relegating the Eucharist to the periphery of our life together.

An important aspect of reform in our time is the restoration of this liturgical norm. We have the tools. May God give us a new spirit of openness to follow in the way the Holy Spirit is leading us in this recovery.

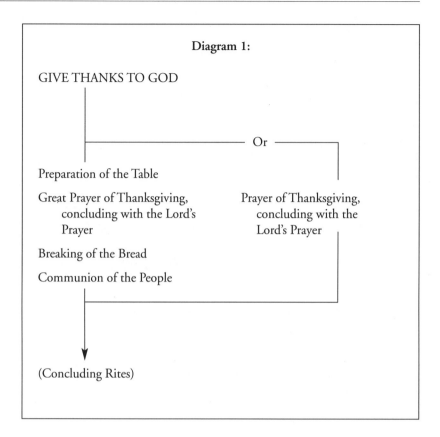

Diagram 1:

GIVE THANKS TO GOD

Or

Preparation of the Table

Great Prayer of Thanksgiving,   Prayer of Thanksgiving,
concluding with the Lord's   concluding with the
Prayer   Lord's Prayer

Breaking of the Bread

Communion of the People

(Concluding Rites)

Diagram 2

THE SERVICE FOR THE LORD'S DAY
Book of Common Worship

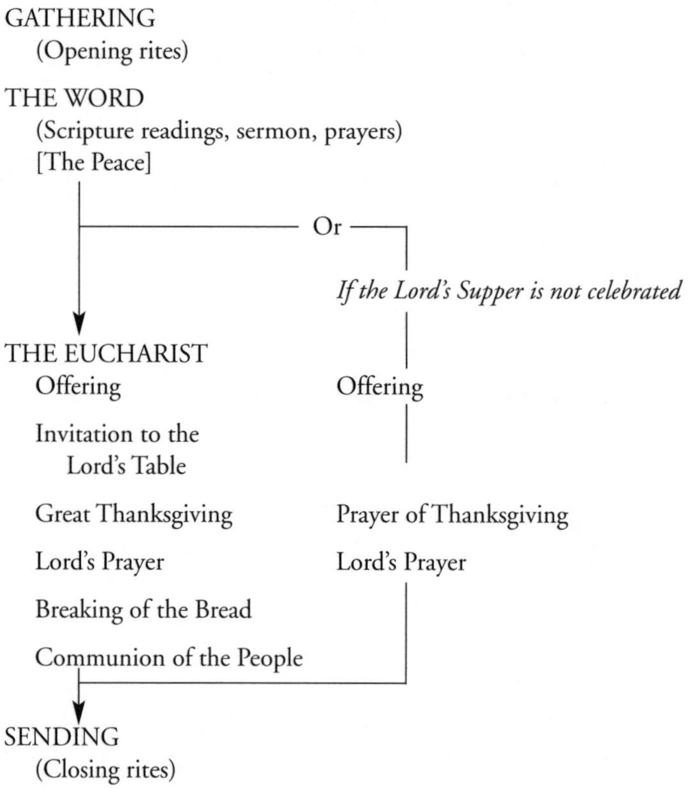

GATHERING
  (Opening rites)

THE WORD
  (Scripture readings, sermon, prayers)
  [The Peace]

——————————— Or ———

                          If the Lord's Supper is not celebrated

THE EUCHARIST
  Offering   Offering

  Invitation to the
    Lord's Table

  Great Thanksgiving   Prayer of Thanksgiving

  Lord's Prayer   Lord's Prayer

  Breaking of the Bread

  Communion of the People

SENDING
  (Closing rites)

Chapter 9

Four Primary
Liturgical Reforms

From its nineteenth-century beginnings until well into the twentieth century, the liturgical movement in the Reformed tradition, as in other traditions, centered on reclaiming a long-forgotten liturgical heritage. In spite of the importance of that recovery, it was sometimes dismissed by its critics as simply romanticism, elitism, and aestheticism. While drawing on the liturgical sources of the past remains important, the liturgical movement in the years leading up to and following Vatican II has shifted its primary focus from restoration to pastoral dimensions of liturgy. It is not enough simply to restore lost rites; the liturgy is not a museum artifact; it is a fountain of living water that flows to quench our thirsting spirits today.

Prompted by pastoral concern, the church needs to recast its liturgical heritage from time to time so that it may fully live in the present. This bifocal emphasis of reclaiming and adapting was the primary guiding light of Vatican II and remains the dominant objective in the modern liturgical movement. The *Book of Common Worship* boldly reclaims the richness of the church's liturgical heritage. At the same time, it is sensitive to present pastoral needs, and it adapts that heritage to meet them. It thus is representative of a living tradition, a script for a lively encounter with the Eternal.

Among the variety of reforms embodied in the *Book of Common Worship,* four are primary, centering on Baptism, the Lord's Supper, the liturgical calendar, and daily prayer. Both the Directory for Worship and the *Book of Common Worship* set forth these reforms as central to the way congregations worship. The anemic manner in which Protestants ordinarily celebrate the faith in each of these areas thwarts the power of the liturgy to shape the faith within us. Underlying each of these reforms is a concern for preserving the integrity of the faith in our life together.

BAPTISM

At the heart of contemporary liturgical reforms is a renewed understanding of the meaning and practice of Baptism, and of the direction it gives for all of the Christian life. This sacrament has far greater power to shape our lives as Christians than is generally realized.

The minimalist ways in which Baptism is often practiced tend to obscure its essential meaning. Baptismal practice is so trivialized that it fails to shape the Christian life in any significant way. The space for Baptism (if there is any) and the sacramental action of the water bath are minimal. Water has all but evaporated from our fonts and practice. Our baptismal practice gives little clue to the rigors of Christian discipleship. Its impact on life following Baptism is negligible. Marginalized, Baptism has become trivialized.

Baptism in the *Book of Common Worship* is clearly portrayed as Baptism with water and the Spirit, signifying cleansing from sin, new birth, death and resurrection with Christ, and incorporation into the body of Christ. These aspects of Baptism are of the very essence of the Christian life. Baptism not only marks the beginning but continues to be the pivotal reference point shaping our discipleship each day of our lives.

In writing about evangelism, Walter Brueggemann underscores the need for integrity in baptismal practice, especially in the face of the "growth of secularism which marginalizes the church," and the "greedy religious right-wing which is only a chaplain for commodity militarism." He adds:

> [W]e must recover the focal drama of baptism, which is a subversive act of renunciation and embrace. The claims of the gospel of God's hidden, decisive victory are fully voiced in our language and in our baptism. We are, however, mostly so kept and domesticated that we cringe from the very news given us. We find ways to skew our language and trivialize the sacrament so that there is nothing left for us except accommodation to cultural expectation.[1]

Recovering the integrity of Baptism hinges on taking Baptism seriously. Perhaps we will continue to have anemic Christians until our baptismal theology and practice overcome anemia. Converts, and those bringing children for Baptism, need to be led to and through a rite that unfolds in word and actions the depths of Baptism's meaning.[2] New converts need to be led to an understanding of the significance of Baptism for life that follows Baptism. The baptismal rites in the *Book of Common Worship* clearly set forth, not only a beginning, but the life that follows Baptism.

Profession

The profession of faith (renunciation of evil and profession) engages the baptizand(s) in renouncing all that is evil and professing Christ as Lord and Savior. It is a sign that the entire life of the Christian is one of *turning from* evil, and *turning to* Christ, a *turning from* all that is destructive of human life and *turning to* the source of all that is true and good. It is a choice to be made each day of our lives.

Thanksgiving

The thanksgiving over the water recalls the waters of salvation history into which we are baptized. This beautiful prayer abounds in watery imagery. Out of a watery chaos the Creator brought forth life. In the waters of the flood God destroyed evil, giving righteousness a new beginning. Through the waters of the sea, God led Israel out of slavery into freedom. In Jordan's waters Jesus was baptized by John and anointed with the Spirit. By the baptism of Jesus' death and resurrection, he set us free from sin and death and opened the way to eternal life. Into that baptism we are buried with Christ in his death, and are raised with Christ to new life. The Spirit is then invoked to make this water "a fountain of deliverance and rebirth," to "wash away the sin of all who are cleansed by it," to "raise them to new life, and graft them to the body of Christ," to "pour out your Holy Spirit upon them, that they may have power to do your will, and continue forever in the risen life of Christ."[3] Just as in the story of creation's beginning "a wind from God swept over the face of the waters" bringing order out of a watery chaos (Gen. 1:2), so in the waters of Baptism the Spirit of God is recreating all things new.

Washing

The washing with water. The heart of the baptismal rite, both in its theology and drama, is a washing with water in the name of the triune God. The rubric in the *Book of Common Worship,* echoing the Directory for Worship, states that whatever the mode, water is to be used "visibly and generously."[4] More than a few drops of water are needed if we are to move beyond the minimalism that has dominated the past.

God speaks to us through our bodies and senses as well as our minds. The water of Baptism can speak with great power in ways words alone cannot. But, if the act of Baptism is to speak clearly, enough water needs to be used so that the one being baptized gets wet, and those gathered can see the water and hear it splash. It will then speak of washing, death, the giving and sustaining of life, refreshment, and creation. We lose that impact when minimalism shapes liturgy.

The word "baptize" means to immerse, and evidence abounds that immersion was the practice of the ancient church. However, immersion is not submersion. In immersion, adults being baptized knelt in the water of the baptismal pool and water was poured over them in abundance. In studying ancient baptismal pools it is clear that immersion, rather than submersion, was the practice. Particularly since Vatican II, churches are moving beyond minimalism in baptismal practice, thereby giving greater regard to the sign value of the water. Increasingly, baptismal spaces have pools of water in which adults may be immersed.[5] The sacrament is thus empowered to express that of which the water is a sign.

Living Out of One's Baptism

Baptism is the beginning of a life that is nourished by Word and Supper and spent in serving God. The significance of Baptism is not confined simply to a single moment of beginning. Baptism occurs but once, but becomes the referent point of our daily lives, filling our days with fresh resolve in discipleship until our Baptism is made complete in death.

Each time we confess our sins and receive God's forgiveness, we renew our resolve to turn from evil and to follow Christ of which the cleansing waters of Baptism are a sign. Each time we affirm our faith in the words of the creeds, we renew our profession of the faith into which we were baptized. Each time we come to the Lord's Table we renew the baptismal covenant. At every occasion of Baptism we are reminded of God's promises given in our Baptism and recommit ourselves to minister in Christ's name. Furthermore, the *Book of Common Worship* provides for liturgies for the reaffirmation of baptismal vows in a variety of circumstances. The need for constant renewing of the baptismal covenant is well stated in these words:

> 30.203   God's faithfulness to us signified in baptism is constant and sure, even when our faithfulness to God is not. Baptism is received only once. The efficacy of baptism is not tied to the moment when it is administered, for baptism signifies the beginning of the life in Christ, not its completion. God's grace works steadily within us, calling us to repentance and newness of life. God's faithfulness needs no renewal. Our faithfulness to God needs repeated renewal. Both for those whose baptism attends their profession of faith and for those who are nurtured from childhood within the family of faith, baptism calls for decision at every subsequent stage of life's way.

> 30.204   Although we receive baptism only once, there are many times in worship (including the celebration of another's baptism, the experience of the sustaining nurture of the Lord's Supper, and occasions for the renewal of our baptismal vows) when we acknowledge the grace of God continually

at work in and among us, confess our ongoing need of that grace, and pledge anew our obedience to God's covenant in Christ.[6]

The baptismal covenant infuses the entire *Book of Common Worship*. There are constant reminders in the texts provided for the Service for the Lord's Day and for the seasons and festivals. We are repeatedly reminded that in our Baptism we are united with all of the baptized from every time and place. The Lenten season is filled with reminders of Baptism, since Lent had its origins as a time of preparing candidates for their Baptism at the Easter Vigil. Baptismal images abound throughout the vigil, in its readings and in its actions.

Since Baptism marks the beginning of a lifelong journey, and is made complete in one's death, it is particularly appropriate that one's Baptism be recalled at the funeral of a faithful Christian. So, as a pall, symbolic of the baptismal garment, is placed upon the coffin, words from Romans (6:3–5) are said (imagine the solemn joy conveyed if these words are sung):

> When we were baptized in Christ Jesus, we were baptized into his death. We were buried therefore with him by baptism into death, so that, as Christ was raised from the dead by the glory of the Father, we too might live a new life. For if we have been united with Christ in a death like his, we will certainly be united with him in a resurrection like his.

Throughout the *Book of Common Worship* we are reminded that the significance of Baptism is to be carried forward through life as the devout Christian seeks to live out all that it means. As the baptized ones, we bear the mark that signifies for us God's unmerited love, the cleansing from sin, our participation in Christ's death and resurrection, and the strengthening and enabling power of the Holy Spirit.[7]

THE LORD'S SUPPER

Chapter 8 provided an extended overview of efforts to restore to each Sunday and festival the full order of Christian worship, a liturgy in which Scriptures are read and interpreted and the Lord's Supper is celebrated. This restoration has the spotlight at the center of the stage of liturgical reform. What follows is a reflection on how the liturgy of Word and Supper contributes to our growth in the faith.

During the past thirty years the church has experienced a significant reform in the liturgy centering on the reading and interpretation of Scripture resulting from the growing acceptance and use of the lectionary. The lectionary's systematic approach to the reading of Scripture in worship, resulting in an enriched diet of Scripture for the faithful, is an important reform in the face of widespread biblical illiteracy. Use of the lectionary has given birth to Bible study based on the lectionary readings, and, since the lectionary is ecumenical, preachers across denominational lines have been meeting together to discuss the readings, thereby fostering a greater sense of unity in Christ's church. The extensive exegetical resources being published on the lectionary readings have resulted in preaching that is more biblical and less topical in nature. This reform in the church's liturgy is important for renewal to take place in the church, for the Spirit speaks to us through the Scripture as in no other way. We are reminded of this whenever the readings are introduced with "Hear what the Spirit is saying to the church."[8] The recovery of a lectionary has made a major impact on the church's worship and is grounding the faithful more firmly in the faith.

However, as we have said above, the church has had less success in recovering the Lord's Supper on each Lord's Day and festival. It remains an unfinished reform. The movement to restore weekly Eucharist among American Presbyterians, beginning with the 1961 adoption of the Directory for Worship of the former United Presbyterian Church in the U.S.A., has brought about an increased frequency in celebration. However, few congregations as yet celebrate the Lord's Supper on each Lord's Day and festival, although the number is growing. On most Sundays, most Presbyterian congregations celebrate half of the liturgy. It is ironic that the portion of the liturgy deriving from the synagogue has remained unbroken in the Protestant tradition, but the portion of the liturgy that from the beginning is uniquely Christian was all but lost, and as yet has not been fully reclaimed.

An inadequate understanding of the Eucharist is undoubtedly the cause. Popular piety often sees it only as a time of contemplating Jesus' death. Congregations that have overcome that limited view too often see it as little more than a means of building unity among members of the congregation. As such, the coffee hour following a preaching service works just as well. While I am tempted to say that a congregation should not move to a weekly celebration until it has an adequate theology of the Sacrament, the fact remains that only as a congregation celebrates the Sacrament in its fullness will it begin to understand it and truly appreciate it. Appreciation will be deepened if the congregation has an opportunity to probe the meaning of the Sacrament in a study setting, as weekly Communion is reclaimed. In making decisions about frequency, each decision should be seen as progressing toward full eucharistic celebration on each Sunday and festival, while leading the congregation with pastoral sensitivity and teaching.

Restoring the weekly celebration of the Lord's Supper is clearly an underlying conviction embodied in the *Book of Common Worship*. The more a congregation grows in its understanding of the Eucharist, the more it will recognize the Lord's Supper as central to Christian worship. Our failure to enlarge our understanding of the Eucharist is a fundamental barrier to recovering the fullness of Christian worship.

When the manifold aspects of eucharistic meaning are seen, the more fully the Sacrament takes on the spirit of *eucharistia*—a joyful and thankful memorial of the mighty acts of God, through which, by the work of the Holy Spirit, we participate in Christ, receiving all that Christ offers us. If we listen to the language of the liturgy it will teach us what the Sacrament is about, for it is most truly what we pray that informs and shapes what we believe. As we pray, so we believe.

Sacraments embody both words and actions. The actions of the Lord's Supper consist of the *taking of bread and wine, giving thanks, breaking the bread,* and *giving it to the people.* The most important words in the Lord's Supper are the eucharistic prayer—the Great Thanksgiving. This prayer is essential to celebrating the Sacrament. Its central themes revolve around creation and redemption, on God who created all things and who is ever redeeming all things. We remember God's promises, and in the light of those promises we pray that through the Holy Spirit, Christ will be effectually present for us. The prayer is central to the action. It is theological in nature, almost credal in tone. In examining texts of this prayer, we find that there are three basic movements: remembering, offering, and invoking.

Gratefully Remembering

"Do this in remembrance of me." The Eucharist is a memorial in which we gratefully remember and give praise to God for all of God's mighty deeds, especially the gift of Jesus Christ. We remember the acts of God that tell us who we are as the people of God, and thus we reclaim our identity, purpose, and direction as disciples. The prayer reminds us that our identity as a people is rooted in the long story of God's calling a people to be God's own. As a community of memory, we are shaped by the story of God's dealings with humankind—creating us in God's own image, persisting in calling us to faithfulness in love and service, establishing covenant with us, taking on flesh in Jesus Christ and dwelling among us, redeeming us through Christ's death and resurrection, and establishing God's promised reign.

Eucharistic remembering is more than being reminded of a past event that we otherwise might forget. It is to be understood in the light of the Jewish understanding of memorial, in which remembering was never static. In the Jewish memorial, the event was brought out of the past, becoming a living part of the present. Thus in the eucharistic memorial Jesus' giving himself for us is not simply an event to be called to mind. Fundamentally, it means that Jesus' once-for-all giving of himself for us is effectual and operative in the present. As Calvin expressed it, we become participants in Christ.

Furthermore, eucharistic remembering is not simply embracing God's grace-filled deeds from the past, but also embracing God's promised future. The faith story conveys the promise of the fulfillment of God's reign. We therefore *remember the future,* the coming reign of God. Eucharistic remembering thus brings both past and future into the present; thus it is filled with hope, giving assurance of the ultimate fulfillment of all God has promised.

Christ, crucified, risen, and coming again, is at the center of every eucharistic celebration. We must never forget that story, for it conveys to us the meaning and direction of life. In gratefully remembering the story of God's grace, beginning with creation and reaching forward to Christ's coming in glory, we receive it as *our* story and discover what it means to be fully human.

Offering

In rehearsing the mighty deeds of God, we take bread and wine, gifts from God's creation, and joyfully celebrate Christ's dying and rising as we await the day of his coming. In taking bread and wine, "we offer our very selves," in words based on Romans 12:1, "as a living and holy sacrifice" given for God's service.[9] In this thankful offering of ourselves to the triune God, we join with all the faithful in heaven and on earth.[10]

Thus, this offering is twofold. First, Christ's self-giving to us in his life, death, and resurrection, a unique, once-for-all offering, is made effectual for us in this Sacrament. Second, the church gives itself to God. In gratitude for God's boundless grace we offer ourselves, all we are, and all we do, in the praise and service of God. Historical theologian Brian A. Gerrish emphasizes this as fundamental in Calvin's theology:

> It is this double self-giving that makes the Supper both embody and represent the perpetual exchange of grace and gratitude that shapes Calvin's entire theology. The sacred banquet prepared by the father's goodness is the actual giving, not merely the remembering, of a gift of grace, and precisely as such it demands and evokes the answering gratitude of God's children.[11]

Invoking

Having gratefully remembered the grace of God for us, and having offered ourselves to God, we call upon God, asking that, through the Holy Spirit, all that God wrought through Jesus Christ for us may be effectually present to us in the Sacrament. We ask "that the bread we break and the cup we bless may be the communion of the body and blood of Christ." Or, as *The Book of Common Order* (1940) of the Church of Scotland, in amplifying the meaning of this, adds, "that we, receiving them, may by faith be made partakers of His body and blood, with all His benefits, to our spiritual nourishment and growth in grace, and to the glory of Thy most holy name."[12] To participate in the communion of the body and blood of Christ is to participate in the fullness of God's grace, to be partakers of all that Christ's coming among us gives and all that his death and resurrection mean for us. In short, it is a participation in, and a grateful receiving of, God's unbounded grace.

The invocation continues, "By your Spirit make us one with Christ, that we may be one with all who share this feast, united in ministry in every place." In the sharing of the body and blood of Christ (1 Cor. 10:16–17) we are made one with the risen Christ, nourished with Christ's body and blood that we may mature into the fullness of Christ.[13] Made one with Christ, we are made one with all God's people. It is important to understand that it is not the act of our eating and drinking together that unites us; we are united only by our being made one with Christ, upon whom we feast in the Sacrament. It is *our union with Christ* that unites us as a people.

Furthermore, we are united not simply with those gathered in a particular assembly. We are one "with the Church in every place, and the whole Church is present," joined "with all the faithful in heaven and on earth."[14] This unity is ours through Baptism, as stated in Great Thanksgiving B: "By your Spirit unite us with the living Christ and with all who are baptized in his name."[15]

Our unity is in order that the church might be "united in ministry in every place."

> As this bread is Christ's body for us,
> send us out to be the body of Christ in the world.[16]

In offering and invoking we commit ourselves "afresh to love and serve God, one another, and our neighbors in the world."[17]

Then we pray that God will strengthen us to be faithful, until that time when we shall sit with Christ at the messianic feast. Gathered about the Lord's Table, we share even now something of that great messianic banquet of God's future, "the joyful feast of the people of God," when "they will come from east and west, and from north and south, and sit at table in the kingdom of God."[18]

Thus the remembering, offering, and invoking in the Eucharist provide us with the primary occasion for reaffirming the covenant into which we were baptized.[19] Receiving the story of God's grace, we gratefully offer ourselves anew in the service of Christ; and in bread and wine Christ gives us his very self as the food of life.

More fully than at any other moment in our life together, we recommit ourselves as Christ's disciples each time we gather at the table our Lord spreads before us. Each time we come to the Lord's Table, we make a choice in doing so. It is a choice to be renewed by God's gift of grace and to reaffirm our resolve to follow him who alone is the way, the truth, and the life. This should be at the heart of our worship each Lord's Day.

Luke tells us (24:13–35) that on the evening of the first day of the week, three days after the crucifixion, some of Jesus' followers, confused and discouraged, were walking gloomily to their home in Emmaus. A stranger joined them on their journey. Hearing their sorrowful dirge, the stranger began to interpret the Scriptures to them, helping them to understand the events that had taken place. Nearing the disciples' home, they invited the traveler to stay with them, for it was evening. Gathered for the evening meal, their guest became the host. He "took bread, blessed and broke it, and gave it to them. Then their eyes were opened, and they recognized him." They knew him to be the Lord, risen from the dead.

Reflecting on what they had seen and heard, they exclaimed in amazement, "Did not our hearts burn within us while he was talking to us on the road, while he was opening the scriptures to us?" Running back to Jerusalem with the good news, they gave witness that Jesus had been "known to them in the breaking of the bread." In this story we have a window into the earliest Christians' understanding of the Lord's Supper—the Scriptures interpreted, and the risen Christ known in the breaking of the bread.

Interpretation of Scripture that causes our hearts to burn and to know the risen Christ "in the breaking of the bread" is what the liturgy should be on each Lord's Day—Word and Sacrament. It is the heart of Christian worship, the centerpiece of liturgical reform.[20]

LITURGICAL CALENDAR

The third major liturgical reform set forth in the *Book of Common Worship* concerns the recovery of the liturgical calendar. The calendar links the way the church keeps time with the gospel story. In festivals and seasons, the church proclaims the mighty acts of God in Jesus Christ, to the end that they may engage us in an encounter with the living God.

Among the Reformed in the sixteenth-century Reformation, the calendar was cleansed of all festivals deemed to be of "human origin." Festivals that detracted from the fullness of the gospel were removed. Only those feast days rooted in the biblical witness, "evangelical feasts," were retained: Christmas, Good Friday, Easter, Ascension, Pentecost. Thus, Advent and Lent were set aside. The Second Helvetic Confession of 1566 clearly encouraged these celebrations of the biblical witness:

> [I]f in Christian liberty the churches religiously celebrate the memory of the Lord's nativity, circumcision, passion, resurrection, and of his ascension into heaven, and the sending of the Holy Spirit upon his disciples, we approve of it highly.[21]

In the Puritan struggles of the seventeenth century, however, all of these were lost, even Christmas and Easter. Although the Reformed in continental Europe were free to preserve festivals and seasons that celebrated the gospel, the Puritans and Scots became increasingly reactionary when confronted with the political and liturgical pressures of the established church. When the Scottish kirk officially recognized the Second Helvetic Confession it deleted from the text the portion cited above, and condemned the observance of all the feasts. So when the Westminster Directory was adopted in 1644, no reference was made to the liturgical calendar.

The first Directory for Worship adopted by American Presbyterians, like the Westminster Directory which was its basis, made no reference to Christian festivals. The result was that no Christian festivals were celebrated by the Reformed in seventeenth-century America. Christmas, Good Friday, Easter, Ascension, and Pentecost had all disappeared.

By the middle of the nineteenth century this began to change through the influence of the Sunday school movement, when Christmas and Easter began to be included in Sunday school literature. But the recovery of the calendar did not really begin until the early twentieth century. By the time the first *Book of Common Worship* was published in 1906, a few festivals had begun to take root, such as Advent, Christmas, Good Friday, and Easter. The next *Book of Common Worship* (1932) gave more attention to the calendar. The season of Lent (although titled "Preparation for Easter"), Palm Sunday, Ascension Day, Pentecost, and All Saints' Day appeared in the calendar. A rudimentary lectionary provided readings for the festivals and seasons. The 1946 *Book of Common Worship* added Maundy Thursday (calling it "Thursday before Easter"), and Trinity Sunday. A fully developed lectionary was added for the first time. In 1961 the United Presbyterian Church, in adopting a new Directory for Worship, officially stated for the first time the appropriateness of observing in public worship: Advent, Christmas, Epiphany, Lent culminating in Holy Week, Easter, and Pentecost. Thus Epiphany was added for the first time, and Lent was no longer called "Preparation for Easter." However, in the South, when the Presbyterian Church in the U.S. published its directory two years later, the continuing strength of Puritanism resulted in defeating the inclusion of any reference to the liturgical year.

In keeping with the 1961 directory, *The Worshipbook* included resources for Sundays and festivals for the "Christian Year," adding a table displaying the traditional liturgical colors. Ash Wednesday appeared in the church's book of services for the first time. The Thursday before Easter became Maundy Thursday. It was perhaps the inclusion of a revised version of the Roman lectionary in *The Worshipbook* that stimulated a growing acceptance of the liturgical calendar, since calendar and lectionary are tightly interrelated.

Following the Second Vatican Council, the trend toward an ecumenical consensus in reference to the liturgical calendar was reflected by all churches as they revised their service books in the 1970s and 1980s. Further development of the calendar was first introduced in the *Presbyterian Program Planning Calendar* for 1983–1984. Appearing for the first time for Presbyterian celebration were: Baptism of the Lord, Transfiguration of the Lord, and Christ the King. Although the Scripture readings for these days had been included in the lectionary in *The Worshipbook,* these festivals were not identified by title. When a new Directory for Worship was adopted in 1989, these festivals were included. Palm Sunday appropriately became Passion/Palm Sunday.

In the publication of the *Book of Common Worship* in 1993, the calendar it embodies reflects the result of this evolution spanning the century. By this time the use of the term "Ordinary Time" was being used for the two periods not included in either the Advent-Christmas-Epiphany cycle or the Lent-Easter-Pentecost cycle, in keeping with ecumenical practice. The Great Vigil of Easter also was included, and the alternative title "Reign of Christ" was given for Christ the King. An abundance of prayers were provided for each season and festival. Full festival liturgies were included for festivals in the paschal cycle. Liturgical texts and orders of service for celebrating the liturgical year are comprehensive, and comprise over one fifth of the volume.

So Presbyterians are invited into one of the rich treasures of the church, its keeping time in relation to the gospel.

What we hear in the Gospel stories of God-with-us is the redeeming work of Christ: incarnation-crucifixion-resurrection-outpouring of the Spirit:

> Christ was born.
> Christ taught.
> Christ was crucified.
> Christ was raised up.
> And the Spirit was poured out on us.
> The saving work of Christ is the story behind the story of Jesus' life.[22]

But the embracing of the liturgical calendar has not been without some misunderstanding of its role. Whenever congregations adopt the church's calendar without being firmly rooted in the lectionary, festivals tend to become encrusted with extraneous meanings that dilute the intrinsic meaning of the gospel event at the center of the festival. There also emerges a fascination in reenacting gospel events. Donkeys appear in Palm Sunday parades; Last Supper tableaus appear on Maundy Thursday; living crèches appear on church lawns during Advent. The festivals in the liturgical calendar are not about reenacting historical moments in the life of Christ, for this tends to trivialize and domesticate gospel events. The purpose of festival liturgies is that through them we may encounter Christ, and in that encounter find spiritual growth. The commentary in *Liturgical Year* (SLR-7) underscores this:

> The festive liturgies throughout the liturgical calendar are not reenacted historical dramas of the past but contemporary encounters with Christ.
>
> In the retelling and commemorating of the stories of God-with-us, the Spirit draws us into the mystery of the saving work of Christ. The liturgical calendar offers a series of celebrations that confront us with who we are in Christ and present us with a pattern for growth in Christ. The liturgical calendar permeates us with the mystery of Christ's redeeming work so we may conform our lives to Christ. It opens to us now the fulfillment of our lives for a future which is already with us in Christ and for which we were created.[23]

Of particular importance is the recovery of a centering on the paschal mystery—Christ's death and resurrection. What is termed The Three Days in the *Book of Common Worship* (the Triduum—Holy Thursday, Good Friday, and Easter Vigil—p. 1041) is at the core of who we are as the people of God.[24] It is the summit of all liturgy centering us in the redeeming work of Christ. The liturgies for these three days form a continuous story, and are to be regarded as one unified liturgy spanning three days (sunset Thursday until sunset Easter Sunday), and not three separate services. One liturgy, with three moments, it is a liturgy that builds toward its climax in the Great Vigil of Easter, the brightest jewel of Christian liturgy. It is the most treasured and richest of Christian festivals.[25]

In the last congregation I served as pastor (St. Andrew Presbyterian in Albuquerque, New Mexico), the renewing power of the Three Days was evidenced again and again. One year, after an intense week of services, Passion/Palm Sunday and then Maundy Thursday, Good Friday, and the Paschal Vigil, a note was slipped through the mail slot in the office. It expressed how meaningful the services had been, and closed with the sentence, "I believe the Holy Spirit was hanging around St. Andrew last week." There was no signature. Immediately I wondered, "Who could have written that note?" With a little detective work, I soon discovered the source. To my amazement, it was a member I least expected. I might have expected someone of pietistic leanings, but this was one actively involved in concerns of justice, one who would prefer engaging in social action to discussing theology. But there it was. "I believe the Holy Spirit was hanging around St. Andrew last week." It illustrated the transforming power of the Holy Spirit to ground us in the faith through our celebrating the paschal mystery. Remembering the story, and receiving it as our story, rejoicing in the power of Christ's death and resurrection, and sealing it by receiving the "bread of heaven" and the "cup of salvation," is life transforming. It revives our fainting spirits and sends us into the world in Christ's name.

The commentary in *Liturgical Year* (SLR-7) unfolds the centrality of the Vigil in the way the church remembers the gospel and appropriates it into its life:

> On the final night of this Easter journey we pause in vigil, at which time we remember stories about who we have been and are now becoming. As the community of faith we recount our centuries-long pilgrimage culminating in the renewal of baptismal promises. The Easter Vigil is akin to sitting around a campfire while listening to the stories of generations past and future. During the Easter Vigil we tell our name to ourselves and to those not of the household of faith. Our name is a very long story—of how we were made, of how God chose us from among all peoples, of how God liberated us from bondage, of how God planted us in the promised land, of how, in these last times, God has given the story a new twist in the life, death, and resurrection of Jesus. Because we have been here for so long, it takes a long time to tell who we are. We will not be hasty folk on that night.[26]

The Vigil has four movements: (1) the Liturgy of Light centering on Christ, the Light of the World, coming into a world of darkness; (2) recalling the story of our faith in a series of Scripture readings; (3) Baptism and reaffirmation of the baptismal covenant; (4) Feasting upon Christ in the Lord's Supper, the resurrection meal and foretaste of the messianic feast of God's kingdom. On this night we dwell upon the work of God for humankind spanning the full expanse of time, from creation to the end of time.

In opening our hearts and lives before God in the Three Days, we become participants in the paschal mystery, engaged in the dying and rising of Christ which is at the heart of the faith. In our Christian pilgrimage these days merit our setting aside all else and allowing the liturgy to aid us in coming to terms with the basic priorities of life. As the most sacred time in the church's calendar, recovery of this liturgy is a critical part of the reforming of our liturgical life. It has great power to convert, to transform, and deepen the Christian life.

DAILY PRAYER

The fourth major reform set forth in the *Book of Common Worship* concerns the recovery of daily prayer, known as the Daily Office.

Across the centuries prayer in the morning and evening has been an important part of the Christian way. With its roots in ancient Judaism, it was continued by the early Christians. The Reformers in the sixteenth century gave renewed attention to daily prayer, recognizing it as a valuable discipline of the Christian life. For centuries the Daily Office has been seen as a discipline for clergy and monks. The Second Vatican Council sought to reclaim the ancient discipline of daily prayer for all Christians.

While the first three editions of the *Book of Common Worship* included services for morning and evening, they were to be viewed as Sunday services of the Word, rather than for daily prayer. *The Worshipbook* was the first American Presbyterian service book to provide liturgies for morning and evening prayer. Coming four years after the end of the Council, it was a clear sign of yet another influence upon the church ecumenical of reforms initiated by the Second Vatican Council.

The Council's ecumenical influence toward the recovery of the Daily Office for all the faithful has come to its fullest bloom among Protestants in the *Book of Common Worship.* The section on daily prayer is one of its richest treasures. The liturgical texts for daily prayer together with the psalms (which are integral to daily prayer) comprise nearly three hundred of its pages, over a quarter of the volume. This portion of the *Book of Common Worship,* published in a separate and smaller volume in deluxe binding, is resulting in a growing ecumenical usage.

Daily Prayer Is Communal

As a tradition shared in common with the whole church, from every time and every place, daily prayer is appropriately ecumenical in scope. That unity is effectively expressed in the prayers. In the morning we are led to pray, in turn throughout the week, for the church in every land: Europe . . . Africa . . . Asia and the Middle East . . . the Pacific region . . . Latin America . . . North America. In the evening we are led to pray, in turn throughout the week, for every segment of the church: the Roman Catholic Church . . . Orthodox and Coptic churches . . . Episcopal and Methodist churches . . . Baptist, Disciples, and other free churches . . . Reformed, Presbyterian, and Lutheran churches . . . ecumenical councils and church agencies. Praying daily for some portion of the church in some part of the world can do much to undergird the unity we share in our Baptism.

Daily prayer is communal, whether it is said by a group gathered for prayer or by one praying alone. It is the prayer of the church. One never prays the Office alone. It is prayer shared in common, expressed in prayers, psalms, and Scripture readings.

The Daily Cycle

Daily prayer follows the natural cycle of the day, sun rising and sun setting. The basic pattern is prayer in the morning and prayer in the evening.

In the morning, we bless God for the awakening of a new day. Our prayers center upon the renewed activity and relationships the day's dawning promises. We pray for guidance as we undertake the day's tasks and for strength to faithfully fulfill our vocation as disciples of Christ. Our prayers center not only on immediate concerns, but encompass the broader concerns of the church's mission and a needy world.

A friend of mine, Richard Rowe, recently shared with me a Christian adaptation of a Native American greeting of the dawn.[27] Standing on the veranda of his home in Santa Fe, New Mexico, in the freshness of a new day, he often greets the morning as the sun rises over the Sangre de Cristo Mountains to the east. Joining his voice with singing birds and with all creation, he prays:

> Spirit of Light,
> Source of Light,
> Light of the World,
> I give you thanks for the return of the sun to the earth;
> the sun that gives light and life to all that is.
> May your light shine in our hearts today.
>
> Spirit of Life,
> Fountain of Life,
> Life of the World,
> I give you thanks for our sister the water,
> from whom all life comes.
> May our thirst be stilled.
>
> Spirit of Life,
> Source of Life,
> Life of the World,
> I give you thanks for the earth our Mother,
> that brings forth and sustains all living creatures,
> both great and small.
> May all have enough food today.
>
> Light and Life of the world,
> you in whom we live and move and have our being,
> I give you thanks that I am alive
> and awake to greet this new day
> with all its possibilities for good and evil.
> May evil be transformed into good,
> and good thereby be strengthened,
> and may I live this day,
> and all the days of my life,
> with my feet rooted in the earth,
> and my heart open to the skies.

The prayer is said while standing, facing the rising sun, with arms raised, and breathing deeply, drawing in the new light. The gesture is repeated with each stanza, taking a step forward each time.

The prayer was composed by Dr. Eva Fleischner, who in her career as a professor of religion, spent considerable time in the Southwest studying Native American religion.[28] It was inspired by her first visit to the Hopi mesas. She said that one day, she rose early before dawn. Upon leaving her tent, she "saw motionless figures, wrapped in blankets, standing silently on top of the flat roofs of their adobe houses, awaiting the sunrise. As the first rays of the sun appeared on the horizon, they raised their arms and breathed in the new light."[29]

The text of the prayer combines Native American and Christian elements. Christian elements are clearly evidenced in the first two lines of the last stanza. This prayer captures something of the essence of daily prayer, rooted in the natural cycle of the day, and in unity with all of creation.[30]

Evening prayer is offered as the day draws to a close. The sun sets, the natural world is hushed, and light fades into darkness. Setting aside the pressures and activities of the day, we quietly reflect on the day just ended. We give thanks for the blessings of the day, bring before God tasks completed or left undone or done amiss, and pray for a broken world in need of the healing grace of God.

Across the ages, prayer in the evening was offered as the lamps were lit. The lighting was often the occasion of special ceremony, the Lucernarium. At the lighting, preceding the singing of the psalms and the readings from Scripture, a Greek evening hymn dating from the third century was sung,[31] and a prayer of thanks for the light was offered. This ceremony, titled "Service of Light" in the *Book of Common Worship,* is a fitting way to begin evening prayer on Saturday and/or Sunday evenings and on special occasions.[32]

Finding some place of quiet after the labor and tasks of the day are set aside provides a valuable time of reflection. At our home in Albuquerque we have a quiet garden spot that looks out across the city, and across the open expanse of the high desert, to Mt. Taylor in the distance. In the evening it is a quiet place to pause for a time of reflection, watch the spectacle of a beautiful Southwestern sunset crescendo into an array of red, orange, yellow, and purple, and then fade to pastel shades and then into darkness. It is a perfect setting for evening prayer offered in union with all creation to the Creator of the universe.

Whether one chooses morning or evening prayer, or both, as a regular discipline, may vary according to circumstances. Prayer services for other times of day are also provided in the *Book of Common Worship,* such as midday prayer and prayer at the close of day.

Midday prayer is a brief moment in the midst of the day's activity, in which we pause to be mindful of living and laboring in God's world, grateful for the wonders of creation and the opportunities for service.

Prayer at the close of day, often known by its Latin name "compline," is loved by many. This beautiful liturgy is offered as we prepare for sleep, and surrender ourselves to God's care and keeping throughout the night. We yield ourselves to a night of sleep, confident of rising at the dawning light of morning. So also, we anticipate our death, confident that God will "raise us to new life" in the promised day of resurrection. The liturgy is simple in structure, and its main elements may be memorized to be recited from memory upon retiring for the night. It may be used by individuals and is effectively used by groups at the end of an evening meeting, or at the end of the day at retreats and conferences.

While one will not often experience the full cycle of prayers in a single day, the liturgical texts of daily prayer can be a valuable part of group retreats, conferences, and meetings of middle governing bodies, in giving spiritual depth to the time together.

Praying without Ceasing

In our discipleship, we often fail to comprehend the meaning of Paul's admonition to "pray without ceasing" (1 Thess. 5:17), the meaning of which is to live all of life in the presence of God. Daily prayer helps us to that end, dissolving the dividing line between sacred and secular.

Arlo Duba tells of once inviting a rabbi to address one of his seminary classes on the subject of Jewish worship and spirituality. He said that when the rabbi

> voiced the expectation that a good Jew will find at least one hundred things each day in his or her experience for which to pause and thank or bless God, one of the seminary students more or less gasped and said quite audibly, "one hundred?!" The rabbi heard the expression of surprise, paused a moment and then said, "If a person can't find at least a hundred things to be thankful for in a day, what kind of an ingrate would he be?"[33]

Daily prayer creates a grateful heart and stretches our compassion to embrace the world in reflecting the compassion of God.

Psalms and Scripture Readings

From ancient times, psalms have been a major part of daily prayer, for both Jews and Christians. The Psalms embrace the full span of human emotion, from the deepest despair to exulting joy, touching our inmost self. They lift our minds and hearts to the God whose glory fills the universe, yet who tenderly cares for the whole human family. Prompting a sense of wonder and awe within us, the Psalms help us to overcome our self-centeredness and refocus our lives on God. Living daily with the Psalms implants them deeply within our minds and souls, giving us strength and assurance in the varying circumstances of life.

The Psalms are most powerful when they are sung. For centuries, singing the Psalms (in meter) was an important part of Reformed worship, reflecting the unvarying God-centeredness that has been a major characteristic of Reformed worship. The Psalms have been the very heart and soul of Reformed piety. In the eighteenth century, however, Presbyterians began to lose tradition of psalm singing as they settled for speaking psalms responsively in worship. Seldom sung, the Psalms lost some of their power to shape us. By the middle of the twentieth century they had virtually disappeared from our worship.[34] The decline in the use of the Psalms may be at the root of an erosion of a God-centered worship and an increasing self-centered focus in worship. If not the cause, it surely is a symptom.

Reclaiming the singing of the Psalms, both in daily prayer and in the Sunday liturgy, is an important aspect of contemporary liturgical reform. Happily, the latter part of the twentieth century witnessed a remarkable rebirth of singing the Psalms in a variety of ways—responsorial chant as well as metered psalm. Hopefully, through singing the Psalms once again, we will refocus our worship away from ourselves and more fully upon God.

Another important part of daily prayer is quiet reflection upon Scripture. A two-year lectionary is provided which can be the basis for reading through the Bible over a period of time. In this lectionary, daily prayer offers a richer diet of Scripture than is possible in the Sunday liturgy, enabling God's Spirit to speak to us in parts of the Bible less familiar to us. Individuals using the lectionary may find a trusted devotional commentary to be of benefit when used along with the lectionary. The texts of the daily Scripture readings are accessible on the Presbyterian Church (U.S.A.) Web site: http://www.pcusa.org. Arrangements can be made to have these readings sent each day to one's e-mail address.

Prayers and Silence

While the Psalms are prayed, and the Scripture readings lead us to pray in reflection on the readings, the Daily Office also includes specific thanksgivings and intercessions. By blending both fixed and free prayer, we are engaged in prayer centering on concerns of the moment in our lives and the life of the world, as well as in prayers from the church's liturgical heritage.

Silent contemplation is also a valuable aspect of daily prayer. Silence is a rare commodity in these frenetic times. Silence before the service begins, silent reflection on the psalm, silent meditation following the Scripture, silence in the midst of the prayers, can help us open ourselves more completely to listening to the prompting of the Spirit.

Occasions for Daily Prayer

Daily prayer is being used in a variety of ways. Small groups within congregations are finding it a valuable discipline, some meeting daily, others weekly, others less often. Engaging in evening prayer at the beginning of session meetings or committee meetings sets the meeting in the framework of prayer, thus helping to establish priorities in the business that follows. The staff of some congregations find regular morning prayer a fitting way to begin a day of ministry. Some congregations are located in towns or neighborhoods where a regular schedule of daily prayer would be possible and welcomed, especially if initiated ecumenically with other churches. In meetings of middle governing bodies, punctuating the routine of business with the daily prayer cycle changes the spirit of the meeting. Congregations engaging in the cycle of daily prayer at retreats keeps in focus the priority of God in all life and relationships. Some families are finding that a brief liturgy of prayer each day brings them closer to one another, keeping before each one the place of God in daily life. The spiritual life of individuals is deepened in a personal discipline of daily prayer; they are strengthened by knowing that they are joined with others in prayer. Furthermore, when individuals regularly pray the church's prayer, and then in groups or committees engage with other members of the faith community in offering the church's prayer, a continuum emerges between one's personal spiritual journey and that of the community of faith. The communal nature of the faith thus becomes most apparent.

Where daily prayer begins to take root in a congregation, the spirit of the congregation is transformed. Just as the Sunday liturgy of Word and Supper undergirds prayer throughout the week, so daily prayer enriches and supports the Sunday liturgy. Engaging in daily prayer throughout the week instills an anticipation to hear the Word proclaimed and quickens the appetite to be renewed at the Lord's Table each Lord's Day.

The recovery of daily prayer is an important reform for our time. It contributes to our conversion, to our growth in Christ, and has the potential of dramatically changing the nature of our life together before God.[35]

INVITATION INTO A DISCIPLINE

The liturgical reforms set forth in the *Book of Common Worship* invite the church into a discipline. In a cultural setting that prizes individualism, discipline is not popular; yet it is essential to any worthy attainment in life. Education requires discipline. To excel in one's vocation requires discipline. To play a musical instrument well, or to be a fine vocalist, requires discipline. Examples abound.

So also our Christian pilgrimage involves discipline if our faith is to mature: the discipline of regularly worshiping with the community of faith, the discipline of prayer and contemplating the mysteries of the faith, the discipline of studying the Scriptures and listening for what God is saying to us today, the discipline of living out the implications of the faith in loving service to God.

In like manner, the church embraces a discipline in ordering its life, a discipline shared in common, toward the end that it may be what the body of Christ is called to be. Without such ordering, confusion as to the meaning and purpose of the church results.

The *Book of Common Worship* offers a discipline. It is not, therefore, simply a resource among other resources upon which to draw to decide what to do next Sunday morning.[36] Its varied parts are interwoven into an integrated whole, each part reinforcing the others. They work together. The *Book of Common Worship* invites congregations into a discipline that has its origin in the church's beginnings and that has been shaped and reshaped across two millennia. To embrace the church's liturgical heritage is to take up a discipline with rich rewards. In the liturgical wisdom of the ages one discovers a discipline that profoundly shapes faith and life, offering growth and maturing. It engages us in a way of life that aims toward reordering our values and the way we live. It guards against the vanity of unbridled ego, and it magnifies the community of faith. It sets us in the embrace of a community that transcends any single time and place, yet a community that finds full expression in this time and place. Unwaveringly, it is a discipline that keeps us centered on the triune God, who created all that is, who through the prophets sought to set us on a course to live justly and to abound in mercy, who came among us in Jesus Christ to heal our brokenness and make us whole, and who is now among us in the Holy Spirit, the giver of true and abundant life.

Chapter 10

The Promise for Renewal

A few years ago a Lutheran liturgical scholar and I were discussing the liturgical climate of our churches. I expressed my discouragement with the slowness of liturgical reform. He quickly replied, "It will never happen until the people are converted." I thought, "Yes, he has a point." How can there be an appreciation of what the liturgy is all about until there is a thirst for God (Ps. 63:1–8), and a desire to live in union with the One who alone is the source and giver of life?

While I was serving as a pastor, one of our most faithful members had an experience in which she encountered God in a way that deepened her commitment, and redirected her life. She shared with me how it changed her feelings about the liturgy. Words said and responses sung, repeated Sunday after Sunday, came alive, rising from the depths of her spirit.

LITURGY AS CONVERSION

Such a moment of awakening can produce a leap in one's faith. Such a moment sometimes marks the beginning of one's Christian pilgrimage. However, even when conversion is marked by a dramatic beginning, being formed in the faith is a gradual conversion process that engages us for as long as we live.

As a process, conversion is marked by a maturing in the knowledge and understanding of the faith, by a deepening of our devotion to the One from whom comes the meaning and purpose of life, and by living out the implications of the faith in every aspect of life. Since our knowledge of the ways of God, our devotion to God, and our service of God are all imperfect, the Christian life involves a lifelong venture of growth. Familiar prayers in the *Book of Common Worship* give it voice:

> . . . may we know you more clearly,
> love you more dearly,
> and follow you more nearly,
> day by day.[1]

And,

> Help us so to know you
> that we may truly love you,
> so to love you
> that we may fully serve you,
> whose service is perfect freedom. . . .[2]

As such, the Christian life is at least as much one of *becoming* Christian as it is of *professing to be* a Christian.

At the core of this life is worship. Our worship forms us in the faith and undergirds every aspect of our discipleship. This is because the offering of ourselves in thankful response to God's grace is the heartbeat of worship. Such offering is expressed in a symbol Calvin cherished at the center of his faith—a hand holding a flaming heart, with the words *prompte et sincere,* which is often represented in English as "My heart I give you, Lord, freely and sincerely." Without such an offering of one's very self to the God "in whom we live and move and have our being,"[3] worship is powerless to transform.

In response to the magnitude of God's glory, Paul implored his readers to fully commit themselves to God:

> O depth of wealth, wisdom and knowledge in God! How unsearchable his judgements, how untraceable his ways! . . . Source, Guide, and Goal of all that is—to him be glory for ever! . . . Therefore, . . . I implore you by God's mercy to offer your very selves to him: a living sacrifice, dedicated and fit for his acceptance, the worship offered by mind and heart. Adapt yourselves no longer to the pattern of this present world, but let your minds be remade and your whole nature thus transformed. Then you will be able to discern the will of God, and to know what is good, acceptable, and perfect. (Rom. 11:33, 36; 12:1–2 NEB)

From ancient times the church's liturgy has been the principal means for conversion. In the waters of Baptism, the proclamation of the Word, and feasting at the Lord's Table, celebrating the mysteries of God in festivals and seasons, and the discipline of daily prayer, Christians are formed in the faith and disciples are made.

In an article appearing in *Reformed Liturgy & Music,* writer Joan Zwagerman Curbow tells how she found the hungers of her spirit fulfilled when she discovered the church's liturgical tradition. Having grown up in a congregation within the Reformed tradition, she describes her journey of discovery and shares the joy of the growth in faith she is experiencing in worship rooted in the liturgical heritage.

Though she early began to hunger for a form of worship that more fully engaged the senses, it was not until attending a Reformed Church college that she first experienced worship drawn from the liturgical heritage. "I was hooked" she wrote. Later she and her husband moved to a community where there was no Reformed Church, and they worshiped with a rather dispirited Lutheran congregation. She said,

> I had expected and yearned for a homecoming on two fronts, one from a common theological and historical background, and the other for my new-found love of formal worship. Instead I was befuddled and set adrift. We mumbled through the music and slogged through the words, as though stuck in a swamp.[4]

In spite of this, the liturgy began to sink in and take hold of her, becoming "an underground spring, whose waters baptized me by stealth."[5]

Her story eloquently describes the experience of those whose earliest Christian experience was within the free church tradition, but who have been led by the Spirit into an ever deepening appreciation of the church's ageless liturgy, finding in it inexhaustible spiritual depth and a source of maturing in the faith:

> For some, tradition might seem oppressive or lifeless, but it has given me a sense of solid standing. I am treading an old road, following an ancient path that is marked by words, words that have been crafted and honed to endure "all times" and "all places" in human history. As I say them, I wonder who has said these words before me, and what of their struggles, their own or others? Likewise, such thoughts help me to consider my fellow worshippers and the joys or sorrows that attend them. Repeating the liturgy takes me in and beyond my own worries. So, it is for those words, those same words repeated week after week, that I go to worship. . . .
>
> The liturgy's language respects and maintains God's mystery. Over the years I've come to appreciate that more and more. This is not worship for the intellect alone; this is worship for all of me, worship that sends depth charges into my innermost being. . . .
>
> Gaining a sense of liturgy was a long time in coming. Perhaps I've had a longer catechumenate than most. Maybe I was just an exceedingly dull student. Whatever the case, in the early days, saying the Lutheran liturgy sometimes felt like boring, mindless work, a chore. That may be why love of liturgy is acquired over time and why, in a culture that demands instant gratification, it may be easily passed over, lying like a rare gem in some forgotten field. I don't repeat the liturgy because it lifts my spirits or "gives me a

boost"; in truth, that seldom happens. I say the liturgy because it has helped to place me more firmly in the community of faith. I am one of many, journeying to God on an ancient road, following a well-worn path that, after centuries, still runs true. It's a reality I can point to and hold onto when so much in life fails or falls away. Discovering the liturgy's depths and richness was a slow process, but once it sank in, it left a stubborn residue.

As I've occasionally worshipped in Reformed and Presbyterian congregations over the past decade, I've been stunned to find many of them using liturgy. After attending a chapel service at Calvin College in Grand Rapids, Michigan, I told a friend that I could have sworn I was in a Lutheran church. Liturgy lurked in my tradition all the time, and I did not know it. Coming to see that has been a joke on me, and it is a good one indeed. In the oddest of ways I seem to have rediscovered my roots. . . .

The great beauty of "converting" to liturgy is discovering that it is God's Word and God's presence working in me, converting "me." It matters little what I feel about it, but it does matter that I do it. It matters that I show up and make the effort, but it is God's Spirit that produces the fruit for my labors. And one of those fruits is joy, a joy that continues to sustain me in this long journey. The labor of liturgy is much like a bee gathering pollen. The honey comes after all the work is done.[6]

In reading her article I recalled a paragraph in Marva J. Dawn's excellent book *Reaching Out without Dumbing Down* in which she shares some insights of Jaroslav Pelikan in meeting accusations that the liturgical tradition is dead. She writes:

> Many complain that old liturgies are dead, and they're often right. In many places they are dead, for churches have turned them into mere traditionalism, which Jaroslav Pelikan calls "the dead faith of the living." Those who advocate using the Church's historic liturgies are searching instead for what Pelikan calls "the living faith of the dead"—that is, worship within a tradition that enables us to be actively conscious of the Church's past as well as of its eschatological future in Christ. As Pelikan insists, tradition has the capacity to develop while still maintaining its identity and continuity. The tradition serves as a mode for relating to the present through contact with both the practices of the past and our collective hope for the future. It places us into the story of God's people and stirs our sense of belonging to a continuing fellowship that stretches throughout time and space.[7]

Gordon Lathrop in speaking of the *Lutheran Book of Worship,* emphasizes that it is not "just a book," but "the record of a common and lively tradition." What he says of the Lutheran book of services may also be claimed for the *Book of Common Worship.* He writes:

> It is better regarded as the fragments and records of the ways many assemblies of Christians have done things, summed up as much as that is possible in print, and passed on as a gift to our present local congregations. The *LBW* is a concrete means of communication and communion between congregations through history. It represents a whole series of actions that cannot be put in print: people gathering, singing, praying, reading the

Scriptures, preaching, baptizing, holding the supper, and, in these things, encountering God, coming to faith, going in mission. The gift from the other congregations to our present congregation needs to be put in motion in each place. It needs to be inhabited, experienced, enacted in a lively way with the book as a resource.[8]

SINGING THE LORD'S SONG IN A FOREIGN LAND

Abiding in a Christian discipline is not easy today, and being in ministry in the church is ever more difficult and demanding. Having lost its place of honor, the church labors in a culture that is increasingly indifferent to the church's claims, if not outright unfriendly. We are constantly reminded of the passing of Constantinian Christendom. It is increasingly apparent that we are moving into a time not unlike that of the early Christians.

To maintain integrity, Christians in our time are probing what it means to be *in and of* the world, but *not belonging to* the world (John 17:14–19), all the while remembering that the church's God-given mission is to be *for* the life of the world. We are learning, with increasing clarity that the Christian faith is a way of being in the world, neither rejecting the world, nor seeking escape from the complex issues facing our common life. While renouncing all of the cultural idols that impact our daily life, we look toward, and labor for, the birth of God's "new creation," enduring the pangs of bearing that attend all birth. This question is crucial. How do we preserve Christian integrity, both in life and ministry, while dwelling in a culture that serves other gods, and where many self-appointed prophets draw attention away from living out what it means to be fully human?

We are beginning to recognize the ways in which the church is countercultural, a colony in an alien culture, resident aliens. Philippians 3:20 describes the church as having its "citizenship in heaven." As James Moffatt translated this verse, "we are a colony of heaven." Building on this image from Philippians, Stanley Hauerwas and William H. Willimon, in their book, *Resident Aliens: Life in the Christian Colony,* consider the implications this has for the contemporary church. In the preface they set the context for what they write. It underscores the conviction that, to maintain integrity in the context in which we live and serve today, the vitality of the church's worship is increasingly crucial:

> The Jews in Dispersion were well acquainted with what it meant to live as strangers in a strange land, aliens trying to stake out a living on someone else's turf. Jewish Christians had already learned, in their day-to-day life in the synagogue, how important it was for resident aliens to gather to name the name, to tell the story, to sing Zion's songs in a land that didn't know Zion's God.
>
> A colony is a beachhead, an outpost, an island of one culture in the middle of another, a place where the values of home are reiterated and passed on to the young, a place where the distinctive language and life-style of the resident aliens are lovingly nurtured and reinforced.

> We believe that the designations of the church as a colony and Christians as resident aliens are not too strong for the modern American church—indeed, we believe it is the nature of the church, at any time and in any situation, to be a colony. Perhaps it sounds a bit overly dramatic to describe the actual churches you know as colonies in the middle of an alien culture. But we believe that things have changed for the church residing in America and that faithfulness to Christ demands that *we* either change or else go the way of all compromised forms of the Christian faith.
>
> The church is a colony, an island of one culture in the middle of another. In baptism our citizenship is transferred from one dominion to another, and we become, in whatever culture we find ourselves, resident aliens.[9]

We are beginning to *re-member* ways of being the church that are new to us, though they have roots in the ages when the Christian faith was formed. This is not easy for churches, once considered "mainline churches," that for centuries saw themselves as inseparably linked with culture, shaping and being shaped by the culture. But with the crumbling of Constantinian Christendom, that relationship is changing.

Secularism, which in its self-sufficiency leaves no room for God, is creeping throughout our culture, and a self-centered individualism plagues our common life. Fundamentalism, with its mindless anti-intellectualism, has heightened its aggressiveness, turning thinking people away from the faith because they assume fundamentalism's strident message is what being Christian is all about. Megachurches with their "marketing techniques" to capture "the spiritual market" may be great "successes," but they trivialize Christian faith and life. Popular religion has domesticated God to serve self-centered interests. Main Street Protestantism is atrophying like aging muscles, its great Reformation legacy, both in spirit and in intellect, weakened. Theologically impoverished and spiritually destitute, it is evident in the typical Protestant worship that Protestantism desperately needs a fresh infusion of the Spirit touching both mind and heart.

Throughout the centuries the Reformed have stressed integrity in theological discourse and biblical interpretation. Presbyterian historian Lefferts A. Loetscher once declared that "Calvinism at its best is a rather fine balance between reason and feeling, between what is definable human knowledge and what is ineffable divine mystery, between formal and experiential elements."[10] Unfortunately, the Reformed have not always maintained this balance, but it remains a coveted objective in any age, no less in the times in which we live.

We have dared to echo the voice of the prophets and champion unpopular issues of justice. We have cherished a strong sense of connectionalism that emphasizes community, believing that we belong to and are for one another. It is important to us that our life and faith be grounded in the tradition of the church catholic. But with declining membership some are tempted to surrender the hallmarks of the tradition and embrace the dubious methods of nineteenth-century revivalism warmed over for our time to "grow churches." But to surrender the tradition is to become something other than what we are called to be. Rabbi Abraham J. Heschel once wisely cautioned his fellow Jews:

> Those who, in order to save the Jewish way of life, bring its meaning under the hammer, sell it in the end to the lowest bidder. The highest values are not in demand and are not saleable on the marketplace.[11]

His caution is equally apropos for Christians. We too need to take care lest we sell the Christian faith to the lowest bidder.

But, in spite of this despairing setting, and all that makes ministry difficult today, there is hope. There are signs of a growing awareness that the cultural idols are false, impotent, and cannot fulfill their promise of a truly satisfying life. There is a growing recognition that the tinsel and glitter of popular forms of religion pander to the self and have little to offer when one is suddenly confronted with the inevitable crises of life. Here and there one finds a yearning for a faith that has integrity, a hungering and thirsting for the "solid food" that is missing in the popular religiosity of our time.

This should prompt us to be on our guard about popularizing the faith. For if we surrender what we are called to be, we will miss the opportunity for enduring ministry when those caught up in currently popular religious sentiments become dissatisfied and search for a deeper faith. Only a faith that engages the mind as well as the heart will endure. Only a faith that accepts the realities of history, affirming the findings of science as it embraces the revealed truth of faith, can fully meet the challenge of evangelism in our time. Only a reasoned faith that probes deeply into the meaning and purpose of human existence can guide us through the complexities of life. Recognizing this, theologian Douglas John Hall has noted: "This presents disciplined and serious-minded Protestant Christians . . . with new opportunities; not opportunities for grandeur and certainly not for worldly power and prestige, but for truth and wisdom. And for hope!"[12]

We must never lose hope by giving in to pressures that would weaken our calling. We need the reassurance of Christ's promise, "Remember, I am with you always, to the close of the age" (Matt. 28:20). There is no greater evidence of the truth of this promise than the signs of the Holy Spirit guiding the church in this time of transition. Many of us believe that the liturgical movement is the work of the Holy Spirit equipping and nurturing the church to preserve the integrity of the faith in the midst of a pervasive secularism and a religious climate that distorts Christian faith.

LITURGICAL INTEGRITY

Throughout history, the church's liturgical tradition has been the very core of the life of the Christian community, for it is primarily in its worship that the church's faith is instilled. The critical importance of worship in forming the faith of the people was clearly seen in the earliest centuries when the church endured great persecution and gathered in secret. Its importance was also at the center in the turmoils of the sixteenth-century Reformation. It is just as important in our time. In the missionary situation into which we are moving, it is crucial that the church begin to understand the critical importance of how it goes about its worship, lest the faithful be ill equipped for witness and service in this age.

Because he understood the formative role of the liturgy, it should not be surprising to learn that Calvin expected the congregations to adhere to prescribed liturgical forms in the turbulent times of the Reformation. Among Calvin's earliest tasks in Geneva was to introduce a reformed liturgy of Word and Sacrament. Adherence to the liturgy, like loyalty to a confessional statement, was meant to ensure that the people were grounded in the faith.

While we would agree that such restrictions are no longer in order, it does underscore that in Calvin's mind, worship—the primary locus of Christian nurture—is not to be taken lightly or done carelessly or recklessly, but to be engaged in with an understanding of the awesomeness of the task that carries the weight of faith formation.

Although offered for voluntary use, there is no better means to convert and to reinforce the faith in the lives of the faithful, than the liturgical heritage embodied in the *Book of Common Worship*. Congregations that have embraced the *Book of Common Worship,* taking it seriously, report that they have experienced a stronger grounding in the faith, more vitality in their worship, and greater intention in their ministry in the world. It is into this discipline that other congregations are invited.

It is expected that congregations, while taking the *Book of Common Worship* seriously, will vary in the way they use it, in keeping with the Reformed liturgical principle of freedom within order. The preface of the *Book of Common Worship* notes that "True freedom does not do away with form. On the contrary, form enables freedom to be truly free. Without structure, freedom can degenerate into license."[13] Consequently, the *Book of Common Worship* provides "for a wide spectrum of styles ranging from free and spontaneous prayer to the use of prayer texts. It is envisioned that while the style of praying will vary from one locale to another, the shape of the service will remain the same."[14] It states further:

> Some will find strength and a sense of unity in the prayers shared in common with the whole church and so will use the liturgical texts as they appear in this book. Others will find it more appropriate to adapt the prayers for use in a particular setting. Others will be prompted to follow the structure of the services as they are outlined and use the texts as models for a free and more spontaneous style of prayer. Each of these styles is appropriate within the provisions of the directories for worship, and it is the intent of the *Book of Common Worship* to provide the necessary resources.[15]

However a congregation may worship, it is critically important to understand the nature of the ordering of worship as set forth in the Directory for Worship and the *Book of Common Worship*. They are to be taken seriously as embodying the wisdom of the church in liturgical matters. Before one begins to tinker with the liturgy, it is essential to know why the church has ordered its worship in the way it has from earliest times, to recognize that it is in worship that we become participants in the grace-filled mysteries of faith, and to have a sensitivity to how the liturgy as a whole and its parts does its work. Not to have this understanding is to play recklessly with the most precious treasure the church has, its worship.

It is not unlike a choir, or an orchestra, offering a masterpiece of great creative beauty. It is important for the conductor to know how to conduct, to be intimately familiar with the musical score, to sense the composer's objective, to be sensitive to the contribution of each voice or instrument to the whole, and to have an ear for balancing and blending the ensemble. It is also essential that singers and instrumentalists have refined skills in reading music, playing their instruments well, or blending their voices.

Such skill and understanding are necessary, for both the conductor and the performers, before any decisions are made about a performance for a given occasion in a specific location. Depending on the occasion, the location, and the musicians, there will be variations in any two performances of the same work, but the musical score of the composer will always set the boundaries.

Yet, more is needed. Musicians must have music in their souls. They must *be* music if the music is to draw those who listen into the music's depths. Playing the notes is not enough. Great music presented by those who live the music touches the soul—mind, emotions, our whole being—and reflects the beauty of the Creator of all things who gave us the gift of music.

So with the liturgy, it is important that one know what the liturgy is all about, know the liturgical heritage and the theology undergirding the liturgy, and know and learn the skills liturgical leadership requires. A firm grounding in the basics is needed before making decisions about variations. Where such an understanding of the nature of Christian liturgy is solidly in place, then variations in keeping with the liturgy's purpose and meaning may be made with integrity.

Just as the musician must have *musical soul,* it is essential for those who lead the people in worship to have *liturgical soul.* Since the essence of the liturgy is prayer, those responsible for preparing and leading worship must *be* prayer, lest worship be merely "playing the notes." Some pastors have said that they cannot pray while leading people in prayer. How unfortunate. How can one expect to engage people in prayer if those who lead in prayer are not themselves engaged in the act of prayer? Prayer needs to be more than words, whether it is free prayer or prayer drawn from a prayer book. It needs to engage the whole person.

Since our abilities and skills will vary, and our understanding will never be complete, no expression of worship will ever be perfect. Nevertheless, the worship of God merits the best we are capable of offering.

THE BUSH THAT BURNS WITHOUT BEING CONSUMED

The burning bush has long been an important symbol in Presbyterian tradition. It is incorporated in the seal of the Church of Scotland as well as Presbyterian churches of other countries. It was prominent in the seals of the Presbyterian Church in the U.S. and the United Presbyterian Church in the U.S.A., the two antecedent churches that formed the Presbyterian Church (U.S.A.). It is presently part of the seal of the Presbyterian Church (U.S.A.), in which the flames of the burning bush share meaning with the tongues of fire at Pentecost. Among other churches within the Reformed tradition, it is part of the seals of The Presbyterian Church in Canada, and of The United Church of Canada, where it signifies the Presbyterian presence in the United Church, formed by a Methodist, Presbyterian, and Congregational merger in 1925.

The symbol of the burning bush is important in the Reformed tradition for it expresses the sovereignty of God, which is at the heart of Reformed thought and worship, and reminds us of God's call to be God's emissary, engaged in God's work in the world.

The meaning conveyed by the image of the burning bush thus centers on both God's presence and God's call. Presence is implicit in the Voice speaking to Moses from the burning bush. Call is implicit in that Voice sending him to be the means by which God would deliver the Hebrew slaves from Egyptian bondage and form them into God's servant people. To the extent that the flames also signify the flames of Pentecost, we recall the outpouring of the Holy Spirit and the charge to proclaim the good news of God's grace-filled love. Once again, presence and call.

The story surrounding the burning bush (Exod. 3:1–15) undoubtedly comes from a long oral tradition and served a defining role in the life of the Hebrews in relation to their God. The children of Israel were slaves in Egypt. Moses had fled the wrath of the Egyptians for killing an Egyptian who was beating a Hebrew slave. The story relates how one day, Moses was in the desert near Mount Horeb, shepherding the flocks of his father-in-law, the priest of Midian. His attention was drawn to a bush that was burning though not consumed by the flames. When Moses turned to see the spectacle, he heard a Voice calling him from out of the bush. When he acknowledged the summons, the Voice prompted him to remove his shoes, for he was standing on holy ground. The Voice said, "I am the God of Abraham, the God of Isaac, and the God of Jacob." Overwhelmed in this unexpected manifestation of the presence of the Holy, Moses hid his face in fear.

From the flaming bush the Voice called him to return to Egypt and be an instrument to free the people of Israel suffering under the heavy yoke of slavery. Confronted by this unexpected and fearsome spectacle, Moses replied, "But who am I, that I should do this?" The Voice assured him that the appointed mission would not depend upon his abilities, but upon the One who was sending him and who would be with him. After raising every possible objection, Moses finally asked, "Then, who shall I say sent me?" And the Voice replied, "I AM WHO I AM.

Say, that I AM has sent you. Say this to the people of Israel, 'The LORD (יהוה), transliterated: YHWH, the God of your fathers, the God of Abraham, the God of Isaac, and the God of Jacob, has sent me to you.' This is my name for ever, and thus I am to be remembered throughout all generations."

The divine name YHWH, the Tetragrammaton (Greek, meaning "having four letters"), appears throughout our English translation of the Hebrew Scriptures as "LORD" and sometimes "GOD." Wherever one of these words is displayed entirely in capital letters, it signifies the divine name YHWH. By the third century B.C., the Name had become so sacred it was never spoken. Only the high priest pronounced the Name, and that only once each year when he entered the holy of holies to pray the ineffable Name of God on the Day of Atonement. After the temple was destroyed in A.D. 70, the Name was never uttered again. To this day the devout avoid the word YHWH, substituting the word "Adonai" (meaning "Lord"), or "Elohim"(meaning "God"). Many Orthodox Jews substitute "ha-Shem" (meaning "the Name").

There is no certainty as to the exact meaning of YHWH. It is a name, yet not a name. It is a verb, rather than a noun or adjective, an archaic form of the verb "to be." It may be interpreted as "I cause to be what I cause to be"; the Creator; the Source of all that is, bringing into being all that is. It may be interpreted as "I am who I am," the Sovereign One, who is beyond every attempt to control, who is present in the midst of events moving toward a divine purpose. Or it may be interpreted as "I will be with you," expressing God's continuing presence in the midst of creation—being there with us, the Beyond in our midst. In the story it is clear that though God is a Presence beyond every attempt to define or describe, God is not aloof from human travail and oppression, but is a Presence in the midst of life and relationships calling all creation to a life that fulfills the purpose and promise for human life, ordained by the Creator. The emphasis is not upon God's being, but upon God's action and presence in human affairs. Bernhard W. Anderson elaborates this meaning:

> Thus the name of God signifies God whose being is turned toward his people, who is present in their midst as deliverer, guide, and judge, and who is accessible in worship. And yet in putting himself at the disposal of his people, so to speak, Yahweh retains his freedom to be present as he will be present, and to show mercy upon whom he will show mercy (Ex. 33:19). As a commandment of the Decalog states (Ex. 20:7), his name cannot be taken in vain—that is, used for human purposes. Perhaps the enigmatic words in 3:14 suggest God's reticence about giving his name. Moses had inquired into the mystery of the divine nature (the name), but his request was handled somewhat evasively, lest by having the name men would hold God himself in their possession and keep him under their (magical) control (see Gen. 32:29 and Judg. 13:17–18). The God who speaks to Moses is the Lord, not the servant of the people; hence the question "Who is God?" would be answered in events that would take place in the future, preeminently the Exodus. "I am Yahweh your God, who brought you out of the land of Egypt, out of the house of bondage" (Ex. 20:2).[16]

Just as the exact meaning of the word is unclear, so also there is no absolute certainty as to how the word is to be pronounced. The ancient Hebrew written language had no vowels. When vowel subscripts were added to Hebrew texts in the Middle Ages, it was unclear how these four consonants were originally pronounced, since they had constituted an unspoken word. Scholars have dismissed the once-popular pronunciation of "Jehovah," still lingering in our hymnody. Nor is there complete assurance that YHWH is to be pronounced "Yahweh," as is the accepted conclusion today. In his book *The Gifts of the Jews,* Thomas Cahill expresses an insightful personal meaning in pronouncing the Name without vowels, "when I attempt to say the consonants without resort to vowels, I find myself just breathing in, then out, with emphasis, in which case God becomes the breath of life."[17]

What the Name seems to convey is that the God we come to know in the Bible is a Presence in our midst that we can never capture and control. The Name given to Moses—a Name that is really not a name—reminds us that God cannot be confined by a name. What we know of God is what God has revealed of God's self.[18] Though we attempt to understand in our theologizing, and in making creeds and confessions, our best thoughts about God are but a shadow of a Presence beyond all we can think or imagine. As such, no creed, confession, or theology is infallible, and properly so, for all our formulations, while formed in response to God's self-revelation, are shaped by the circumstances of a particular time and place. This mystery in the depths of our life will always defy all we can think or imagine. It is as Paul has reminded us, "For now we see in a mirror, dimly, but then we will see face to face. Now I know only in part; then I will know fully, even as I have been fully known" (1 Cor. 13:12). To make absolute any description of God is to serve something less than the God of the Bible.[19]

While full knowledge of God lies beyond our grasp, the theological task will always be important, not only in giving form to our understanding about God and God's grace-filled acts, but in unfolding meaning and purpose for human life. In a very real sense, to speak of God is to speak of the meaning of human existence at its deepest level. Our attempts to explain the truth of God point us toward that Eternal Presence in the depths of existence that is the Source, Guide, and Goal of all that is, the One in whom we live and move and have our being, the Fountain of all that is true and good and beautiful. Though knowledge of the essence of God is denied us, it is enough to know how God has acted and acts toward us, and what God requires of us.[20] As God is toward us, so we are to be in all our relationships. The God who is "full of compassion and mercy" calls us, made in God's image, to acts of compassion and mercy, and thus to be icons of God. Wherever humans engage in acts of compassion and mercy, God's image is shown.

So also, as imperfect as our liturgies may be, the biblical story we celebrate is a progression of God's self-revelation in the midst of human life, giving direction and purpose to our life together as humans. God is revealed as a delivering Presence in the exodus, freeing from all that holds humans in bondage. God is revealed as a just God in the Law given at Sinai, expecting just dealings in all human relationships. In the cries of the prophets, God is revealed as a God of mercy and forgiveness, of justice for the oppressed and compassion for the poor, of infinite love for all creation, a God who calls humans to walk in ways that are just and true.

In Jesus the Christ, God is revealed as in no other—a God of grace who is among us forgiving and offering abundant life, who with compassion brings a healing touch to our deepest need, who shows us what it means to be truly human, who sets before us the command of love, a command that embraces all. And so we confess Jesus the Christ as "Emmanuel, God with us" (Matt. 2:23; Isa. 7:14), as the Word who became flesh and lived among us, full of grace and truth (John 1:14), through whom God was reconciling the world to God's self (2 Cor. 5:19). At Pentecost, God is revealed as a living Presence, beckoning us and all creation into a new creation. In our worship we become participants in this story.

WONDER-FILLED WORSHIP

The bush that burns without being consumed thus becomes a symbol of worship focused unswervingly upon God. It is in worship when, like Moses, we "turn aside to see," that we know we are standing on holy ground. While we may know this Presence in unexpected moments of life, it is in worship that we open ourselves most fully to that Presence. While we may hear that still small Voice in the silent moments of daily life, it is in hearts made still in worship that we listen with greatest care for the Voice of the One who is with us and who calls us into servanthood. In sacrament, Scripture, sermon, prayer, and song—here indeed is our burning bush and holy ground.

While we ask for no spectacular theophanies, our spirits need to encounter the living God. Worship should strip away our callousness to the mystery at the depths of life, opening us to encounter the God of glory who alone is the pathway to true meaning and wisdom. Overburdened with life's cares, we need times when we are moved to exultation, overwhelmed with wonder in the presence of the God who is beyond all we can think or imagine, yet who is as near as the air we breathe. Our hungering spirits need such glimpses of the holy, touching us with wonder.

It is in encountering this Sacred Presence that we are confirmed in the faith, receive the grace of God's loving forgiveness, find our spirits renewed, and are impelled into ministries of compassion, peace, and justice. The object of the *Book of Common Worship*, and the reforms it sets forth, is to bring us into such an encounter. And in that encounter our lives are transformed. Here is the promise for renewal. Philip H. Pfatteicher emphasizes the power of the liturgy to transform and renew:

> When we are confronted with God's life-giving power, our lives cannot remain the same. Worship does more than simply suggest or teach or urge. Worship in fact requires our renewal because we cannot worship the living

God and not be made new. We cannot be washed in God's holy water and cannot eat God's life-giving meal and remain as we were. We are inevitably changed by our encounter with God. Our relationship to God is changed; our relationship to each other is changed; our relationship to the world is changed. We are changed by that encounter precisely because it is an encounter with God.[21]

Liturgical reform holds promise for the renewal of every aspect of the church's life and of our individual lives as Christians. But if that promise is to come to fruition, we must be willing to open ourselves to the Holy Spirit, who alone can touch our hearts through word, ritual, and song.

> To God,
> from whom comes
> all that is true,
> all that is good,
> all that is beautiful,
> *soli Deo gloria.*

PART II
THE SOURCES OF THE
BOOK OF COMMON WORSHIP

Introduction

Service books like the *Book of Common Worship* reflect the lively tradition of Christian worship of God across the ages. It is a tradition that is old and yet new. Service books present an old tradition rooted in the faith and life of the earliest Christians, embracing a language that has been spoken for many centuries. Yet it becomes new when it takes on flesh today in a lively expression of life lived in the presence of God. Such worship thus joins us with the faithful of every time and place, and unites us with all who today gather to give praise to God, and to be nourished in Word and Sacrament.

Service books embody theology cast in the metaphor of ritual—words and actions. As we experience and enact these words and actions in a lively way, we claim the faith they embody, and in turn, that faith shapes and reshapes us, directing the way we live in all aspects of life.

The pages that follow seek to step behind the words of the *Book of Common Worship*. The commentary provided gives information on the origins and continuing life of the texts and the actions that accompany them; it seeks to convey a bit of the meaning of the metaphoric language they embody. Thus, it is hoped, readers may come to see how the church's prayer has shaped the faith in the past and continues to do so in the present.

Perhaps, with this to guide them, those who use the *Book of Common Worship* will have a glimpse into the rich heritage we have in the church's book of prayer, finding a sense of union with the faithful, past and present, as a vital and inseparable part of their very being. Then we shall begin to know the meaning of *common* worship.

The glossary on pp. 152–170 defines many of the terms that follow in the commentary on the texts (pp. 171–259). The significance of ritual actions associated with certain of the texts is elaborated in the glossary and the commentary on texts.

Abbreviations are used to denote sources from which the texts are derived (pp. 147–151). Where texts have been included in previous editions of the service books of American Presbyterians, these are cited, beginning with Charles W. Shields's Presbyterian *Book of Common Prayer*, published in 1864, proceeding through the 1906, 1932, and 1946 editions of *The Book of Common Worship,* the two provisional liturgies, the *Service for the Lord's Day and Lectionary for the Christian Year, The Book of Common Worship—Provisional Services,* and *The Worshipbook.* Also cited is *The Book of Common Order* of the Church of Scotland, published in 1940, since it significantly influenced the creation of the 1946 edition of the *Book of Common Worship.*

In reference to texts taken from other sources, care was taken to determine the original source. However, in some instances the text may not be original with the source cited, since (as noted in the *Book of Common Worship,* p. 1101), "many liturgical texts that are widely shared are derived from a longer tradition and appear in a number of contemporary service books." Where a particular prayer is included in other English-language service books within the Reformed tradition, that has been noted. If information concerning the original source is not known, the source from which the prayer was taken is noted. For example, some of the prayers cited as from *The Book of Alternative Services of the Anglican Church of Canada* and *A New Zealand Prayer Book* (as well as other service books) are undoubtedly from earlier sources. Since information concerning the original source is not available to us, the entry simply cites as source the service book from which the prayer was taken (in our example: BAS or NZPB, the abbreviations for these service books). Other than citing the book from which a text was taken, no attempt has been made to indicate service books of other traditions, or even service books of other Reformed churches, that include the prayer. To do so would have meant a far greater project than was feasible.

In preparing notes on *Book of Common Worship* texts included in *The Book of Common Prayer* and/or the *Lutheran Book of Worship,* the following commentaries were particularly valuable: Marion J. Hatchett, *Commentary on the American Prayer Book* (New York: Seabury Press, 1980, 1995), and Philip H. Pfatteicher, *Commentary on the Lutheran Book of Worship: Lutheran Liturgy in Its Ecumenical Context* (Minneapolis: Augsburg Fortress, 1990).

EXPLANATION OF FORM USE IN COMMENTARY ON TEXTS

The number preceding each entry refers to the corresponding number in brackets at the end of each prayer in the *Book of Common Worship;* for example, [268]. Commentary on texts other than prayers appears in sequence with the commentary on the prayers.

In general, each entry proceeds from the original or earliest available source, cites authorship if known, then documents the inclusion of the prayer or text in American Presbyterian service books. Where a specific service book states "altered," it signifies an alteration of the text as it appears in the service book listed immediately before it. Example:

110. LBW, p. 204; SLR-1, p. 83, altered.

This entry tells us that prayer [110] derives from the *Lutheran Book of Worship* (Minister's edition), and was altered for inclusion in *The Service for the Lord's Day* (Supplemental Liturgical Resource 1).

Other examples of information supplied in abbreviated form are:

64. WBK, p. 39; SLR-1, p. 122, altered. Altered further for BCW.

This entry informs us that prayer [64] derives from *The Worshipbook.* It was altered when included in *The Service for the Lord's Day* (Supplemental Liturgical Resource 1), and altered further when included in the *Book of Common Worship* (1993).

241. BAS, p. 300; SLR-7, p. 150.

This entry tells us that prayer [241] was derived from *The Book of Alternative Services* of the Anglican Church of Canada for inclusion (without alteration) in *Liturgical Year* (Supplemental Liturgical Resource 7).

292. Derives from Gelasian and Gregorian sacramentaries; English translation from Cranmer's BCP (1549). LBW, p. 155 [69]; SLR-7, p. 214.

This entry tells us that prayer [292] derives from two Roman sacramentaries, which the glossary informs us date from as early as the fifth and sixth centuries. It also informs us that at the time of the Reformation, Archbishop Thomas Cranmer translated the prayer for the English liturgy for inclusion in *The Book of Common Prayer* of 1549. The entry also tells us that the text was included in *Liturgical Year* (Supplemental Liturgical Resource 7), taken without alteration from the *Lutheran Book of Worship*.

512. A Gelasian collect for vespers, this prayer dates from at least the ninth century. It was included in PBCP, pp. 24, 358; BCW (1906), p. 15; BCW (1932), pp. 15, 47, 217; BCO (1940), p. 55; BCW (1946), p. 364; BCP, p. 133; SLR-5, p. 202. Biblical allusion: 2 Sam. 22:29.

This entry informs us that prayer [512], from the Roman liturgical tradition (a Gelasian collect for vespers), dates from at least the ninth century and has long been included in American Presbyterian service books. Charles W. Shields included it in his Presbyterian *Book of Common Prayer* in 1864, and it appeared in the 1906, 1932, and 1946 editions of *The Book of Common Worship,* as well as the 1940 *Book of Common Order* of the Church of Scotland. The text was taken from the current edition of *The Book of Common Prayer* and included in *Daily Prayer* (Supplemental Liturgical Resource 5) without alteration. Some portion of the text alludes to 2 Sam. 22:29.

CONCERNING AUTHORSHIP

Those preparing the liturgical resources leading to and culminating in the *Book of Common Worship* recognized their task as that of preparing the prayer of the church. Since it is the church's prayer, service books do not display authorship. Such identity would intrude upon the spirit of prayer. The only exception to this in the *Book of Common Worship* is for a few prayers in the prayer collections (nos. 1–37, 669–790), where knowing the source may result in a greater appreciation of the prayer.

Authorship is, however, sometimes preserved in archives or scholarly books. Following publication of the *Book of Common Worship,* it seemed appropriate to preserve whatever information is available concerning authorship. The entries that follow seek to provide such source and authorship information as is readily available. However, in the process leading to the publication of the *Book of Common Worship,* task force and committee minutes are not often clear as to authorship. Furthermore, many of the texts were so revised by the task forces or committees that they transcend the work of one individual. Where authorship can be identified, it is given. Where authorship cannot be identified, or where texts have been revised extensively by committee process, the source will be identified by the Supplemental Liturgical Resource from which the text was taken. It is sincerely hoped that no one will feel slighted if proper credit is not given because of incomplete records or faulty memory. Authorship of texts taken from other service books is also noted where available.

Abbreviations

The following abbreviations are used to indicate sources which include a particular text.

AC
: William Bright, *Ancient Collects and Other Prayers Selected for Devotional Use from Various Rituals,* with an Appendix, On the Collects in the Prayer-Book (Oxford and London: J. H. and Jas. Parker, 1862)

ASB
: *The Alternative Service Book* 1980. Church of England

BAS
: *The Book of Alternative Services of The Anglican Church of Canada* (Toronto: Anglican Book Centre, 1985)

BCO (1874)
: *The Book of Common Order.* Scotland Church Service Society, 1874

BCO (1940)
: *The Book of Common Order.* Church of Scotland, 1940

BCO (1979)
: *The Book of Common Order (1979).* Church of Scotland, 1979.

BCO (1994)   *Book of Common Order of the Church of Scotland* (Edinburgh: Saint Andrew Press, 1994)

BCP (1549)   *The Book of Common Prayer*. Church of England, 1549

BCP (1552)   *The Book of Common Prayer*. Church of England, 1552

BCP (1662)   *The Book of Common Prayer*. Church of England, 1662

BCP (1928)   *The Book of Common Prayer*. Episcopal Church, U.S.A., 1928

BCP   *The Book of Common Prayer*. Episcopal Church, U.S.A., 1979

BCW   *Book of Common Worship*. Presbyterian Church (U.S.A.), 1993

BCW (1906)   *The Book of Common Worship*. Presbyterian, U.S.A., 1906

BCW (1932)   *The Book of Common Worship*. Presbyterian, U.S.A., 1932

BCW (1946)   *The Book of Common Worship*. Presbyterian, U.S.A., 1946

BCW-CSI   *The Book of Common Worship*. The Church of South India, 1963

BCW-PCC   *The Book of Common Worship*. The Presbyterian Church in Canada, 1991

BCWP   *The Book of Common Worship: Provisional Services*. United Presbyterian, U.S.A., 1966

BW-UCC   *Book of Worship*. United Church of Christ, 1986

CB   Consultation on Common Texts, *A Celebration of Baptism* (Nashville: Abingdon Press, 1988)

CBW   *Covenant Book of Worship* (Chicago: Covenant Publications, 1981)

ELLC   English Language Liturgical Consultation, *Praying Together* (Abingdon Press, 1988)

GA74   "Report of the Special Joint Committee on the Worshipbook," *Minutes of the General Assembly, United Presbyterian Church in the U.S.A.*, 1974

HCY   *The New Handbook for the Christian Year* (Abingdon Press, 1992)

ICEL   International Commission on English in the Liturgy (Roman Catholic)

ION   *The Iona Community Worship Book* (Iona Community/Wild Goose Publications, Scotland, 1988)

ISIT   In Spirit and in Truth: A Worshipbook (World Council of Churches, 7th Assembly, 1991)

KJV   King James Version of the Bible

LBW	*Lutheran Book of Worship.* Lutheran, U.S.A., 1978
LH	*The Liturgy of the Hours: According to the Roman Rite* (International Commission on English in the Liturgy, 1975)
LHP	*Lord Hear Our Prayer,* comp. by Thomas McNally and William G. Storey (Notre Dame, Indiana: Ave Maria Press, 1978)
MPE	*Morning Praise and Evensong,* ed. William G. Storey, D.M.S.; Frank C. Quinn, O.P.; and David F. Wright, O.P. (Notre Dame, Ind.: Fides Publishers, Inc., 1973)
MR	*Messale Romano* (the Italian Sacramentary) (Libreria Editrice Vaticana, 1983)
NEB	*The New English Bible*
NRSV	New Revised Standard Version of the Bible
NZPB	*A New Zealand Prayer Book,* The Church of the Province of New Zealand (Anglican), 1989
OCF	*Order of Christian Funerals,* International Commission on English in the Liturgy, Inc., 1985
OS	*Occasional Services: A Companion to the Lutheran Book of Worship* (Augsburg Fortress, 1982)
OW	Commission on Worship of the Consultation on Church Union, *An Order of Worship for the Proclamation of the Word of God and the Celebration of the Lord's Supper* (Cincinnati: Forward Movement, 1968)
PBCP	Presbyterian *Book of Common Prayer* (*The Book of Common Prayer and Administration of the Sacraments . . .*), ed. Charles W. Shields, 1864
PCS	*Pastoral Care of the Sick: Rites of Anointing and Viaticum* (Washington, D.C.: International Commission on English in the Liturgy, 1982)
PG	*Praise God: Common Prayer at Taizé* (New York: Oxford University Press, 1977)
PGIS	*Praise God in Song,* ed. John Allyn Melloh, S.M., and William G. Storey (Chicago: G.I.A. Publications, 1979)
PH	*The Presbyterian Hymnal: Hymns, Psalms, and Spiritual Songs* (Louisville, Ky: Westminster/John Knox Press, 1993)
PNW	*Prayers for a New World,* ed. John Wallace Suter (New York: Charles Scribner's Sons, 1964)

PR	*Prayers of the Reformers,* compiled by Clyde Manschreck (Philadelphia: Muhlenberg Press, 1958)
PTWS	*Praying Together in Word and Song,* 2d ed. (Taizé) (London and Oxford: Mowbray, 1988)
RS	*The Roman Missal: The Sacramentary* (various editions)
RSV	Revised Standard Version of the Bible
SB-UCC	*Service Book.* United Church of Canada, 1969
SB-URC	*Service Book.* United Reformed Church in the United Kingdom, 1989
SBK-92	*1992 Sourcebook for Sundays and Seasons.* Liturgical Training Publications, Chicago
SLDL	*Service for the Lord's Day and Lectionary for the Christian Year.* Presbyterian, U.S.A., 1964
SLR-1	*The Service for the Lord's Day* (Supplemental Liturgical Resource 1), Presbyterian, U.S.A., 1984
SLR-2	*Holy Baptism and Services for the Renewal of Baptism* (Supplemental Liturgical Resource 2), Presbyterian, U.S.A., 1985
SLR-3	*Christian Marriage* (Supplemental Liturgical Resource 3), Presbyterian, U.S.A., 1986
SLR-4	*The Funeral: A Service of Witness to the Resurrection* (Supplemental Liturgical Resource 4), Presbyterian, U.S.A., 1986
SLR-5	*Daily Prayer* (Supplemental Liturgical Resource 5), Presbyterian, U.S.A., 1987
SLR-6	*Services for Occasions of Pastoral Care* (Supplemental Liturgical Resource 6), Presbyterian, U.S.A., 1990
SLR-7	*Liturgical Year* (Supplemental Liturgical Resource 7), Presbyterian, U.S.A., 1992
SP	*The Scottish Collects from the Scottish Metrical Psalter of 1595*, ed. Patrick Millar (Edinburgh: Church of Scotland Committee on Publications, n.d.)
SPJP	*Singing Psalms of Joy and Praise,* by Fred R. Anderson (Philadelphia: Westminster Press, 1986)
TEV	The Bible in Today's English Version
TO	*The Taizé Office* (London: Faith Press, 1966)

UMBW	*The United Methodist Book of Worship.* United Methodist, 1992
UW	*Uniting in Worship.* Uniting Church in Australia, Australia, 1988
WAGP	*With All God's People: The New Ecumenical Prayer Cycle* (Orders of Service) (Geneva: World Council of Churches, 1989)
WBK	*The Worshipbook—Services.* Presbyterian, U.S.A., 1970
WBK-SH	*The Worshipbook—Services and Hymns.* Presbyterian, U.S.A., 1972
WTL	*Worship the Lord.* Reformed Church in America, 1987

Glossary

Agnus Dei. Lamb of God (Latin). An anthem in the form of a litany, repeated three times, each time ending with the petition *Miserere nobis* (Have mercy on us). It was inserted into the Roman rite in the seventh century (probably an influence from the Eastern church) as an accompaniment to the breaking of the bread. It is based on the announcement of John the Baptist concerning Jesus (John 1:29; see also Isa. 53:7 and Rev. 5:6ff.). In the tenth and eleventh centuries the third repetition was altered to end with *Dona nobis pacem* (Grant us your peace). In order to reveal more clearly aspects of the meaning of "Lamb of God, you take away the sin of the world," a new text, prepared by ELLC, adds the name of Jesus and alterations that seek to bring out the dual meaning of the Greek verb translated "take away" in John 1:29, namely "bear" and "lift up." See text C, p. 55, and elsewhere in the BCW. For further commentary see ELLC, pp. 37–38.

Ambrosian rite. A rite in use in northern Italy, centering in Milan. This rite, of great antiquity, bears the name of St. Ambrose (ca. 340–397). Much loved, Ambrose was seized by the Christians of Milan and made their bishop in 374, even before he was baptized. Ambrose introduced the custom of singing hymns and psalms in the manner of Eastern regions. He is the earliest Latin hymn writer. Among his hymns is "O Splendor of God's Glory Bright" (PH, no. 474). The Milanese community resisted unification attempts by Rome and by secular powers, and was given special dispensation by Rome to preserve its rite.

Amen. A Hebrew word used by ancient Jews as an expression of concurrence. Liturgically it expresses the affirmation of the people, "So be it." It is thus an expression of affirmation, the people's assent to what has been offered for them in prayer. It is not unlike signing one's name to a document one agrees to. Justin Martyr (ca. 100– ca. 165), in describing worship in the middle of the second century, made particular note that at the end of the thanksgivings over the bread and wine "the congregation assents, saying the Amen." Jerome (d. ca. 420) said that the Amen at the end of the eucharistic prayer so thundered in Rome's churches that it caused the pagan temples to tremble.

anamnesis. A Greek word translated "remembrance" or "memorial" in Paul's account of the Last Supper (1 Cor. 11:24): "Do this in remembrance (as a memorial, NEB) of me." It refers to that portion of the eucharistic prayer through which we remember the redemptive work of Christ. Eucharistic remembering is more than thinking about a past event. It is a calling forth the saving acts of Christ that they may be effectual in our lives today. In a sense, then, the past becomes present.

anointing with oil *in Baptism.* From at least the third century, anointing with chrism accompanied the laying on of hands (q.v.) following the water bath in Baptism. Chrism is a high-quality olive oil to which a fragrance, such as balsam, has been added; it is set apart by prayer for use in Baptism. In anointing the newly baptized, the minister lays hands on the baptizand's head. Then the minister, using her or his thumb, traces with the oil the sign of the cross (q.v) on the baptizand's forehead.

In Western Christendom, since this ritual act was performed only by a bishop, it became separated from Baptism, reserved for the visit of a bishop. Separated from Baptism, this anointing became the rite of confirmation. In the East, this division never occurred, since anointing could be administered by a priest. As in the BCW, many contemporary rites seek to correct this separation, restoring anointing to the baptismal rite. In the BCW it is an optional ceremonial act in relation to the laying on of hands (q.v.).

Anointing with oil in Baptism has many layers of meaning. While Baptism with water alone is complete, anointing conveys tactile expression of aspects of Baptism's meaning. It expresses ritually that Christian baptism is a baptism with water *and* the Holy Spirit, and it has its ritual basis in Jesus' baptism. Jesus' baptism in the waters of Jordan marked his Messianic anointing, in which the Holy Spirit descended as a dove upon him. In ancient Israel, kings and priests were anointed; this set them apart for their office (e.g., 1 Sam. 10:1; Exod. 28:41). They were frequently spoken of as God's anointed. Linked with this ancient ceremony, Jesus' anointing marked his being set apart as Messiah, proclaiming the kingdom of God, and being our high priest. Jesus' baptism provided the church with the ritual basis for washing and anointing in Christian Baptism.

Anointing is thus a ritual metaphor of New Testament images (John 3:3–6; Acts 10:38; 2 Cor. 1:21, 22; Eph. 1:13, 14; 1 John 2:20), expressing the meaning of the name Christian. Christ (Gk. *Christos*), Christian and chrism are etymologically rooted in the Greek word *chriein,* meaning "to anoint." Christians are thus *the anointed ones,* in union with Christ, *the Anointed One.* Anointing is thus a sign that in Baptism, one takes the name of Christ. As God's baptized and Spirit-filled people, Christians share in the priesthood and rule of Christ (1 Pet. 2:5, 9; Rev. 1:6; 5:10).

In ministry with the sick. Anointing the sick has been a part of Christian ministry with the sick since New Testament times (Mark 6:13; Jas. 5:14-15). Its use is an option in relation to the laying on of hands in the service of wholeness in the BCW. Its origins lie in its medicinal use from early times (e.g., Luke 10:34), just as healing ointments are used today. Christian anointing with oil in pastoral care is a sign of Christ's presence and the grace of God in making the human spirit whole. It is ordinarily administered by tracing the sign of the cross (q.v.) on the forehead of the one being anointed.

antiphon. An antiphon is a text sung (or said) "in reply," i.e., sung antiphonally. It can be two choirs alternating in singing a psalm. Or, as more commonly understood, it may be a verse from Scripture sung as a response to one or more verses of a psalm, or sung at the beginning and end of a psalm.

Apostles' Creed. Originating in Rome, this creed may be traced back to at least the early third century. In its present form it dates to an eighth-century Latin text. From its origin, it has been associated with Baptism, where it commonly had a question-and-answer form (*see* baptismal formula). Because it has been associated with a personal expression of faith at Baptism, it retains the singular pronoun "I," rather than "we" as in the Nicene Creed. It is called "Apostles'" in that it seeks to express the faith of the apostles. The text in the BCW is an ELLC text. For further commentary see ELLC, pp. 29–32.

Apostolic Constitutions. A Syrian document from about A.D. 380, using three earlier documents: the *Didache* (q.v.), the *Apostolic Tradition of Hippolytus* (q.v.), and the *Didascalia* (a third-century Syrian document). Not available until 1563, it provided the oldest known liturgical texts then available. The sixteenth-century Reformers thus did not have access to it in reforming the liturgy. See prayer texts [448], and [521].

Apostolic Tradition of Hippolytus, the. Usually considered Roman, ca. A.D. 215, this document has great ecumenical significance in providing a record of pre-Nicene Christian worship. It includes the oldest extant texts for the Eucharist. For an adaptation of the eucharistic prayer from these eucharistic texts, see Great Thanksgiving G, prayer text [120] in the BCW. Hippolytus is also important for an early third-century A.D. description of baptismal practice (*see* baptismal formula), daily prayer, the Great Vigil of Easter (q.v.), ministry with the sick, and ordination practice. This ancient document was unavailable until 1891. Therefore the sixteenth-century Reformers did not have access to it in reforming the liturgy. See prayer text [451].

baptismal formula. Words said as a person is baptized. In Western Christianity individuals are baptized as the minister says, "N., I baptize you in the name of the Father, and of the Son, and of the Holy Spirit." In Eastern Christianity, persons are baptized with this formula beginning, "You are baptized in the name of . . ."

The baptismal formula is based on Matthew 28:19 and is reflected in the *Didache* (q.v.). However, the Matthew and *Didache* references may represent a succinct statement of the faith into which one was baptized, rather than specific words spoken as a person is baptized. Furthermore, the Acts of the Apostles indicates that baptism was "in the name of Christ" (Acts 2:38; 8:16; 10:48; 19:5; see also Rom. 6:3; 1 Cor. 1:13; 6:11; Gal. 3:27). Again, it is not clear whether these were words spoken as a person was baptized.

It is clear, however, that by the beginning of the third century, a confession of faith constituted the baptismal formula, evidenced in the *Apostolic Tradition of Hippolytus* (q.v.). This was made in response to three formulaic questions, to which the candidate replied. With each response the candidate was immersed. The creeds developed from these formulas, amplified over time in combating heresies that threatened the integrity of the church's faith (*see* Apostles' Creed; Nicene Creed). A threefold affirmation of faith accompanied by a threefold immersion continued until the eighth century, as evidenced by the Gelasian sacramentary (q.v.). However, sometime after the third century the use of a formula based on Matthew 28:19 was introduced in some places; it seems to have been in a Syrian adaptation of the

Apostolic Tradition of Hippolytus. In the West it is evidenced in eighth-century Gallican liturgies (q.v.). It was introduced into the Roman rite in the eighth century.

The passive form of the Eastern formula ("N., you are baptized . . . ,", instead of "N., I baptize you . . .") makes it clear that Baptism is ultimately not an act of the clergy but the action of the triune God, to which we are witnesses. The use of "I" in Western tradition should be so understood, the minister acting as the principal witness to what God is doing.

In our time, much attention is being focused on the baptismal formula, particularly on its patriarchal images. In this regard, it is important to note that "name of" (whether in the New Testament references noted above or in the baptismal formula) means God's self-revelation, which cannot be confined by names we may employ in our seeking to understand that revelation. Issues surrounding the baptismal formula are manifold and complex and press to the very heart of the Christian faith, namely, how we understand and express faith in a triune God (for more on the Trinity *see* Trisagion). Related discussions are thus highly sensitive and controversial.

The implications for ecumenical relations are also a major concern. Across the past century, churches have come to recognize each other's baptisms, namely, baptisms with water using the traditional formula based on Matthew 28:19. In this recognition, we have come to a clearer understanding that we are baptized into the church of Jesus Christ—the one holy catholic and apostolic church—rather than individual churches. In expressing the essential unity of the church, no church can thus move unilaterally in innovating change, without threatening this accord. The issue of ecumenical recognition of each other's baptisms is thus no small issue.

Alternatives to the traditional baptismal formula need to be the result of ecumenical discussions and agreement. We may soon see specific statements emerging from ecumenical discussions being presented to the churches for consideration. For example, the North American Academy of Liturgy presently has a task group focusing on the Triune Name that anticipates offering such a statement in the near future.

Benedictus. *See* Canticle of Zechariah.

berakah (pl. berakoth). Jewish prayer form of blessing God. In Jewish tradition, something is blessed by blessing God, i.e., by giving thanks to God for it. A berakah is an act of praise-filled remembering which names God and remembers God's grace-filled deeds. BCW prayers [520], [532], and [534] are examples of mealtime berakoth. The Thanksgiving for Light, in the Service of Light (q.v.) of evening prayer [448]–[455], is an example (with [508] drawn from Jewish liturgies), as is the Thanksgiving Over the Water (q.v.) in Baptism [411], [412], [419], and [420]. The canticles of Zechariah (q.v.) and Mary (q.v.) also share the berakah form. The eucharistic prayer (Great Thanksgiving), the central prayer in Christian worship, has its roots in the berakah, the word Eucharist being a Greek translation of the Hebrew word *berakah.* The eucharistic prayer is therefore to be understood as the great praise of God for the goodness of God, especially for creation, covenant, and redemption, in which past and present are entwined, enabling us to have hope in the future because of God's faithfulness in the past. The dialogue that precedes the Thanksgiving for Light, the Thanksgiving Over the Water, and the Great Thanksgiving in the Eucharist are typical of the dialogue introducing the Jewish berakoth when offered in assemblies of the faithful.

bidding prayer. Prayers of the people in third- and fourth-century Rome are believed to have been bidding prayers in which the deacon bid the people to pray for a given concern. After a period of silence, the celebrant summed up the prayers of the people in a brief collect. This sequence comprised a series of biddings. Although the bidding prayer was dropped from normal use, it was preserved in the Good Friday liturgy (see at [252]). A leader/people response, such as "God of mercy, **hear our prayer**," may conclude each bidding sequence. In BCW see Prayers of the People A [90–91] and B [92], as well as [252].

Byzantine rite. The rite of Eastern Orthodoxy, e.g., the Liturgy of St. Basil (q.v.), and a shortened form of it, the Liturgy of St. Chrysostom (q.v.).

canonical hours. A series of services held throughout the day. In Benedictine monastic practice the pattern consists of eight daily periods of prayer. The hours in use by congregations are morning prayer (matins), evening prayer (vespers), and prayer at the close of day (compline).

canticle. A biblical song other than a psalm. *See* BCW, pp. 573–591.

Canticle of Mary—the Magnificat (Luke 1:46–55). A song of praise attributed to Mary when Elizabeth, her cousin, greeted her. One of the gospel canticles, this canticle has traditionally been sung in the Western churches at evening prayer since at least the sixth century (the Rule of St. Benedict, A.D. 540). There is a striking resemblance to the Canticle of Hannah (BCW, p. 582). The text of the Canticle of Mary in the BCW is an ELLC text. For further commentary see ELLC, pp. 49–51. For more on gospel canticles, *see* Canticle of Zechariah.

Canticle of Miriam and Moses—Long known as the Canticle of Moses, this canticle is an abbreviation of the song that, according to Exodus 15, was sung by the children of Israel after crossing the sea. From very early this canticle was sung in the Easter Vigil, and it was early used in liturgies during the Easter season, the Christian Passover.

Canticle of Simeon—Nunc Dimittis (Luke 2:29–32). The joyous song attributed to Simeon on the occasion of the presentation of the infant Jesus by his parents in the temple. This canticle is the traditional gospel canticle for compline—prayer at the close of day. The Canticle of Zechariah (q.v.), sung in morning prayer, anticipates the birth of John the forerunner. The Canticle of Mary (q.v.), sung in evening prayer, anticipates the birth of the Messiah. Now, the Canticle of Simeon, the third Lukan song, expresses the confidence of completion. From as early as the fourth century it was associated with evening prayer, as evidenced in the *Apostolic Constitutions* (q.v.). Its images of peace and light are particularly appropriate for the evening. This canticle has also been associated with the Eucharist in the Liturgy of St. Chrysostom, where it was sung after Communion. It was also sung following Communion in early Reformed and Lutheran liturgies. The refrain "Guide us waking, O Lord . . ." is invariably used with the Canticle of Simeon at compline (q.v.). It was introduced into compline during the Middle Ages. The text in the BCW is an ELLC text. For further commentary see ELLC, pp. 53–54.

Canticle of Zechariah—the Benedictus (Luke 1:68–79). This canticle is based on phrases from the Greek version of the Old Testament, the Septuagint. Luke attributes it to Zechariah at the birth of his son, John the Baptist. The first portion of the canticle gives praise to God for fulfilling Israel's hopes for the Messiah. The portion beginning with "And you, child . . ." addresses his son, the Messiah's forerunner.

From ancient times this canticle has been associated with morning prayer, in both the East and the West. It is one of the gospel canticles (so called not because they are from the Gospels, but because they proclaim the gospel), along with the Canticle of Mary (q.v.) and the Canticle of Simeon (q.v.). The text in the BCW is an ELLC text. For further commentary see ELLC, pp. 45–48.

collect. A brief prayer that has a formal structure, peculiar to Western liturgies. The collect, along with the Great Thanksgiving (q.v.) and the litany (q.v.), constitute the three basic forms of Western liturgical prayer. Although there are variations in the structure of the collect, the following is the most common form:

a. Address to God (with few exceptions, to the first person of the Trinity)
b. A clause describing the particular divine attribute(s) being relied on for the petition that follows.
c. The petition, usually beginning with a strong verb.
d. The hoped-for result, usually beginning with "that" or "so that."
e. A Trinitarian doxology emphasizing the mediating work of Christ.

Most prayers of the day (q.v.) in the BCW fit this structure.

With few exceptions, collects also conform to a long tradition that all Christian prayer is addressed *to* the first person of the Trinity, *through* Jesus Christ, *in* the Holy Spirit. A few collects are addressed to Christ, but none earlier than the Gregorian sacramentary (q.v.) A few collects, primarily Mozarabic in origin, are addressed to the Holy Spirit. *See* Mozarabic liturgy; Roman liturgy.

compline. Prayer at the close of day. The last of the canonical hours (q.v.) in a monastic community, said just before retiring for the night.

confession and pardon. Shaped by the medieval emphasis of penitential preparation to receive Holy Communion, the sixteenth-century Reformers introduced public confession to begin worship. The precedent for this was the mutual confession and absolution of priest and server at Mass in the late medieval period. Calvin saw it as the proper way to begin worship, which he led from the Communion table. Since "in every sacred assembly we stand before the sight of God and the angels," Calvin saw no other way to begin worship than to acknowledge our unworthiness. Indeed, it was for him the key that opened the gate to prayer. By acknowledging our unworthiness, we "show forth the goodness and mercy of God" (*see* Calvin, *Institutes,* 3.4.10f.).

Calvin, furthermore, had a high view of absolution, which he maintained should follow confession. For Calvin, the absolution was a "seal" of the gracious promises of the Word in the hearts of believers. He thus recognized the pronouncing of the absolution to be part of the minister's sacred office, and only to be given by ministers. He maintained that, while all Christians "ought to console one another and confirm one another in assurance of divine mercy, we see that the ministers themselves have been ordained witnesses and sponsors of it to assure our consciences of forgiveness of sins . . ." (*see* Calvin, *Institutes* 3.4.12ff.). After admonishing all to acknowledge that they are sinners, to humble themselves before God, and to trust in God's graciousness, he pronounced the absolution, "To all those that repent in this wise, and look to Jesus Christ for their salvation, I declare that the absolution of sins is effected, in the name of the Father, and of the Son, and of the Holy Spirit. Amen."[1]

Confiteor (Latin, "I confess"). A penitential rite at the beginning of the Roman Mass. Early liturgies had no penitential rite. However, in medieval times an emphasis began to be placed on the need for private confession before receiving the Sacrament. The Confiteor reflected that emphasis. It began as a private prayer of the priest, said while vesting, in preparation for Mass, and later it became a general confession by the people. *See* confession and pardon, and at [49] and [503].

daily office. The ordered daily prayer of the church. The word "office" derives from the Latin *officium,* meaning duty, obligation, service. Authorized by ecclesiastical authorities, it has been the official prayer of the church, to be said daily. *Also see* canonical hours.

declaration of forgiveness. *See* confession and pardon.

Didache, the. Or, Teaching of the Twelve Apostles. One of the earliest known Christian writings, dating from the late first or early second century. Though its existence was known through other writings, it was not discovered until 1875 at Constantinople. It was thus unavailable to the sixteenth-century Reformers as they reformed the liturgy. Its discovery is important for the study of the primitive church. It is believed to have originated in Syria, perhaps in Antioch. *See* prayer text [59].

doxology. An ascription of glory from the Greek word *doxa,* thus "word of glory." The Gloria in Excelsis (q.v.) is regarded as the Greater Doxology, and the Gloria Patri (q.v.) as the Little Doxology. The word "doxology" is also identified with a format that praises God in three persons. Many prayers in the BCW have a doxological ending. The Great Thanksgiving has an expanded doxological ending. *See* collect.

Easter Vigil. *See* Great Vigil of Easter.

epiclesis. A Greek word usually translated "invocation." It refers to that part of the Great Thanksgiving that petitions God to pour out the Holy Spirit upon us and upon the gifts of bread and wine, that our eating and drinking may be the communion in the body and blood of Christ. In invoking God, we acknowledge the sacrament to be the work of God, not ours. The epiclesis is of Eastern origin or influence.

eucharistic prayer. *See* Great Thanksgiving.

Gallican liturgies. In the early centuries of missionary expansion, local liturgical traditions developed with different characteristics. Liturgies emerging in the East retained ancient forms and structures and were characterized by highly developed ceremonial and hymnody. Liturgies emerging in the West were principally the Roman liturgy (q.v.), which was characterized by simplicity and brevity, and the Gallican liturgies. Like the Eastern liturgies, the Gallican rites of Western Europe were characterized by a great variety of texts, of high poetic quality, and elaborate ceremonial. Until late in the eighth century, the Roman liturgy was limited to the city of Rome, Western North Africa, and Roman missionary outposts. The various local (Gallican) liturgies characterized worship in Western Europe until they were gradually supplanted by the Roman liturgy between the eighth and eleventh centuries. For texts deriving from the Gallican liturgies *see* prayer texts [251], [294], [349], and the Easter Proclamation (the Exsultet) in the Great Vigil of Easter (see note following [254]).

Gelasian sacramentary. *See* Roman liturgy. And see prayer texts [8], [25], [46], [162], [237], [252], [258], [263], [286], [292], [363], [378], [388], [512], and [776] and the preface for Trinity Sunday (p. 136).

Gloria in Excelsis. Glory to God in the Highest (Latin). (PH, nos. 566, 575, paraphr. 133) A Greek "Christian psalm." The hymn begins with the song of the angels (Luke 2:14), which gives it its name. This verse is in the form of an antiphon (refrain), and has been so used. Author and source are unknown. Since the fourth century it has been a part of morning prayer in the Byzantine rite. It later found its way into the Roman eucharistic liturgy, first in the Easter and Christmas liturgies, and then as a regular part of the Roman Mass since the twelfth century. The translation in the BCW is an ELLC text. For further commentary see ELLC, pp. 19–21. *Also see* doxology.

Gloria Patri. Glory to the Father (Latin). An ascription of praise to the Trinity, a doxology similar to the doxology at the end of the Lord's Prayer, and to Christian doxologies such as Rom. 16:27; Phil. 4:20; and Rev. 5:13. The text dates from as early as the second century to emphasize the Trinity, as in the baptismal formula (q.v.) and Matt. 28:19. The original text is believed to have been simply *Gloria Patri per Filium in Spiritu Sancto* (Glory to the Father through the Son in the Holy Spirit) (*see* collect). In response to fears that this text subordinated the Son, the present form was adopted in the fourth century. Some maintain that the present form suggests a tritheism and have proposed returning to the more ancient text.

The latter portion of this text evolved later. First "forever," then "now" was added ("now and forever," and then in the West, "as it was in the beginning," where in the sixth century it was intended to undergird the doctrine of Christ's preexistence. The thrust of this doxology, however, is not upon the nature of the Trinity. The subject, instead, is "Glory." Glory to the triune God. Glory to God, just as in the dawn of creation, so now, and forevermore.

In later centuries the Gloria Patri was sung to conclude the singing of a psalm, to "Christianize" it (*see* psalm prayer). The translation in the BCW is an ELLC text. For further commentary see ELLC, pp. 39–40. *See also* collect; doxology; and psalm prayer.

Glory to God in the Highest. *See* Gloria in Excelsis.

Glory to the Father. *See* Gloria Patri.

Great Thanksgiving (eucharistic prayer). The central prayer in Christian liturgy (often called "the canon of the Mass" in the Roman tradition). Its Trinitarian structure was a development in the East, in which the prayer first centers on the work of God in creation and redemption, then on the redeeming work of Jesus Christ, and finally on invoking the Spirit upon the meal, with a petition for receiving the benefits of grace.

The predominant character of the Great Thanksgiving is blessing the God of all creation with thanksgiving and praise in response to God's boundless grace. It thus mirrors the essential character of Christian worship, the result of which is to know God in a way that completely reorders human priorities and relationships. There is no prayer in Christian liturgy of greater importance. It is central in forming the faith within us, in knowing God as God, and in knowledge, knowing who we are and are called to be as humans.

Eucharistic meals described in the Gospels followed a pattern of taking, thanking, breaking, and giving. From the beginning eucharistic thanking was without doubt a Jewish berakah (q.v.), modified to include the Christ event. The earliest nonbiblical reference to the prayer derives from the *Didache* (q.v.; see also prayer text [59]). The oldest actual text of a eucharistic prayer is included in the *Apostolic Tradition of Hippolytus* of Rome (q.v.; *see* prayer text [170]). In their essential character, eucharistic prayers today continue to follow the ancient berakah form of prayer.

In their reactions, the Reformed in the sixteenth century rejected the canon of the Latin Mass because of the medieval doctrine that had come to be inextricably woven into it. It is important, however, to understand that the documents cited above, along with the *Apostolic Constitutions* (q.v.), were not yet discovered. These ancient sources were important in providing texts and descriptions of worship dating from the earliest Christian centuries. Lacking the knowledge these documents now provide, the Reformers had no early models to shape eucharistic praying, and so they set aside the Roman canon. They replaced it with exhortations and petitions for worthy reception. The institution narrative (q.v.) was retained, but was separated from the prayer.

It was not until the liturgy proposed in 1857 by the Mercersburg (q.v.) theologians that the historic structure of the eucharistic prayer began to be restored in the Reformed tradition. The historic shape of the eucharistic prayer has been incorporated in American Presbyterian service books since the BCW (1906). *See also* Sursum Corda; preface; Sanctus; institution narrative; memorial acclamation; anamnesis; epiclesis; doxology; amen; and berakah.

Great Vigil of Easter (Paschal Vigil) BCW, pp. 296–314. Each year the people of Israel observed the night of Passover as a vigil to keep the past alive (Exod. 12:41–42). It kindled both memory of God's mighty act of deliverance and hope in God's future acts on their behalf. The Great Vigil of Easter became the Christian Passover.

Early Christians understood Jesus' dying and rising as a fulfillment of the Passover hope, and began keeping vigil through the night preceding the dawn of

Easter Day. The *Apostolic Tradition of Hippolytus* (q.v.) describes the vigil as it had developed from at least as early as the second century, as the occasion of the baptism "at the time when the cock crows" of those who had been prepared, and of their sharing for the first time with the faithful in Holy Communion. The occasion of commemorating Christ's death and resurrection was recognized as the most fitting time for baptism to take place, for in baptism we die with Christ and are raised with him. The sacramentaries of the fifth and sixth centuries evidence an evolution of the vigil, with the adding of the blessing of the new fire, the singing of the Exsultet (see note "Rejoice, heavenly powers" after [254]), and the series of readings (interspersed with psalms, canticles, and prayers) recounting the faith story into which we are baptized. The readings began with the story of creation and included the stories of the flood, the exodus, the calls of the prophets, Paul's teaching on dying and rising with Christ (Rom. 6), and they climaxed in the resurrection story. Baptisms followed and the Eucharist was celebrated, as the first service of Easter, in the darkness of night. The Vigil had thus evolved into four parts, the Service of Light (q.v.), the readings, Baptism, and the Eucharist.

In the centuries that followed, the vigil was essentially lost in the West. The mid-twentieth century witnessed a recovery of the Great Vigil of Easter, beginning among Roman Catholics. Among Presbyterians the first celebrations of this ancient liturgy seem to have been at Princeton Theological Seminary in the 1970s when Arlo Duba, as dean of the chapel, guided students each year in planning and leading a creative vigil filled with drama and music. It spawned wide and continuing interest among Presbyterians.

Gregorian sacramentary. *See* Roman liturgy. And see prayer texts [12], [162], [165], [237], [251], [252], [270], [292], [349], [356], [366], [378], [388], [768], [834], and preface for Christmas, p. 134.

Hermann's Consultation. Early in the sixteenth-century Reformation, the elector archbishop of Cologne, Hermann von Wied, in preparing the reform of his electorate, formed a consultation. Martin Bucer (the Strassburg reformer) and Philip Melanchthon (a reformer associated with Luther) were asked to draft the liturgy. It was published in 1543, and thereafter was published in England. When the emperor declared war on the German Protestants, Bucer as well as his proposals went to England. The liturgy from *Hermann's Consultation* was an important source for Archibishop Thomas Cranmer in preparing the BCP (1549), and some of it continues in the present edition of the BCP.

Holy, Holy, Holy Lord. *See* Sanctus.

Hymn to Christ the Light (Phos Hilaron). (PH, trans., no. 548; paraphr., nos. 549 and 550) An ancient Greek hymn dating from the third century. It is the oldest existing hymn traditionally used in the Service of Light (q.v.) and has been sung at evening prayer, day after day, throughout the centuries. St. Basil the Great (ca. 330–379) spoke of the singing of this hymn as one of the cherished traditions of the church, and how even then, in the fourth century, it was so old no one remembered who composed it. It is a hymn to Christ, "light from light" (Nicene Creed), the "light of the world" (Fourth Gospel). It proclaims that the light of the world is not the sun that shines by day, nor the evening lamps that illumine the night, but the eternal Son of God, from whom radiates the brightness of the Father's glory.

institution narrative (words of institution, or Verba). Paul's narrative of the institution of the Lord's Supper, an essential part of the eucharistic liturgy. The narrative has had particular importance for the Reformed in expressing the warrant from Scripture for celebrating this sacrament.

invocation. *See* epiclesis.

Iona Community. An ecumenical community, international in scope, seeking to build community in a divided and broken world. Members of the community are committed to obedience to Christ through prayer and political action. Founded in 1938 by George F. MacLeod, it is under the auspices of the Church of Scotland. While centered in Glasgow, it has strong identity with the Isle of Iona. In A.D. 563 St. Columba, an Irish monk, established a monastic settlement on Iona that became a leading center for spreading the Christian faith into Scotland and England and as far as northern Germany and Russia. In the thirteenth century it was the site of a Benedictine monastic community. Through the inspiring leadership of George MacLeod, the Abbey buildings were rebuilt in an expression of the integration of work and worship, prayer and politics. Rebuilding was completed in 1967. The center is used for many conferences, especially for youth.

Kyrie Eleison. Lord, Have Mercy (Greek). In the fourth century the Kyrie Eleison was used as a response in Eastern liturgies, and in the fifth century it was introduced into the Roman rite. Used as a response to the petitions in a litany, it remains such in Eastern liturgies (*see* Prayers of the People E [95]). The origin of the line "Christ, have mercy" is unclear. Threefold and sixfold forms of the Kyrie are most common. The phrase "Lord, in your mercy, hear our prayer" in the prayers of the people is a variant of the Kyrie (see prayer text D [94]). When sung in Greek, it links us with the early Greek liturgies as the use of Amen, Alleluia, and Hosanna link us with Hebrew worship. For further commentary see ELLC, p. 17.

Lamb of God. *See* Agnus Dei.

laying on of hands. A ceremonial act adopted from Judaism. It is an act signifying God's blessing, and a setting apart for God's service. In the BCW baptismal rites, the minister lays hands on the head of each person immediately following her or his baptism while offering a prayer of blessing invoking the gifts and guidance of God's Spirit (pp. 413, 427–428, 441–442). The act is repeated when one makes a public profession of faith (pp. 444, 452), and on every other occasion of the reaffirmation of the baptismal covenant (pp. 461, 470–471, 483–484, 487–488). The laying on of hands in Baptism and the reaffirmation of the baptismal covenant may be accompanied with anointing with oil (q.v.) with the sign of the cross (q.v.). It is also included in the service for wholeness (BCW, pp. 1013, 1020–1021), and may be accompanied with the anointing with oil. In ordination to the ministry of Word and Sacrament, the laying on of hands sets the candidate apart for God's service, ordained into the succession of proclaiming the apostolic faith. Hands lifted by the minister in giving the blessing at the conclusion of worship, sometimes tracing the sign of the cross (q.v.) toward the congregation, is a symbolic laying on of hands upon the faithful, a gesture signifying the blessing of God. As the minister's hands are lifted and the blessing is spoken, the faithful bow their heads as a gesture of receiving the blessing of God pronounced by the minister (2 Cor. 13:13; Num. 6:24–26).

Lectionary. An ordered list of Scripture readings appointed for use in worship on particular Sundays and festivals, providing a system for the reading of Scripture in worship. The word "lectionary" also refers to the bound volume of the appointed readings used in some liturgical traditions.

The reading and exposition of the Scriptures was a central aspect of synagogue worship. The early Christians continued this Jewish practice, soon adding Christian writings to the readings from the Hebrew Scriptures. Among the earliest Christians, readings from Christian writings varied, depending on what writings were available to them.

It was not until the second century, when various writings could be assembled into a leaf-form collection (codex), rather than individual scrolls, that the idea of a canon emerged, a list of those writings deemed authoritative, and therefore acceptable for reading in worship. Consensus was slow in coming. There was wide agreement among the churches on most of the writings by the end of the second century. The sifting continued through the third century. Athanasius in A.D. 367 was the first to name the twenty-seven books of the New Testament as canonical. Ecclesiastical pronouncements followed, accepting the Athanasian list. The New Testament canon thus emerged from among Christian writings that were in general use in the church's worship. The purpose of establishing an authoritative canon was to regularize the body of Christian writings to be read in Christian assemblies. Criteria for inclusion centered on whether writings were deemed apostolic in origin (or reflected apostolic teaching) and possessed a spiritual quality that elevated them to the rank of apostolic.

The *Apostolic Constitutions* (q.v.) shows that in fourth-century Antioch there were two readings from the Law and the Prophets, one from the Epistles or Acts, and one from the Gospels. More commonly, three readings began to be standard, a reading from the Old Testament, one from the Epistles, and another from the Gospels. Psalms were interspersed with the readings. Ultimately, the Roman rite reduced the selections to two readings, one (with few exceptions) from the Epistles and one from the Gospels.

Readings gradually began to be fixed, beginning with Easter and widening to include other days and seasons. The first complete lectionaries, with readings appointed for each day of the liturgical year, date from the seventh century and were bound together in books.

In the sixteenth-century Reformation, Lutherans and Anglicans retained the historic readings, with modifications. The Reformed, however, preferred to read the Scriptures in course, *lectio continua,* rather than follow the established principle of *lectio selecta,* a lectionary of selected readings.

The last half of the twentieth century saw a remarkable recovery of lectionary usage among American Presbyterians. A two-year lectionary was included in the BCW (1946), consisting of a reading from the Old Testament, one from the Epistles, and one from the Gospels, together with a psalm (see p. 36 of this volume). Since publication of the WBK in 1970, American Presbyterians, along with other churches, have witnessed a remarkable acceptance of the ecumenical lectionary. This lectionary combines both principles, *lectio selecta* and *lectio continua.* (For an account of the formation of the Common Lectionary, and its successor, the Revised Common Lectionary, see pp. 69–70, 258–259 of this volume. For notes on the daily lectionary, see p. 259.)

Leonine sacramentary. *See* Roman liturgy. And see prayer texts [162], [306], [356], [376], [378], [513].

Lift up your hearts. *See* Sursum Corda.

litany. The litany is an ancient form of prayer that engages the congregation in responding with a repeated response or refrain [93], [94], [95], [97], [131], [150], [170], [177], [213], [269], [333], [315], [317], [390], [419], [666], [667], [668], [818], [856]. Responsive prayers (e.g., [236], [243], and [267]) are sometimes called litanies, though technically they are not, since the people's responses are not repetitive. Psalms 118 and 136 are Old Testament examples of a litany. In the Christian East, litanies date to at least the second half of the fourth century in Antioch, as evidenced in the *Apostolic Constitutions* (q.v.). Various types of litanies evolved in East and West over the centuries. Some were sung in processions, not only in church but in public as well.

Liturgy of Malabar. An ancient Syriac liturgy used by the Church of St. Thomas in South India (Malabar is India's southwestern coastal area). A long-standing tradition maintains that the apostle Thomas (one of the Twelve) first introduced Christianity to India. While Christianity was implanted early in India, it cannot be proved that St. Thomas ever went to India. See prayer texts [36] and [124].

Liturgy of St. Basil. An Alexandrian (Egypt) liturgy in Greek from a very early date, later reedited by St. Basil the Great, bishop of Caesarea (329–379). It is one of the principal Byzantine (q.v.) liturgies. See prayer texts [12], [95], [96], [108], and [119].

Liturgy of St. John Chrysostom. A Byzantine liturgy in Greek, attributed to St. John Chrysostom, bishop of Constantinople (died 407), but of a much later date. It is in general use in the Eastern Orthodox Churches and is a shortened version of the Liturgy of St. Basil (q.v.). See prayer texts [95], [96], and [108].

Liturgy of St. Mark. A Greek, Alexandrian liturgy of great antiquity. It is preserved in twelfth- and thirteenth-century manuscripts, and in fragments from the fourth and fifth centuries. The later manuscripts evidence Byzantine assimilation. *See* prayer text [787].

Lord, Have Mercy. *See* Kyrie Eleison.

Lord's Prayer. The prayer that, according to the Gospels, was taught by Jesus to his disciples (Matt. 6:9–13; Luke 1:2–4). The doxology was added early and is cited in the *Didache* (q.v.). The doxology is common in the Byzantine rite (q.v.), but not in the Roman liturgy (q.v.). In the early centuries of the church's life this prayer was given to the catechumens during Lent along with the creeds in preparation for their baptism at the Great Vigil of Easter (q.v.). About A.D. 400, the Lord's Prayer was included in the Eucharist, to be said after the bread was broken, as a devotional preparation for receiving the Sacrament. Gregory the Great placed the Lord's Prayer immediately after the Amen of the eucharistic prayer. The prayer is used in a majority of church traditions. The text beginning, "Our Father in heaven . . ." is an ELLC text. For further commentary see ELLC, pp. 13–16.

Lucernarium. *See* Service of Light.

Magnificat. *See* Canticle of Mary.

Matins. Morning prayer. *See* canonical hours.

memorial acclamation. One of the people's portions of the Great Thanksgiving, the memorial acclamation derives from the liturgies of the Eastern church. It succinctly recalls the threefold nature of the paschal mystery—the death, resurrection, and coming again of Christ. Memorial Acclamation 3 (BCW, p. 71, and elsewhere) is a literal translation of the form appearing most frequently in Eastern liturgies and is found in some Ethiopian eucharistic prayers. The wording is that of BCP, p. 368. The first and second acclamations are clearly based on the Eastern acclamation and are from the RS. The fourth acclamation is also from the RS. The words introducing acclamations 1, 2, and 4 are borrowed from drafts of proposed revisions of the liturgy of the Mass prepared by the International Commission on English in the Liturgy (ICEL).

Mercersburg Movement. The first steps toward liturgical reform to be made by a Reformed denomination in North America emerged within the German Reformed Church in the middle of the nineteenth century. Its birth was in a German Reformed theological seminary in Mercersburg, Pennsylvania, which gave the name to the reforming movement that followed. This movement has had significant and lasting influence on subsequent efforts to reshape worship, not only within the German Reformed Church (later merging into the Evangelical and Reformed Church, and then later into the United Church of Christ), but also within other branches of the Reformed tradition in North America. See further on the Mercersburg movement on p. 26 of this volume.

missal. *See* Roman liturgy.

Mozarabic liturgy (or rite). Also called the Old Spanish liturgy, dating from at least as early as the sixth century and continuing until the Roman liturgy became predominant. The Mozarabic liturgy is still used in a chapel of the cathedral in Toledo, Spain. See prayer text [11].

Nicene Creed. In its present form, this creed dates from the Council of Chalcedon (451). It was accepted as the creed of the Council of Constantinople (381), which in turn had confirmed it as expressing the Nicene Faith. The Council of Nicaea (325) had stated orthodox faith in response to the Arian heretics, emphasizing that the Son is of the same essential Being (*homoousios*) as the Father. It is believed that this creed is based on an earlier baptismal creed perhaps from Jerusalem or Antioch. In addition to the essential clauses from Nicaea, it addressed later heresies as well. The creed is cast in the first person plural ("we believe") since it is a statement of faith of an ecumenical council. Its use is, therefore, particularly appropriate in corporate worship, since we are expressing the faith of the whole church of every time and place, rather than simply the faith of individual believers, or even that of a local congregation. Its use in the Eucharist probably dates from the late fifth century in Antioch. Later it spread to the West, Rome introducing it early in the eleventh century.

Controversy continues surrounding the introduction, in 589 at the Third Council of Toledo, of a *filioque* clause ("and the Son") in the portion on the Holy Spirit, indicating that the Holy Spirit "proceeds from the Father and the Son." Its inclusion spread throughout the West and ultimately was embraced in Rome early in the eleventh century. It was firmly resisted in the East and became a point of major contention in the conflicts between East and West that led to the great schism between Western and Eastern Christianity in 1054. Today, there are persuasive arguments, both historical and theological, for the deletion of this clause added to the Nicene-Chalcedonian creed. For further commentary on this creed see ELLC, pp. 23–28.

Nunc Dimittis. *See* Canticle of Simeon.

Ordinary, the. The invariable parts of the Eucharist, as distinct from the propers (q.v.), which vary with the day and season. In the Western liturgical tradition the Ordinary has included the Kyrie, the Gloria in Excelsis, the Nicene Creed, the Sursum Corda, the Sanctus, and the Agnus Dei (qq.v.).

Peace, the. Jesus taught that one should not come before God before being reconciled with one's neighbor (Matt. 5:23–24). The peace in the liturgy is a ritualization of this admonition, as well as the admonition of Paul to his readers to "Greet one another with a holy kiss" (Rom. 16:16; 1 Cor. 16:20; 2 Cor. 13:12; 1 Thess. 5:26). In ancient times it was a greeting of the communicants after the catechumens were dismissed. The traditional placement, therefore, followed the readings, sermon, and prayers and was shared immediately before the liturgy of the Supper. The BCW places it immediately after the declaration of forgiveness, whether the prayer of confession is said during the Gathering, or following the prayers of the people (the traditional placement). Alternatively, the BCW suggests that it may be exchanged after the Lord's Prayer before the bread is broken.

Phos Hilaron. *See* Hymn to Christ the Light.

prayer for illumination. The prayer for illumination is a Reformed creation by which we pray that the Holy Spirit may give us receptive hearts as the Scriptures are read, and illumine our minds and hearts. Following confession, pardon, and the singing of the Ten Commandments, it was Calvin's custom to leave the Communion table, enter the pulpit, and offer such a prayer. Bard Thompson provides a translation of one such prayer Calvin used, derived from Martin Bucer:

> Almighty and gracious Father, since our whole salvation standeth in our knowledge of thy Holy Word, strengthen us now by thy Holy Spirit that our hearts may be set free from all worldly thoughts and attachments of the

flesh, so that we may hear and receive that same Word, and, recognizing thy gracious will for us, may love and serve thee with earnest delight, praising and glorifying thee in Jesus Christ our Lord. Amen.[2]

The prayer for illumination marks the beginning of the portion of the liturgy titled "The Word" in the BCW.

prayer of confession. *See* confession and pardon.

prayer of the day. A collect (q.v.) assigned to a particular day, usually relating to the Gospel reading for the day in the lectionary. Many of these prayers date back to the Roman sacramentaries (*see* Roman liturgy). Traditionally, this prayer concludes the opening rite (the Gathering). The BCW places this prayer at the beginning of the liturgy, or alternatively has it conclude the prayers of the people. By so doing, this enables the use of a prayer that is uniquely Reformed, the prayer for illumination (q.v.), to be said before the first reading. However, to use the prayer of the day in its traditional location concluding the Gathering remains an option, in which case the prayer for illumination is not used.

In practice, when the prayer is used at the beginning of the liturgy, the Trinitarian ending of the prayer, by echoing the baptismal formula (q.v.), reaffirms that we are a gathering of those claimed as God's own through baptism. Since the prayer of the day serves a different function when concluding the prayers of the people, the full doxological ending may be deleted, the prayer concluding simply with "through Jesus Christ our Lord."

prayers of the people. Prayers of intercession, or prayers on behalf of others offered by the faithful. Intercessions have always been a part of Christian worship, as evidenced in 1 Tim. 2:1–2. Typically, prayers of the people are in the form of a bidding prayer (q.v.), a litany (q.v.), or a responsive prayer such as [216], [243], [267]. (Prayers of the People G [98–99] is a responsive prayer incorporating free prayer). Such prayer forms effectively assist the people in offering prayer to the end that they may truly be the people's prayers for the life of the world. Such prayers include intercessions for the church universal, for all humankind, and for civil authorities, as well as concerns that are local in nature, for the sick and bereaved, and those in distress or need (see rubrics in the BCW, pp. 66, 99, and Directory for Worship, W-3.3506).

preface. The beginning section of the Great Thanksgiving, following the Sursum Corda (q.v.) and ending with the Sanctus (q.v.). It is an ascription of praise and thanksgiving centering on the mighty acts of the first person of the Trinity. In eucharistic prayers that have variable prefaces, it expresses the theme of the particular feast or season of the liturgical year (*see* Great Thanksgivings B, C, and D, [115], [116], [117]).

propers. The variable parts of the liturgy, in contrast to the parts of the Ordinary (q.v.), which tend to be the invariable portions. The propers would include, for example, the opening sentences from Scripture, the prayer of the day, the Scripture readings for the day, and the preface to the Great Thanksgiving if one is used that has variable seasonal prefaces.

psalm prayer. A collect (q.v.) following the singing or speaking of a psalm in the daily office (q.v.), reflecting some theme or image from the psalm and usually adding Christian implications. Psalm prayers help one pray the Psalms, and they follow moments of silent reflection on the psalm. They are of ancient origin, mentioned in documents as early as the fourth century. The purpose of a psalm prayer was to give a Christian interpretation to the psalm. Early in the fifth century, psalm prayers were replaced by the Gloria Patri (q.v.) to defend against Arianism. The restoration of the psalm prayer, following the Second Vatican Council, replaces singing or saying the Gloria Patri at the conclusion of a psalm. Within the

Reformed tradition, psalm prayers appeared in the French Psalter in 1561 and were translated into English for inclusion in the Scottish Metrical Psalter of 1595. Some of the psalm prayers in the BCW are based on these Scottish prayers; see [546], [548], [575], [613], [615], [618], [659], [662].

psalmody. Singing the Psalms in worship has great antiquity, shaping the prayer of Jews and Christians alike for many centuries. Singing a psalm following the Old Testament reading is the oldest regular use of psalmody in Christian liturgy. The psalms have also been at the core of the daily office (q.v.). Psalms have been sung in a variety of ways.

Responsorial singing is the earliest, in which a cantor sang the psalm, with the people answering by singing a refrain (usually a verse of the psalm) after each of the psalm's sections. The Psalms have also been sung directly, with the entire community singing the psalm in unison. Another practice is singing the psalm alternately: the congregation is divided into two parts that alternate in singing the verses of the psalm.

Antiphonal singing of the Psalms appeared in fourth-century monastic practice in which the community was divided into two parts, one section singing the psalm verses, the other responding with an antiphon (q.v.; refrain not necessarily scriptural) after each verse. A common practice today is to sing an antiphon, or refrain drawn from the psalm, at the beginning and at the end of the psalm.

Each of these methods have utilized chant tones in singing the psalm texts. Chanting most easily accommodates the irregularities of a psalm text without forcing it into a particular metrical mold. The integrity of the psalm is thus more readily preserved.

The sixteenth-century Reformation brought a resurgence of congregational singing of the Psalms, by introducing metrical psalmody. A metrical psalm is a psalm translated into poetic meter, enabling it to be sung to a tune. Among the Reformed on the continent, each metered psalm text had its own tune. The text determined composition of the tune, resulting in a close affinity between text and tune. These psalms continue to be cherished by the Reformed on the Continent. In Scotland, however, psalm texts were translated into common poetic meters so that they could be sung to a variety of tunes with the same meter. Thus the tune determined the poetic meter of the text. In forcing texts to fit a set tonal structure, strictures of meter and rhyme unduly burdened the translations, often resulting in awkward syntax and loss of vivid textual imagery. In spite of these limitations, many metrical psalms in common meter are fine examples of metrical psalmody. Metrical psalms long constituted the major sung praise within the Reformed tradition. In time, loose paraphrases, such as those of Isaac Watts, who introduced interpretations alien to the psalm text, gained popularity. The result is that today many so-called metrical psalms, though they may be regarded as such, are no more than hymns inspired by a psalm text. When metrical psalms are truly metered translations, they have integrity as psalms. These merit full recovery alongside other ways, old and new, for singing the psalms, e.g., plainsong, Gelineau psalmody, Anglican chant, and the simple and popular chant forms introduced since the Second Vatican Council.

renunciations. Vows made at baptism renouncing all that is evil, a turning from all that is destructive of human life and relationships. Renouncing evil at baptism derives from a time very early in the church's life, and through the centuries it has been part of baptismal rites both in West and East. Dating from the beginning of the third century, the *Apostolic Tradition of Hippolytus* cites the following: "I renounce you, Satan, and all your service and all your works." Other ancient sources cite similar forms. While such a vow is cast in mythic terms, evil forces are nevertheless very real and powerful in the world today. Renunciation is prelude to affirming—to accepting Jesus Christ as Lord and Savior. Thus, from ancient times a profession of faith immediately followed the renunciations. The central aspects of life by which Christians seek to live each day are brought to focus—*turning from* all that is destructive of human life and relationships (both personal and in society), and *turning to* Jesus Christ and seeking to live as his faithful disciples. Charles Shields included renunciations in PBCP, p. 297. In the rite for the baptism of adults in BCW (1906), p. 44; (1932), p. 62; and (1946), p. 127, some expression of "turning from evil, and turning to Christ" was included. BCW (1906) expressed it as follows: "Do you confess your sins, and turn from them with godly sorrow, and put all your trust in the mercy of God, which is in Christ Jesus; and do you promise in His strength to lead a sober, righteous, and godly life . . . ?" In BCW (1932) the first portion was revised to read: "Do you confess your sins, and repent of them . . . ?"

Roman liturgy. The sacramentary contains the liturgy for the Mass, including the propers (q.v.) as well as the Ordinary (q.v.), and is used by the clergy. The missal is the liturgy for use by the people. The most important ancient Roman sacramentaries are the Leonine, the Gelasian, and the Gregorian. They are named after the popes with whom it is believed they were connected. The Leonine sacramentary (q.v.), the earliest of the sacramentaries, was completed in the sixth century and is purported to be connected with Pope Leo I "the Great" (440-461). The heart of the Gelasian sacramentary (q.v.) may go back to the time of Pope Gelasius I (492-496). There are also manuscripts incorporating Gelasian and other Roman and Gallican elements, known as the Frankish Gelasian sacramentary. The Gregorian sacramentary (q.v.) probably originated with Pope Gregory I (590–604) but passed through considerable revision until the ninth century. Alcuin of Tours (c. 735–804), born in England, religious advisor to Emperor Charlemagne, is noted for editing the Gregorian liturgical material and making numerous additions to it. *See also* Gallican liturgies.

sacramentary. *See* Roman liturgy.

Sancta Sanctis. "The gifts of God for the people of God." Derives from fourth-century Eastern liturgies. *Sancta sanctis* means, literally, "The holy for the holy" or "Holy things for holy people," i. e., "Set-apart things for set-apart people." It is the invitation to the people to come to commune.

Sanctus. Holy, Holy, Holy Lord (Latin). The sung (or spoken) response of praise of the people concluding the preface in the Great Thanksgiving. This response belongs to the people. In singing it the people participate in offering the Great Thanksgiving. It is a hymn of adoration based on Isa. 6:3 and Rev. 4:8. It thus is the song of the angels in which we are invited to join. It seems to have originated in the East, spreading throughout East and West. By the fourth century it was universally a part of the eucharistic prayer. Ordinarily it is combined with "Blessed Is He Who Comes" (the Benedictus Qui Venit), from Ps. 118:25–26, sung by the crowds in praise of Jesus as he rode into Jerusalem (Matt. 21:9; Mark 11:9–10; Luke 19:38). The text in the BCW was prepared by the International Consultation on English Texts (ICET), subsequently reviewed and concurred with by the successor to ICET, the ELLC. For further commentary see ELLC, pp. 35–36.

Sarum liturgy (or rite). One of a number of local variants of the liturgy in use in England. The Sarum liturgy was the liturgy associated with Salisbury Cathedral. It dates from the eleventh century, with a revision in the thirteenth century, and was the most generally used liturgy in England just before the Reformation. See prayer texts [31], [44], [258], [270], [286], [349], [356], [378], [388], first paragraph of [795], and the text "Depart, O . . ." (BCW p. 464).

Service of Light. The lucernarium. Thanksgiving (blessing) for the evening lights, a Jewish ritual at the lighting of the lamps, a practice embraced within the earliest Christian tradition, as evidenced in the *Apostolic Tradition of Hippolytus* (q.v.). It was followed by psalmody and prayers and sometimes included an agape meal. When transferred to church buildings, this lamp-lighting ceremony preceded a brief service of singing psalms and prayer, and sometimes readings from Scripture. It continued as the core of vespers in Eastern Orthodoxy, and in the West in the Mozarabic (q.v.) and Ambrosian rites (q.v.). However, it died out in much of the West as the monastic hours of prayer replaced the congregational (or cathedral) services. The lighting of a new fire and paschal candle in the Great Vigil of Easter (q.v.) is a remnant of the primitive lucernarium. In recent years the lucernarium has been revived because of its beauty and significance. It is included in the BCW as the Service of Light (pp. 505–513), which may begin Evening Prayer.

sign of the cross. A gesture tracing the cross on oneself, or by a minister on or toward others. Since the second century the cross has been traced on the forehead of the newly baptized immediately upon their baptism, as a sign of God's ownership and their engagement to serve Christ. Oil, set apart for the purpose, may be used in tracing the sign (*see* anointing with oil). Second-century sources state that this sign was repeated often by individual Christians throughout their lives—tracing the sign on the forehead as in his or her baptism—as a reminder of one's identity as a Christian. The gesture of crossing oneself from forehead to heart and across one's chest dates from a later time. On Ash Wednesday the cross is traced with ashes on the forehead of those who present themselves for the imposition of ashes (see following note on prayer text [210]). As a sign of God's blessing, ministers may trace the cross toward the people in pronouncing the apostolic benediction (2 Cor. 13:13). With its Trinitarian focus in both word and sign, it further underscores our identity as the community of the baptized.[3]

Sursum Corda. Lift Up Your Hearts (Latin). The introductory dialogue to the eucharistic prayer, between the celebrant and the congregation. It dates from as early as the third century in the West, and fourth century in the East. The first pair of verses derives from Ruth 2:4. The second pair of verses are cited in the *Apostolic Tradition of Hippolytus* (q.v.). Cyprian (ca. 252), comments on the verses as admonishing that all worldly thought be suppressed and minds be turned solely to the Lord. Augustine also refers to them, seeing in them the Pauline injunction to "seek the things that are above" (Col. 3:1–2; see also Ps. 86:4). The original intent of these verses, however, seems to have been a command to the people to stand, assuming the priestly posture of prayer. The third pair of verses follows the basic form that introduces the prayer of thanks (berakah, q.v.) in Jewish prayer. As in Jewish prayer, Christian liturgies give thanks by blessing God, praising God for God's mighty works. "Let us give thanks . . ." is a request by the celebrant to be allowed to proceed in giving thanks in the name of all who are present. The response of the people is the people's assent to the request. The text in the BCW was prepared by the International Consultation on English Texts (ICET), subsequently reviewed and concurred with by its successor, the English Language Liturgical Consultation (ELLC). The only change is from "him" to "our" in the last line. For further commentary see ELLC, pp. 33–34.

Taizé Community. An ecumenical monastic community founded in the early 1940s by Roger Schutz (Swiss Reformed). Originally it was a community of Reformed and Lutheran "brothers," both ordained and lay. Anglicans and Roman Catholics joined the community in the 1960s. The hope of the Taizé Community has been expressed as follows: "To live out, in the lives of a few men, a parable of reconciliation that would put into the dough of the divided churches a leaven of communion." Located in the Burgundy region of France, it has a strong ministry with youth, attracting thousands of young people during the summer. It also is engaged in ministries of compassion with the poor in various places in the world. Its music has a deeply spiritual character and is widely used by Catholics and Protestants alike throughout Europe and the United States. Taizé has also inspired the introduction of services of evening prayer in many Presbyterian congregations. See prayer texts [148], [150], [170], [171], [177], [213], [243], [253], [267], [269], [300], [478], [479], [670], and [722].

Te Deum Laudamus. *See* We Praise You, O God.

Thanksgiving Over the Water. *See* prayer texts [411], [412], [419], [420]. Use of a prayer over the water in baptism dates from at least as early as the beginning of the third century (the *Apostolic Tradition of Hippolytus* [q.v.]). In the fifth-century Gelasian sacramentary (*see* Roman liturgy) and the sixth-century Mozarabic liturgy (q.v.), the Easter baptismal vigil included prayers over the water rich in biblical imagery in unfolding the richness and depth of Baptism's meaning. The Flood Prayer in Luther's baptismal rite (1523), is an adaptation of this tradition, drawing on biblical images of Noah's flood and the exodus through the sea as typologically portraying the destruction and salvation implicit in Baptism. Thomas Cranmer included a version of Luther's prayer in the BCP (1549). This was incorporated from the BCP tradition into PBCP, pp. 254–255, 295–296. The prayer in today's service books is parallel to the Great Thanksgiving of the Eucharist and is similar in structure and language. The prayer begins with the Sursum Corda (q.v.), though the last two lines are omitted, since these are reserved only for the Eucharist. Images of the mighty acts of God's saving grace are gratefully remembered—creation, the flood, the exodus, Jesus' baptism—and the Spirit is invoked, that those who are baptized may receive the new life promised in the gospel.

Triduum. Latin: the Three Days. It refers to Maundy Thursday, Good Friday, and Holy Saturday. This is the holiest time of the year for Christians, centering on the crucifixion and resurrection of Jesus. The liturgies for Maundy Thursday, Good Friday, and the Easter Vigil are interrelated and inseparable. Together they proclaim the story. For this reason the liturgies on these three days are regarded as a single liturgy in three extended moments. Therefore, there is no benediction after the Maundy Thursday and Good Friday portions; the benediction is said only at the conclusion of the Easter Vigil.

Trisagion. "Holy God, Holy and Mighty . . ." BCW, p. 55. (Latin: thrice holy.) An ancient hymn of the Eastern churches. It found its way into the Gallican liturgies (q.v.), and into the Roman liturgy with the Gallican reproaches for Good Friday, where it was used as a response to the reproaches (BCW, pp. 288–291). Like the Sanctus (q.v.), the Trisagion derives from the seraph's hymn in Isaiah's vision (Isa. 6:3), and in the same hymn of praise heard by John on the Isle of Patmos (Rev. 4:8). It is sung in praise of the triune God. In comparing it with the traditional way of expressing the Trinity (based on Matt. 29:19), "Holy God" refers particularly to the Father; "Holy and mighty" refers especially to the Son (based on Isa. 9:6, "a child has been born for us, a son given to us; . . . and he is named . . . Mighty God"); "Holy Immortal One" refers to the Holy Spirit, "the Lord, the giver of life" (Nicene Creed). It is repeated three times, once for each *persona* of the Trinity. Though each is addressed, none is considered apart from the others. While each expresses a distinct aspect of the Trinity, God is one. The intent of the doctrine of the Trinity is to affirm the oneness of God, not deny it. In a time when a functioning tritheism is so prevalent in popular expressions of Christianity, use of the Trisagion may help us to refocus on the oneness of the triune God.[4]

When we listen to the debates that surrounded the formation of the doctrine of the Trinity in the Eastern church of the third and fourth centuries, we witness human minds attempting to fathom the unfathomable, stretching the imagination in seeking to comprehend how God accommodates God's self to the limits of human understanding. Rooted firmly in Hebrew monotheism, they took great care to reaffirm belief in the oneness of God, in the face of how God was experienced, especially as revealed in and through Jesus Christ.

Just as the church's doctrine of the Trinity was formed from lived experience of God, so we shall come to "know" the Trinity more from our lived relationship with God than from the reasoning of our minds. Nevertheless it is important that we seek understanding, to love God with the mind as well as the heart and soul (Matt. 22:37). When we contemplate the workings of the One who is beyond all we can think or imagine, an awe of God is implanted deep within us, guiding us in the life to which God calls us. At the same time, we need always to be reminded that our reasonings are but metaphors of the One who is beyond all efforts to fathom or describe, even in a doctrine of Trinity. *See* baptismal formula.

Vespers. Evening prayer. *See* canonical hours.

We Praise You, O God. The Te Deum Laudamus. A Latin hymn, the church's great song of thanksgiving. A popular legend surrounding it (beginning perhaps in the eighth century) was a belief that it was extemporaneously composed by Ambrose at Augustine's baptism in the Great Vigil of Easter in Milan in 387. Modern scholars attribute the Te Deum to Niceta, bishop of Remesiana in Dacia (ca. 392–414), modern Nish in Yugoslavia. The hymn "Holy God, We Praise Your Name" (PH, no. 460) is a nineteenth-century hymn based on the Te Deum. The translation in the BCW (p. 577) is an ELLC text. For further commentary see ELLC, pp. 41-44.

words of institution. *See* institution narrative.

Chapter 1

Commentary on Preparation for Worship

PRAYERS FOR USE BEFORE WORSHIP (PP. 17–28)

1.   SLDL, p. 11; BCWP, p. 11; WBK, p. 15; SLR-1, p. 29, altered.

2.   BCO (1940), pp. 38, 259; BCW (1946), p. 28; SLR-1, p. 29, altered; doxology expanded in BCW. Lines 1–2 draw on Acts 17:28; lines 3–5 derive from St. Augustine (Conf. 1:1).

3.   Derives from AC, p. 233; BCP (1928) for which it was altered; BCP, p. 833; BCW (1946), p. 3; SLR-1, p. 29, altered. Biblical allusions: Zech. 12:10 and John 4:23.

4.   SLDL, p. 12 (opening lines incorporated from BCW [1946], p. 5); BCWP, p. 11; WBK, pp. 15–16; SLR-1, p. 30, altered. Altered further for BCW.

5.   *The Book of Common Prayer* of St. Giles Cathedral, Edinburgh, Scotland. SLR-1, p. 30, altered.

6.   From the Gelasian liturgy. BCP (1549) and subsequent editions, BCP, p. 230. PBCP, p. 383 (as in early tradition, commemorating St. Simon and

St. Jude); BCW (1906), p. 130; BCW (1932), p. 179; BCW (1946), p. 323 (in part); SLDL, p. 12; BCWP, p. 12; BCP, p. 230; SLR-1, p. 30, altered. See SLR-7, p. 255 for a different version of this text. See also text [380]. Biblical allusion: Eph. 2:20-22.

7.   BCW (1946), pp. 3, 109; SLR-1, pp. 30–31, altered.

8.   Portions of this prayer are from the Gelasian liturgy. First four lines included in BCO (1874); BCW (1906), p. 12; BCW (1932), p. 12; and BCO (1940), p. 70; BCW (1946), p. 344; SLR-1, p. 31, altered. See also at [25] and [46].

9.   LBW, p. 111 [206]; altered for LBW from *Collects and Prayers for Use in Church* (United Lutheran, 1935, p. 41). SLR-1, p. 31.

10.   Based on a prayer in BCP, p. 834. The BCP prayer first appearing in BCP (1549) for use after worship, and reflecting the sixteenth-century Reformation emphasis on the Scriptures. It appeared in PBCP, p. 44; BCO (1874); BCW (1906), p. 17; BCW (1932), p. 17.

11.   Derives from the ancient Mozarabic liturgy. BCW-CSI, p. 14; BCP, p. 834; SLR-1, p. 31. Altered as it appears in LBW, prayer [207], p. 111. The form of the ancient text may be stronger, beginning, "Be present, be present, O Jesus, our great High Priest . . . ."

12.   In the Anglican tradition since BCP (1549). It came to be known as the Prayer of Humble Access. BCP, p. 337 (Rite 1), as an optional Communion devotion following the breaking of the bread and prior to Communion. The prayer contains phrases or concepts from the Liturgy of St. Basil, a Gregorian collect, and allusions to Mark 7:28 and John 6:56. A form of this prayer is in PBCP, p. 242; BCO (1979), pp. 34–35. SLR-1, p. 31, altered. Altered further for BCW.

13.   UW (leader's edition), p. 598, altered. Biblical allusions: Deut. 8:3; Matt. 4:4; Luke 4:4.

14.   Source information lost. Another version of this prayer reads "Lord of glory," instead of "Lord Jesus."

15.   This prayer is included in PNW, p. 133 (no. 308), as from *The Church in Germany in Prayer*. Altered.

16.   Source information lost.

17.   SB-UCC, p. 299 (no. 433). Biblical allusions to John 15:5 and Phil. 4:13.

18.   Christina Rossetti (1830–1894).

19.   Desiderius Erasmus (ca. 1466–1536).

20.   Attributed to Nels Ferré.

21. Cardinal John Henry Newman (1801–1890).

22. Dag Hammarskjöld (1905–1961), from *Markings* (1964). The text in the first printings of the BCW included lines that were not a part of the original text, reflecting the secondary source from which the text was taken. Although the publisher's permission had been granted, the family of Dag Hammarskjöld, understandably, requested that the text that was not in the original be removed from all subsequent printings and not included in the software edition.

    Therefore, only lines 2 through 5 should be included in any reproduction of this text for church bulletins. Lines 1, 6–8 are deleted in later printings of the BCW, including the software edition. A preferred translation of this text is included in the edition of *Markings* translated by Leif Sjöberg and W. H. Auden (London: Faber & Faber, 1964), p. 176, since this prayer is cast in first-person plural language.

23. Richard, bishop of Chichester (1197–1253).

24. Howard Thurman (1900–1981), from *Meditations of the Heart* (1953).

25. Attributed to Augustine of Hippo, though this is questionable. Lines 2–4 immediately follow the first four lines of prayer [8] above in a prayer in BCW (1906), p. 12; BCW (1932), p. 12; BCO (1940), p. 70, which is the form of prayer [46]. BCW (1932) identifies the prayer appearing in these servicebooks as an altered version of a prayer from the Gelasian liturgy. Form of prayer [25] is from UW (people's edition), p. 213. See also [8] and [46].

26. Augustine, bishop of Hippo (354–430).

27. Archbishop William Temple (1881–1944).

28. Archbishop William Laud (1573–1645).

29. Attributed to Benedict of Nursia (ca. 480–547). Versions of this prayer abound, which may indicate that it has evolved over time. While most variations have little significance, one version found after publication of the BCW adds the line "intelligence to understand you" to the first portion of this prayer. Another adds instead "intellect to understand you, reason to discern you."

30. Alcuin of Tours (ca. 735–804).

31. From Sarum Primer (ca. 1514).

32. Maria Ware (1798).

33. Attributed to Francis of Assisi (1181–1226).

34. Patrick of Ireland (389–461).

35.   Clement, Bishop of Rome (d. ca. 99).

36.   From the Liturgy of Malabar (fifth century). A prayer for use after celebrating the Eucharist.

37.   Patrick of Ireland (389–461). This prayer is known as St. Patrick's Breastplate. Translation by Cecil Frances Alexander (1818–1895), slightly altered. A musical setting of this text (tune: St. Patrick's Breastplate) may be found in *The Hymnal 1982* of the Episcopal Church, no. 370. An abbreviated paraphrase (Joseph W. Clokey, 1964) is included in WBK-SH, no. 428, "I Sing as I Arise Today."

PRAYERS FOR WORSHIP LEADERS (PP. 29–30)

38. BCO (1940), p. 6; BCW (1946), p. 6; SLR-1, p. 32, altered.

39. WBK, p. 16; SLR-1, p. 32.

40. SLDL, p. 12; BCWP, p. 12; SLR-1, p. 32, altered.

41. WBK, p. 16; SLR-1, p. 33, altered.

42. SLDL, p. 11; BCWP, p. 11; WBK, p. 16; SLR-1, p. 33, altered.

43. SLDL, p. 12; BCWP, p. 12; WBK, p. 16; SLR-1, p. 33.

Chapter 2

Commentary on the Service for the Lord's Day

THE SERVICE FOR THE LORD'S DAY— ORDER WITH TEXTS (PP. 48–85)

Call to Worship (pp. 48–50)

On the use of Ps. 124:8 (p. 49) in Reformed worship, see note in Evening Prayer, following [456].

"Praise the Lord . . ." (p. 50). SLDL, p. 13; BCWP, p. 21; WBK, p. 25; SLR-1, p. 36. This versicle appeared in the Scottish Prayer Book of 1637.

Prayer of the Day or Opening Prayer (pp. 50–52)

44. This well-known collect can be found in an eleventh-century missal and the Sarum rite. In the Sarum rite it was part of the priest's personal preparation as he vested for Mass. It was also the collect of the day in a Mass invoking the graces of the Holy Spirit. It was included at the beginning of the eucharistic liturgy in the BCP (1549) and each succeeding edition of the BCP (BCP, pp. 323, 355). PBCP, p. 37; BCW (1906), p. 20; BCW

(1932), pp. 42, 49; BCO (1940), p. 144; BCW (1946), p. 155; SLDL, p. 11; BCWP, p. 11; BCO (1979), pp. 1, 15, 289; SLR-1, p. 40, altered. It is reminiscent of Ps. 51.

45.   SLR-1, p. 40. Based on a prayer written by James F. White and Susan J. White.

46.   Derives from the Gelasian sacramentary. BCO (1874); BCW (1906), p. 12; BCW (1932), p. 12; BCO (1940), p. 70; SLR-1, p. 41, altered. See also [8] and [25].

47.   A prayer written by Henry van Dyke for BCW (1906), p. 109; revised for inclusion in BCW (1932), p. 22; BCO, p. 24, altered; BCW (1946), p. 11; SLR-1, p. 41, altered. Altered further for BCW.

48.   Written for SLR-1, p. 42, incorporating phrases from a prayer in SB-UCC, p. 224.

Confession and Pardon (pp. 52–57)

49.   This prayer derives from John Hunter, *Devotional Services for Public Worship* (London: Dent, 1901, p. 52). A revised version was included in BCW (1946), pp. 39–40. The Joint Liturgical Group (JLG), a British ecumenical liturgical body, included a version of this prayer in *The Daily Office* (London: S.P.C.K., 1968, p. 77), substituting the line "that we may delight in your will" for much lengthier prose. The JLG version was further altered for inclusion in the BCP, pp. 79, 116–17, 331, 360. An abbreviated version appeared in BCO (1979), p. 30. The Hunter prayer is also the basis for the penitential rite in the LBW (pp. 195, 233, 269). The prayer was included in SLR-1, p. 48. The BCW text draws from the BCW (1946) version, revisions made by the JLG, and revisions incorporated in BCP. Biblical allusions: Matt. 22:34–40; Mark 12:28–31; Luke 10:25–28; Ps. 1:2; Mic. 6:8. The line that we [originally: I] have sinned "in thought, word, and deed," *quia peccavi nimis cognitatione, verbo, et opere,* is part of the ancient Confiteor ("I confess"), a prayer the priest silently prayed at the beginning of the Mass, originally while he vested in the sacristy. After these words were spoken the priest struck his breast three times saying: *mea culpa, mea culpa, mea maxima culpa* (through my fault, through my own fault, through my own grievous fault). The Roman Confiteor dates from 1314. See glossary: Confiteor.

50.   A prayer written by Henry van Dyke for BCW (1906), pp. 20–21; revised for inclusion in BCW (1932), pp. 5, 42; BCO (1940), p. 12; BCW (1946), p. 12; SLDL, p. 14; BCWP, p. 22; SLR-1, p. 51, altered.

51.   BCWP, p. 22; SLR-1, p. 48, altered. Altered further for BCW. Biblical allusions: Gen. 3:8; Luke 10:31–32.

52.   BCW (1946), pp. 26–27; SLR-1, p. 50, altered. Biblical allusions: Ps. 51:1, 2, 10–12; Mic. 6:8.

"Lord, have mercy . . ." (p. 55). BCW (1946), p. 156; SLR-1, p. 52. See glossary: Kyrie Eleison.

"Holy God . . ." (p. 55), the Trisagion. It is included in a prayer in BCO (1940), p. 43. SLR-1, p. 55. See glossary: Trisagion.

"Jesus, Lamb of God" and "Lamb of God . . ." (p. 55). BCO (1940), p. 121; BCW (1946), p. 163; SLDL, p. 15; BCO (1979), pp. 12, 25, 37. See glossary: Agnus Dei.

"The mercy of the Lord . . ." (p. 56). SLR-1, p. 53, based on declarations of pardon contained in PBCP, p. 241; BCW (1906), p. 29; BCW (1932), p. 51; BCW (1946), pp. 118, 157, 294, 305; SLDL, p. 15; BCWP, p. 23; BCP, pp. 80, 117, 353.

"Hear the good news! Who is in a position to condemn . . ." (pp. 56–57). WBK, pp. 26–27 (based on J. B. Phillips's translation); SLR-1, p. 54, altered. Altered further for BCW. The ending, "Know that you are forgiven and be at peace," is from NZPB, pp. 408, 443, 449.

"Glory to God . . ." (p. 58). PBCP, p. 41; BCW (1946), p. 66; BCO (1979), p. 3; SLR-1, p. 55. See glossary: Gloria in Excelsis.

"Worthy Is Christ, the Lamb . . ." (p. 59). LBW, pp. 199–200, 237–238, 273; SLR-1, p. 56. Based on Rev. 5:9, 12–13; 15:2–4; 19:5–7, 9; 11:17. In LBW it is an alternative to the "Glory to God." This hymn (PH, no. 594) expresses the gladness of feasting in God's kingdom, anticipating the messianic feast of the kingdom of God.

"Glory to the Father . . ." (p. 59). See glossary: Gloria Patri.

Prayer for Illumination (p. 60)

53.   UMBW, p. 34; SLR-1, p. 59, altered. First appeared in United Methodist liturgical publications preparatory to UMBW.

54.   SLDL, p. 15; BCWP, p. 24; WBK, p. 28; SLR-1, p. 59, altered.

55.   WBK, p. 28; SLR-1, p. 59, altered. Altered further for BCW.

56.   BCO (1940), p. 41; SLR-1, p. 60, altered. Biblical allusion: Ps. 119:105.

"Hear what the Spirit . . ." (p. 61). NZPB, p. 460 (where it is followed by a congregational response: "Thanks be to God"). John, exiled on the island of Patmos, "in the spirit on the Lord's day," received messages from the exalted Christ for each of the seven churches in the Roman province of Asia (Rev. 1:4-3:22). This exhortation, "Hear what the Spirit is saying to the church [NRSV: churches]" accompanies each message. This text from Revelation in the BCW seeks to give added clarity to the intent of the words that introduced the readings in the WBK, p. 28, "Listen for the Word of God." While the WBK words precede each reading, the BCW text is said once, to introduce the series of readings.

The Confession of 1967 clearly expresses the manner of our engagement, how we are to hear: "The church has received the books of the Old and New Testaments as prophetic and apostolic testimony in which it hears the word of God and by which its faith and obedience are nourished and regulated." While "given under the guidance of the Holy Spirit," the Scriptures are nevertheless the words of men and women, and reflect an ancient past. They are to be received in the light of the context in which they were written. The Confession then affirms that just as God has spoken "in diverse cultural situations" of an ancient past, the church is confident that

> [God] will continue to speak through the Scriptures in a changing world and in every form of human culture.
>
> God's word is spoken to his church today where the Scriptures are faithfully preached and attentively read in dependence on the illumination of the Holy Spirit and with readiness to receive their truth and direction.[5]

The same admonition to hear a living Word in the reading of Scripture, characterizes the introduction of each reading in the Taizé liturgy. The reading from the Old Testament is introduced with "Come, Holy Spirit of truth; lead us into all truth." The source of the reading is then cited. The Epistle reading is introduced with "Lord, sanctify us in the truth: Thy Word is truth." The source of the reading is then cited. Before the Gospel reading the deacon says, "Let us hear the wisdom of Christ!" and then the Gospel reading is cited. Also see glossary: lectionary; prayer for illumination.

"The Word of the Lord . . ." (p. 61). SLR-1, p. 62. In the Roman Mass the reader says, "This is the Word of the Lord." The shorter version here is that of the Taizé Office. It avoids the confusion introduced by the word "this," which may be interpreted as refering to the biblical text itself rather than to a living Word we hear through the readings.

The response of the people, "Thanks be to God," dates from medieval times as an acknowledgment of having heard what was said. It is now understood to be an expression of thanks by the faithful for the good news of the gospel.

"Glory to you, O Lord . . . Praise to you, O Christ" (p. 62). BCW (1946), p. 157; SLDL, p. 16; BCO (1979), p. 4, adapted; SLR-1, p. 62; LBW, pp. 202, 239, 275; BCP, pp. 357–358; RS. Revised in accordance with

LBW. The acclamations before and after the Gospel reading came into the Western liturgy very early from northern Europe. Signing one's forehead with the sign of the cross at the announcement of the reading was practiced in the ninth century. Signing one's forehead, mouth, and breast, dates from about the eleventh century. The forehead being considered to be the seat of shame, this form has been interpreted as confessing, "I am not ashamed of the gospel, but confess it with lips and heart." It may also be a prayer, "May your Holy Gospel illumine my mind +, be confessed with my lips +, and treasured in my heart +."

Affirmations of Faith (pp. 64–65)

Nicene Creed (p. 64). See glossary.

Apostles' Creed (p. 65). See glossary.

Offering (p. 67)

"Let us return . . ." BCW-PCC, p. 77. This text, in contrast to the one on p. 79, implies that the elements of bread and wine as well as the gifts of money are presented at this time.

57.   NZPB, p. 420.

Invitation to the Lord's Table (pp. 68-69)

"Friends, this is the joyful feast . . ." (p. 68). WBK, p. 34; SLR-1, p. 87, altered. Biblical quotations from Luke 13:29 and Luke 24:30–31. The verses from the Emmaus story (Luke 24) are particularly significant, for they expand the focus of the Lord's Supper to include not simply the upper room feast preceding Jesus' death, but a postresurrection meal as well. The meal at Emmaus on the Sunday of the resurrection transforms the upper room meal of the previous Thursday. The joy of the Emmaus meal should dominate the spirit of the eucharistic celebration, not the somber mood of the Last Supper.

The taking, blessing, breaking, and giving of bread in the upper room and at Emmaus are inseparable from the taking, blessing, breaking, and giving of the bread in the sacramental meal on the Lord's Day. The Eucharist is a feast that joins inseparably Jesus' death and resurrection.

The words from Luke 13:29 introduce an image of the joy of the messianic feast in God's eternal realm, of which the Eucharist is a foretaste. Thus three meals—upper room, Emmaus, and an anticipation of feasting in the messianic banquet of God's future—are inseparable from the celebration of the Supper on the Lord's Day. In the Supper we celebrate Christ's death and resurrection and anticipate with joy the hope of God's eternal kingdom.

Great Thanksgiving (pp. 69–73)

58. This Great Thanksgiving was prepared for the BCW by Marney Ault
     Wasserman as a prototype of the eucharistic prayers for celebrating litur-
     gical days and seasons, prayers she shared in editing: [133], [153], [173],
     [180], [205], [211], [218], [240], [248], [272], [320], [327], [396], [409].
     For sources of elements shared in common in eucharistic prayers, see glos-
     sary: Great Thanksgiving; Sursum Corda; preface; Sanctus; anamnesis;
     institution narrative; memorial acclamation; epiclesis; doxology; Amen.

Lord's Prayer (p. 73)

"Let us pray for God's rule . . ." SLR-1, p. 125.

"And now, with the confidence . . ." UMBW, p. 38. Based on RS; SLR-1, p. 125.

"As our Savior Christ has taught us . . ." BCP, p. 336 (Rite I), altered. A render-
    ing of the invitation from earlier Roman missals. BCW (1946), p. 163,
    reads "we humbly pray" rather than "we are bold to pray." BCP, p. 363 (Rite
    II), provides an alternative, "we now pray." The thrust of "we are bold to
    say" is an expression of confidence (not presumption), grounded in Christ's
    words instructing and promising life that is abundant, making us whole.

"Our Father in heaven . . ." See glossary: Lord's Prayer.

Communion of the People (pp. 75–76)

"The gifts of God for the people of God" (p. 75). SLR-1, p. 127. See glossary:
    Sancta Sanctis.

59. From the *Didache*. This text is therefore one of the oldest known nonbib-
     lical liturgical texts. Unfortunately the lines that immediately follow in the
     Didache were not included in the BCW. Including them as the response
     by the people, would have been a more fitting use of this text:

> Creator of all,
> just as this broken bread
> was first scattered upon the hills,
> then was gathered and became one,
> so may your church be gathered
> from the ends of the earth into your kingdom
>
> **For yours is the glory and the power
> through Jesus Christ forever.**

The final lines of the hymn "Father, We Thank You that You Planted" (WBK-
SH, no. 366, paraphrased by F. Bland Tucker), are based on the *Didache* text:

> As grain, once scattered on the hillsides,
> Was in this broken bread made one,
> So from all lands your church be gathered
> Into your kingdom by your Son.

"The body of Christ, given for you . . . The blood of Christ, shed for you" (p. 75). LBW, pp. 227, 263, 300; SLR-1, p. 128. "The body of Christ, the bread of heaven . . . The blood of Christ, the cup of salvation" (p. 76). BCP, p. 365; SLR-1, p. 128. The words said in administering the bread and wine, "The body of Christ," and "The blood of Christ" have been used since early times, and are those in the RS. Through long tradition, these words of delivery have expressed a profession of faith, to which the recipients of the bread and wine give assent with the word "Amen." In the *Apostolic Tradition of Hippolytus,* in giving the bread the words were, "The bread of heaven in Christ Jesus." In the *Apostolic Constitutions,* the words were "The body of Christ" and "The blood of Christ, the cup of life."

Prayer After Communion (pp. 76–77)

The use of a post-Communion prayer dates from the fourth or fifth century. In some Eastern rites, a hymn was sung after a post-Communion prayer. Calvin's rite included a metrical psalm after the prayer.

60.   UW (leader's edition), p. 655. SLR-1, p. 130, altered. Doxological ending added for BCW.

61.   *An Australian Prayer Book,* as in UW (leader's edition), p. 129. SLR-1, p. 130, altered.

62.   SB-URC, pp. 20–21; SLR-1, p. 129, altered. Altered further for BCW.

63.   Prayer drafted by the Rev. Dr. Leo Malania. BCP, p. 365; SLR-1, p. 131, altered.

Charge and Blessing (pp. 78, 82–83)

The charge is a dismissal, which dates from at least the fourth century. In the *Apostolic Constitutions* and other Eastern liturgies it was a simple dismissal by the deacon, "Depart in peace." A blessing at the end of the Eucharist dates from at least the fourth century. In early liturgies, and continued in many Eastern liturgies, the blessing is said by the celebrant with or without the laying on of hands. See glossary: laying on of hands.

"Go out into the world in peace . . ." (pp. 78, 82). From proposed BCP (1928). BCW (1946), p. 133 (confirmation); WBK, pp. 38, 40; SLR-1, p. 132, altered.

"Go in peace . . ." (pp. 78, 83). BCP, p. 366; SLR-1, p. 133.

"Go forth into the world . . ." (pp. 78, 83). BCP, p. 366; SLR-1, p. 133. Altered for BCW.

Offering (p. 79)

"With gladness, let us present . . ." (p. 79). BCP, p. 377, SLR-1, p. 85, altered. Altered further for BCW.

Prayer of Thanksgiving (pp. 80–81)

64. WBK, p. 39; SLR-1, p. 122, altered. Altered further for BCW.

65. SB-UCC (people's edition), p. 263. Altered.

66. Based on a prayer by Louis F. Benson. BCW (1906), p. 111; BCW (1932), p. 24; BCO (1940), p. 32; BCW (1946), p. 15; SLR-1, p. 122, altered. Altered further for BCW.

Diane Karay Tripp has traced the core text of this prayer to the Church of Scotland's *Prayers for Social and Family Worship* (first published in 1859):

> Thy power hath created us;
> Thy bounty hath sustained us;
> Thy patience hath spared us;
> Thy love hath redeemed us.

Bensen reworked and improved these lines as follows:

> For Thy goodness that hath created us,
> Thy bounty that hath sustained us,
> Thy fatherly discipline that hath chastened and corrected us,
> Thy patience that hath borne with us;
> Thy love that hath redeemed us.

ADDITIONAL TEXTS FOR THE SERVICE FOR THE LORD'S DAY (PP. 87–161)

Prayer of Confession (pp. 87–89)

67. Revision of prayer by Henry van Dyke. BCW (1906), p. 11; BCW (1932), p. 11; BCW (1946), p. 53; SLR-1, p. 49, altered. Altered further for BCW. Biblical allusion: Acts 17:28.

68. This prayer dates to BCP (1552). It is based on Rom. 7:8–25 and appears in BCP, pp. 41–42 in Rite I, Morning Prayer; PBCP, pp. 3, 18; BCW (1932), p. 5; BCW (1946), p. 21; SLDL, p. 14; BCWP, p. 22; SLR-1, pp. 49–50, altered. Other scriptural allusions include Isa. 53:6; Ps. 119:176; 1 Pet. 2:25; Ps. 51:13; Rom. 15:8; 1 John. 2:12; Titus. 2:11–12; and John 14:13.

69. BW-UCC, p. 211, included in an order for Tenebrae for use during Holy Week .

70. BCW-PCC, p. 28, altered.

71. WBK, p. 26; SLR-1, p. 50, altered. Altered further for BCW.

72. UMBW, p. 35; SLR-1, pp. 48–49, altered. Altered further for BCW.

Prayer for Illumination (pp. 90–91)

73. BCWP, p. 24; SLR-1, p. 58, altered.

74. Original source not found, altered. Biblical allusions: Matt. 4:4 and Deut. 8:3.

75. Original source not found. SLR-1, p. 60, altered. Altered further for BCW.

76. Ulrich Zwingli. From Ulrich Zwingli, *A Short Pathwaye to the Ryghte and True Understanding of the Holye and Sacred Scriptures,* trans. Jhon Vernon (Worcester: Jhon Oswen, 1550).

77. Ancient collect, source unknown. BCO (1940), p. 22; SLR-1, pp. 60–61, altered. Biblical allusions: Jas. 1:17; Eph. 1:17; 2 Pet. 1:3.

78. Original source unknown. SLR-1, p. 61. Altered further for BCW.

79. Written for BCP (1549). PBCP, p. 50; BCW (1946), p. 291; BCP, p. 236; SLR-1, p. 61, altered. Based on Rom. 15:4.

Affirmation of Faith (pp. 94–98)

A Brief Statement of Faith (pp. 94–96). Adopted by the Presbyterian Church (U.S.A.) in 1991, as a brief statement of the Reformed faith.

"This is the good news . . ." (p. 96). BCWP, p. 26; WBK, p. 30; SLR-1, pp. 69–70, altered.

Prayers of the People (pp. 99–120)

80. SLDL, p. 17; BCWP, p. 26; SLR-1, p. 72, altered. Altered further for BCW. The line "and to present our petitions to you in his name" is from the BCW-PCC (p. 32) revision of this prayer, replacing "and promised that what we ask in his name will be given us."

81. SLDL, p. 18; BCWP, p. 27; WBK, p. 31; SLR-1, p. 72, altered. Altered further for BCW.

82. WBK, p. 31. SLR-1, p. 73, altered. Altered further for BCW. the line "and live in the light of your truth" is from the revision of this petition in BCW-PCC, p. 32.

83. SLDL, p. 18; BCWP, p. 27; WBK, p. 32, altered.

84. SLDL, p. 18; BCWP, p. 27; WBK, p. 32, altered.

85. SLDL, p. 18; BCWP, pp. 27–28; WBK, p. 32, altered.

86. WBK, p. 32, altered.

87. SLDL, p. 19; BCWP, p. 28; WBK, pp. 32–33, altered.

88. SLDL, p. 19; BCWP, p. 28; WBK, p. 33. Biblical allusion: Rom. 8:38–39.

89. SLDL, p. 19; BCWP, p. 28; WBK, p. 33, altered.

90. BCWP, p. 33; WBK, p. 33, altered.

91. WBK, p. 33, altered.

92. Written by Diane Karay Tripp for BCW. Biblical allusions: Rom. 8:26 (opening petition, p. 103); Song 8:6 (thanksgiving for departed, p. 106); Rom. 8:22, 23 (concluding petition, p. 106).

93. Written by Diane Karay Tripp for BCW.

94. Written by Harold M. Daniels for BCW.

95. Based on litanies from the Eastern liturgies of St. Basil and St. John Chrysostom. Adapted from text in BCP (pp. 383–385) and LBW, pp. 65–68. SLR-5, pp. 287–289. Revised further for BCW. It is most appropriately sung, as is the custom in the Eastern church.

96. From the Eastern Orthodox liturgies of St. John Chrysostom and St. Basil. Biblical allusion: Matt. 18:20. Use in the Anglican liturgy dates to before the 1549 BCP was published (BCP, p. 102). PBCP, pp. 15, 27, 35; BCW (1906), p. 26; BCW (1932), pp. 9, 47; BCO (1940), pp. 47, 260; BCW (1946), pp. 52, 64, 99; SLDL, p. 19; BCWP, p. 28; SLR-1, p. 84. Slight alteration in BCW.

97. BCP, pp. 389–391, altered. This is an adaptation of the Eastern litany form.

98. NZPB, pp. 413–414, altered.

99. NZPB, p. 414, altered.

100. Written for SLR-1, pp. 78–79, by Donald K. Campbell, based on intercessions in BCW (1946). Altered for BCW.

Commemoration of Those Who Have Died in the Faith (pp. 121–122)

101. UW (leader's edition), p. 641.

102. SB-UCC, p. 185. SLR-1, p. 80, altered.

103. Written for SLR-1, pp. 80–81, based on three prayers in BCW (1946), pp. 43, 17, 37. Altered further for BCW. Biblical allusions: 2 Tim. 4:7; 1 Cor. 2:9.

104. Derives from the burial service in the *Lutheran Service Book and Hymnal* (1958), p. 266; LBW, p. 335, prayer [285]; SLR-1, p. 81, altered. The opening clause is from the BCO (1940), p. 176. Altered further for BCW.

105. Derives from the *Lutheran Service Book and Hymnal* (1958), p. 8; LBW, p. 117; SLR-1, p. 81, altered with addition of salutation.

106. BCW-PCC, p. 33, altered.

Prayers of the People: Concluding Collects (pp. 123–124)

107. BCP, p. 394; SLR-1, p. 82, altered.

108. This collect dates from the eighth century and derives from the Eastern Orthodox liturgies of St. Basil and St. John Chrysostom. BCP, p. 395; SLR-1, p. 82, altered.

109. WBK, p. 58; SLR-1, p. 82. Altered for BCW.

110. LBW, p. 204; SLR-1, p. 83, altered.

111. The original text was written by George Edward Lynch Cotton, a nineteenth-century Anglican missionary bishop of Calcutta. BCP, pp. 100, 257. SLR-1, p. 83, altered. Biblical allusions: Acts 17:26; Eph. 2:17; Isa. 57:19; Joel 2:28; Acts 2:17. Altered slightly for BCW.

112. SLR-1, p. 84. The first portion of this prayer, "O God . . . perfect freedom," is from a prayer in ASB, p. 59.

113. An adaptation of a collect dating to Archbishop Thomas Cranmer and BCP (1549). BCP, p. 394; SLR-1, p. 84, altered.

114. ASB, p. 60. SLR-1, p. 84, altered.

Great Thanksgiving (pp. 126–156)

For sources of elements shared in common in eucharistic prayers 115–120 and 122, see glossary: Great Thanksgiving; Sursum Corda; preface; Sanctus; anamnesis; institution narrative; memorial acclamation; epiclesis; doxology; Amen.

115. Prepared by Marney Ault Wasserman for BCW using portions of a prayer written by J. A. Ross Mackenzie for SLR-1, pp. 98–101.

116. Revision of the WBK (pp. 34–36) eucharistic prayer, as was SLR-1, pp. 88–97.

Sources of proper prefaces for use with Great Thanksgivings B and C are as follows:

Ordinary Time I—WBK, p. 35, SLR-1, p. 93, altered. Altered further for BCW.

Ordinary Time II—SLR-1, p. 98. Altered for BCW. Original text written by J. A. Ross Mackenzie as part of the Great Thanksgiving in SLR-1, pp. 98–101.

Ordinary Time III—WBK, p. 42; SLR-1, p. 93, altered.

Advent—SLR-1, p. 88. Altered for BCW. Biblical allusion: Amos 5:24.

Christmas—SLR-1, p. 88. Altered for BCW. The line "a new and radiant vision of your glory" comes from the preface for Christmas I in the RS and may be traced to the Gregorian sacramentary. Biblical allusions: John 1:14; Phil. 2:9; Isa. 9:6; 1 Pet. 2:9.

Epiphany—SLR-1, p. 89. Altered for BCW.

Baptism of the Lord—SLR-1, p. 89. Altered for BCW. Biblical allusions: Matt. 3:16, 17; Mark 1:9–11; Luke 3:21, 22; John 1:32; Luke 4:18 (Isa. 61:1).

Transfiguration of the Lord—SLR-1, p. 89. Biblical allusions: Matt. 17:1–5; Mark 9:2–8; Luke 9:28–36; Matt. 5:17.

Lent—SLR-1, p. 90, based on WBK, p. 41. Biblical allusion: Gen. 3:8–10.

Passion/Palm Sunday—SLR-1, p. 90. Altered for BCW. The words "lifted high upon the cross, that the whole world might be drawn to him" are adapted from BCP, p. 379, and are from John 12:32. The words "The tree of defeat became the tree of victory; where life was lost, life has been restored" are adapted from RS (preface for the Triumph of the Cross—Sept. 14), and are from a sermon of Leo the Great (fifth century).

Maundy Thursday—WBK, p. 41; SLR-1, p. 90, altered. Altered further for BCW.

Easter—WBK, p. 41; SLR-1, p. 91, altered. Altered further for BCW. Biblical allusions: John 6:47; Luke 24:30, 31.

Ascension of the Lord—SLR-1, p. 91. Biblical allusions: Phil. 2:9, 10; Matt. 28:20.

Day of Pentecost—SLR-1, p. 91 (based in part on WBK, pp. 41–42) altered. Biblical allusions: Acts 1:8; 2:2–4; John 16:13.

Trinity Sunday—SLR-1, p. 92. Lines 1–5 follow closely the preface for Holy Trinity in RS and date from the middle of the eighth century; Gelasian sacramentary.

All Saints' Day—SLR-1, p. 92. Altered for BCW. Biblical allusions: Heb. 12:1; 1 Pet. 5:4.

Christ the King (or Reign of Christ)—Adapted from the preface for Christ the King in the RS. SLR-1, p. 92.

Baptism—SLR-1, p. 94. Lines 3–5 based on BCP, p. 381. Biblical allusions: Rom. 6:4; John 16:13.

Reaffirmation of the Baptismal Covenant—SLR-1, p. 94. Biblical allusions: John 16:13; Acts 1:8; 1 Pet. 2:9.

Ordination—SLR-1, p. 94. Biblical allusions: Matt. 20:28; Mark 10:45.

Christian Marriage—Written by Marney Ault Wasserman for BCW. Biblical allusion: Gen. 1:26, 27.

Funeral (or Memorial Service)—SLR-1, p. 95. Biblical allusion: Rom. 8:38, 39.

117. BCW (1946), pp. 161–163. SLR-1, pp. 102–105, altered. Altered further for BCW. The institution narrative has been added as an option, and the acclamation has been included. Neither was part of the BCW (1946) text. The prayer included in BCW (1946) is a revision of the eucharistic prayer in BCW (1906), pp. 36–37 and BCW (1932), pp. 66–67. The prayer has its origin in the eucharistic prayer prepared by Archbishop Thomas Cranmer in the BCP (1549), which included elements from the eucharistic prayer in the Latin Mass, the Eastern liturgy of St. Basil, as well as other sources. In Anglican usage, the prayer has passed through numerous revisions across the centuries. It is included in the BCP (1979), Rite I, pp. 333–336. Charles Shields included a revised text of the prayer in his PBCP (pp. 243–246) in 1864. Biblical allusions: At the "offering of ourselves": Rom. 12:1. In the prefaces: *Epiphany*—John 1:14; 8:12; 1 Pet. 2:9. *Lent*—Heb. 4:15; Heb. 2:18; Matt. 16:24 (Mark 8:34; Luke 9:23). *Easter*—John 1:29. *Day of Pentecost*—1 Pet. 2:9.

118. ICEL, Eucharistic Prayer A (1986), altered. Alterations to this text in BCW-PCC, pp. 94–97, were included.

119. This prayer is the work of a group of American scholars, Catholic, Episcopalian, Lutheran, Methodist, and Presbyterian, who in 1974 gathered to draft a prayer that the major American churches might approve. To this end they adapted the eucharistic prayer in the Alexandrine Liturgy of St. Basil (fourth century). The Liturgy of St. Basil was particularly suited, not only because it has ancient roots but because it has appeal in both Eastern and Western traditions and possesses a breadth of scope. Episcopalians have included it in the BCP (1979), pp. 372–375; the Consultation on Church Union included it in *Word Bread Cup* (1978); and the Inter-Lutheran Commission on Worship has authorized its use. It was included in SLR-1, pp. 108–110, and has been slightly altered for BCW. Eucharistic prayer IV in the RS is also an adaptation of the eucharistic prayer in the Alexandrine Liturgy of St. Basil.

120. A translation of the ancient eucharistic prayer of Hippolytus of Rome, dating from about 215. It is the earliest-known eucharistic prayer text, and it therefore has great ecumenical significance. The text is based on a translation

made by the ICEL, *Eucharistic Prayer of Hippolytus: Text for Consultation* (Washington, D.C., 1983). It was included in SLR-1, pp. 106–107, and has been slightly altered for BCW.

121. Written for SLR-1, p. 118 by J. A. Ross Mackenzie. Altered for inclusion in SLR-6, pp. 77–78. Altered further for inclusion in BCW. Biblical allusion: Ps. 96:11.

122. Prepared for BCW from common elements of the other eucharistic prayers in BCW with rubrics based on the Directory for Worship in the *Book of Order* of the Presbyterian Church (U.S.A.), W-2.4003, 4, 5, 6, 7 and W-3.3613.

Great Thanksgiving J (p. 156) draws on the Directory for Worship in the *Book of Order* of the Presbyterian Church (U.S.A.), W-2.4003, 4, 5, 6, 7 and W-3.3613.

Prayer After Communion (pp. 157–158)

123. UMBW, p. 39; SLR-1, p. 129.

124. From the Liturgy of Malabar, fifth century. Cf. [36]. UW (leader's edition), p. 658, altered. A text in BAS, p. 214 (drawn from two post-Communion prayers in ASB, pp. 144–145) seems to be inspired by this prayer from the Malabar liturgy. Found too late for inclusion in the BCW, it is an ideal post-Communion prayer and lends itself well for repeated use prayed in unison by the congregation (as in BAS and ASB):

> Gracious God
> we thank you for feeding us
> with the body and blood of your Son, Jesus Christ.
> May we, who share his body,
> live his risen life;
> we, who drink his cup,
> bring life to others;
> we, whom the Spirit lights,
> give light to the world.
> Keep us firm in the hope you have set before us,
> so that we and all your children shall be free,
> and the whole earth live to praise your name;
> through Christ our Lord.   Amen.

125. RS prayer after Communion for the Fifth Sunday in Ordinary Time. SLR-1, p. 129, altered. Altered further for BCW.

126. This prayer was used by the Westminster divines in 1647. SLDL, p. 23; BCWP, p. 33; SLR-1, p. 130, altered.

127. RS prayer after Communion for the Twenty-second Sunday in Ordinary Time. SLR-1, p. 130, altered.

128. LBW, p. 111 [no. 209]. A revision of a prayer from *The Kingdom, the Power and the Glory* (*The Grey Book*, Part III), 3d ed. (London, 1925), p. 69. SLR-1, p. 136. Biblical allusion: John 15:4–5.

Prayer of Thanksgiving (pp. 158–159)

129. Derives from BCP (1662), continuing to the present in the Anglican tradition. The prayer was composed by Bishop Edward Reynolds (Norwich). Some believe that it was inspired by a private prayer of Queen Elizabeth I dating from 1596. Others have noted the parallels between this prayer and the guidelines for a eucharistic prayer found in the Directory for the Publique Worship of God (Westminster Assembly, 1644). Still others theorize that it may have been composed for use as a eucharistic prayer (or an abbreviated version of a eucharistic prayer) during the period of the Westminster Assembly when the *Book of Common Prayer* was banned. One alteration merits comment. BCW substitutes "to us and all people" for the BCP Rite II (pp. 101, 125) text "to us and to all whom you have made." The BCP text might be taken to imply that some people are not God's creation. The substitution of "to us and all people" is clearer, and preserves the intent of the original prayer "for all thy goodness and loving-kindness to us, and to all men." However, a better alteration might have been "to us and to all living creatures," or, "all living things" in keeping with the environmental concerns of our time. PBCP, pp. 14, 26–27; BCW (1906), p. 110; BCW (1932), p. 20; BCO (1940), pp. 38–39; BCW (1946), p. 22; SLDL, pp. 23–24; BCP, pp. 58–59, 101, 125, SLR-1, p. 123, altered. Biblical allusions: Col. 1:27; Ps. 51:15; Luke 1:75.

130. This prayer was written by J. A. Ross Mackenzie for SLR-1, pp. 123–124 for non-sacramental use. Altered for BCW. It is an adaptation of Great Thanksgiving H [121]. Biblical allusion: Ps. 96:11.

"The peace of God, which passes all understanding . . ." (p. 161). The first portion of this prayer, "The peace of God . . . Christ our Lord," was the blessing in the 1548 Order of the Communion, the first Anglican liturgy after separation from Rome. When the first prayer book was published in 1549, a Trinitarian blessing from *Hermann's Consultation* (see glossary) was added: "And the blessing of God . . . remain with you alway." It is this form that has endured and is included in BCW. BCW (1906), pp. 9, 18; BCW (1932), pp. 9, 19; BCO (1940), pp. 17, 42, 49, 131, 143, 148, 311; BCW (1946), pp. 25, 38, 99, 165; BCWP, p. 35 (first portion only); BCO (1979), pp. 38-39; BCP, p. 339; SLR-1, p. 134, altered.

Chapter 3

Commentary on Resources for the Liturgical Year

ADVENT (PP. 165–177)

Lighting of the Advent Candles (pp. 165–166). Prepared by Peter C. Bower for SLR-7, pp. 61, 62. Slightly revised for BCW.

131. This litany comprises a series of texts called "O Antiphons," so called because each of them begins with the interjection "O." Of uncertain origin, they were in use by the eighth century, and were highly regarded during the Middle Ages. For centuries they have been sung before and after the Magnificat in evening prayer during the final days of Advent, as follows: Dec. 17—O Wisdom; Dec. 18—O Adonai; Dec. 19—O Root of Jesse; Dec. 20—O Key of David; Dec. 21—O Radiant Dawn; Dec. 22— O Ruler of the Nations; Dec. 23—O Emmanuel. The antiphons follow an exact form. Each begins with an invocation to the Messiah, using a title from the Hebrew Scriptures. An amplification of the title follows, using other biblical images. Each antiphon then concludes with a petition that begins with the word "Come" and is based on the invocation. Biblical and apocryphal allusions: *O Wisdom:* Ecclus. (Sirach) 24:3, 5; Wisd. Sol. 8:1;

Isa. 40:3–5. *O Adonai:* Exod. 6:2–3, 12; 3:2; 6:6. *O Root of Jesse:* Isa. 11:1, 10; Rom. 15:12; Isa. 5:15; Hab. 2:3; Heb. 10:37. *O Key of David:* Isa. 22:22 (cf. Rev. 3:7); Isa. 42:7; Ps. 107:14; Luke 1:79. *O Radiant Dawn:* Zech. 6:12; 2 Pet. 1:19; Heb. 1:3; Mal. 4:2; Isa. 9:2; Luke 1:78, 79. *O Ruler of the Nations:* Hag. 2:8; Isa. 28: 16; Eph. 2:14; Gen. 2:7. *O Emmanuel:* Isa. 7:14; 8:8; 33:22. These antiphons are the basis of the well-known Advent hymn "O Come, O Come, Emmanuel" (PH, no. 9). Taken in reverse order, using the first letter of each messianic title, in Latin, these spell ERO CRAS ("I shall be there tomorrow"), becoming Christ's answer to the pleas. Plays on words such as this were popular in the Middle Ages. The text is based on English-language versions in LBW (p. 92–93) and other sources. SLR-5, pp. 297– 298. The concluding prayer was written by Harold M. Daniels for SLR-5, p. 97.

132. Revision by Joseph D. Small III of a prayer in WBK, p. 135.

133. Revision of eucharistic prayer written for SLR-7 (pp. 63–65). Drafted by Donald Wilson Stake and Harold M. Daniels; Marney Ault Wasserman revised it for BCW. For sources of elements shared in common in eucharistic prayers see glossary: Great Thanksgiving; Sursum Corda; preface; Sanctus; anamnesis; institution narrative; memorial acclamation; epiclesis; doxology; Amen.

134. Written for SLR-7 (pp. 65–66) by Donald Wilson Stake. Altered for BCW.

135. Written for SLR-7, p. 66.

136. WBK, p. 136. SLR-7, p. 67, altered. Altered further for BCW.

137. Based on prayer in WBK, p. 135.

138. Written by Horace T. Allen Jr., *A Handbook for the Lectionary* (Philadelphia: Geneva Press, 1980), p. 175. SLR-7, p. 68. Altered for BCW.

139. BCP, p. 211, for Second Sunday in Advent.

140. ICEL, from SBK-92, p. 19, for Second Sunday in Advent. Altered.

141. WBK, p. 136; SLR-7, p. 69, altered. Altered further for BCW.

142. Based on collect for Third Sunday of Advent in BCP from 1662 through the 1928 edition. LBW, p. 122 [3]; SLR-7, p. 69, altered. Altered further for BCW.

143. ICEL, from SBK-92, p. 19, for Third Sunday in Advent.

144. A revision of a prayer in ASB, p. 437, for BAS, p. 272. SLR-7, p. 70, altered. Altered further for BCW.

145. SLR-7, pp. 70–71. Lines 2–4 are adapted from the opening prayer in RS for the Fourth Sunday of Advent. Altered for BCW.

146. ICEL, from SBK-92, pp. 19–20, for Fourth Sunday in Advent. Biblical allusions: Luke 1:68 and 1:41.

CHRISTMAS (PP. 178–190)

147. BCW (1946), p. 293; SLR-7, p. 73, altered.

148. Based on a litany from the daily office of the Taizé Community, PG, pp. 58–60, and TO, pp. 70, 72; SLR-5, pp. 300–301. Biblical allusions: John 1:14; Ps. 24:7–10; Mal. 4:2; Isa. 9:6; Ps. 23; John 10:11, 14; 1 Cor. 1:24, 30; John 14:6.

149. Traditional Byzantine Christmas prayer. Taken from UMBW, p. 271.

150. Based on a litany from the daily office of the Taizé Community, PG, pp. 76–77; and TO, pp. 71, 101–102. SLR-5, pp. 299–300. Altered further for BCW. Biblical allusion: Ps. 98:3, 4.

151. LH (December 29); SLR-5, p. 110, altered. Altered further for BCW.

152. Written for BCW by Joseph D. Small III, incorporating phrases from a prayer in WBK, p. 137.

153. Revision of eucharistic prayer written for SLR-7, pp. 74–76. Donald Wilson Stake and Harold M. Daniels drafted SLR-7 text; Marney Ault Wasserman revised it for BCW. For elements shared in common with other eucharistic prayers, see glossary: Great Thanksgiving; Sursum Corda; preface; anamnesis, institutional narrative; memorial acclamation; epiclesis; doxology; Amen.

154. Prayer written by Donald Wilson Stake for SLR-7, pp. 76-77. Altered for BCW.

155. WBK, p. 137; SLR-7, p. 77, altered. Slight alteration in doxological ending for BCW.

156. ICEL, *Second Progress Report on the Revision of the Roman Missal,* p. 53. Biblical allusion: Luke 2:12.

157. BCWP, pp. 117–118; WBK, p. 136 altered; SLR-7, p. 78. Altered further for BCW.

158. WBK, p. 136; SLR-7, p. 78, altered. Altered further for BCW.

159. WBK, p. 137; SLR-7, p. 79, altered using GA74, p. 393. Altered further for BCW.

160. ICEL, from SBK-92, p. 43.

161. This collect was composed for BCP (1549). BCW (1906), p. 122; BCW (1932), p. 162; BCO, p. 237; BCW (1946), p. 297; BCO (1979), p. 136; BCP, p. 213, altered.

162. This prayer dates to the Leonine sacramentary; it was also included in the Gelasian and Gregorian sacramentaries. Line 6 parallels words attributed to Pope Leo the Great (fifth century): "The Son of God became the Son of Man that the sons of men might become the sons of God." BCP, p. 214; SLR-7, p. 80, altered.

163. BAS, p. 276; SLR-7, p. 80.

164. ASB, p. 450, altered.

165. Dates from the Gregorian sacramentary. BCP (1928), p. 106, Collect for Second Sunday after Christmas. SLR-7, p. 81, altered using changes to the text of this collect in LBW, p. 124 [9]. Altered further for BCW.

166. WBK, p. 138. SLR-7, p. 81, altered. Altered further for BCW. Biblical allusion: Ps. 90:4.

EPIPHANY—JANUARY 6 (PP. 191–197)

167. ICEL, from SBK-92, p. 44. Altered.

168. ASB, p. 460. SLR-7, p. 85, altered. Altered further for BCW.

169. This collect is from the Latin sacramentaries, fifth–seventh centuries. BCW (1946), p. 298; UMBW, p. 296, altered.

170. Based on a litany from the daily office of the Taizé Community (PG, p. 85, and TO, pp. 100, 108). Biblical allusion: Ps. 98:3, 4. SLR-5, pp. 303–304.

171. From the daily office of the Taizé Community (PG, p. 83; TO, p. 106). SLR-5, pp. 118–119, altered.

172. Written for BCW by Harold M. Daniels, incorporating phrases from prayer in WBK, p. 139.

173. Revision of eucharistic prayer written for SLR-7 (pp. 86–88). Donald Wilson Stake and Harold M. Daniels drafted SLR-7 text; Marney Ault Wasserman revised it for BCW. For sources of elements shared in common in eucharistic prayers, see glossary: Great Thanksgiving; Sursum Corda; preface; Sanctus; anamnesis; institution narrative; memorial acclamation; epiclesis; doxology; Amen.

174. Prayer written by Donald Wilson Stake for SLR-7, p. 89. Slight alteration in doxological ending for BCW.

BAPTISM OF THE LORD (PP. 198–204)

175. Drafted for the BCP by Charles M. Guilbert, based on Roman collects for the day in the RS. BCP, p. 214, altered.

176. WBK, p. 140; SLR-7, p. 93, altered using GA74. Doxological ending added in BCW.

177. Based on a litany from the daily office of the Taizé Community (PG, p. 82, and TO, p. 108–109). SLR-5, pp. 302–303.

178. Based on ASB, p. 463, and LH (Baptism of the Lord); SLR-5, p. 122. Expanded doxological ending added for BCW.

179. A prayer written for BCW by Joseph D. Small III based on prayer in SLR-7, p. 94 written by Judith Kolwicz.

180. Revision of eucharistic prayer written for SLR-7 (pp. 94–96). Donald Wilson Stake and Harold M. Daniels drafted the SLR-7 text; Marney Ault Wasserman revised it for BCW. For sources of elements shared in common in eucharistic prayers, see glossary: Great Thanksgiving; Sursum Corda; preface; Sanctus; anamnesis; institution narrative; memorial acclamation; epiclesis; doxology; Amen.

181. Prayer written by Donald Wilson Stake for SLR-7, p. 97. Slight alteration in doxological ending for BCW.

SUNDAYS BETWEEN BAPTISM OF THE LORD AND TRANSFIGURATION OF THE LORD (PP. 205–213)

182. BAS, p. 349. SLR-7, pp. 98–99.

183. NZBB, p. 623, altered.

184. WBK, p. 140; SLR-7, p. 99. Altered for BCW.

185. BAS, p. 351; SLR-7, p. 100.

186. UW (leader's edition), p. 233; SLR-7, p. 100; altered. Doxological ending added for BCW.

187. LBW, p. 125 [13]; SLR-7, p. 100, altered. Altered further for BCW.

188. BAS, p. 352; SLR-7, p. 101.

189. UW (leader's edition), p. 234; SLR-7, p. 102, altered. Altered further for BCW.

190. SLR-7, pp. 101–102, altered.

191. WBK, p. 140; SLR-7, p. 103, altered. Doxological ending added in BCW.

192. MR, translated by Fr. Peter Scagnelli. Taken from UW (leader's edition), p. 162. SLR-7, p. 103, altered.

193. ICEL, from SBK-92, p. 72, for Fifth Sunday in Ordinary Time.

194. WBK, p. 141; SLR-7, p. 104. Altered for BCW.

195. BAS, p. 355; SLR-7, p. 104.

196. SLR-7, pp. 104–105. Altered for BCW.

197. BAS, p. 356; SLR-7, p. 105. Altered for BCW.

198. Written for BCP (1549). PBCP, p. 83; BCO (1940), p. 273; BCW (1946), p. 341; BCP, p. 216; SLR-7, p. 248, altered. Altered for BCW. Biblical allusions: 1 Cor. 13:1–3; Col. 3:14.

199. BAS, p. 358; SLR-7, p. 106. Altered for BCW.

200. NZBB, p. 608. Altered.

TRANSFIGURATION OF THE LORD (PP. 214–219)

201. Translation of a Latin collect that is believed to date from the fifteenth century and may have been written by Pope Calixtus III (1455-1458). In the RS it is assigned to the Transfiguration (Aug. 6). LBW, p. 128 [21]; SLR-7, p. 108, altered. Minor alteration for BCW.

202. Collect written by William Reed Huntington for the 1892 *Book of Common Prayer* (the Feast of Transfiguration—Aug. 6). BCP, p. 217; SLR-7, pp. 108–109, altered. Altered further for BCW. The prayer is based on the Lukan account of the transfiguration (Luke 9:28–36). It is unfortunate that the SLR-7 and BCW texts substitute "Give us faith to perceive his glory, that being strengthened by his grace we may . . ." for the BCP lines, which more fully reflect the Lukan account (e.g., Luke 8:23; 9:29, 32: "Grant to us that we, beholding by faith the light of his countenance, may be strengthened to bear our cross, and . . ." A better reading would be "Give us faith to perceive his glory, that we may be strengthened to bear our cross, and . . ." The parallelism of Christ's cross (line three) and our cross would thereby strengthen the text.

203. MR, translated by Fr. Peter Scagnelli, from SBK-92, p. 98 altered.

204. Revision, by Joseph D. Small III, of a prayer written by Judith Kolwicz for SLR-7, p. 109.

205. Revision of eucharistic prayer written for SLR-7 (pp. 109–111). Donald

Wilson Stake and Harold M. Daniels drafted SLR-7 text; Marney Ault Wasserman revised it for BCW. For sources of elements shared in common in eucharistic prayers, see glossary: Great Thanksgiving; Sursum Corda; preface; Sanctus; anamnesis; institution narrative; memorial acclamation; epiclesis; doxology; Amen.

206.   Prayer written for SLR-7, pp. 111–112. Biblical allusions: Ps. 104:1, 2; John 3:16; Col. 1:15, 16.

ASH WEDNESDAY (PP. 220–234)

207.   Prayer written by Peter C. Bower for SLR-7, p. 116. Doxology added in BCW.

208.   Prayer written by Thomas Cranmer for the BCP (1549). PBCP, p. 86; BCP, pp. 217, 264; SLR-7, p. 117, altered (alterations influenced by version of text in LBW, p. 128 [22]). Doxology altered in BCW. The opening clause is based on Wisd. Sol. 11:24, 25, 27, which was the introit for Ash Wednesday in the Roman missal in the sixteenth century. The petition is based on Ps. 51:10.

"Friends in Christ . . ." (pp. 223–224). BAS, p. 281–282; SLR-7, p. 118 altered. Altered further for BCW.

209.   BCP, pp. 267–268, altered. The litany was drafted by Massey H. Shepherd Jr. for BCP. The litany begins with petitions from prayers of confession [49] (Service for the Lord's Day) and [503] (Prayer at the Close of Day). The concluding words of the litany immediately preceding the imposition of ashes are based on Ps. 85:4 and Ps. 69:16. The text following the imposition of ashes in the BCW is included as part of the litany in the BCP (pp. 268–269) and forms its conclusion. The insertion of the imposition of ashes into the litany follows the practice in the LBW, pp. 129–131. Along with Psalm 51 this litany forms the confession of sin at the beginning of Lent. Since Lent is a time of penitence, it is traditional not to pronounce a declaration of forgiveness (in this service and throughout Lent) until the Eucharist is celebrated on Maundy Thursday. The declaration of forgiveness before receiving Communion on Maundy Thursday thus marks the conclusion of the weeks of preparation before celebrating the Triduum, the Three Days (Maundy Thursday, Good Friday, and the Great Vigil of Easter).

210.   Prayer written by Howard E. Galley for the BCP, p. 265. SLR-7, pp. 118–119, altered. Altered further for BCW.

"Remember that you are dust . . ." (p. 227). The imposition of ashes is a sign both of penitence and of human mortality, and is the basis for the title: Ash

Wednesday. In ancient Judaism, ashes were used as a sign of penitence and of mourning. The imposition of ashes on the heads of the faithful at the beginning of Lent dates from at least the eleventh century. In the Roman Catholic rite, the words "Turn away from sin and be faithful to the gospel" (Mark 1:15) are said as the ashes are administered. As a sign of penitence, these words look toward Lent as a season of repentance and renewal. The Roman rite also provides an alternative text based on Gen. 3:19, "Remember, man, you are dust and to dust you will return." The BCW, the LBW, and the BCP, only provide one text for the imposition, "Remember that you are dust, and to dust you shall return." In these words we are reminded of the fragility of human life, thus prompting us to sift the priorities by which we live.

"Accomplish in us . . ." (p. 227). BCP, pp. 268–269; LBW, p. 131. These words conclude the confession. In the BCP and LBW these words are followed by a prayer which is an abbreviation of a prayer from the BCP (1552) that incorporated phrases from Calvin's liturgy, perhaps taken from Bucer.

211. Revision of eucharistic prayer written for SLR-7 (pp. 120–122). Donald Wilson Stake and Harold M. Daniels drafted the SLR-7 text; Marney Ault Wasserman revised it for BCW. For sources of elements shared in common in eucharistic prayers, see glossary: Great Thanksgiving; Sursum Corda; preface; Sanctus; anamnesis; institution narrative; memorial acclamation; epiclesis; doxology; Amen.

"The gifts of God for the people of God" (p. 233). See glosssary: Sancta Sanctis.

"Jesus, Lamb of God," and "Lamb of God . . ." (p. 233). See glossary: Agnus Dei.

"The body of Christ, given for you" and "The blood of Christ, shed for you" (p. 233). See notes following prayer [59].

212. BAS, p. 286; SLR-7, p. 124.

"Go in peace . . ." (p. 234). BCP, p. 366.

LENT (PP. 235–250)

213. Based on a litany from the daily office of the Taizé Community (PG, p. 90, and TO, p. 131). SLR-5, pp. 308–309. The people's petitions in the BCW are included in the leader's part in the Taizé office, the people's response after each of the petitions being: "Hear us, Lord of glory."

214. Prayer based on two prayers written for SLR-5, pp. 134, 135–136. Biblical allusion: John 14:6.

215. Prayer by Joseph D. Small III, based on prayers in SLR-7, p. 128, and WBK, p. 142.

216. Written by Donald Wilson Stake for SLR-5, p. 306.

217. LH (alternative prayer for Fourth Sunday in Lent); SLR-5, p. 147, altered. Biblical allusion: 1 Cor. 13:13.

218. Revision of eucharistic prayer written for SLR-7 (pp. 128–131). Donald Wilson Stake and Harold M. Daniels drafted SLR-7 text; Marney Ault Wasserman revised it for BCW. For sources of elements shared in common in eucharistic prayers, see glossary: Great Thanksgiving; Sursum Corda; preface; Sanctus; anamnesis; institution narrative; memorial acclamation; epiclesis; doxology; Amen.

219. Written by Donald Wilson Stake for SLR-7, p. 131. Altered for BCW.

220. Written by Donald Wilson Stake for SLR-7, pp. 131–132 Altered for BCW.

221. BAS, pp. 286–287; SLR-7, p. 133. Altered for BCW.

222. LBW, p. 131 [24]; SLR-7, p. 133, altered.

223. ICEL. *Second Progress Report on the Revision of the Roman Missal,* p. 53, altered.

224. UW (leader's edition), p. 241; SLR-7, p. 134, altered. Altered further for BCW. Biblical allusion: Ps. 145:8.

225. UW (leader's edition), p. 170; SLR-7, p. 135, altered. Doxological ending added for BCW.

226. NZBB, p. 622, altered.

227. NZBB, p. 567. Doxological ending added.

228. LBW, p. 133 [28]; SLR-7, pp. 135–136, altered.

229. MR, translated by Fr. Peter Scagnelli. Taken from SBK-92, p. 98, altered.

230. A prayer written by Diane Karay Tripp for BCW. Biblical allusions: Heb. 5:14; John 8:12.

231. A prayer written by Harold M. Daniels for BCW. Following an allusion to Ps. 103:8, the prayer draws inspiration from the Gospel reading for Year C: Luke 15:1–3, 11b–32.

232. LBW, p. 133 [30], altered.

233. NZPB, p. 572, altered.

234. BAS, p. 293; SLR-7, p. 138. Doxology added in BCW.

PASSION/PALM SUNDAY (PP. 251–267)

235. BCP, p. 271, which is based in part on Roman prayers. SLR-7, pp. 141–142, altered. Altered further for BCW.

236. BW-UCC, pp. 187–188; SLR-7, p. 142. Biblical allusions: 2 Cor. 5:1; Rev. 21:2.

Procession into the Church. The tradition of a procession with palms originated in Jerusalem during the fourth century. The oldest liturgical texts portrayed the branches as symbols of hope, life, and victory. Bishop Theodulph of Orleans (ca. 750–821), while imprisoned on charges of conspiring against the king, composed "All Glory, Laud, and Honor" (PH, no. 88) to be sung in the procession. John Mason Neale, the nineteenth-century translator of the hymn as we know it, noted concerning the hymn that another verse was usually sung until the seventeenth century (understandably not surviving): "Be thou, O Lord, the Rider, / And we the little ass, / That to God's Holy City / Together we may pass."

237. The prayer derives from a collect in the Gelasian and Gregorian sacramentaries and is inspired by the second reading (Phil. 2:5–11), a reading appointed for the day in the earliest Roman lectionary. The second line is based on an addition to the prayer by Cranmer, "of thy tender love for mankind." BCP, p. 219; BCW (1906), p. 118; BCW (1932), p. 163; SLR-7, p. 143, altered incorporating some of the revisions of this prayer in LBW, p. 134 [31].

238. From *Alternative Collects, 1985,* The Anglican Church of Australia. Taken from UW (leader's edition), p. 246; SLR-7, p. 143, altered. Inspired by second reading, Phil. 2:5–11.

239. BW-UCC, p. 190; SLR-7, p. 144, altered.

240. Revision of eucharistic prayer written for SLR-7, pp. 145–148. Donald Wilson Stake and Harold M. Daniels drafted SLR-7 text; Marney Ault Wasserman revised it for BCW. For sources of elements shared in common in eucharistic prayers, see glossary: Great Thanksgiving; Sursum Corda; preface; Sanctus; anamnesis; institution narrative; memorial acclamation; epiclesis; doxology; Amen.

"The gifts of God for the people of God" (p. 261). See glosssary: Sancta Sanctis.

"The body of Christ, given for you" and "The blood of Christ, shed for you" (p. 261). See notes following prayer [59].

"Jesus, Lamb of God" (p. 262). See glossary: Agnus Dei.

241. BAS, p. 300; SLR-7, p. 150.

242. WBK, p. 147; SLR-7, p. 151, altered. Altered further for BCW.

"The peace of God . . ." (pp. 263, 265). See note following prayer [130].

"Go in peace . . ." (pp. 263, 265). BCP, p. 366.

243. Based on a litany from the Taizé Daily Office appointed for Maundy Thursday noon (PG, pp. 145–146); SLR-5, pp. 310–311, altered. The major alteration is that the people's responses in the BCW version are included in the leader's part in the Taizé office. In the Taizé litany, the people respond to each petition saying: "O Christ, we adore you." The text of the "Jesus, Lamb of God . . ." is an ELLC alternative text for the Agnus Dei. See glossary: Agnus Dei.

244. Written for SLR 5, p. 149. This prayer is identical to prayer 486.

MAUNDY THURSDAY (PP. 268–279)

"On this day . . ." (p. 269). BAS, p. 304; SLR-7, p. 160. Altered for BCW.

245. BAS, p. 307, an edited version of LBW [37], pp. 136–137; SLR-7, pp. 160–161. Biblical allusion: John 13:34. The word "Maundy" (Old French *mande*) is from the Latin *Mandatum novum,* the new commandment of John 13:34. The verse used as the call to worship makes this clear.

246. BCWP, p. 122; WBK, p. 146; SLR-7, p. 161. Altered for BCW.

247. Revision, by Joseph D. Small III, of prayer of confession in WBK, p. 146.

"The mercy of the Lord . . ." (p. 272). SLR-1, p. 53, based on declarations of pardon contained in PBCP, p. 241; BCW (1906), p. 29; BCW (1932), p. 51; BCW (1946), pp. 118, 157, 294, 305; SLDL, p. 15; BCWP, p. 23; BCP, pp. 80, 117, 353. As noted above, at Ash Wednesday, the declaration of forgiveness traditionally is postponed during Lent until it is said in the Maundy Thursday Eucharist, thus bringing to a close the time of preparation, and beginning the Triduum, the Three Days.

Footwashing. The washing of feet in the Maundy Thursday liturgy has its origins as a simple act of humility and servanthood, reflecting John 13:2b–17. It has been practiced in the church since at least the fourth century. The hymn "Where Charity and Love Prevail" (WBK-SH, no. 641) is traditionally sung during the washing. The hymn is a translation of a Latin antiphon based on 1 John, and associated with the washing of feet.

248. Revision of eucharistic prayer written for SLR-7, pp. 165–167. Donald Wilson Stake and Harold M. Daniels drafted SLR-7 text; Marney Ault Wasserman revised it for BCW. For sources of elements shared in common in eucharistic prayers, see glossary: Great Thanksgiving; Sursum Corda;

preface; Sanctus; anamnesis; institution narrative; memorial acclamation; epiclesis; doxology; Amen.

"The gifts of God for the people of God" (p. 278). See glosssary: Sancta Sanctis.

"The body of Christ, given for you" and "The blood of Christ, shed for you" (p. 278). See notes following prayer [59].

"Jesus, Lamb of God" (pp. 278–279). See glossary: Agnus Dei.

249. BAS, p. 304; SLR-7, p. 169, altered.

Stripping of the Church (p. 279). Not only does this action serve a utilitarian purpose, facilitating the cleaning of linens, paraments, Communion vessels, table, and fixtures, but the stark, unadorned space remaining bare until the Easter Vigil dramatically depicts the desolation following Jesus' abandonment in Gethsemane, the night before his crucifixion.

GOOD FRIDAY (PP. 280–293)

250. BCWP, p. 122; WBK, p. 147; SLR-7, pp. 172–173, altered.

251. This prayer is from the Gregorian sacramentary, where it was used at the end of Mass on Wednesday of Holy Week. It was included in Gallican daily office liturgies for Maundy Thursday, Good Friday, or Holy Saturday. The Sarum missal included it as a post-Communion prayer on Good Friday. BCP, p. 276; SLR-7, p. 173, altered.

252. The Solemn Intercessions derive from the Gelasian sacramentary and were also included in the Gregorian sacramentary. The prayer form is a bidding prayer. These intercessions are a distinctive and important feature of the Good Friday liturgy, Roman Catholic, Episcopal, and Lutheran, as well as the rite in the BCW. The intercessions reach out to embrace the whole church, all nations and peoples of the earth, all who suffer and all who sorrow, etc. Someone has commented that these prayers reach out as far as the arms of the cross in an all-encompassing embrace. BCP, pp. 277–280; SLR-7, pp. 173–177, altered. In the invitation to prayer, John 3:16–18 is paraphrased. Fourth collect. Biblical allusion: John 10:16. The concluding collect (from RS where it follows the Ez. 36 reading in the Easter Vigil) is altered in BCW.[6]

"Behold the cross . . ." (p. 287). This act was included in a Good Friday rite in the Gelasian sacramentary. SLR-7, p. 178. Based on texts in LBW, p. 142; BAS, p. 313; and RS (Good Friday).

Solemn Reproaches of the Cross (pp. 288–289). The Solemn Reproaches are of ancient origin, perhaps of Byzantine origin. Traces of it have been found dating from the seventh century. The first three stanzas of this moving hymn existed in the late ninth and early tenth centuries, the remaining stanzas are not found until the eleventh century. Philip Pfatteicher describes this as a "powerful and moving hymn in which the church hears the disappointed voice of Christ as an anguished parent."[7] RS; SLR-7, pp. 178–181, altered. Alterations were informed by HCY, pp. 187-189, a text acceptable to the Anti-Defamation League of B'nai B'rith. This revised text overcomes the problems with earlier texts regarded by many as anti-Semitic.

"Holy God, Holy and mighty . . ." See glossary: Trisagion.

253. A litany from the Taizé Daily Office, PG, p. 123. SLR-5, pp. 311–312, altered. For notes on text "Jesus, Lamb of God . . . ," see glossary: Agnus Dei.

THE GREAT VIGIL OF EASTER (PP. 294–314)

"Sisters and brothers in Christ . . ." (pp. 297–298). SLR-7, p. 184. First portion adapted from RS.

254. SLR-7, p. 185, based on prayers in RS; and BAS, p. 322.

"Rejoice, heavenly powers! . . ." RS; SLR-7, pp. 186–190, altered. The proclamation, called the Exsultet (from its opening Latin word) is very ancient. It draws from the thought of Ambrose and Augustine of Hippo, and even older texts. The form in use today is believed to be of Gallican liturgical origin, dating from the beginning of the seventh century. It is one of the richest treasures of the liturgy of the Western church.[8]

"Friends in Christ . . ." SLR-7, p. 190, based on BAS, p. 325.

255. RS (Easter Vigil, collect for creation reading); BAS, p. 325; SLR-7, p. 191.

256. BCP, p. 289; SLR-7, p. 191, altered. Alteration based on BAS, p. 289, revision of text.

257. UMBW, p. 374; SLR-7, p. 192, altered.

258. Based on a prayer in the Gelasian sacramentary and Sarum missal associated with this reading. BCP, p. 289; LBW, p. 148 [54]; BAS, p. 326; SLR-7, p. 192, altered.

259. BCP, p. 290 (based on a collect of the Rev. Dr. H. Boone Porter); SLR-7, p. 193, altered.

260. Written for SLR-7, p. 193.

261. UMBW, p. 375; SLR-7, p. 194, altered.

262. BCP, p. 291 (based on a collect by the Rev. Dr. H. Boone Porter); SLR-7, p. 194 (the BAS, p. 328, version of the text). The prayer alludes to the seal of Baptism.

263. Derives from the Gelasian sacramentary. RS; SLR-7, p. 195, altered. Altered further for BCW. Same prayer as the concluding collect of [252], without the expanded doxological ending.

264. BAS, p. 329; SLR-7, p. 195.

"Friends, this is the joyful feast . . ." (p. 310). See note after [57].

"The gifts of God for the people of God" (p. 313). See glossary: Sancta Sanctis.

"The body of Christ, the bread of heaven" and "The blood of Christ, the cup of salvation" (p. 313). See notes following prayer [59].

265. Written for SLR-7, p. 202.

EASTER SUNDAY THROUGH SEVENTH SUNDAY OF EASTER (PP. 315–337)

266. BCW (1946), p. 304; SLR-7, p. 204, altered. Altered further for BCW.

267. Based on an Easter litany from the Taizé Daily Office (PG, pp. 171–172), SLR-5, pp. 313–314. The people's petitions in the BCW are included in the leader's portion in the Taizé office, the people's response after each petition being "Hear us, Lord of glory."

268. RS and LH (alternative prayer for Second Sunday of Easter); SLR-7, p. 211, altered. Doxology added for BCW.

269. Based on an Easter litany from the Taizé Daily Office (TO, p. 232); SLR-5, pp. 314–315, altered.

270. Derives from the Gregorian sacramentary, also included in the Sarum rite. BCP, p. 222; SLR-7, pp. 209–210, altered (incorporating some alterations in LBW, p. 153 [62] version of text). Altered further for BCW.

271. Written for BCW.

272. Revision of eucharistic prayer written for SLR-7, pp. 204–207. Donald Wilson Stake and Harold M. Daniels drafted SLR-7 text; Marney Ault Wasserman revised it for BCW. For sources of elements shared in common in eucharistic prayers, see glossary: Great Thanksgiving; Sursum Corda; preface; Sanctus; anamnesis; institution narrative; memorial acclamation; epiclesis; doxology; Amen.

273. Written for SLR-7, pp. 207–208, by Donald Wilson Stake. Altered for BCW.

274. BCW (1946), p. 26; SLR-7, p. 208, altered.

275. WBK, p. 148; SLR-7, p. 208. Biblical allusion: Rom. 8:38–39.

276. BAS, p. 335; SLR-7, p. 209, altered; NZPB, p. 592, altered, combining elements from each version.

277. Prayer written by Henry van Dyke for BCW (1932), pp. 166–167; BCW (1946), p. 309, altered.

278. Collect from MR (in SBK-92, p. 157), rewritten by Diane Karay Tripp.

279. SLR-5, p. 172. Altered for BCW by adding doxological ending. Original source uncertain. Biblical allusions: Gospel readings, Years ABC.

280. ICEL, in SBK-92, p. 157. Altered for BCW. Biblical allusions: Gospel readings, Years ABC.

281. Prayer written by Diane Karay Tripp for BCW. Biblical allusions: Gospel readings, Years ABC.

282. BAS, p. 336; SLR-7, p. 211. Biblical allusions: Gospel readings, Years ABC.

283. Prayer by Janet Morley, *All Desires Known* (London: Movement for the Ordination of Women, 1988), p. 17. Biblical allusions: Gospel readings, Years ABC. The ending "To you belong honor and glory forever and ever" was added. Following reception of permission from the publisher to include this prayer with the ending, the author asked that the addition be removed, regarding it as superfluous liturgical verbage. The addition was deleted in the software edition of the BCW and subsequent printings of the BCW. Apart from theological reasons for including doxological endings, they assist people to know when to respond with their assent of "Amen." See glossary: collect; prayer of the day.

284. NZPB, p. 599. Doxological ending added.

285. Prayer written by James F. White. UMBW, p. 390 [394].

286. Derives from the Gelasian sacramentary and was included in the Sarum rite. BCP, p. 222, altered.

287. Collect prepared for BCP (1928) by the Rev. Dr. John W. Suter Sr. BCP, pp. 223, 224; SLR-7, p. 212, altered. Altered further for BCW. Biblical allusion: Luke 24:35.

288. LBW, p. 155 [67]; SLR-7, p. 212. Biblical allusions: Heb. 13:20–21: Gospel readings, Years ABC.

289. WBK, p. 149; SLR-7, pp. 212–213, altered. Doxology added in BCW. Biblical allusions: Gospel readings, Years ABC.

290. NZPB, p. 596, altered. Biblical allusions: Gospel readings, Years ABC.

291. BAS, p. 340. SLR-7, pp. 213–214. Altered for BCW. Biblical allusions: John 14:6 (Gospel, Year A); John 13:34 (Gospel, Year C).

292. Derives from Gelasian and Gregorian sacramentaries; English translation from Cranmer's BCP (1549). LBW, p. 155 [69]; SLR-7, p. 214.

293. ICEL, in SBK-92, p. 158. Fifth Sunday of Easter.

294. Prayer found in several Gallican liturgies. A version appeared in Cranmer's BCP (1549). PBCP, p. 186; BCO, p. 112; BCW (1946), p. 41; BCP, p. 225; SLR-7, p. 240, altered. Altered further for BCW. Biblical allusion: 1 Cor. 2:9.

295. NZPB, p. 537, altered. Biblical allusion: Rom. 6:3–5.

296. ICEL in SBK-92, p. 158, altered. Biblical allusions: Gospel, Years AC (John 14); Col. 1:18.

ASCENSION OF THE LORD (PP. 332–335)

297. ICEL in SBK-92, p. 158. Biblical allusions: Second reading; Gospel, Years ABC; Col. 1:18.

298. BAS, p. 343. SLR-7, p. 216. Altered for BCW.

299. NZPB, p. 601, altered.

300. Based on a litany in the daily office of the Taizé Community (PG, pp. 211–212). SLR-5, p. 316.

301. SLR-5, p. 170. Original source uncertain. Biblical allusions: John 14:16–17; 15:26. "Amen" is missing from end of prayer in BCW, but should be added.

302. WBK, p. 150; SLR-7, p. 217, altered. Altered further for BCW.

303. Written by Donald Wilson Stake for SLR-7, pp. 217–218.

304. Written for SLR-7, p. 218, with lines 8–10 based on prayer in WBK, p. 150. Altered for BCW.

305. WBK, p. 149, altered.

306. Dates to the earliest of the sacramentaries, the Leonine. BCW (1946), p. 309. BCP, p. 226, altered. Biblical allusions: Eph. 4:10; Matt. 28:20.

307. Based on a prayer by Archbishop William Temple. BCP, p. 255, altered. Biblical allusion: Gospel, Year C (John 17:20–21).

DAY OF PENTECOST (PP. 338–347)

308. NZPB, p. 541, altered.

309. NZPB, p. 605, altered.

310. LBW, p. 158 [76]; SLR-7, p. 221, altered. Altered further for BCW. Biblical allusions: First reading (Acts), Years ABC; Genesis reading, Year C.

311. SBK-92, p. 161, altered. Biblical allusions: Exod. 19:16, 18–20:1–21; Acts 2:2–3; and First reading (Acts).

312. NZPB, p. 541.

313. Prepared by Harold M. Daniels for the liturgy at the 192nd General Assembly of the United Presbyterian Church in the U.S.A., and the 120th General Assembly of the Presbyterian Church in the U.S., meeting jointly in Detroit, Michigan in 1980. The assemblies convened in the days immediately following Pentecost Sunday. In their liturgies, they were thus mindful of the day of Pentecost of Acts 2. It is of special significance that at this same General Assembly the United Presbyterians initiated the development of the BCW. In its action, the assembly expressed the fervent hope that the new service book might be "an instrument for the renewal of the church at its life-giving center." The BCW was thus envisioned in the context of a meeting that gave particular attention to praying for a fresh outpouring of the Spirit, the source of all renewal. SLR-7, pp. 221–222. Biblical allusions: Gen. 1:1–2; 2:7, 19; Acts 2:3; 1 Cor. 3:16; Rom. 8:26–27; Isa. 11:2.

314. LH (Pentecost); SLR-5, p. 183, altered; SLR-7, p. 222. Used in the liturgy at the 1980 joint meeting of the General Assemblies (see note for [313]). Biblical allusions: Day of Pentecost, First reading (Acts), Years ABC.

315. Prepared by Harold M. Daniels for the liturgy at the 192nd General Assembly of the United Presbyterian Church in the U.S.A. and the 120th General Assembly of the Presbyterian Church in the U.S., meeting jointly in Detroit, Michigan, in 1980 (see note for [313]). SLR-5, pp. 317–318; SLR-7, pp. 223–224. Biblical allusions: Gen. 2:7; Acts 2:3.

316. LBW, p. 158 [75], altered.

317. From *Praise Him* (Notre Dame, Ind.: Ave Maria Press, 1973), pp. 154–155; SLR-5, pp. 318–319, altered with the addition of lines 1 and 2. Biblical allusion: Isa. 11:2.

318. SLR-5, p. 186. Used at the 1980 joint meeting of the General Assemblies to conclude the litany [313]. (See note at [313] above.)

319. Prayer written for BCW by Joseph D. Small III, incorporating phrases from WBK, p. 152.

320. Revision of eucharistic prayer written for SLR-7, pp. 224–227. Donald Wilson Stake and Harold M. Daniels drafted SLR-7 text; Marney Ault Wasserman revised it for BCW. For sources of elements shared in common in eucharistic prayers, see glossary: Great Thanksgiving; Sursum Corda; preface; Sanctus; anamnesis; institution narrative; memorial acclamation; epiclesis; doxology; Amen.

321. NZPB, p. 542, altered.

322. Written by Donald Wilson Stake for SLR-7, p. 227. Doxology altered for BCW.

TRINITY SUNDAY (PP. 348–353)

323. BCW (1946), p. 311, altered.

324. Derives from late medieval prayers. BCP, p. 228; SLR-7, pp. 231–232, altered. Altered further for BCW.

325. BAS, p. 346; SLR-7, p. 231.

326. Written for BCW by Joseph D. Small III.

327. Revision of eucharistic prayer written for SLR-7, pp. 233–235. Donald Wilson Stake and Harold M. Daniels drafted SLR-7 text; Marney Ault Wasserman revised it for BCW. For sources of elements shared in common in eucharistic prayers, see glossary: Great Thanksgiving; Sursum Corda; preface; Sanctus; anamnesis; institution narrative; memorial acclamation; epiclesis; doxology; Amen.

328. SLR-7, p. 235.

SUNDAYS BETWEEN TRINITY SUNDAY AND CHRIST THE KING (PP. 354–393)

329. LBW, p. 159 [79]; SLR-7, p. 236, altered.

330. Composed for BCP (1549). PBCP, p. 156; BCP, pp. 167, 219; Altered for BCW, using alterations in NZPB, p. 640.

331. BAS, p. 360; SLR-7, p. 237.

332. NZPB, p. 623. Doxology added.

333. NZPB, p. 612, altered. (Cf. SLR-7, p. 238, which was taken from BAS, p. 362.)

334. Written for BCW.

335. NZPB, p. 623, altered.

336. Ignatius of Loyola (1491–1556). BCW (1932), p. 198; BCO, p. 260; BCW (1946), p. 97, altered.

337. MR, translated by Fr. Peter Scagnelli. Taken from UW (leader's edition), p. 201. SLR-7, p. 239, altered.

338. LBW, p. 160 [82]; SLR-7, p. 239, doxological ending added. Biblical allusion: Gospel reading, Year B.

339. ICEL, in SBK-92, p. 205, altered.

340. NZPB, p. 625. Doxology added.

341. BAS, p. 366. SLR-7, p. 241.

342. Written for BCW.

343. From *The Sunday Missal,* new edition, William Collins Publishers Ltd., 1982; taken from UW (leader's edition), p. 268, altered. Doxological ending added.

344. LBW, p. 162 [85]; SLR-7, p. 242. Doxology added in BCW. Biblical allusion: Gospel reading, Year A.

345. BAS, p. 365; SLR-7, p. 242, altered. Biblical allusion: Gospel reading, Year C (Luke 10:27).

346. BAS, p. 369; SLR-7, p. 243, altered.

347. Prayer by Henry van Dyke. BCW (1906), p. 17; BCW (1932), p. 18, altered.

348. ICEL, in SBK-92, p. 205, altered.

349. Gregorian and Gallican sacramentaries, and Sarum missal. PBCP, p. 182; BCO (1940), p. 259; BCW (1932), pp. 8, 210; BCW (1946), pp. 312, 361; BCP, p. 231, altered.

350. UW, p. 269 (leader's edition); SLR-7, p. 244, altered.

351. ICEL in SBK-92, p. 205, altered. Biblical allusion: Gospel reading, Year C.

352. NZPB, p. 578, altered. Doxology added.

353. BAS, p. 371, altered. Biblical allusion: Gospel reading, Year B.

354. LBW, p. 163 [91]; SLR-7, p. 245, altered. Altered further for BCW. The BCW alteration (lines 5 and 6) unfortunately weakens the text, since it tends to shift the blessing toward ourselves, rather than outward toward the world. The original LBW and SLR-7 text reads:

> that our possessions may not be a curse in our lives,
>> but an instrument of blessing;

A better altered reading would have been:

> that our possessions may not be a curse,
> but a means of blessing;

Biblical allusion: Gospel reading, Year C.

355. BAS, p. 373.

356. Leonine and Gregorian sacramentaries and Sarum missal. BCW (1946), p. 313; BCP, p. 232, altered. (Cf. LBW, p. 162 [87].)

357. From *Alternative Collects, 1985,* The Anglican Church of Australia, in UW (leader's edition), p. 206; SLR-7, p. 246, altered. Biblical allusion: Gospel reading, Year B.

358. BAS, p. 374; SLR-7, p. 247. Altered for BCW.

359. NZPB, p. 619, doxology added. Biblical allusion: Gospel reading, Year B.

360. BAS, p. 387; SLR-7, pp. 247–248. Biblical allusion: Second reading (Heb. 12:1, 2).

361. NZPB, p. 615. Doxology added.

362. MR, translated by Fr. Peter Scagnelli. Taken from UW (leader's edition), p. 209; SLR-7, p. 249, altered. Biblical allusions: Gospel reading, Year A (Matt. 16:16); 1 Pet. 2:4, 5.

363. From Gelasian sacramentary, and included in Sarum missal. Paraphrased by Cranmer. The phrase "bring forth in us the fruit of good works," is an addition in the BCP. The phrase completes the metaphor of farmer or gardener, good works being brought forth by God who plants and nourishes. The BCW version drops the salutation "Lord of all power and might," retaining "author and giver of all good things." BCO (1940), p. 261; BCW (1946), 313; BCP, p. 233, altered.

364. BCO, p. 275; BCW (1946), p. 340, altered.

365. MR, translated by Fr. Peter Scagnelli. Taken from UW (leader's edition), p. 333; SLR-7, p. 250. Altered for BCW. Biblical allusion: Gospel reading, Year C.

366. See notes for prayer 768, of which this text is a revision.

367. BCW (1946), p. 314, altered.

368. ICEL in SBK-92, p. 206; SLR-7, p. 251. Altered for BCW.

369. BAS, p. 380. SLR-7, p. 252.

370. NZPB, p. 535, altered.

371. ICEL in SBK-92, p. 206, altered.

372. BAS, p. 381. SLR-7, p. 253. Altered for BCW.

373. MR, translated by Fr. Peter Scagnelli. Taken from UW (leader's edition), p. 276. SLR-7, p. 253, altered. Altered further for BCW. Biblical allusion: Gospel reading, Year B.

374. ICEL in SBK-92, p. 207, altered. Biblical allusion: Gospel, Year C.

375. BAS, p. 383. SLR-7, p. 254.

376. From the Leonine sacramentary; reflects the turbulent times during the barbarian invasions. BCP, p. 234, altered. Biblical allusion: Col. 3:2.

377. An original prayer included in the appendix of William Bright's *Ancient Collects* (Oxford, 1902). Biblical allusions: Ps. 25:8; Isa. 11:2; Ps. 36:9; Jer. 31:9. BCP (1928); BCO (1940), p. 274; BCW (1946), p. 369; BCP, p. 832. Doxology added in BCW.

378. Leonine, Gelasian, and Gregorian sacramentaries, Sarum missal. PBCP, pp. 198, 357; BCO (1940), p. 261; BCW (1946), p. 312; BCP, p. 234; SLR-7, pp. 245–246, altered. Doxology added in BCW.

379. BCO, p. 38; BCW (1946), p. 28, altered.

380. BCW (1946), altered. See notes for prayer [6], from which lines 1–4 are taken. Biblical allusion: Eph. 2:20.

381. BAS, p. 385; SLR-7, pp. 255–256.

382. Written for BCW. Biblical allusion: Matt. 7:13.

383. BCO (1940), p. 274; BCW (1946), p. 341, altered.

384. BCP, p. 235; SLR-7, p. 256.

385. NZPB, p. 569. Doxology added. Biblical allusion: Second reading, Year B.

386. ICEL in SBK-92, p. 207, for Twenty-ninth Sunday in Ordinary Time.

387. BCW (1946), p. 310, altered.

388. Gelasian and Gregorian sacramentaries, Sarum missal. PBCP, pp. 24, 358; BCO, p. 277; BCW (1946), pp. 58, 104, 372–373; BCP, p. 69, altered. Biblical allusion: John 14:27.

389. ICEL in SBK-92, p. 207, altered. Biblical allusion: Gospel reading, Year C.

390. BCW (1946), p. 372, altered.

391. Written by John W. Suter Jr., and published in *A Book of Collects* (1919); included in BCP (1928). BCW (1946), p. 373; BCP, p. 832, altered. Biblical allusion: Isa. 30:15; Ps. 46:10.

392. UW (leader's edition), p. 342, altered. Biblical allusion: Gospel reading, Year C.

393. UW (leader's edition), p. 224; SLR-7, pp. 261–262, altered. Altered further for BCW.

394. Composed for BCP (1549); BCW (1946), p. 314; BCP, p. 245.

395. Revison of prayer of confession proposed for All Saints' Day in GA 74. SLR-7, p. 262, altered. Altered further for BCW.

396. Revision of eucharistic prayer written by Harold M. Daniels for SLR-7, pp. 262–264. Marney Ault Wasserman revised it for BCW. For sources of elements shared in common in eucharistic prayers, see glossary: Great Thanksgiving; Sursum Corda; preface; Sanctus; anamnesis; institution narrative; memorial acclamation; epiclesis; doxology; Amen.

397. This text was prepared for SLR-7, pp. 264–265. It borrows extensively from a prayer by Henry van Dyke, first appearing in BCW (1932), p. 128, and included in BCW (1946), p. 315. A few lines derive from GA 74, p. 395. Henry van Dyke's prayer merits preservation in a revision free of Tudor English, thus made available here for use:

> We give you thanks, O Lord,
> for all your saints and servants,
> who have lived justly, loved mercy,
> and walked humbly with their God.
>
> For all the high and holy ones,
> who have wrought wonders
> and been shining lights in the world,
> we give you thanks.
>
> For all the meek and lowly ones,
> who have earnestly sought you in darkness,
> and held fast their faith in trial,
> and done good to all people as they have had opportunity,
> we give you thanks.
>
> Especially for those whom we have known and loved,
> who by their patient obedience and self-denial,
> steadfast hope and helpfulness in trouble,
> have shown the same mind that was in Christ Jesus,
> we bless your holy name.

> As they have comforted and upheld our souls,
> grant us grace to follow in their steps,
> and at last to share with them
> in the inheritance of the saints in light;
> through Jesus Christ our Savior.
>
> Amen.

398. UW (leader's edition), p. 218; SLR-7, p. 258, altered. Doxology added in BCW.

399. Written for BCP (1662). BCP, p. 236; SLR-7, p. 258, altered. Altered further for BCW.

400. ICEL in SBK-92, p. 208, altered.

401. LBW, p. 170 [107]; SLR-7, p. 259, altered. Doxology added in BCW. Inspired by Ps. 90.

402. From *Alternative Collects, 1985,* The Anglican Church of Australia. Taken from UW (leader's edition), p. 344; SLR-7, pp. 259–260.

403. ICEL in SBK-92, p. 208. Biblical allusions: Rev. 1:8; 4:8; Mal. 4:2.

CHRIST THE KING (OR REIGN OF CHRIST) (PP. 394–400)

404. RS (alternative collect for Christ the King); SLR-7, p. 266, altered. Further altered for BCW.

405. A collect by Capt. Howard E. Galley, based on a Roman collect for Christ the King. BCP, p. 236; SLR-7, pp. 266–267, altered.

406. SLR-7, p. 267.

407. ICEL in SBK-92, p. 208.

408. Written for BCW by Harold M. Daniels.

409. Revision of eucharistic prayer written by Donald Wilson Stake for SLR-7, pp. 267–269. Marney Ault Wasserman revised it for BCW. For sources of elements shared in common in eucharistic prayers, see glossary: Great Thanksgiving; Sursum Corda; preface; Sanctus; anamnesis; institution narrative; memorial acclamation; epiclesis; doxology; Amen.

410. Written by Donald Wilson Stake for SLR-7, p. 270. Altered for BCW.

Chapter 4

Commentary on Baptism and Reaffirmation of the Baptismal Covenant

THE SACRAMENT OF BAPTISM (PP. 402–417)

Presentation (pp. 403–406)

"Obeying the word . . . this sacrament" (pp. 404–405). SLR-2, p. 26. Altered.

"Relying on God's grace . . . your child?" (p. 406). SLR-2, p. 27.

"Do you promise . . . faithful Christian?" (p. 406). SLR-2, p. 27.

"Do you, as members . . . his church?" (p. 406). Written for BCW.

Profession of Faith (pp. 406–410)

"Through baptism we enter . . . in which we baptize" (pp. 406–407). SLR-2, pp. 27–28. Altered for BCW.

Renunciations No. 1 (p. 407), prepared for BCW.

Renunciations No. 2 (pp. 407–408). SLR-2, p. 28. Altered for BCW.

Renunciations No. 3 (p. 408), first question written for BCW; second question and answer, WBK, p. 44; third question, WBK, p. 44, altered for BCW.

The Apostles' Creed (pp. 408–409). See glossary.

"Will you be . . . with God's help" (pp. 409, 438), written for BCW.

"Will you devote . . . with God's help" (p. 410), BCP, p. 304, altered. Based on Acts 2:42.

Thanksgiving over the Water (pp. 410–412)

411. Prepared for BCW, based on thanksgivings over the water in SLR-2, pp. 29–30, 35–37. Fifth paragraph ("We thank you, O God . . . power of the Holy Spirit") is based on a paragraph in the thanksgiving over the water drafted by Lionel Mitchell in BCP, pp. 306–307.

412. Prepared for BCW, based upon thanksgivings over the water in SLR-2, pp. 29–30, 35–37. Fourth paragraph ("We praise you . . . royal priesthood") is based on a paragraph in BAS, p. 157.

The Baptism (p. 413)

"N., I baptize you . . ." (p. 413). See glossary: baptismal formula.

Laying on of Hands (pp. 413–414)

See glossary: laying on of hands; sign of the cross; and anointing with oil.

413. SLR-2, p. 31. Based on Isa. 11:2. BCO (1940), p. 102 (Confirmation); BCW (1946), pp. 132–133 (Confirmation). Cf. LBW, p. 311 [246]; and RS. By the fifth century, anointing and prayer after baptism were virtually universal. By early in the sixth century, in the Gelasian sacramentary (and in later Western books), the prayer included the sevenfold gifts of the Spirit (Isa. 11:2 in Vulgate trans.). Enumeration of the seven gifts of the Spirit were perhaps made in Rome in the fourth century.

414. Dating from BCP (1552), this is an abbreviated form of a prayer accompanying the laying on of hands in various sixteenth-century German confirmation rites. In BCW (1906), pp. 45, 48; BCW (1932), pp. 63, 73; BCO (1940), p. 262; BCW (1946), pp. 129, 133; BCP, p. 309. In the BCW (1906), (1932), and (1946), it accompanies the laying on of hands in the baptism of adults and in the confirmation of baptismal vows.

"N., child of the covenant" (p. 414). SLR-2, p. 31, based on BCP, p. 308.

"N., child of God" (p. 414). SLR-2, p. 39.

Welcome (p. 414)

"N. and N. have been received . . ." SLR-2, p. 32. Revised for BCW.

"With joy . . ." SLR-2, p. 32. Revised for BCW.

PRAYERS . . . FOR INCLUSION IN THE PRAYERS OF THE PEOPLE (PP. 416-417)

415. SLR-2, p. 42.

416. SLR-2, pp. 42–43.

417. SLR-2, p. 43.

418. SLR-2, p. 43.

AN ALTERNATIVE SERVICE FOR THE SACRAMENT OF BAPTISM (PP. 419–429)

This liturgy was prepared by the Consultation on Common Texts in response to a proposal from the Baptism task force that prepared SLR-2 (through the Joint Administrative Committee of the Joint Office of Worship) that a baptismal rite be developed ecumenically. All texts are from CB.

419. CB, pp. 14–16.

420. CB, pp. 16–17.

421. CB, p. 24.

BAPTISM AND REAFFIRMATION OF THE BAPTISMAL COVENANT (PP. 431–445)

This liturgy is a composite of texts from the Sacrament of Baptism (pp. 403–415) and Reaffirmation of the Baptismal Covenant for Those Making a Public Profession of Faith (pp. 446–453), with slight alterations. See commentary on each of those rites.

422. SLR-2, p. 76. Revised for BCW.

423. Written for BCW.

REAFFIRMATION—PUBLIC PROFESSION OF FAITH (PP. 446–453)

Presentation (p. 447)

"N. and N. are presented . . . the gospel of Jesus Christ." SLR-2, pp. 73–74. Altered for BCW.

Profession of Faith (pp. 448–452)

"Now, as you . . ." (p. 448). SLR-2, pp. 74–75.

Renunciations and Profession are as displayed in the baptismal rite (pp. 407–408), with alterations in the introduction.

424. SLR-2, p. 77.

Welcome (p. 453)

"N. and N., by publicly professing . . . in him" (p. 453). Written for BCW. A modification of the Welcome in the baptismal rite (p. 414).

REAFFIRMATION—THOSE UNITING WITH A CONGREGATION (PP. 454–462)

Presentation (pp. 455–457)

"You come to us . . . our baptism" (p. 456). Written for BCW by Joseph D. Small III.

Profession of Faith (pp. 457–461)

Renunciations and Profession are as displayed in the baptismal rite (pp. 407–408), with slight alterations in the introduction.

425. WBK, pp. 50, 52; SLR-2, p. 97.

426. SLR-2, p. 80. Altered for BCW.

Laying On of Hands (p. 461)

Texts 1 and 2 are those used in the baptismal rite (p. 413).

Welcome (p. 462)

"Welcome to this . . ." SLR-2, p. 97. Altered for BCW.

REAFFIRMATION—CONGREGATION (PP. 464–477)

Profession of Faith (pp. 465–468)

"Sisters and brothers in Christ . . . in which we were baptized" (p. 465). SLR-2, pp. 82–83. Altered for BCW.

Renunciations and Profession, as displayed in the baptismal rite (pp. 407–408).

Thanksgiving for Baptism (pp. 468–470)

427. Adaptation of Thanksgiving Over the Water [411].

428. Adaptation of Thanksgiving Over the Water [412].

"Remember your baptism . . ." (p. 470). SLR 2, p. 84. The inclusion of a portion of the baptismal formula, "In the name of . . ." intensifies the focus on reaffirming of the baptismal covenant.

Laying On of Hands (pp. 470–471)

Texts 1 and 2 are those used in the baptismal rite (p. 413).

ADDITIONAL LITURGICAL TEXTS FOR THE SERVICE FOR THE LORD'S DAY (PP. 472–477)

429. Written by Harold M. Daniels. Biblical allusions: John 3:3–5; Rom. 8:18–25.

430. NZPB, p. 398.

431. Written by Harold M. Daniels.

432. Written by Harold M. Daniels. Biblical allusion in sixth petition, "we rely on ourselves, and refuse to trust your direction": Prov. 3:5.

433. Based on a prayer in WAGP, p. 105. The original source of the prayer is not known.

REAFFIRMATION—GROWTH IN FAITH (PP. 478–484)

Call to Discipleship (pp. 478–480)

"The call of Christ . . . in renewing their baptism" (pp. 479–480). SLR-2, p. 88.

Profession of Faith (pp. 480–483)

"The grace bestowed . . . holy catholic church" (p. 480). SLR-2, p. 88.

Renunciations and Profession (pp. 480–483) are as displayed in the baptismal rite (pp. 407–408).

Laying On of Hands (pp. 483–484)

Texts A and B are those used in the baptismal rite (p. 413).

"N., and N., you are . . ." (p. 484). SLR-2, p. 91, altered.

REAFFIRMATION—PASTORAL COUNSELING (PP. 485–488)

Profession of Faith

"In your baptism . . . we are baptized" (pp. 485–486). SLR-2, p. 94.

Renunciations and Profession are as displayed in the baptismal rite (pp. 407-408).

Laying On of Hands (pp. 487–488)

Texts A and B are those used in the baptismal rite (p. 413).

Chapter 5

Commentary on
Daily Prayer

MORNING PRAYER (PP. 491–503)

Opening Sentences (pp. 491–492)

"O Lord, open my lips . . ." (p. 491). Ps. 51:15. The earliest descriptions of the
morning office indicate that the rite opened with Ps. 51 or at least the versicle Ps. 51:15.

Morning Psalm (pp. 492–494)

The BCW provides four psalms to introduce the psalmody of morning prayer:
Ps. 95:1–7 (Venite); Ps. 100 (Jubilate); Ps. 63:1–8; Ps. 51:1–12. Each has
long been associated with morning prayer. In Western monasticism, Benedict of Nursia directed that Ps. 95 be sung in the liturgy in the middle of
the night (nocturns or matins). Psalm 100 was a morning psalm in the
Jerusalem temple. In Western monasticism Ps. 100 has been an opening
psalm at dawn (lauds) on Sundays and festivals, and daily upon rising
(prime). In the Eastern church, Ps. 51 is often sung at the beginning of
morning prayer. John Chrysostom (ca. A.D. 347–407) and the *Apostolic*

Constitutions (ca. A.D. 380) indicate that Ps. 63 was the traditional morning psalm. Psalm 24 and Ps. 67 (the most ancient morning psalm) are alternatives in LH for introducing the psalmody in morning prayer.

Canticle (pp. 495–496)

Canticle of Zechariah. See glossary, and see note on p. 228.

Prayers of Thanksgiving and Intercession (pp. 496–499)

"Satisfy us . . . joy and praise" (p. 496). SLR-5, p. 52 and elsewhere throughout the book.

434– A series of prayers of thanksgiving and intercession for use in the morning,
440. written by Donald Wilson Stake. In addition to centering on thanksgivings and intercessions appropriate to the particular day of the week, during the course of the week the prayers focus on every part of the church throughout the world. The ellipses denote pauses for silent prayer, thereby engaging the people in prayer. SLR-5, pp. 279–286; [434], p. 279; [435], p. 280; [436], p. 281; [437], p. 282; [438], pp. 283–284; [439], pp. 284–285; [440], pp. 285–286.

441. Written by Donald Wilson Stake. SLR-5, p. 58.

442. Written by Donald Wilson Stake. SLR-5, p. 62. Altered for BCW.

443. LH (alternative prayer for Seventeenth Sunday in Ordinary Time); SLR-5, p. 62–63, altered. Altered further for BCW.

444. Written by Donald Wilson Stake. SLR-5, p. 66.

445. Prayer by Donald Wilson Stake, based on a prayer in NZPB, p. 92.

446. A prayer from Eric Milner-White and George Wallace Briggs, *Daily Prayer* (London: Oxford, 1941), p. 14. Taken from LBW, p. 52 [251]; SLR-5, p. 192–193, altered.

447. NZPB, p. 60.

EVENING PRAYER (PP. 504–523)

Service of Light (pp. 505–513)

Opening Sentences (pp. 505–507)

See glossary: Service of Light.

"Jesus Christ is the light . . ." (p. 505). LBW, p. 58; SLR-5, pp. 53, 81. The first pair of verses are based on John 8:12 and 1:5; the second pair are based on Luke 24:29; the third pair are based on 2 Cor. 4:6 and the lines from the

Exsultet: "Rejoice, O mother church! Exult in glory! The risen Savior shines upon you!" (BCW, p. 301).

"Light and peace . . ." (p. 505). PGIS, p. 136.

"The Spirit and the church . . ." (p. 506). LBW, p. 92; SLR-5, pp. 86, 105. Based on Rev. 22:17, 20; 2 Tim. 4:8; and Rom. 8:22.

"The people who walked . . ." (p. 506). LBW, p. 93; SLR-5, pp. 111, 119, altered. References as indicated with text.

"Behold, now is the . . ." (p. 506). LBW, p. 94; SLR-5, pp. 126–127, 151–152. References in addition to those with the text: Ps. 4:6b; Mal. 4:2; Ps. 113:7.

"Jesus Christ is risen . . ." (p. 507). LBW, pp. 94–95; SLR-5, pp. 156, 178–179, 183–184. Based on Rom. 6:9 and Isa. 60:3 (RSV).

Evening Hymn (p. 507)

Hymn to Christ the Light. See glossary.

Thanksgiving for Light (pp. 507–511)

448. From the *Apostolic Constitutions* (ca. A.D. 380) (see glossary). An ICEL translation from a draft of evening prayer, February 1992, altered. LBW, p. 95; SLR-5, p. 54, alt., was another version of this prayer.

449. Jewish berakah of the evening, based on Jewish texts, traditional and Reform. SLR-5, pp. 54–55. See glossary: berakah.

450. A new prayer from an ICEL draft of evening prayer, February 1992.

451. Thanksgiving for light from the *Apostolic Tradition of Hippolytus* (see glossary). An ICEL translation (in a February 1992 draft of Evening Prayer). SLR-5, pp. 82–83, contained another version of this prayer.

452. Text by John Allyn Melloh, S.M., PGIS, pp. 230–231 (plainsong setting). SLR-5, pp. 87–88, 106, altered.

453. Text by John Allyn Melloh, S.M., PGIS, p. 232 (plainsong setting). SLR-5, pp. 112, 120–121. Altered further for BCW.

454. Text by John Allyn Melloh, S.M., PGIS, pp. 234–235 (plainsong setting). SLR-5, pp. 127–128, 152–153. Altered further for BCW.

455. Text by John Allyn Melloh, S.M., PGIS, pp. 236–237 (plainsong setting). SLR-5, pp. 184–185.

Evening Psalm (p. 512)

Psalm 141 is the traditional evening psalm. The earliest reference to this psalm being used in the evening is from Origen (ca. A.D. 185–ca. 254). The writings of Chrysostom (ca. A.D. 347–407) evidence that in Antioch Ps. 63 was used in the morning and Ps. 141 in the evening.

456.   MPE, p. 59; SLR-5, p. 245, altered. Altered further for BCW.

Opening Sentences (p. 513)

For use when the Service of Light is not included at the beginning of Evening
   Prayer.

"Our help is in the name . . ." (p. 513). It is not Ps. 24:34 as stated here, but Ps.
   124:8. This verse, referred to by the Reformed as the Votum (Latin, vow),
   has long been used to begin worship in the Reformed tradition (see also
   BCW pp. 49, 545). This bold proclamation, the first words in Calvin's
   liturgy, affirms the dominant character of classic Reformed worship, worship that unswervingly centers on a sovereign God, the source of all things
   and our continuing help.

"O God, come . . ." (p. 513). BCP and Roman daily office. Dates from pre-
   Reformation times; in English-language liturgies it may be traced to the
   Sarum offices, from which it made its way into the BCP (1549). Though
   it derives from Ps. 70:1, it echoes a recurring plea in the Psalms, e.g., Pss.
   22:19; 31:2; 38:22; 40:13.

"Light and peace . . ." (p. 513). PGIS, p. 136.

Canticle (p. 516)

Canticle of Mary. See glossary, and see note on p. 228.

Prayers of Thanksgiving and Intercession (pp. 517–520)

457– A series of prayers of thanksgiving and intercession for use in the evening,
463.   written by Donald Wilson Stake. In addition to centering on thanksgivings and intercessions appropriate to the particular day of the week, during the course of the week the prayers focus on all of the major Christian
   traditions. The ellipses denote pauses for silent prayer, thereby engaging
   the people in prayer. SLR-5, pp. 279–286: [457], pp. 279–280; [458], pp.
   280–281; [459], pp. 281–282; [460], p. 283; [461], p. 284; [462], p. 285;
   [463], p. 286.

464.   LH, SLR-5, p. 78, altered. Doxology added for BCW.

465.   Written by Donald Wilson Stake. SLR-5, p. 60.

466.   Written by Donald Wilson Stake. SLR-5, p. 65. Altered for BCW.

467.   Written by Donald Wilson Stake. SLR-5, p. 69. Altered for BCW.

468.   Written by Donald Wilson Stake. SLR-5, p. 73.

469.   SLR-5, pp. 180–181. Altered for BCW.

470.   Attributed to James Burns (twentieth century) in *The Minister's Prayer
   Book,* ed. John W. Doberstein (Philadelphia: Muhlenberg Press, n.d.),
   p. 30, altered.

ALTERNATIVE TEXTS FOR SEASONS AND FESTIVALS: MORNING AND EVENING PRAYER

Advent (pp. 524–528)

"The Lord shall come . . ." (p. 524). SLR-5, p. 95.

"Like the sun . . ." (p. 524). LH, Antiphon for Canticle of Zechariah, Dec. 19, morning prayer. SLR-5, p. 101, altered.

471. LH, First Sunday of Advent, evening prayer. SLR-5, p. 86, altered.

472. SLR-5, pp. 98–99.

473. SLR-5, p. 104. Altered for BCW.

"Drop down the dew . . ." This translation of Isa. 45:8 is that of Massey H. Shepherd Jr. in *A Liturgical Psalter for the Christian Year* (Minneapolis: Augsburg Publishing House, 1976).

474. SLR-5, p. 91.

475. SLR-5, p. 94. Altered for BCW.

476. SLR-5, p. 97.

477. There is no prayer numbered 477.

Christmas (pp. 528–530)

"Today Christ is born . . ." (p. 529). Based on LH, antiphon for the Canticle of Mary for Christmas Day, evening prayer II. SLR-5, p. 112.

478. PG, p. 77; SLR-5, p. 113, altered. Altered further for BCW. Biblical allusions: John 1:5, 14; Rev. 21:6.

479. PG, p. 80; SLR-5, p. 116, altered. Biblical allusions: John 3:16; 1:14.

Epiphany (pp. 531–533)

"Sealed with the sign . . ." (p. 531). PG, p. 63, altered. Biblical allusion: John 1:29–34.

480. Written by Diane Karay Tripp for BCW.

"This is a holy day . . ." (p. 532). Adaptation of LH, antiphon for Canticle of Mary, Epiphany evening prayer II; SLR-5, p. 123, altered. In the Eastern church, Epiphany centered on the baptism of Jesus and the wedding feast at Cana. In the Western church, Epiphany included not only these two events but also the visit of the magi. In the East, the visit of the magi was part of the celebration of Jesus' birth. The Cana wedding feast has its place in the Revised Common Lectionary on the Sunday following Baptism of the Lord in Year C. Thus the three foci that have been associated with Epiphany in the Western church are clustered around Epiphany, and are embodied in this text.

481. LH, alternative prayer for Epiphany morning prayer. SLR-5, pp. 123-124, altered.

482. SLR-5, p. 122.

Lent (pp. 533–537)

483. SLR-5, p. 126.

484. SLR-5, p. 134. Altered for BCW.

485. SLR-5, p. 151.

486. SLR-5, p. 149. This prayer is identical to prayer 244.

487. SLR-5, p. 129. Altered for BCW.

488. Written by Anglican Bishop Charles Henry Brent (1862–1929). BCP, p. 101.

489. There is no prayer numbered 489.

Easter (pp. 538–541)

490. SLR-5, p. 163.

491. LH, Monday Evening–Week IV. SLR-5, pp. 158–159 , altered. Altered for BCW. Biblical allusion: Luke 24:13–35.

492. SLR-5, p. 172. Altered for BCW.

493. Based on prayer in SLR-5, p. 166.

Pentecost (pp. 541–543)

494. Written for BCW. Lines 1–4 based on prayer in SLR-5, p. 129; lines 9–11 based on a prayer in NZPB, p. 541.

495. Written by Diane Karay Tripp for *Liturgy* 10, no. 1 (spring 1992): 67. Altered by the author for BCW.

Midday Prayer (pp. 544–549)

496. Dates from BCP (1928). BCP, p. 107; SLR-5, p. 192, altered.

497. Prayer written by Donald Wilson Stake for SLR-5, p. 192. Altered for BCW.

498. Written by John Underwood Stephens (1901–1984), an American Presbyterian minister. In John Underwood Stephens, *Prayers of the Christian Life for Private and Public Worship* (New York: Oxford University Press, 1952), p. 147.

499. Written by Donald Wilson Stake for BCW.

500. WBK, p. 57; SLR-5, p. 192, altered.

501. Based on a prayer by Episcopal Bishop Arthur Cleveland Coxe (1818–1896). BCP, p. 107. Biblical allusion: John 12:32.

502. LH, Wednesday midday prayer. SLR-5, p. 194.

PRAYER AT THE CLOSE OF DAY (PP. 550-561)

Opening Sentences (p. 551)

"O God, come . . . (p. 551). For the opening two lines, see note on opening sentences at the beginning of Evening Prayer. The third line is a post-Reformation addition to the office and is found in BCP, LBW, and LH (where it concludes the liturgy). It echoes the well-known prayer attributed to Cardinal John Henry Newman [504].

Prayer of Confession (pp. 551–553)

"Almighty God, Maker of all things . . ." (p. 551). Information for the source of this versicle was lost. The three sections of the Nicene Creed are echoed in this versicle.

503. An adaptation of the Roman Confiteor (see glossary). The Confiteor is included at the beginning of the Roman Mass and in communal celebrations of the penitential rite in night prayer, where its use dates from the sixteenth century. A revision of the Confiteor is used at the abbey in the Iona Community (Church of Scotland), and is reciprocal in form as here in [503]. This reciprocal form of confession underscores the priesthood of all believers and is particularly appropriate during penitential seasons. In Roman usage, the Confiteor is not reciprocal. SLR-5, p. 196. Altered for BCW. The petition for pardon following confession, "May Almighty God . . . ," is from ION, p. 25.

Prayer (p. 555)

"Into your hands . . ." The first two lines, Ps. 31:5, comprise a traditional text for compline. The following two lines, Ps. 17:8, are found in the medieval

Sarum and Roman forms. The last two lines, Ps. 17:15, have been added as in LBW. For comparison see the LH liturgy for night prayer, BCP (p. 132), and LBW (pp. 73–74).

504. Prior to 1876 this prayer was found in (or composed by George W. Douglas from) a collection of sermons by Cardinal John Henry Newman.[9] It was added to the BCP (1928) as a night prayer. In the BCP, p. 833, it is used as an evening prayer. In BCW (1906) it was included among the family prayers (p. 165). In BCW (1932) it was included in the family prayers for evening (p. 217) and the funeral rite (p. 100). In BCW (1946) it was included in evening worship (p. 75) and at the grave following the words of committal (p. 214). In BCWP (p. 86), WBK (p. 87), BW-UCC (p. 389), SLR-4 (p. 46), and BCW-PCC (p.245), it is included in the committal. SLR-5 (p. 200) includes it in Night Prayer. In BCO (1994) p. 299, it is included in a collection of additional prayers for use in funeral services. BCW includes it in Prayer at the Close of Day (p. 556) and the Committal (p. 942).

505. BCWP, p. 86; WBK, p. 87; SLR-4, pp. 46–47, altered; SLR-5, p. 200.

506. Derives from writings of Augustine of Hippo. BCP, p. 134; SLR-5, p. 200.

507. BCO (1940), p. 265; BCW (1946), p. 362; SLR-5, p. 201, altered.

508. The traditional Roman collect for compline. LH; PBCP, p. 360; BCP, p. 133; SLR-5, p. 201.

509. Based on an intercession in a version of compline published in *Authorized Services* (New York: Church Hymnal Corporation, 1973), p. 195, as part of the revision process leading to the BCP. LBW, p. 76; SLR-5, p. 202.

510. From the Church of South India, as adapted in WAGP, p. 69.

511. A prayer by Henry van Dyke. BCW (1906), p. 165; BCW (1932), p. 217; BCW (1946), p. 364, altered.

512. A Gelasian collect for vespers, this prayer dates from at least the ninth century. It was included in PBCP, pp. 24, 358; BCW (1906), p. 15; BCW (1932), pp. 15, 47, 217; BCO (1940), p. 55; BCW (1946), p. 364; BCP, p. 133; SLR-5, p. 202. Biblical allusion: 2 Sam. 22:29.

513. This prayer dates from at least the sixth-century Leonine sacramentary. BCO (1940), p. 263; BCW (1946), p. 365; BCP, p. 133; SLR-5, pp. 202–203.

514. LH, night prayer, Monday; SLR-5, p. 203. Altered for BCW.

515. A prayer by Russell L. Dicks, from his book: *The Art of Ministering to the Sick* (New York: Macmillan, 1961), p. 225, altered.

Canticle of Simeon (p. 561). See glossary, and see note on p. 228.

Dismissal (p. 561)

"May Almighty God . . ." (p. 561). Source information for this text was lost.

VIGIL OF THE RESURRECTION (PP. 562–572)

This is not to be confused with the Easter Vigil. It is recommended for weekend
retreats and conferences as an alternative to Evening Prayer on Saturday.
This liturgy is based on BAS, pp. 133–137, and PGIS, pp. 280–307.

Opening Sentences (p. 563)

"Light and peace . . ." (p. 563). PGIS, p. 136.

Evening Hymn (p. 564)

Hymn to Christ the Light (p. 564). See glossary.

Thanksgiving for Light (pp. 564–565)

516. PGIS, pp. 284–285 (plainsong setting), altered.

517. Thanksgiving for Light for Easter in ICEL draft of Evening Prayer (1992),
altered.

Psalm 118 (pp. 565–567)

518. PGIS, p. 287, altered.

The Resurrection Gospel (pp. 567–568)

"The gospel of the Lord . . ." (p. 568). See note "Glory to you . . ." following
[56].

Thanksgiving for Our Baptism (pp. 568–571)

"Remember your baptism . . ." (p. 569). SLR-2, p. 84. The inclusion of a portion of the baptismal formula, "In the name of . . ." intensifies the focus
on reaffirming of the baptismal covenant.

Canticle (pp. 570–571)

Canticle of Miriam and Moses (p. 570). See glossary, and see note on p. 228.

We Praise You, O God (pp. 570–571). See glossary, and see note on p. 228.

Prayer (p. 571)

519. BAS, p. 137, altered.

Dismissal (p. 572)

"May God the Father, who . . ." (p. 572). PGIS (plainsong setting), pp. 300–301; BAS, p. 137, altered.

CANTICLES AND ANCIENT HYMNS: TEXTS (PP. 573–591)

This section provides a variety of canticles, along with three ancient hymns for use in the liturgy. Nos. 1, 2, and 3 are the three gospel canticles associated with the Daily Office. Nos. 4, 5, and 6 are hymns that are non-biblical in origin. Nos. 7–16 are songs drawn from the Hebrew Scriptures. Nos. 17–19 are songs from the Apocrypha. Nos. 21–29 are drawn from the New Testament. Translations used in preparing these texts include BCP, RSV, NEB, TEV, and NRSV. Notes are provided in the glossary on those texts long associated with the liturgy, especially the daily office.

1. Canticle of Zechariah—The Benedictus (pp. 573–574). PBCP, pp. 9–10; BCW (1906), pp. 259–260; BCW (1932), p. 327; SLR-5, p. 260; ELLC, p. 46. See glossary.
2. Canticle of Mary—The Magnificat (pp. 575–576). PBCP, pp. 20–21; BCW (1906), p. 259; BCW (1932), p. 326; BCW (1946), p. 72; SLR-5, pp. 261–262; ELLC, p. 50. See glossary. For notes on the "O Antiphons" traditionally sung with the Magnificat between Dec. 17 and 23, see notes on Litany for Advent [131].
3. Canticle of Simeon— Nunc Dimittis (p. 576). PBCP, p. 22; BCW (1906), p. 260; BCW (1932), pp. 327–328; BCW (1946), p. 58; SLR-4, p. 36; SLR-5, p. 263; ELLC, p. 53. See glossary.
4. Hymn to Christ the Light—Phos Hilaron (pp. 576–577). SLR-5, p. 263. See glossary. Translated by William G. Storey.
5. We Praise You, O God—Te Deum Laudamus (p. 577). PBCP, pp. 6–8; BCW (1906), p. 256; BCW (1932), pp. 324–325; BCW (1946), pp. 60–61; SLR-4, pp. 52–53; SLR-5, pp. 264–265; ELLC, p. 41. See glossary.
6. Glory to God—Gloria in Excelsis (p. 578). PBCP, p. 41; BCW (1906), p. 257; BCW (1932), pp. 325–326; BCW (1946), pp. 66, 294; SLR-5, p. 265; ELLC, p. 19. See glossary.
7. Canticle of Miriam and Moses—Cantemus Domino (pp. 578–579). SLR-5, p. 266. Text based on NRSV. See glossary.
8. God's Chosen One (p. 579). Text based on RSV, NRSV.
9. The Desert Shall Bloom (pp. 579–580). NZPB, p. 96, altered.
10. Canticle of Thanksgiving (p. 580). Also known as First Song of Isaiah. SLR-5, p. 267; NZPB, p. 77, altered.

11. Seek the Lord (pp. 580–581). Also known as Second Song of Isaiah. SLR-5, pp. 267–268; NZPB, pp. 87–88, altered.
12. The New Jerusalem (p. 581). Also known as Third Song of Isaiah. SLR-5, p. 268; NZPB, p. 61, altered.
13. The Spirit of the Lord (p. 582). Text based on NEB, NRSV.
14. Canticle of Hannah (p. 582). Text based on RSV.
15. Canticle of David (p. 583). Text based on NRSV. SLR-5, pp. 271–272.
16. The Steadfast Love of the Lord (p. 583). Text based on RSV, NEB.
17. Canticle of Judith (p. 583). NZPB, pp. 66–67.
18. A Canticle of Creation—*Benedicite, omnia opera Domini* (pp. 584–586). This apocryphal text is an expanded paraphrase of Ps. 148. The first part calls upon all creation to the praise of God, the second calls the earth and all its creation (including humanity) to praise God; the final part calls the people of God, living and dead, to praise God. Probably a composition of an Alexandrian Jew, it is part of the book of Daniel in the Septuagint, though not in the Hebrew Old Testament book of Daniel. From late in the fourth century this canticle was sung with the Psalms in morning prayer. In the Eastern rite it continues in use daily in morning prayer. The Trinitarian doxology at the end is added. Text based on RSV, NEB, BCP. BCW (1906), pp. 257–259; SLR-5, pp. 269–270. Text revised for BCW.
19. A Canticle of Penitence—Prayer of Manasseh (pp. 585–586). This text was included in some Greek versions of the Old Testament, but not in the Hebrew canon. It is supposedly the prayer of repentance spoken of in the reign of Manasseh (2 Chr. 33:1–20). It continues to be sung during Lent in the Mozarabic and Byzantine rites. SLR-5, pp. 270–271; NZPB, pp. 98–99.
20. A Canticle to the Lamb (p. 586). This hymn, sung to the One seated on the throne and to the Lamb in the heavenly vision of Rev. 4–5, may be an early Christian hymn incorporated by the author of Revelation. SLR-5, p. 272, revised in BCW based on NRSV and BCP.
21. Canticle of the Redeemed (p. 587). A mosaic of Old Testament phrases in the vision of Rev. 15:3–4. BCP, p. 94. SLR-5, pp. 272–273. Altered for BCW.
22. A Canticle for Pentecost (pp. 587–588). Text based on NEB and NRSV. SLR-5, p. 273. Altered for BCW.
23. A Canticle of Love (p. 588). Text based on RSV, NEB, NRSV. Alan Luff adapted these texts from the RSV for an antiphonal anthem by Erik Routley (Galliard Ltd., 1969), included in *New Songs for the Church*, ed. Reginald Barrett-Alyres and Erik Routley (Galliard Scottish Churches Council, Book 2, Canticles), printed in Great Britain by Galliard Limited, Great Yarmouth, Norfolk, England. SLR-5, p. 274. Altered for BCW.

24. Christ, the Head of All Creation (p. 589). Text based on NEB, NRSV. SLR-5, pp. 274–275. Altered for BCW.

25. Jesus Christ Is Lord (p. 589). Text based on RSV, NRSV. SLR-5, p. 275. Altered for BCW.

26. The Mystery of Our Religion (p. 590). Text based on RSV, NRSV.

27. The Beatitudes (p. 590). PBCP, pp. 40–41; BCW (1906), pp. 31–32; BCW (1932), pp. 52–53; Cf. BCW (1946), pp. 138–142. Text based on NEB, NRSV. SLR-5, p. 276. Revised for BCW.

28. Christ the Servant (p. 591). Text based on NRSV. SLR-5, pp. 276–277. Revised for BCW.

29. Christ Our Passover (p. 591) is from BCP, p. 83; SLR-5, p. 277, altered. Altered further for BCW.

PRAYERS AT MEALTIME (PP. 592–595)

520. A Jewish blessing from the Jewish *Authorized Daily Prayer Book*. Typically, Jewish mealtime prayers were blessings of God rather than petitions to bless the food or those about to eat. The prayer is reminiscent of Ps. 104:1, 14c–15:

> Bless the Lord, O my soul;
> O Lord my God, how excellent is your greatness! . . .
> You make grass grow for flocks and herds
> and plants to serve humankind;
> that they may bring forth food from the earth,
> and wine to gladden our hearts,
> oil to make a cheerful countenance,
> and bread to strengthen the heart.[10]

SLR-4, p. 321. See note at 532–533 below.

521. *Apostolic Constitutions* (ca. A.D. 380). SLR-5, p. 321. Altered for BCW.

522. A portion of a mealtime blessing from Jewish tradition. Included in a collection of mealtime blessings: Gabe Huck, *Table Prayer Book* (Chicago: Liturgy Training Publications, 1980), p. 10; SLR-5, p. 321. See note at 532–533 below.

523. BAS, p. 694.

524. A Roman Catholic prayer at mealtime. SLR-5, p. 320.

525. A commonly used mealtime prayer.

526. A prayer commonly sung at mealtime.

527. A prayer commonly sung at mealtime.

528. An Eastern Orthodox prayer before a meal, based on Ps. 145:15–16. SLR-5, p. 320. Altered for BCW.

529. BCW (1906), p. 167; BCW (1932), p. 218; BCW (1946), p. 374; SLR-5, p. 320, altered.

530. A prayer by Henry van Dyke. BCW (1906), p. 167; BCW (1932), p. 218; BCW (1946), p. 374; SLR-5, p. 320.

531. Of unknown origin. BCP, p. 835. Compare with the prayer by Henry van Dyke in BCW (1906), p. 167; BCW (1932), p. 218; BCW (1946), p. 374: "Heavenly Father, make us thankful to Thee, and mindful of others, as we receive these blessings; in Jesus' name. Amen." SLR-5, p. 320.

532 and 533. A two-part table prayer based on ancient Jewish mealtime prayers and assimilated early into Christian practice. These prayers are comparable to prayers that would have been said at meals in Jesus' family as he was growing up and with his followers during his ministry. They are typically Jewish in form, blessing God rather than food or participants. In Jewish tradition, there are hundreds of brief blessings covering every conceivable occasion of life. "Blessed are you O Lord our God, ruler of the universe, for you . . ." Or, "Blessed are you, Lord, God of all creation, for you . . ." Examples abound: on awakening in the morning, on washing, on having body eliminations, and on dressing, on going to work, on coming home from work, on going to bed, on meeting a friend for the first time following convalescence from illness, on hearing bad news, on eating the first fruit in a season, on eating particular foods, on purchasing a new set of dishes, on first sight of an ocean, on smelling the fragrance of a forest, on seeing lightning, meteorites, a rainbow, lofty mountains, or vast deserts. Such prayers express the attitude by which we are to live as people of faith, a way of seeing and understanding all of life, a way of being in this world and in the human community. It is a way of life, marked by living day after day in gratitude and praise. Blessing God for the food and drink that sustains and delights us each day is one of the most basic occasions of life lived in gratitude and praise. SLR-5, p. 322.

Chapter 6

Commentary on the Psalms

The translation of the Psalms in the BCW (pp. 597–783) derives from the BCP. It was a revision of the Miles Coverdale Psalter, which was preserved in the Great Bible of 1539. The text in use today is the result of careful revision in the light of modern scholarship and linguistic study. Care has been taken to preserve the beauty of the rhythm of Coverdale's translation. It lends itself to a variety of musical forms, and has beauty in recitation. It is printed in lines of poetry that correspond to the Hebrew versification, thereby preserving a sense of the parallelism and symmetry of form of the Psalms.

This Psalter was included in the LBW for use by Lutherans. Thus Episcopalians, Lutherans, and Presbyterians share the same translation of the Psalms.

At the time of the publication of the BCW, a revision of this Psalter in gender-inclusive language became available, the work of two Lutheran liturgical scholars, Gordon Lathrop and Gail Ramshaw. It is this revision of the BCP Psalter that is included in the BCW.[11]

YHWH (the name of God) is translated "LORD," and Adonai (Lord) is translated "Lord." Small capital letters are used in the one instance and not in the other.

In the BCW the numbering of the lines will occasionally differ from the LBW and the BCP, since an attempt was made in the BCW to have the numbering correspond with the versification in the Bible (see, for example, Ps. 7). However, the line divisions of the BCP were maintained in order to preserve the parallelisms of the Hebrew text and to facilitate chanting the Psalms.

The Psalter in the BCW includes all of the psalms appointed in the Revised Common Lectionary and in the Daily Lectionary. The assigning of psalms in the daily lectionary is, with few variations, in harmony with Lutheran usage (see LBW, p. 96). While the BCP and the LBW include all 150 psalms, the BCW includes only those appointed in the lectionaries.

Throughout the BCW, the psalms and canticles are pointed, enabling them to be sung to simple and readily available tones. However, the shortcomings of the pointing in the BCW reflect inadequate testing prior to publication. The BCW introduced a tie where it was thought singing two syllables on a single note would improve communication of the text. Whatever the merits might have been in the use of the tie, it introduced a complication into an otherwise simple system. Furthermore, in singing, there is a tendency to emphasize the tied syllables, which is invariably inappropriate. Some musicians have corrected this by using whiteout to blot out the tie, and then have placed a dot appropriately over the last of the tied syllables, thereby giving consistency with the rest of the text. This correction relieves any confusion that may result when using tones that are commonly available.[12] The correction also brings the pointing in the BCW into conformity with pointed psalms in *The Psalter—Psalms and Canticles for Singing* (Louisville, Ky.: Westminster/John Knox Press, 1993).

For more on the use of psalms in worship, see glossary: psalm prayer; psalmody.

534. Based on a psalm prayer for Ps. 1 in LH, altered. 2d and 3d lines reflect alteration in LBW, p. 340.

535. Written by Diane Karay Tripp for BCW.

536. BAS, p. 708, altered.

537. Written for BCW, borrowing phrases from SLR-5, p. 208.

538. SLR-5, p. 208.

539. Revision of a draft of an alternative prayer for LH for Ps. 36, appearing in LBW, p. 362 [314]. SLR-5, p. 208, altered. Altered further for BCW.

540. Written for BCW, based on a psalm prayer for Ps. 8 by Philip H. Pfatteicher in LBW, pp. 343–344 [286], which was altered for inclusion in SLR-5, p. 209.

541. SLR-5, p. 209. Altered for BCW.

542. Written by Fred R. Anderson, SPJP, p. 16, altered.

543. SLR-5, p. 210. Altered for BCW.

544. BAS, p. 717.

545. SLR-5, p. 210, altered.

546. A revision, by Donald Wilson Stake, of a psalm prayer for Ps. 15 in the Scottish Psalter (1595). SP, p. 13; SLR-5, p. 210. In the BCW text "God of love" is substituted for the word "Father" in the 1595 prayer and SLR-5 text.

547. Written for BCW, based on BAS, p. 720.

548. A revision, by Donald Wilson Stake, of a psalm prayer for Ps. 17 in the Scottish Psalter (1595). SP, p. 14; SLR-5, p. 211. Altered for BCW.

549. BAS, p. 725, altered.

550. Prayer prepared for SLR-5, p. 212. Lines 2 and 3 are based on a psalm prayer for Ps. 19 in LH. Remainder of prayer is based on a prayer in BCP (1928), p. 596, "For Joy in God's Creation," written by John W. Suter Jr.

551. SLR-5, p. 212, altered.

552. BAS, p. 731, based on a psalm prayer for Ps. 22 in LH, altered. Cf. SLR-5, p. 213.

553. Psalm prayer for Ps. 23 in LH, SLR-5, p. 213, altered. Altered further for BCW, using some revisions of this prayer in BAS, p. 731.

554. SLR-5, p. 214, altered.

555. Written by Diane Karay Tripp for BCW. Concerning the prayer, she writes (June 27, 1992): "Covenant Friend: a common reference for God in Reformed devotional material. Perhaps they derived their reference from v. 14 of this psalm."

556. Written by Harold M. Daniels for BCW.

557. Written by Donald Wilson Stake, SLR-5, p. 215. Altered for BCW.

558. An altered version of a draft of an alternative prayer for LH in LBW, p. 356 [306], for Ps. 28. SLR-5, p. 215, altered. Altered further for BCW.

559. BAS, p. 738.

560. BAS, p. 739, altered.

561. BAS, p. 742.

562. SLR-5, p. 217, altered.

563. Revision of a draft of an alternative psalm prayer for LH, in LBW, p. 360 [311]. SLR-5, p. 218, altered. Altered further for BCW.

564. Based on a psalm prayer for Ps. 34 in LBW, p. 360 [312], and BAS, p. 746, each altered versions of a psalm prayer for Ps. 34 in LH; SLR-5, p. 218. Altered further for BCW.

565. BAS, p. 748.

566. SLR-5, p. 219.

567. BAS, p. 752.

568. BAS, p. 754.

569. BAS, p. 755, altered. Lines 2 and 3 based on a psalm prayer for Ps. 39 in LH.

570. Written by Diane Karay Tripp for BCW.

571. BAS, p. 758, altered.

572. BAS, p. 759.

573. Written for BCW. First two lines from a psalm prayer for Ps. 43 in LH.

574. Written by Diane Karay Tripp for BCW. Biblical allusions: Phil. 2:10; Rev. 19:9.

575. A revision, by Donald Wilson Stake, of a psalm prayer for Ps. 46 in the Scottish Psalter (1595). SP, p. 22; SLR-5, p. 221. Altered for BCW.

576. SLR-5, p. 221, altered.

577. BAS, p. 766, altered.

578. SLR-5, p. 222, altered.

579. Psalm prayer for Ps. 50 in LH; SLR-5, p. 222, altered. Altered further for BCW.

580. Prayer prepared for BCW, combining portions of two prayers for Ps. 51 in SLR-5, p. 222.

581. Psalm prayer for Ps. 52 from LH.

582. Psalm prayer for Ps. 53 in LH. SLR-5, p. 223, altered. Altered further for BCW.

583. Revision of a draft of an alternative prayer for LH, appearing in LBW, p. 374 [332]. SLR-5, p. 223, altered. Altered further for BCW.

584. BAS, p. 776.

585. (Unnumbered in early printings.) Prepared for BCW, incorporating lines

2, 3, and 6 from BAS, p. 777, with lines 4 and 5 from a psalm prayer for Ps. 56 in SLR-5, p. 223.

586. SLR-5, p. 223, altered.

587. Psalm prayer for Ps. 59 in LH, altered.

588. BAS, p. 783. Lines 3 and 4 are based on a psalm prayer for Ps. 62 in LH. Cf. SLR-5, p. 224.

589. Prayer written by Donald Wilson Stake for SLR-5, p. 224, altered.

590. Written by Mark Felde in LBW, pp. 380–381 [343], altered.

591. BAS, p. 788, based on LH psalm prayer for Ps. 66.

592. SLR-5, p. 225. Biblical allusion: John 1:5.

593. SLR-5, p. 225, altered.

594. BAS, p. 794, altered.

595. Written for BCW.

596. Based on a psalm prayer for Ps. 71 in LH. Cf. LBW, p. 386 [349].

597. BAS, p. 798, altered.

598. Written for BCW with lines 4a, 5, and 6 based on SLR-5, p. 226, psalm prayer for Ps. 73.

599. Psalm prayer for Ps. 77 in LH. Altered using revisions made for LBW, p. 390 [355].

600. BAS, p. 811.

601. BAS, p. 812.

602. LH for Ps. 80; SLR-5, p. 227, altered.

603. Prepared for BCW. Lines 2–4 adapted from SLR-5, p. 227 (psalm prayer for Ps. 81). Lines 5–6 adapted from BAS, p. 815 (psalm prayer for Ps. 81).

604. BAS, p. 816.

605. Written by Fred R. Anderson, SPJP, p. 45, altered.

606. BAS, p. 819, altered.

607. SLR-5, p. 228. Ending altered for BCW.

608. BAS, p. 823.

609. BAS, p. 826.

610. SLR-5, p. 229. Altered for BCW.

611. SLR-5, p. 230.

612. Written by Diane Karay Tripp for BCW.

613. A revision, by Donald Wilson Stake, of a psalm prayer for Ps. 93 in the Scottish Psalter (1595). SP, p. 37; SLR-5, p. 231. Altered for BCW.

614. Based on a psalm prayer for Ps. 94 in LBW, p. 403 [372]. A revision of LH psalm prayer for Ps. 94; SLR-5, p. 231.

615. A revision, by Donald Wilson Stake, of a psalm prayer for Ps. 95 in the Scottish Psalter (1595). SP, p. 38; SLR-5, p. 231. Altered for BCW.

616. Revision of a draft of an alternative psalm prayer for LH, as a psalm prayer for Ps. 96 in LBW, p. 404 [374]. SLR-5, p. 232.

617. SLR-5, p. 233. Lines 2 and 3 are based on LH psalm prayer for Ps. 97. Ending added in BCW.

618. A revision, by Donald Wilson Stake, of a psalm prayer for Ps. 98 in the Scottish Psalter (1595). SP, p. 39; SLR-5, p. 234.

619. Written for BCW. Lines 4 and 5 are based on lines from a psalm prayer for Ps. 99 in SLR-5, p. 234.

620. Based on LH psalm prayer for Ps. 100. SLR-5, p. 235. Altered for BCW.

621. A draft of an alternative prayer for LH; a psalm prayer for Ps. 102 in LBW, p. 408 [380]. SLR-5, p. 235, altered. Ending added in BCW.

622. SLR-5, p. 236.

623. SLR-5, p. 236, altered.

624. Based on LH psalm prayer for Ps. 105 in BAS, p. 848.

625. Based on LH psalm prayer for Ps. 106 in LBW, p. 413 [384], altered.

626. BAS, p. 855, altered.

627. BAS, p. 856.

628. BAS, p. 859, altered.

629. Prayer written by Donald Wilson Stake for SLR-5, p. 238.

630. Prayer written by Donald Wilson Stake for SLR-5, p. 238, altered.

631. BAS, p. 862, altered.

632. SLR-5, p. 239, altered.

633. BAS, p. 864, altered.

634. SLR-5, p. 239.

635. A draft of an alternative prayer for LH, in LBW, p. 419 [395]. SLR-5, p. 240, altered.

636. BAS, p. 868, altered.

637. SLR-5, p. 241. Ending added in BCW.

638. SLR-5, p. 241, altered. Lines 2 and 3 are from a psalm prayer by Fred R. Anderson in SPJP, p. 64.

639. Written by Diane Karay Tripp for BCW.

640. Written by Bill Schreiber, LBW, p. 427 [401].

641. BAS, p. 884.

642. SLR-5, p. 242.

643. SLR-5, p. 243.

644. Revision of LH psalm prayer for Ps. 127 in LBW, p. 428 [405].

645. BAS, p. 887.

646. SLR-5, p. 243, altered.

647. Revision of LH psalm prayer for Ps. 131 in LBW, p. 430 [409], altered.

648. SLR-5, p. 244, altered.

649. BAS, p. 891.

650. A draft of a psalm prayer for LH in LBW, p. 431 [412]. SLR-5, p. 244. Altered for BCW.

651. SLR-5, p. 244, altered.

652. A draft of an alternative prayer for LH in LBW, p. 432 [414]. SLR-5, p. 244.

653. BAS, p. 895.

654. BAS, p. 896.

655. SLR-5, p. 245.

656. Written by Diane Karay Tripp for BCW.

657. BAS, p. 902.

658. BAS, p. 903.

659. A revision, by Donald Wilson Stake, of a psalm prayer for Ps. 145 in the Scottish Psalter (1595). SP, p. 54; SLR-5, p. 247.

660. Based on LH psalm prayer for Ps. 146. (Cf. LBW, p. 438 [424], and SLR-5, p. 248).

661. LH psalm prayer for Ps. 147:1–11. SLR-5, p. 249, altered.

662. A revision, by Donald Wilson Stake, of a psalm prayer for Ps. 147 in the Scottish Psalter (1595). SP, p. 55; SLR-5, p. 250.

663. A draft of a psalm prayer for LH in LBW, p. 439 [426]. SLR-5, p. 251.

664. Written by Diane Karay Tripp for BCW.

665. Prepared for BCW, formed by combining two psalm prayers in SLR-5, p. 254.

Chapter 7

Commentary on Prayers for Various Occasions

The General Assembly of the United Presbyterian Church in the U.S.A. in 1980 called for the preparation of a treasury of prayer, in response to a special report by the Advisory Council on Discipleship and Worship's Task Force on Communal and Personal Prayer. The development of that treasury became a part of the process of preparing the BCW. Each of the predecessors of the BCW in American Presbyterianism have included such a collection of prayers, a treasury of devotion for personal and family worship as well as public worship.

THE GREAT LITANY (PP. 787–791)

666. The Great Litany is the result of an evolution across time, surviving the Reformation (with revisions) in the Anglican and Lutheran traditions. Based on texts in BCP (pp. 148–154), ASB (pp. 99–102), BAS (pp. 138–143), LBW (pp. 86–91), PBCP (pp. 28–34), and BCW (1946) (pp. 100–104). SLR-5, pp. 289–294.

LITANIES AND PRAYERS FOR
VARIOUS OCCASIONS (PP. 792–837)

667. WBK, pp. 114–115, altered.

668. WBK, pp. 109–110, altered.

669. BCP, p. 815, from *Occasional Prayers Reconsidered* (London: SPCK, 1930), altered.

670. A prayer by Brother Roger of the Taizé Community in France. PTWS, p. 28, altered.

671. WBK, p. 179, altered.

672. Written by Caroline Rose. BCP, p. 840, altered.

673. A prayer by Episcopal Bishop Edward Lambe Parsons, first appearing in BCP (1928). BCP, p. 816, altered. Biblical allusions: Jas. 3:18; Rev. 11:15.

674. Attributed to Wanda Lawrence, a twentieth-century Chippewa. The prayer bears a footnote concerning the reference to "eagle" in the prayer: An eagle in the Native American tradition is often a carrier of prayer. UMBW, p. 521.

675. Written by Charles P. Price. BCP, p. 815, altered.

676. WBK, p. 179, altered.

677. From *Textes liturgiques: Louons Dieu et celebrons la vie,* Masamba ma Mpolo et Mengi Kilandamoko (Zaire, 1988). ISIT, p. 20.

678. Written by Donald Wilson Stake for BCW.

679. A prayer from the Mainau Prayerbook. Other source information was lost.

680. WBK, p. 189, altered.

681. WBK, p. 179, altered.

682. A Samoan prayer of The Uniting Church in Australia Assembly Commission on Liturgy. ISIT, p. 17, altered.

683. Francis of Assisi, "Canticle of the Sun."

684. Written by revisers for a proposed revision of the BCP in 1689 for use on Sunday before the rogation days. BCP, p. 824, altered.

685. Based on a prayer for the harvest in BCP, p. 840, which dates from revisions of the BCP proposed in 1789. LBW, p. 113 [217].

686. WBK, p. 179.

687. Written by the Rev. Charles W. F. Smith. BCP, p. 827, altered.

688. Written for the BCP by Caroline Rose. BCP, p. 840.

689. This text was formed from dialogue in Dostoyevsky's novel *The Brothers Karamazov*.[13] Information as to who formed this text into a prayer was not available.

690. WBK, p. 180, altered.

691. Written for the BCP, based on a prayer from the 1929 revision of the Scottish prayer book (Anglican). BCP, p. 817, altered.

692. Written by Donald Wilson Stake for BCW.

693. WBK, p. 198, altered.

694. WBK, p. 198, altered.

695. WBK, p. 200, altered.

696. WBK, p. 196, altered.

697. WBK, p. 197.

698. WBK, p. 198, altered.

699. WBK, pp. 194–195, altered.

700. Written for BCP by Caroline Rose. BCP, p. 838.

701. A revision of a collect written by William Bright, and included in AC (pp. 234–235), in BCP (1928), p. 596. LBW, p. 111 [204], altered.

702. A prayer of Toyohiko Kagawa, originally published in *The Willows and the Bridge,* by T. Kagawa and Franklin Cole (New York: Association Press). Taken from PNW, p. 110 (no. 256), altered.

703. WBK, p. 196.

704. LBW, p. 110 [197], based on a prayer in BCP, p. 819. The BCP prayer is the prayer of the Royal School of Church Music, revised to include the petition for other artists as well as musicians.

705. WBK, p. 192.

706. Written by Donald Wilson Stake for BCW.

707. LBW, p. 109 [194], from *The Lutheran Hymnal,* 1941.

708. Written by Donald Wilson Stake for BCW.

709. Philip Melanchthon (1497–1560). PR, p. 98.

710. WBK, p. 200.

711. Written by Donald Wilson Stake for BCW.

712. WBK, p. 199, altered.

713. WBK, p. 195, altered.

714. WBK, p. 197, altered.

715. Written by Donald Wilson Stake for BCW.

716. A prayer from *Textes liturgiques: Louons Dieu et celebrons la vie,* Masamba ma Mpolo et Mengi Kilandamoko (Zaire, 1988). ISIT, p. 20.

717. WBK, p. 200, altered.

718. A prayer by Dionysius of Alexandria. The source information was lost.

719. WBK, p. 201, altered.

720. WBK, p. 196, altered.

721. WBK, p. 202, altered.

722. Revision of the commemoration of saints in the Eucharist of the Taizé Community, taken from the 1968 liturgy of the Consultation on Church Union. OW, p. 26; BCP, p. 838; LBW, p. 109 [193].

723. Written by Donald Wilson Stake for BCW.

724. BCO (1940), p. 59, altered. Error in sense lining: "here," beginning line 5, should be at end of line 4.

725. Written by Donald Wilson Stake for BCW.

726. Written by Donald Wilson Stake for BCW.

727. Woodrow Wilson (1856–1924), PNW, p. 24 (no. 52). This prayer could not be included in the software edition of the BCW because of permission problems.

728. This prayer, though sometimes regarded as "George Washington's prayer for his country," was written by the Rev. George Layman Locke in 1882 and first appeared in the BCP (1928). BCP, p. 820; LBW, pp. 105–106 [169], altered.

729. Written for BCP (1928), revised from prayer for the sovereign in the Church of England prayer books. BCP, p. 820; LBW, p. 106 [172].

730. Written for BCP (1928). BCP, p. 821; LBW, p. 106 [173]. Biblical allusion: Ps. 9:4.

731. A revision of a prayer from the Anglican Church of Canada *Prayer Book* (1959). BCP, p. 822; LBW, p. 106 [170], altered.

732. WBK, p. 180, altered.

733. WBK, p. 187, altered.

734. WBK, p. 180, altered.

735. By an unknown author, BCP, p. 823. LBW, p. 105 [167], altered.

736. WBK, p. 189.

737. Martin Luther King Jr. (1929–1968) From *Martin Luther King, Jr.: A Documentary . . . Montgomery to Memphis,* ed. Flip Schulke (New York and London: W. W. Norton & Co., 1976). This prayer could not be included in the software edition of the BCW because of permission problems.

738. Drafted by Charles W. F. Smith. BCP, p. 831; LBW, p. 114 [227].

739. WBK, p. 191.

740. Modeled after a prayer in the Anglican Church of Canada *Prayer Book* (1959) for BCP, p. 259. LBW, p. 107 [178].

741. Drafted by J. Robert Zimmerman for the BCP, p. 825. LBW, p. 106 [174], altered.

742. Prayer written for LBW, p. 107 [176]. Biblical allusion: Jer. 29:7.

743. WBK, pp. 193–194.

744. WBK, p. 184, altered.

745. Drafted by Caroline Rose in the form of a litany for BCP, pp. 821–822. LBW, p. 106 [171].

746. Written by Charles P. Price for BCP, p. 823. LBW, p. 108 [187].

747. WBK, p. 184.

748. WBK, pp. 184–185.

749. Written by Frederick Dan Huntington, included in BCP (1928). BCP, pp. 828–829; LBW, p. 115 [230], altered. Biblical allusions of BCP text are from KJV: Ps. 68:6; Heb. 12:15; Gal. 5:26; 2 Pet. 1:5–6; Gen. 2:24; Mal. 4:6.

750. Robert Louis Stevenson (1850–1894). PNW, p. 94 (no. 209), altered.

751. Drafted by Paul E. Langpaap, BCP, p. 829. LBW, p. 115 [234].

752. John W. Suter Jr. wrote this prayer based on a longer prayer by William Austin Smith. Appeared in BCP (1928). BCP, p. 829; LBW, p. 115 [232], altered. Biblical allusion: Phil. 4:8.

753. WBK, p. 183, altered.

754. Written by Ann Brooke Bushong. BCP, p. 829. LBW, p. 115 [233], altered.

755. WBK, p. 184, altered.

756. WBK, p. 183.

757. Written by Charles P. Price. BCP, p. 830.

758. Angus Dun, Episcopal bishop of Washington (1944–1962), wrote this prayer. It was included in the *Book of Prayers for Church and Home,* ed. Howard Paine and Bard Thompson (Philadelphia: Christian Education Press, 1963), no. 203. BCP, p. 444. See prayer [794], paragraphs 2 and 3, in the marriage rite.

759. WBK, p. 186, altered.

760. WBK, p. 186.

761. WBK, p. 186, altered.

762. Written by Donald Wilson Stake for BCW.

763. Attributed to Augustine of Hippo (354–430). *Little Book of Prayers* (Mount Vernon, N.Y.: Peter Pauper Press, 1960).

764. Attributed to Teresa of Lisieux (1873–1897). The source information was lost.

765. Thomas à Kempis (ca. 1380–1470).

766. Written by William Temple, Archbishop of Canterbury (1942–1944). BCP, pp. 832–833, altered.

767. Thomas Aquinas (ca. 1225–1274).

768. Dates to the Gregorian sacramentary and Sarum missal. Retained in BCP (1549), BCP (1552); BCP (1662); PBCP, pp. 45, 360; BCW (1906), p. 97; BCW (1932), pp. 142, 201; BCW (1946), p. 342; BCP, p. 832. Prayer [366] is another version of this prayer.

769. BCW (1946), p. 140, altered.

770. BCP, p. 458; LBW, p. 114 [226].

771. Attributed to Ambrose of Milan. The source information was lost.

772. Written by Donald Wilson Stake for BCW.

773. Written by Donald Wilson Stake for BCW.

774. Written by James G. Birney. BCP, p. 825; LBW, p. 109 [188].

775. A prayer of Henry van Dyke (1852–1933). Concluding part of prayer in BCW (1906), p. 154; BCW (1932), p. 206; BCW (1946), p. 354, altered.

776. Lines 1–5 derive from the Gelasian sacramentary. English translation

originates with Eric Milner-White, *The Occasional Prayers of the 1928 Book Reconsidered* (London, 1930), p. 25. BCW (1906), p. 136; BCW (1932), p. 188. Lines 6–9 derive from the Liturgy of St. Mark. LBW, p. 114 [223], altered.

777. WBK, p. 181, altered.

778. WBK, p. 185.

779. Composed by Charles W. F. Smith and Ivy Watkins Smith, BCP, p. 830. LBW, p. 114 [229].

780. Introduced in the 1789 revision of the BCP. BCP, p. 831. LBW p. 114 [225], altered. Biblical allusions: Lam. 3:33; conclusion, Num. 6:26.

781. WBK, p. 182.

782. Prayer drafted by Caroline Rose. BCP, p. 826, altered.

783. Written by Donald Wilson Stake for BCW.

784. Mother Teresa of Calcutta. LHP, p. 48.

785. WBK, p. 185, altered.

786. WBK, p. 185, altered. After publication of the BCW, line 7 was revised in subsequent printings and in the software edition of BCW to read,

> Unmask your veiled image in us, O Lord

787. The Liturgy of St. Mark. Information as to the immediate source was lost.

788. WBK, p. 181, altered.

789. WBK, p. 183, altered.

790. A revision of the prayer of the Industrial Christian Fellowship, published in *The Prayer Manual,* ed. F. B. Macnutt (London: A. R. Mowbray, 1951), no. 117. BCP, p. 824, altered.

Chapter 8

Commentary on Christian Marriage

CHRISTIAN MARRIAGE: RITE I (PP. 840-851)

Statement on the Gift of Marriage (p. 842)

"We gather in the presence of God . . ." (p. 842). Drafted by Thomas G. Long for SLR-3, pp. 12–13. The text varies slightly in Marriage Rites II (p. 858) and III (p. 884). Portions of the text derive from BCO (1979), pp. 73–74; BCP, pp. 423–424; and ASB, p. 288. Altered for BCW.

791. Written for SLR-3, p. 13. Lines 1 and 2 are based on a prayer in BW-UCC, p. 328. Lines 6 and 7 are based on a prayer in BCP, p. 425, that was drafted by Charles M. Guilbert.

Declaration of Intent (p. 843)

"N., understanding that . . ." (p. 843). SLR-3, p. 14, altered.

"N., in your baptism . . ." (p. 843). SLR-3, p. 14.

Affirmations of the Families (p. 844)

"N., N. [Names of family members] . . ." (p. 844). SLR-3, p. 14, adapted from UMBW, p. 118.

"We (I) give our . . ."(p. 844). SLR-3, p. 15.

Affirmation of the Congregation (p. 844)

"Will all of . . ." (p. 844). SLR-3, p. 15, adapted from UMBW, p. 118.

Reading from Scripture (pp. 844–845)

792. Adapted from SLR-1, p. 61 ([78] in BCW), for SLR-3, p. 15. Altered for BCW.

Vows (pp. 845–846)

"N. and N., since it is . . ." (p. 845). SLR-3, p. 16.

"I, N., take you, N., to be . . ." (p. 845). Adapted from BCW (1946), pp. 185–186, and other English-language liturgies.

"Before God and these . . ." (p. 846). SLR-3, p. 16–17.

Exchange of Rings (or Other Symbols) (pp. 846–847)

793. ASB, p. 292. SLR-3, p. 17, altered.

"N., I give you this ring . . . I receive this ring . . ." (p. 847). SLR-3, p. 18.

"This ring I give you . . ." (p. 847). SLR-3, p. 18. Based on ring vows in BCW (1946), p. 186.

Prayer (pp. 847–849)

794. This prayer was drafted by Robert H. Greenfield from a variety of sources. The first paragraph is an adaptation of a prayer dating to the Sarum rite. The second and third paragraphs are from a prayer by Angus Dun (see BCW [758]). Paragraph four is new to the BCP. Paragraph five is based on a prayer by Virginia Harbour. The optional paragraph seven is based on a prayer from the Scottish BCP revision of 1912. Paragraphs eight and ten are based on intercessions drafted by Virginia Harbour. Paragraph nine was inserted by the SLR-3 task force. BCP, pp. 429–430; SLR-3, pp. 18–19, altered. Altered further for BCW.

795. Prepared for SLR-3, p. 20. First part of prayer adapted from WBK, p. 67; last part adapted from CBW; SLR-3, p. 20. Altered for BCW.

Announcement of Marriage (p. 850)

"Before God . . ." (p. 850). SLR-3, p. 21.

"Those whom God has joined . . ." (p. 850). SLR-3, p. 21. Based on Matt. 19:6; Mark 10:9.

Charge and Blessing (p. 851)

"The grace of Christ attend you . . ." (p. 853). Lines 1–3 from BW-UCC, p. 337; SLR-3, p. 22.

CHRISTIAN MARRIAGE: RITE II (PP. 852–881)

For texts shared in common with rite I, see notes above for Christian Marriage: Rite I (pp. 247–249).

Confession of Sin (p. 855)

796. WBK, p. 65; SLR-3, p. 27, altered.

"Hear the good news! Who is . . ." (p. 856). See note on p. 177.

Blessing of the Couple (pp. 866–867)

797. Drafted by H. Boone Porter. Marion J. Hatchett writes of this prayer: "The imagery is from the marriage rite: the ring is a seal; the festal clothing normally associated with a wedding, the mantle; and the crowns, still associated with a wedding in the Eastern churches (of which we have a remnant in the wedding veil), the crown. The reference to the heavenly banquet anticipates the conclusion of the service in the Eucharist."[14] BCP, p. 430. SLR-3, pp. 38–39, altered. Minor alteration in BCW.

Great Thanksgiving (pp. 869–872)

798. Written by Harold M. Daniels for SLR-3, pp. 40–42. Altered for BCW. For sources of elements shared in common in eucharistic prayers, see glossary: Great Thanksgiving; Sursum Corda; preface; Sanctus; anamnesis; institution narrative; memorial acclamation; epiclesis; doxology; Amen.

Prayer After Communion (p. 875)

799. Based on portions of prayers in SLR-1, p. 130. (In BCW, [60] and [61].) SLR-3, p. 45.

Prayer of Thanksgiving (pp. 877–878)

800. Written by Harold M. Daniels. An adaptation of prayer [798] for SLR-3, pp. 47–48. Altered for BCW.

CHRISTIAN MARRIAGE: RITE III (PP. 882–892)

Texts in Christian Marriage: Rite III are based on those in Christian Marriage: Rite I, altered for differing circumstances. See notes above for Christian Marriage: Rite I.

Chapter 9

Commentary on The Funeral: A Service of Witness to the Resurrection

COMFORTING THE BEREAVED (PP. 905–909)

801. Written for SLR-4, p. 19.

802. Adapted from a litany in BCP, pp. 465–466, which is dependent on the form used at Gethsemani Abbey in Kentucky. SLR-4, p. 19. The people's response is based on words Jesus spoke from the cross (Luke 23:46, taken from Ps. 31:5). Other biblical allusions are Matt. 11:28; Matt. 25:34; Heb. 4; and 1 Pet. 5:4.

803. Written for SLR-4, p. 20.

804. Written by Bishop Charles Lewis Slattery of Massachusetts (d. 1930); included in BCP (1928) as the final prayer in a brief graveside rite for the burial of a child. BCP, p. 505; SLR-4, p. 20, altered (incorporating alterations in LBW, p. 332 [280]). Biblical allusion: Matt. 5:4, the second of the Beatitudes.

805. Written for SLR-4, p. 20. Altered for BCW.

806. A prayer by John Dowden, appearing in the 1912 Scottish BCP. BCP, p. 494; SLR-4, p. 21, altered. Altered further for BCW.

807. Based on prayer in BCW (1946), pp. 211–212. SLR-4, pp. 55–56. Altered for BCW.

"The Lord bless us . . ."(p. 909). SLR-4, p. 21.

THE FUNERAL: A SERVICE OF WITNESS TO THE RESURRECTION (PP. 910–938)

808. Written for BCW, based in part on SLR-4, pp. 26–27, and BCW (1946), p. 204–205.

809. UMBW, p. 142; SLR-4, p. 27, altered.

810. UMBW, p. 143; SLR-4, pp. 27–28, altered.

811. Based on BCW (1946), p. 205; SLR-4, p. 28. Altered further for BCW. Biblical allusions: Ps. 39:4–5; Isa. 40:6–8; Ps. 23:4; Ps. 39:4, 12.

"Let us now ask . . ." (p. 917). SLR-4, p. 28.

812. SLR-4, pp. 28–29.

"Here the good news! Who is . . ." (p. 918). See note on p. 177.

"The mercy of the Lord . . ." (pp. 918–919). See note on p. 177.

813. SLR-4, p. 30.

814. BCO (1940), pp. 165–166; BCO (1979), pp. 89–90; BCO (1994), p. 293; BCW (1946), pp. 193–194; SLR-4, p. 30, altered. Altered further for BCW.

815. BCW (1946), pp. 205–206; WBK, pp. 84–85; SLR-4, pp. 31–32. altered. Biblical allusion: Rom. 8:38–39.

816. WBK, p. 85; SLR-4, p. 32, altered. Altered further for BCW.

817. WBK, pp. 85–86; SLR-4, pp. 32–33, altered.

818. OCF, pp. 116–117; SLR-4, p. 33, altered. See also BCP, p. 497.

819. Based on the first and second paragraphs of a prayer in the BCO (1940), pp. 184–185, and its revision in BCO (1979), p. 116 (third paragraph); SLR-4, p. 34. See also BCW-PCC, p. 250. Altered for BCW.

820. BCW (1946), p. 212; SLR-4, p. 56, altered. Altered further in BCW.

821. Prepared for BCW drawing from two prayers in NZPB, p. 857 (nos. 7 and 9).

"You only are immortal . . ." (p. 925). From the Byzantine rite, attributed to Thesphanes (d. ca. 842). BCP, p. 499; SLR-4, p. 34, altered.

822. Slightly abbreviated form of "A Commendatory Prayer When the Soul Is Departed," in the litany for the dying, new to BCP (1928). It derives from *Collection of Private Devotions* (1627), by John Cosin, who played an important role in the BCP (1662). BCP, p. 499; SLR-4, p. 35, altered slightly. See: LBW, p. 336; UMBW, p. 150; BW-UCC, pp. 365–366, 381. This prayer also links with Prayer at the Close of Day (lines from versicle A, BCW, p. 555, ". . . I commend my spirit; for you have redeemed me . . ."), which is an appropriate tie. Biblical allusion: Luke 23:46. Philip H. Pfatteicher writes of this prayer:

> The prayer is a concluding statement of trust to console the living with the knowledge of God's care for all his children now and forever. With joy the church once again relies on what God has done in Holy Baptism and commends the servant of God to Christ as "your own . . . your own . . . your own."[15]

It recalls the words and action of Baptism: "N., child of the covenant, you have been sealed by the Holy Spirit in baptism, and marked as Christ's own forever" (BCW, p. 414). So in death, Baptism reaches its consummation. The child of God is truly God's own.

823. BW-UCC, p. 381; SLR-4, p. 35, altered. See BCW-PCC, p. 240. Ending altered in BCW.

"May God in endless mercy . . ." (p. 926). ASB, p. 315; SLR-4, p. 36, altered.

"Now, Lord, you let . . ." (p. 927). The Canticle of Simeon. See glossary.

824. Written by Harold M. Daniels for SLR-4, pp. 37–40. Altered for BCW. For the sources of elements shared in common in eucharistic prayers, see glossary: Great Thanksgiving; Sursum Corda; preface; Sanctus; anamnesis; institution narrative; memorial acclamation; epiclesis; doxology; Amen.

"Jesus, Lamb of God . . ." and "Lamb of God . . ." (p. 935). See glossary: Agnus Dei.

825. Post-Communion prayer in the burial rite in BCP, Rite II, drafted by Massey H. Shepherd Jr. BCP, p. 498; SLR-4, p. 42.

"You only are immortal . . ." (p. 935). See note above on this page.

"May God in endless mercy . . ." (p. 937). See note above on this page.

"Now, Lord, you let . . ." (p. 938). See note above on this page.

THE COMMITTAL (PP. 939–946)

"Christ is risen from the dead . . ." (p. 940). Not a scriptural text. It is based on an antiphon sung in the Eastern Orthodox Easter liturgy when, at a burial during the Easter season, it is sung as the body is carried to the grave. BCP, p. 500. SLR-4, p. 44, included a slightly altered version. BCW returns to the BCP text, which is in keeping with Eastern usage.

"In sure and certain hope . . ." (pp. 940–941), dates from the BCP (1552), which was taken from the beginning of a funeral sermon in *Hermann's Consultation*. BCP, p. 501; BW-UCC, p. 387; SLR-4, pp. 44–45; BCW-PCC, p. 244. Singing or speaking the words from Rev. 14:13 concluded the words of committal in the PBCP, p. 332; BCW (1906), p. 71, BCW (1932), p. 102; BCW (1946), p. 214; SLR-4, pp. 44–45; BCW-PCC, p. 244.

826. UMBW, p. 155; WBK, p. 87; SLR-4, pp. 46–47, altered. This has been in the Methodist funeral rite from at least 1965.

827. This prayer has been attributed to Bishop Charles Lewis Slattery of Massachusetts. Was included in BCP (1928). BCP, pp. 489, 505; SLR-4, p. 47, altered. See BCWP, p. 87; BCO (1979), p. 115; UW (leader's edition), p. 489; BCW-PCC, p. 259. Biblical allusion: Matt. 5:4 (the second of the Beatitudes).

828. WBK, p. 88; SLR-4, p. 47.

829. Prayer written by Lewis A. Briner for SLR-4, pp. 47–48.

830. Prayer written by Lewis A. Briner for SLR-4, p. 48.

831. UW (leader's edition), p. 488, altered.

832. UW (leader's edition), p. 489, altered.

833. Written for SLR-4, p. 49, based on a prayer in the committal of the Roman Catholic funeral rite.

834. Based on 2 Esdras 2:34–35. Can be traced back to the supplement to the Gregorian sacramentary, where it was used as an antiphon to the psalms of the burial office. The term Requiem, the Mass for the departed, derives from the first word of the Latin text of this antiphon. This text is part of the concluding words in the Roman rite—the Song of Farewell in the funeral Mass (OCF, p. 90), and appears as a versicle in the committal (OCF, p. 120), and elsewhere. (Compare the Lutheran rite, LBW, p. 339; OS, p. 127; BCP, p. 502.) SLR-4, p. 49. See also: BCO (1979), p. 91; BCO (1994), p. 257.

835. WBK, p. 88, altered.

Chapter 10

Commentary on Pastoral Liturgies

MINISTRY WITH THE SICK (PP. 967–993)

836. Based on a prayer in *Anointing of the Sick,* Alternative Futures for Worship 7 (Collegeville, Minn: Liturgical Press, 1987), pp. 117–118. SRL-6, p. 64.

837. WBK, p. 183. SLR-6, pp. 64–65, altered.

838. SLR-6, p. 65.

839. Based on a prayer by Theodore Parker Ferris, *Prayers* (New York: Seabury Press, 1981), p. 57. SLR-6, p. 65.

840. SLR-6, p. 65.

841. SLR-6, p. 66.

842. SLR-6, p. 66.

843. SLR-6, p. 66. The last three lines derive from WBK, p. 191.

844. SLR-6, p. 67.

845. SLR-6, p. 67.

846. WBK, p. 181. SLR-6, pp. 67–68, altered.

847. SLR-6, p. 68.

848. SLR-6, p. 68.

849. SLR-6, pp. 68–69.

850. SLR-6, p. 69.

851. SLR-6, p. 69. Biblical allusion: Isa. 53:4 (RSV).

852. SLR-6, pp. 69–70. Biblical allusion: Ps. 46:1.

853. Written for BCW.

854. OS, p. 106 [487]; SLR-6, p. 70.

855. UW (leader's edition), p. 491; SLR-6, p. 70.

HOLY COMMUNION (PP. 995–1002)

"In the Lord's Supper . . ." (p. 996). SLR-6, p. 75.

"The mercy of the Lord . . ." (p. 997). SLR-6, 76. See note on p. 177.

"Here the good news! Who is . . ." (pp. 997–998). See note on p. 177.

A SERVICE OF WHOLENESS FOR USE
WITH A CONGREGATION (PP. 1003–1015)

"Jesus said, "Ask . . ." (p. 1006). BW-UCC, pp. 312–313; SLR-6, p. 87 altered. Altered further for BCW.

"The mercy of the Lord . . ." (p. 1008). SLR-6, p. 88. See note on p. 177.

"Here the good news! Who is . . ." (p. 1008). SLR-6, p. 89. See note on p. 177.

856. Based on a litany in WTL, pp. 37–38. The concluding collect is from LBW, p. 204; SLR-6, pp. 90-92. Altered for BCW.

857. SLR-6, pp. 92–93.

858. Modification of prayer [857]; SLR-6, p. 93.

859. SLR-6, p. 93, altered.

860. Modification of prayer [857]; SLR-6, p. 93–94.

"N., may the God of all mercy . . ." (p. 1013). Based on a portion of a prayer in BCP, p. 456; SLR-6, p. 94.

"N., may God deliver you . . ." (p. 1013). SLR-6, p. 95.

"Spirit of the living God . . ." (p. 1013). This is based on a petition (spoken by all assembled) in the Service of Prayer for Healing in use in the Iona Community, ION, p. 38; SLR-6, p. 95. Altered for BCW.

"N., may the . . ." (p. 1013). SLR-6, p. 95.

"I anoint you . . ." (p. 1013). SLR-6, p. 95.

"As you are anointed . . ." (p. 1014). SLR-6, p. 95

861. SLR-6, pp. 95–96. Biblical allusion: Mal. 4:2.

A SERVICE FOR WHOLENESS FOR USE WITH AN INDIVIDUAL (PP. 1016–1022)

862. SLR-6, p. 105.

For texts accompanying the laying on of hands and anointing with oil (pp. 1020–1021), see notes above on this page.

863. Prayer written by J. A. Ross Mackenzie for SLR-6, p. 108.

A SERVICE OF REPENTANCE AND FORGIVENESS (PP. 1023–1024)

"The mercy of the Lord . . ." (p. 1024). See note on p. 177.

PRAYER AT THE TIME OF DEATH (PP. 1025–1030)

864. SLR-4, p. 11; SLR-6, p. 123, altered.

865. Based on the Roman Catholic Rite for the Commendation of the Dying, PCS, p. 179, incorporating revisions of this prayer in OS, p. 106. SLR-4, p. 13; SLR-6, pp. 124–125, altered.

866. An abbreviation of a prayer in Anglican Bishop Charles Gore's *A Prayer Book Revised* (1913), based on a translation of "A prayer for a soul going to judgment" in the Eastern Orthodox rite for the dying. BCP, p. 464; SLR-4, p. 12, altered; SLR-6, p. 124.

867. SLR-4, p. 12; SLR-6, p. 124, altered.

868. WBK, p. 185; SLR-4, p. 12, altered; SLR-6, p. 124, altered further. Revised for BCW, it is now essentially a new prayer, bearing little resemblance to the original WBK prayer.

"Depart, O Christian soul, in peace . . ." (p. 1028). BCP, 464; SLR-4, pp. 13–14, altered; SLR-6, p. 125, altered further. Also see OS, p. 106; BW-UCC, p. 365; BCO (1994), p. 302.

869. Prayer written by Lewis A. Briner for SLR-4, pp. 14–15; SLR-6, p. 126, altered.

870. Prayer written by Lewis A. Briner for SLR-4, p. 15; SLR-6, p. 127, altered.

871. Prayer written by Lewis A. Briner for SLR-4, p. 16; SLR-6, p. 127, altered.

872. SLR-6, p. 127, based on a prayer from UW (leader's edition), p. 450. Altered for BCW.

Chapter 11

Commentary on Calendar and Lectionaries

LECTIONARY FOR SUNDAYS
AND FESTIVALS (PP. 1035–1048)

The Calendar and Lectionary for Sundays and Festivals is the work of the Consultation on Common Texts, and is taken from its publication *The Revised Common Lectionary* (Nashville: Abingdon Press, 1992). It is widely used by churches throughout the world.

Following the Second Vatican Council, Presbyterians, Episcopalians, Lutherans, and the Consultation on Church Union each made revisions, for their own use, in the lectionary prepared by the Roman Catholics. The result was five versions of the lectionary. The differences in the versions led to problems related to preparing exegetical and homiletical materials based on the readings for ecumenical use. The Consultation on Common Texts, which included representatives from all of the churches that were using variations of the Roman lectionary, undertook the task of examining the readings and working toward a consensus lectionary. This work resulted in the publication of a trial-use Common Lectionary in 1982. Extensive testing followed. A revision was then published in 1992. It is this revised lectionary that is embodied in the BCW.

The Revised Common Lectionary includes an alternative track of Old Testament readings based on the readings in the original Roman lectionary and on variants in the revisions made by other churches (e.g., WBK). That track is typological in nature; the Old Testament readings tend to be linked to the Gospel readings. It was not included in the BCW, preference being given to the track introduced in the 1982 Common Lectionary that was circulated for trial use. The latter was immediately implemented for Presbyterian use in a variety of publications. The church, therefore, had a decade of familiarity with it before BCW. While the Consultation on Common Texts desired participating churches to include both tracks on an equal basis, a decision was made, in order to avoid confusion, that the typological track would not be included in the BCW. That track is available for those who choose to use it; see Consultation on Common Texts, *The Revised Common Lectionary* (Nashville: Abingdon Press, 1992), which includes all of the lectionary readings and a valuable introduction on the use of the lectionary.

DAILY LECTIONARY (PP. 1049–1095)

The Daily Lectionary is taken from the BCP (pp. 933–1001), incorporating some modifications made to it for inclusion in the LBW (pp. 96–104). There are two major differences between the BCP daily lectionary and the daily lectionary included in the LBW. Wherever the BCP lists an apocryphal reading, the LBW provides an alternative canonical reading. The second difference is that the LBW follows a psalm table that differs from the schedule of the Psalms in the BCP daily lectionary. The BCW follows the lead of the LBW, providing the canonical readings as alternatives to apocryphal readings. It also incorporates the Psalms based on the psalm table in the LBW.

Notes

Preface

1. Philip Pfatteicher, *Prayer with the Church: An Introduction to Prayer in Daily Life* (Minneapolis: Augsburg Fortress, 1995), p. 49.

1. Rebuilding the Church from the Ground Up

1. Geddes MacGregor, *The Coming Reformation* (London: Hodder & Stoughton, 1960), 9. This is one of many books written by Dr. MacGregor, who was educated at the University of Edinburgh and Oxford University and ordained in the Church of Scotland. Moving to the United States in 1949, he held the first Rufus Jones Chair of Philosophy and Religion at Bryn Mawr College in Pennsylvania. In 1961 he became Dean of the Graduate School of Religion at the University of Southern California. Eight years after *The Coming Reformation* was published, at the age of fifty-nine, he concluded that there was little hope for reform within the Presbyterian Church. He became an Episcopalian and served as Canon Theologian at St. Paul's Cathedral in San Diego. As an Episcopal priest, he continued to have a most distinguished career as a theologian and was a visiting professor at major North American universities. He died late in 1998. As a Presbyterian, MacGregor was a strong advocate for liturgical reform, catching the attention of the committee charged with service book revision that led to *The Worshipbook*. Since he left the Presbyterian Church in 1968, two service books embodying broad liturgical reforms have appeared—*The Worshipbook—Services* (1970) and the *Book of Common Worship* (1993)—as well as a major directory revision adopted in 1989. One is left to wonder whether these reforms might have instilled within him some tangible hope for the reforming of the church. On the other hand, it remains to be seen whether the renewed hope for renewal embodied in these reforms will come to fruition.
2. Ibid., 55.
3. Ibid., 22.
4. Ibid, 10.
5. Ibid., 46.
6. Ibid., 126.
7. Ibid., 129.
8. Ibid., 130.
9. Ibid., 55–56.
10. A communication from James H. Blackwood to chairperson Scott F. Brenner, dated December 29, 1960, quoted in Harry Ernest Winter, "Catholic, Evangelical and

Reformed: The Lord's Supper in the (United) Presbyterian Church USA, 1945–70" (Ph.D. diss., University of Pennsylvania, 1976), 344.

11. In the statement of the General Assembly Mission Council to the 192nd General Assembly, UPCUSA (1980), in support of the recommendation of the assembly committee on Liturgy and Worship for a new service book, Psalter, and hymnal.

12. *Book of Common Worship* (Louisville, Ky.: Westminster/John Knox Press, 1993), 1.

13. For a treatise on this motto, see Harold B. Nebelsick, "Ecclesia Reformata Semper Reformanda," *Reformed Liturgy & Music* 18, no. 2 (1984): 59–63, republished in: *Exploring Presbyterian Worship: Contributions from Reformed Liturgy & Music* (Louisville, Ky.: Christian Faith and Life, Congregational Ministries Division, Presbyterian Church (U.S.A.) 1994), 3–10.

14. Gordon W. Lathrop, *Holy Things: A Liturgical Theology* (Minneapolis: Fortress Press, 1993), 225. A study of Dr. Lathrop's book will deepen one's understanding of the liturgy and kindle one's love for it.

15. *Book of Common Worship,* p. 58.

16. *Book of Common Worship,* pp. 404–405.

17. *Book of Common Worship,* p. 414.

18. *Book of Common Worship,* p. 410.

19. Max Thurian, *Our Faith: Basic Christian Belief,* trans. Emily Chisholm (London: Mowbray, 1978), 115.

20. Max Thurian, *The Eucharistic Memorial,* Part II—*The New Testament* (Richmond: John Knox Press, 1961), 124.

21. Ibid.

22. *Book of Common Worship,* p. 72 and elsewhere.

23. *Book of Common Worship: Daily Prayer* (Louisville, Ky.: Westminster/John Knox Press, 1993), p. 3.

24 James Hastings Nichols, *Corporate Worship in the Reformed Tradition* (Philadelphia: Westminster Press, 1968), 14, 15. Reformed liturgical scholar William D. Maxwell in *The Liturgical Portions of the Genevan Service Book Used by John Knox While a Minister of the English Congregation of Marian Exiles at Geneva, 1556–1559* (Westminster, England: Faith Press, 1931), 34, 35, makes the point similarly:

> It was not the intention of the Reformers to depart from the central tradition of Christendom and innovate according to mere whim or mood. Rather they counted themselves as the faithful trustees of Catholic tradition, and if they simplified the Roman worship of their day, they did so with the intention of removing all mediaeval and sacerdotal accretions in order to achieve the simplicity and purity of the primitive rites.

> Calvin's liturgy (Geneva, 1542; Strassburg, 1545), *La forme des prieres et chantz ecclesiastiques: Avec la maniere d'administrer les Sacremens, et consacrer le Mariage; selon la coustume de L'eglise ancienne* (The Form of Church Prayers and Hymns, with the Manner of Administering the Sacraments and Consecrating Marriage, According to the Custom of the Ancient Church) is included in English translation in Bard Thompson, *Liturgies of the Western Church* (Cleveland and New York: World Publishing Company, Meridian Books, 1961), 197–210.

25. James F. White, "Book of Common Worship," *Theology Today* 51, no. 1 (April 1994): 168.

26. See Daniell C. Hamby, "Liturgical Implications of the Church of Christ Uniting," *Reformed Liturgy & Music* 29, no. 3 (1995): 186–190.

27. *Book of Common Worship,* p. 70.

28. These are two of the four choices of acclamations included in each eucharistic prayer in the *Book of Common Worship.*

29. *The Constitution of the Presbyterian Church (U.S.A.),* Part II, *Book of Order* (Louisville, Ky.: Office of the General Assembly, 1992–1993), W-2.4003.
30. *Book of Common Worship,* 73, 171, 183, 197, 203, 321, 346, 352, 399, 872.
31. *Book of Common Worship,* 129.
32. Ibid., 132.
33. MacGregor, *Coming Reformation,* 124–125.
34. Although liturgical training for pastors has long been minimal, this is beginning to change. Even though most Presbyterian seminaries still do not require liturgical training, some have added professors of liturgy to their faculties.
35. In his last published writings, C. S. Lewis emphasized the importance of familiarity with the words and acts of liturgy. Familiarity frees us from having to think about the service itself, freeing us to worship. He wrote, "As long as you notice, and have to count, the steps, you are not yet dancing but only learning to dance. A good shoe is a shoe you don't notice." He continued saying that novelty introduced into worship can only have an entertainment value, turning our attention away from God, fixing it upon the one leading worship and on the service itself. "It lays one's devotion waste." We don't go to worship to be entertained, but to use or to enact the service. "Every service is a structure of acts and words through which we receive a sacrament, or repent, or supplicate, or adore." He argued for familiarity and uniformity. (C. S. Lewis, *Letters to Malcolm: Chiefly on Prayer,* in Lyle W. Dorsett, ed., *The Essential C. S. Lewis* [New York: Simon & Schuster, 1988], 408.)

   Here are cautionary words to those who would introduce novelty into worship, and to those who fear repetition. At the same time, they are cautionary words for all who engage in reforming the liturgy as set forth in this book. The caution touches on the perennial discontent that arises from the tension between where we are and where we ought to be. Faced with inadequate ways of worship that still remain familiar and meaningful for many, raises an issue of pastoral responsibility. Leadership that begins to replace the familiar with the unfamiliar, even though based on the ageless wisdom of the church, calls for pastoral sensitivity.

   Not to grow is to be stunted. Not to embrace change that broadens the mind and deepens the affections of the heart, is to stagnate. But change can be traumatic when proposed to those secure in familiar and trusted paths in worshiping God. How fast changes can be effectively made is a pastoral issue. Responsible pastoral leadership will sensitively recognize the gravity of moving beyond ways that are inadequate, though trusted, into ways that promise maturity and growth. It calls for respect for where people are. It requires a lot of love and patience, careful teaching, and understanding of people's feelings as they move into what is new and unfamiliar. Pastoral sensitivity will recognize when the unfamiliar begins to be familiar, and when once trusted ways will lose their allure, supplanted by ways that lead into the presence of God, in a manner the old ways could never do.
36. An excellent analysis of current alternative worship styles is: Frank C. Senn, "'Worship Alive': An Analysis and Critique of 'Alternative Worship Services'" *Worship* 69, no. 3 (May 1995): 194–224.
37. Gordon Lathrop, *Holy Things,* 175.

2. A Book of Services Is Recovered

1. *Eutaxia, or the Presbyterian Liturgies: Historical Sketches.* By a minister of the Presbyterian Church (New York: M. W. Dodd, Publisher, 1855). This book was republished in 1957 by Baker Book House, Grand Rapids, with the title: *Presbyterian Liturgies: Historical Sketches.*

2. James Hastings Nichols, *Corporate Worship in the Reformed Tradition* (Philadelphia: Westminister Press, 1968), 57.

3. James Hastings Nichols, "The Liturgical Tradition of the Reformed Churches," *Theology Today* II (July 1954): 215.

4. *Eutaxia,* 5.

5. Ibid., 260.

6. Julius Melton, *Presbyterian Worship in America: Changing Patterns Since 1787* (Richmond, VA: John Knox Press, 1967), 75, summarizing Charles Hodge, "Review of Eutaxia," *Biblical Repertory and Princeton Review* 27 (1855).

7. Another nineteenth-century stimulus for liturgical reform centered in a Presbyterian congregation, St. Peter's Church in Rochester, New York. Organized early in the 1850s, the liturgy used in this church was principally the work of Levi A. Ward, a layperson, the church's founder and a man who respected the liturgical traditions of the church catholic. For the remainder of the nineteenth century, this church served as a liturgical laboratory, providing hope for better worship among Presbyterians.

8. Nichols, *Corporate Worship*, 155, 156.

9. Ibid., 163–164.

10. Ibid., 165.

11. *The Book of Common Prayer and Administration of the Sacraments, and Other Rites and Ceremonies of the Church, as Amended by the Westminster Divines in the Royal Commission of 1661 and in Agreement with the Directory for Public Worship of the Presbyterian Church in the U.S.A.* (Philadelphia: William S. and Alfred Martien, 1864). (This is referred to elsewhere for convenience as the Presbyterian *Book of Common Prayer* [PBCP].)

12. Melton, *Presbyterian Worship in America,* 85ff.

13. While stirrings for liturgical reform were being felt among Anglicans, Lutherans, Reformed, the origin of the liturgical movement is generally regarded as beginning in Benedictine monasticism and most particularly in the refoundation of the Abbey of Solesmes in France by Dom Prosper Guéranger in 1832. Although romantic in its focus in the early part of the century, the movement began to take on its modern perspective toward the end of the century among Benedictines in Germany and Belgium. Slow to emerge in America, it began with the Benedictines of St. John's Abbey at Collegeville, Minnesota, in 1925. The movement had little impact on American Catholics before the sweeping liturgical reforms of the Second Vatican Council, which placed liturgical reform at the very heart of the church. The impact for liturgical reform set in place by Vatican II has impacted the liturgical life of all of Western Christianity.

14. *Minutes, General Assembly of the Presbyterian Church in the United States of America,* new series, vol. 4, no. 2, 1904. *Proceedings, etc., of the 116th General Assembly* (Philadelphia: Office of the General Assembly, 1904), 65–66.

15. A quotation from the *Interior,* contained in Tertius van Dyke, *Henry van Dyke: A Biography* (New York: Harper & Brothers, 1935), 273, 274.

16. *Minutes of the General Assembly of the Presbyterian Church in the United States of America, 1905,* 165, 173.

17. Melton, *Presbyterian Worship in America,* 131, 132. From "The Liturgic Trend in Presbyterianism," *Literary Digest* 30 (June 10, 1905): 862f., quoting *The Herald and Presbyter.*

18. *The Book of Common Worship* (Philadelphia: Presbyterian Board of Publication and Sabbath-School Work, 1906).

19. T. van Dyke, *Henry van Dyke,* 274.

20. *Minutes of the General Assembly of the Presbyterian Church in the United States of America, 1906,* 122.

21. T. van Dyke, *Henry van Dyke,* 396.

22. Quoted in ibid., 401.

23. Henry van Dyke often said he believed that his work in preparing a service book for the church was the most important task of his life.

24. *The Book of Common Worship,* revised ed. (Philadelphia: Presbyterian Board of Christian Education, 1932).

3. Liturgical Reform in the Mid-Twentieth Century

1. Jules Bonnet, ed., *Letters of John Calvin* (Philadelphia: Presbyterian Board of Publication, 1858) 2:348 (Letters to Cranmer, April 1552).

2. Pehr Edwall, Eric Hayman, William D. Maxwell, eds., *Ways of Worship: The Report of a Theological Commission of Faith and Order* (London: SCM Press Ltd., 1951), 24.

3. Cited in Howard Hageman, *Pulpit and Table* (Richmond: John Knox Press, 1962), 15.

4. *The Book of Common Worship* (Philadelphia: Board of Christian Education of the Presbyterian Church in the United States of America, 1946).

5. The eucharistic prayer caught the attention of the Episcopalians as they began the long process toward prayer book revision that ultimately led to the 1979 *Book of Common Prayer.* In *Prayer Book Studies IV, Eucharistic Liturgy,* prepared by the Standing Liturgical Commission of the Protestant Episcopal Church in the U.S.A. (New York: Church Pension Fund, 1953), 269–271, the Commission noted how the Presbyterians in the 1946 *Book of Common Worship* had moved in similar revisions as their own. They called attention to commendable aspects of the prayer in the 1946 *Book of Common Worship,* and commented,

> [I]t must be acknowledged that this Consecration Prayer has a simplicity of plan, a clarity of expression, and a forceful directness and economy of movement, which make it distinctly superior to our present American text. . . . Evidently it was inspired by the same objectives which we have had in mind in our construction of the Draft Liturgy, and has arrived at remarkably comparable results. The existence of such a piece of work is a strong argument for the adoption of something along the lines of what we have worked out. We simply cannot afford to let our Presbyterian brethren make better use of the valuable materials, new and old, which have been attained in the latest revisions of the Liturgy by our sister Provinces of the Anglican Communion (p. 271).

6. For more on the first three editions of *The Book of Common Worship,* see David Rodney Bluhm, "Trends of Worship Reflected in the Three Editions of the 'Book of Common Worship' of the Presbyterian Church in the U.S.A" (Ph.D. dissertation, University of Pittsburgh, 1956).

7. Quoted in Harry Ernest Winter, "Catholic, Evangelical and Reformed: The Lord's Supper in the (United) Presbyterian Church USA, 1945–70" (Ph.D. diss., University of Pennsylvania, 1976), 287.

8. Scott F. Brenner, *Way of Worship: A Study in Ecumenical Recovery* (New York: Macmillan Co., 1944), 77.

9. By 1974 the society had disbanded and its journal was taken over by the Program Agency of the United Presbyterian Church in the U.S.A.

10. In adopting the recommendation, the General Assembly of the United Presbyterian Church in the U.S.A. added "truly evangelical." This then became part of the objective of the Consultation on Church Union—a church that was "truly reformed, truly catholic, and truly evangelical."

11. Commission on Worship and the Executive Committee of the Consultation on Church Union. *An Order of Worship for the Proclamation of the Word of God and the Celebration of the Lord's Supper with Commentary* (Cincinnati, Ohio: Forward Movement Publications, 1968).

12. "C.O.C.U. and Worship," cited in Harry Ernest Winter, "Catholic, Evangelical and Reformed," 228n.
13. See special issue of *Reformed Liturgy & Music* 31, no. 2 (1997), on "Lutherans and Reformed in Dialogue." While Lutheran and Reformed theologians engaged in dialogue for a quarter of the century, Lutheran writers often wrote in *Reformed Liturgy & Music,* and Lutheran musicians were frequent clinicians at Worship and Music Conferences sponsored by the Presbyterian Association of Musicians. Thus Lutheran liturgical leaders helped shape Presbyterian understanding of the church's liturgy and have contributed to the professional and spiritual development of the musicians of Presbyterian congregations.
14. P. C. Rodger and Lukas Vischer, eds., *Fourth World Conference on Faith and Order* (New York: Association Press, 1964), 29.
15. International Consultation on English Texts, *Prayers We Have in Common,* 2d ed. (Philadelphia: Fortress Press, 1975).
16. *Service for the Lord's Day and Lectionary for the Christian Year* (Philadelphia: Westminster Press, 1964).
17. *The Book of Common Worship, Provisional Services and Lectionary for the Christian Year* (Philadelphia: Westminster Press, 1966.)
18. *The Worshipbook—Services* (Philadelphia: Westminster Press, 1970).
19. Directory for Worship, United Presbyterian Church in the U.S.A., 1980–81, 21.01. Cf. *The Worshipbook,* p. 34.
20. Scott Francis Brenner, *The Art of Worship: A Guide in Corporate Worship Techniques* (New York: Macmillan Company, 1961), 33. The quotation is from John Williamson Nevin, *The Liturgical Question.* These comments are just as apropos in response to often expressed opposition to use of a book of services.
21. A. Allan McArthur. *Christian Year and Lectionary Reform* (London: SCM, 1958), 65–70.
22. *Service for the Lord's Day . . . ,* pp. 33–38, and *The Book of Common Worship: Provisional Services . . . ,* pp. 129–135.
23. *Service for the Lord's Day. . . .*
24. *The Book of Common Worship: Provisional Services . . . ,* 36–45.
25. *Minutes of the General Assembly of the United Presbyterian Church in the U.S.A. (1971), Journal,* Part I, *Journal,* 313.
26. It must be added, however, that while *The Worshipbook* was in fact a service book in the hands of the people, most churches regarded it as a hymnal rather than a service book, and it was used as such. Ordinarily, when texts from *The Worshipbook* were used, they were placed in the worship bulletin. The exceptions might be in celebrating the sacraments, reception of members, and the occasional use of a litany.
27. Two years before *The Worshipbook* was published, Westminster Press published a small volume of orders for worship, prayers, liturgical music, and hymns, titled *Worship and Hymns for all Occasions* (Philadelphia: Westminster Press, 1968). Three members of the Joint Committee on Worship were on the compiling committee. A recording accompanying the book demonstrated the singing of the liturgy contained in the book. In several ways the volume anticipated *The Worshipbook—Services and Hymns* that was soon to follow in 1972.

4. A New Book of Services Is Called For

1. Letter to Virginia Robertson, Stated Clerk of the Presbytery of the Cascades, from the Rev. Duncan Hanson, pastor of First Presbyterian Church, Lakeview, Oregon, dated March 29, 1979.

2. Minutes of the Joint Administrative Committee of the Joint Office of Worship, March 19, 1980.
3. "Proposal: Development of a New Liturgical Resource: Joint Office of Worship, The United Presbyterian Church in the United States of America and The Presbyterian Church in the United States," 1.
4. Ibid., 2.
5. Ibid. Attachment: "Proposed Schedule for Development of a New Liturgical Resource."
6. *Minutes of the 192nd General Assembly (1980) of The United Presbyterian Church in the U.S.A.,* Part I, *Journal,* 63, 64.
7. Ibid., 64.
8. The minority report was contained in the report of the Liturgy and Worship Committee.
9. Addition to the Report of the General Assembly Mission Council to the 192nd General Assembly (1980), Reference Y-8. June 2, 1980.

5. The *Book of Common Worship* Is Prepared

1. The exception was *The Presbyterian Hymnal,* which required only the action of the Theology and Worship Ministry Unit to approve it for publication. None of the named entities were responsible for oversight of the development of the hymnal.
2. Directory for Worship, *The Constitution of the Presbyterian Church (U.S.A.),* Part II, *Book of Order* (Louisville, Ky.: Office of the General Assembly). Within the same time frame the Cumberland Presbyterian Church also prepared a new Directory for Worship and it was available to the task forces preparing the Supplemental Liturgical Resources.
3. James F. White, "Sources for the Study of Protestant Worship in America," *Worship* 61, no. 6 (November 1987): 530.
4. *Baptism, Eucharist and Ministry,* Faith and Order Paper No. 111 (Geneva: World Council of Churches, 1982), viii.
5. See p. 41.
6. The North American Academy of Liturgy was formed in 1974. Fr. John Gallen, S.J., was the driving force behind its formation. Arlo Duba, who was then teaching at Princeton Theological Seminary, was the sole Presbyterian in the founding group. Within four years the Presbyterian membership had grown, and today it constitutes one of the largest Protestant constituencies.
7. The Consultation on Common Texts, *A Celebration of Baptism* (Nashville: Abingdon Press, 1988).
8. English Language Liturgical Consultation, *Praying Together* (Nashville: Abingdon Press, 1988).
9. Consultation on Common Texts, *The Revised Common Lectionary* (Nashville: Abingdon Press, 1992).
10. This revision of the Psalter in *The Book of Common Prayer* by liturgical scholars Gail Ramshaw and Gordon Lathrop was later published as *An Inclusive-Language Psalter of the Christian People* (Collegeville, Minn.: Liturgical Press, 1993).
11. See pp. 48–49 and 53.
12. Two of the festival keynote addresses were published by the Office of Theology and Worship in Cynthia M. Campbell and J. Frederick Holper, *Praying in Common,* Theology and Worship Occasional Paper No. 6, Presbyterian Church (U.S.A.). DMS #70420-94-200.
13. *Book of Common Worship: Software Edition* (Louisville, Ky.: Westminster John Knox Press, 1995).

14. *Book of Occasional Services: A Liturgical Resource Supplementing the Book of Common Worship, 1993* (Louisville, Ky.: Geneva Press, 1999).
15. Bryan Spinks, "Glorifying God in Two Recent Presbyterian Worship Books," *Spectrum* 19, no. 1 (spring 1999): 10. *Spectrum* is a publication of Yale Divinity School.
16. A remark by the late Archbishop George Patrick Dwyer of Birmingham, England, noted in W. Jardine Grisbrooke, "Liturgical Reform and Liturgical Renewal," *Studia Liturgica* 21, no. 2 (1991): 154.

6. The Book of Common Worship: What's New?

1. The full title of John Knox's liturgy (1556) was *The Forme of Prayers and Ministration of the Sacraments, &c. vsed in the English Congregation at Geneua: and Approued, by the Famous and Godly Learned Man, Iohn Caluyn.* Geneva M.D.LVI. The text of this liturgy is included in Bard Thompson, *Liturgies of the Western Church* (Cleveland: World Publishing Co., 1961), 295–307.
2. When the Church of South India published its book of services in 1963, it chose the title *The Book of Common Worship.* The book of services for The Presbyterian Church in Canada has long been *The Book of Common Order.* When it published its new book in 1991, it chose instead the title: *The Book of Common Worship.*
3. *Book of Common Worship*, pp. 99–124.
4. Ibid., pp. 126–156.
5. *The Worshipbook*, pp. 31–33, 111–113.
6. *Book of Common Worship*, pp. 99–102.
7. Portions of *The Worshipbook* prayer appear in Great Thanksgiving C, ibid., pp. 130–132 and in the proper prefaces pp. 133–137.
8. Ibid., pp. 165–400.
9. *Book of Common Worship*, pp. 597–783.
10. Such as those in Hal Hopson's excellent collection in *Refrains and Psalm Tones* (Hope Publishing Company, 1988, 1992). See review in *Reformed Liturgy & Music* 23, no. 1 (1989): 50.
11. *Baptism, Eucharist and Ministry,* Faith and Order Paper No. 111 (Geneva: World Council of Churches, 1982).
12. When the baptismal rite first appeared, pastors feared that it was much longer than previous rites. Addressing this fear, Laurence Hull Stookey, in reviewing the rite, commented:

> The basic baptismal service is spread across twelve pages. This may seem to compare quite unfavorably with the rites of four pages in *The Worshipbook,* or with *The Book of Common Worship* of 1946, in which the service for infants is four pages long and that for adults four and a half pages in length. But a page count is a very inaccurate gauge for several reasons. First, both page and font sizes can vary greatly. Second, recent rites tend to provide many more options, so that three prayers may be printed, for example, but only one of the three will be used on a given occasion. Third, in the older books, type was spread all across the pages, margin to margin. Now what is to be said aloud (as distinct from the rubrics) is set out in "sense lines"—lines of greatly varying length, and often quite short, to allow the reader's eye to flow down the page, rather than across; this facilitates interpretation and ease of public speech. Finally, even counting words can be misleading; because the new rites tend to use less complex vocabulary, an actual syllable count is the only accurate basis of comparison.
>
> To illustrate: On the third page (p. 123) of the 1946 rite, when one infant was to be baptized 292 syllables were spoken, exclusive of the names of the

candidate. But the third page (p. 405) of the new rite contains only 91 syllables for use in the comparable situation. Thus, while the page size of the 1993
book is literally twice that of the 1946 page, it contains less than one-third
the verbiage. The new rite is also significantly shorter than the corresponding
third page of *The Worshipbook*—91 syllables compared with 241 syllables.
Hence the question so ingrained in students—"How many pages long is this
assignment?"—is totally inappropriate when comparing new rites to old.

Yet another consideration is that the new book provides one rite for candidates of any age. This was the case with the 1970 joint book; but in older
collections of rites, on a day when both children and adults were to be baptized it was necessary to work one's way through two separate sets of texts.

(From Laurence Hull Stookey, "Baptismal Rites in the Book of Common Worship (1993)," *Princeton Seminary Bulletin*, n.s., 16, no. #2 [1995]: 150–151.)

13. The *Daily Prayer* edition of the *Book of Common Worship* has found wide ecumenical reception. Ministers, professors, and laypersons of other traditions, even those
traditions having a Daily Office, have chosen to use it regularly.

14. "Language About God—Opening Doors" (1975), and "The Power of Language
Among the People of God" (1979).

15. Task Force on the Service for the Lord's Day, Minutes (unpublished), February
11–15, 1982, p. 5.

16. A recommended resource to help one understand the nature of liturgical language
is: Gail Ramshaw, *Reviving Sacred Speech: The Meaning of Liturgical Language*
(Akron, Ohio: OSL Publications, 2000). This book is a revision of her earlier book
Christ in Sacred Speech.

17. Walter Wangerin Jr. "What's a Good Story?" *The Lutheran*, July 11, 1990, p. 5.

18. The recommendations are contained in a letter dated August 14, 1984, following
action by the Executive Committee of the Presbyterian Association of Musicians
(PAM), in which it asked its president, John Weaver, to send a letter to the "Hymnal Formulation Committee" expressing "the strong interest, hopes, and concerns
of PAM in the formulation of a new hymnal" and to include the specific recommendations the Executive Committee adopted. The letter was addressed to staff and
elected leadership of the Program Agency of the former UPCUSA, the Division of
National Mission of the former PCUS, and to the director of the Joint Office of
Worship.

The letter reminded those to whom it was addressed of the place of PAM in the
church's life: "membership of approximately 2,000 persons" representing "the major
geographical sections of the nation." After stressing that PAM's primary reason for
existence continues to be "concern for worship and music of integrity," it expressed
its hope that great care be taken in selecting members of the committee. It then stated
the recommendations passed by the Executive Committee:

> We hope the hymns may, perhaps in some way, be easily identified with the
> lectionary readings provided by our denomination.
>
> We strongly recommend that this proposed hymnal contain these basic
> liturgical materials: (1) the Service for the Lord's Day, which is basically the
> Communion Service; (2) the Service of Baptism; (3) the Marriage Service; (4)
> the Funeral Service; and (5) a selective Psalter along with other scriptures. . . .

19. Congregations are finding ways to provide worshipers with appealing worship folders that engage the people in worship with ease. Such a task is now made easier with
the availability of computer software designed for Presbyterian churches, and other
service book, hymnal, and Psalter resources. Recently, in attending worship in a congregation where I do not customarily worship, I was handed a very attractive worship

folder to guide me through the liturgy. It was printed in-house on 8½ x 14 paper with two folds, providing six pages for the liturgy. All of the service music was included within the order of the service, as well as the congregation's refrain to a psalm sung by the choir. The singing of the hymns depended upon the availability of the hymnal. The texts of the prayers to be prayed together by the people, and the creed, were included. The texts of prayers offered by those leading worship (prayers not needed by the people for their participation) were not included. The folder was simple and dignified, well-designed, and had an inviting visual appeal. It enabled worshipers to participate in the service with ease. There was no fumbling with books, or loose pieces of paper, just the liturgy and a hymnal. Such a user-friendly guide to the liturgy is an especially hospitable gesture to visitors unfamiliar with the order of service.

Some congregations avoid such a weekly task by preparing several basic settings of the service music. These might include a different setting for each of the major seasons of the liturgical calendar, and two or three for the long period in Ordinary time following Pentecost. These settings of the service music are printed on a heavy paper or card stock, the size of the weekly worship folder when folded. Unlike the weekly worship folder, they are reused each Sunday during the particular season for which they are designed. While not as convenient as having everything in a single folder each week, this is a viable alternative, especially for small congregations.

20. Fritz A. Rothschild, ed., *Between God and Man: An Interpretation of Judaism From the Writings of Abraham Joshua Heschel* (New York: Free Press, 1959), 208. This quotation is part of an excerpt, in Rothschild's book, from Heschel's *Man's Quest for God: Studies in Prayer and Symbolism* (New York: Charles Scribner's Sons, 1954).

21. Scott Francis Brenner, *The Art of Worship: A Guide in Corporate Worship Techniques* (New York: Macmillan Co., 1961), 21.

22. George F. MacLeod, *Only One Way Left: Church Prospect,* 3d ed. (Glasgow: Iona Community, 1961), 100.

7. Future Service Books

1. See chapter 2.

2. J. V. L. Casserley, "The Significance of the Liturgical Movement," *Religion in Life* 29 (spring, 1960): 211.

3. See pp. 40–41, 59–60.

4. Among the traditions regularly represented on the board of directors are Roman Catholic, Lutheran, Presbyterian, Episcopalian, and Methodist.

5. Paul Waitman Hoon, *The Integrity of Worship: Ecumenical and Pastoral Studies in Liturgical Theology* (Nashville: Abingdon Press, 1971), 17.

6. Eugene L. Brand, "Response to the Berakah Award: Ecumenism and the Liturgy," *Worship* 58 (1984): 307–308.

7. Ibid., 315.

8. Eugene L. Brand, "An Ecumenical Enterprise" in Ralph R. Van Loon, ed., *Encountering God: The Legacy of Lutheran Book of Worship for the 21st Century* (Minneapolis: Kirk House Publishers, 1998), 20.

9. The Rt. Rev. Robert E. Terwilliger, "Fantasy," *Anglican Digest* 32, no. 6 (Advent-Epiphany), A.D. 1990): 13. (The author's middle initial is E., not T., as given in the *Anglican Digest*.)

10. A summary of his address may be found in American Academy of Ecumenists, *From Organization through Dialogue to Decision: The Third Stage of Ecumenism,* Occasional Papers 45, November 1995.

11. Ibid., 11.

12. Ibid.
13. Ibid.
14. Ibid., 16.
15. Ibid.
16. See p. 34.
17. As we have already noted, however, the Consultation on Common Texts has ecumenically prepared not only a common lectionary, but a wedding rite and a baptismal rite. With the English Language Liturgical Consultation it has prepared common texts for common parts of the liturgy, as well as a eucharistic prayer for ecumenical use. Also, the Commission on Worship of the Consultation on Church Union has produced liturgies for use by participating churches, such as a service of Word and Sacrament, a baptismal liturgy, and a collection of eucharistic prayers.
18. See Paul Westermeyer, "Three books of worship: An ecumenical convergence," *Christian Century,* October 27, 1993, 1055–1057.
19. With the adoption of the Formula of Agreement between Reformed churches and the Evangelical Lutheran Church in America, the Episcopal/Lutheran Concordat, and the adoption of the Joint Declaration on the Doctrine of Justification by Lutherans and Roman Catholics, it seems that Lutherans will have an exciting ecumenical challenge in developing their next book of services. It suggests the propriety of including Reformed, Episcopal, and Catholic representatives on the commission to prepare the next Lutheran service book.
20. In reference to the North American Academy of Liturgy, Societas Liturgica, the Consultation on Common Texts, and the English Language Liturgical Consultation, see p. 60.
21. See pp. 269–270, note 19.
22. *Common Worship: Services and Prayers for the Church of England* (London: Church House Publishing, 2000).
23. Publishing in 1989, the Church of the Province of New Zealand (Anglican) broke new ground in publishing *A New Zealand Prayer Book, He Karakia Mihinare o Aotearoa* (Auckland: William Collins Publishers Ltd.). Its major contribution was to give expression to a liturgy that, while faithful to tradition, reflects the Pacific cultural setting. Furthermore, it provides rich and diverse liturgical texts. It is of ecumenical interest that the Church of England's *Common Worship* marks that church's adoption of the Revised Common Lectionary.

8. Eucharistic Recovery, the Centerpiece of Liturgical Reform

1. See also the account of worship on the Lord's Day in Acts 20:7–12.
2. Eucharistic theology is particularly evident in John 6. See Oscar Cullmann, *Early Christian Worship,* trans. A. Stewart Todd and James B. Torrance, Studies in Biblical Theology 10 (London: SCM Press, 1953).
3. Justin Martyr, *First Apology* (ca. 155), trans. Edward Rochie Hardy. Quoted in James F. White, *Documents of Christian Worship: Descriptive and Interpretive Sources* (Louisville, Ky.: Westminster/John Knox Press, 1992), 185–186.
4. *Book of Common Worship,* p. 41.
5. Means of grace: a means, or instrument, given to us by God by which we are assured of God's grace—of our forgiveness, our salvation, our adoption as children of God.
6. "According to the liturgy of Zurich, the Lord's Supper is not actually an integral part of the service at all, but is appended to it after a formula of dismissal which, with God's blessing, dismisses from the church all those 'who cannot or do not wish to communicate.'" Kathi La Roche, "Report from Europe," *Reformed Liturgy & Music,* Special Issue, 1995, p. 26.

7. Following the Second Vatican Council, Roman Catholic theologians began to explore the meaning of the real presence in the Eucharist in ways that are in harmony with modern physics, setting it free from Aristotelian concepts. Even though the Roman Catholic Church still officially adheres to the definitions of Trent, the contribution of these Catholic theologians holds a promise that there may someday be a convergence among Catholics and Reformation traditions, concerning the nature of the real presence in the Eucharist. The concepts of these theologians have been labeled transsignification. Transsignification centers on meaning and purpose in the sacramental signs, recognizing that meaning is an aspect of the reality of something. In the Sacrament, therefore, there is an ontological change. It is a change in what the bread and wine signifies, rather than a change in substance, as we now understand the word substance. A common analogy is that of a sheep's wool. On the sheep its significance is a coat of hair to ward off wet and cold. When sheared and woven into cloth, its significance is a raw material for use in industry. When tailored into a garment, its significance is that of clothing to be worn by humans. Other analogies have included the change of sign that takes place in the making of an American flag or the minting of coins. A flag, like a coin, signifies far more than its raw materials. So also, the Eucharist effects a change in sign. In the Eucharist, the elements are no longer merely bread and wine, for the sign has changed. In partaking of them we feast upon Christ. It has been suggested that this concept of the Sacrament is not unlike that of Calvin. For a Catholic exposition of transsignification, see E. Schillebeeckx O.P., *The Eucharist,* trans. N. D. Smith (London and Sydney: Sheed & Ward, 1968). For comments by a Reformed theologian, see: Alasdair I. C. Heron, *Table and Tradition: Toward an Ecumenical Understanding of the Eucharist* (Philadelphia: Westminster Press, 1983), 164–165.

8. *Calvin: Institutes of the Christian Religion,* Library of Christian Classics, ed. John T. McNeill, trans. Ford Lewis Battles (Philadelphia: Westminster Press, 1960), pp. 1403–1404 (4.17.32). For Calvin's sacramental theology see pp. 1276–1303 (4.14). For his eucharistic theology in particular see pp. 1359–1428 (4.17). And see John Calvin, "Short Treatise on the Holy Supper of our Lord and only Saviour Jesus Christ," in *Calvin: Theological Treatises,* Library of Christian Classics, trans. and with introduction and notes by J. K. S. Reid (Philadelphia: Westminster Press, 1954), 140–177. The following secondary sources are very useful: B. A. Gerrish: *Grace and Gratitude: The Eucharistic Theology of John Calvin* (Minneapolis: Fortress Press, 1993); and Alasdair I. C. Heron, *Table and Tradition: Toward an Ecumenical Understanding of the Eucharist,* 108–145.

9. Calvin: *Institutes,* p. 1023 (4.1.9). This is comparable with the Augsburg Confession (Art. VII), which defines the church as "the congregation of saints in which the gospel is rightly taught and the sacraments are rightly administered."

10. "Articles concerning the Organization of the Church and of Worship at Geneva proposed by the Ministers at the Council, January 16, 1537," in *Calvin: Theological Treatises,* 49.

11. Ibid.

12. Ibid., 50.

13. Ibid., 66 n. 58.

14. Karl Gottlieb Bretschneider, *Corpus Reformatorum,,* vol. 38, i, p. 213.

15. "The Westminster Directory" in Bard Thompson, *Liturgies of the Western Church* (Cleveland and New York: World Publishing Co., Meridian Books, 1961), 368.

16. The Directory for the Worship of God (adopted 1788, amended, 1789–1933), chapter IX, par. 1.

17. For an overview of the work of Shields, see Julius Melton, *Presbyterian Worship in America: Changing Patterns Since 1787* (Richmond: John Knox Press, 1967), 83–88.

18. Charles W. Shields, "Liturgica Expurgata; or, The Prayer-Book Amended According to the Presbyterian Revision of 1661 and Historically and Critically Reviewed," an essay appended to Shields's prayer book, *The Book of Common Prayer and Administration of the Sacraments*, 107. (See chap. 2, note 11.)

19. Ibid., 118.

20. Shields, *The Book of Common Prayer and Administration of the Sacraments*, 231.

21. *The Book of Common Worship* (1906), pp. 34–39.

22. "Directory for the Worship of God," in *The Constitution of The United Presbyterian Church in the United States of America*, Part II, *The Book of Order* (New York: Office of the General Assembly of the United Presbyterian Church in the United States of America, 1961 through 1981), par. 21.01.

23. "Directory for the Worship and Work of the Church," in *The Book of Church Order*, Presbyterian Church in the United States (Atlanta: Office of the Stated Clerk of the General Assembly, The Presbyterian Church in the United States, 1961–1982), par. 211.2.

24. *Service for the Lord's Day and Lectionary*. . . .

25. Ibid., 20.

26. *The Book of Common Worship: Provisional Services*. . . .

27. However, two texts were provided, one in Elizabethan English, and the other in contemporary language.

28. *The Book of Common Worship: Provisional Services* . . . , p. 29.

29. Ibid., pp. 34–35.

30. *The Worshipbook—Services*, pp. 38–40.

31. See *Service for the Lord's Day*, Supplemental Liturgical Resource 1 (Philadelphia: Westminster Press, 1984), p. 21. See also pp. 12, 13, 21–25.

32. See *Book of Common Worship*, pp. 46, 47, 220, 251, 402, 418, 430, 446, 454, 463, 852.

33. Ibid., p. 66.

34. Ibid., pp. 33, 41–42.

35. "It is appropriate to celebrate the Lord's Supper as often as each Lord's Day. It is to be celebrated regularly and frequently enough to be recognized as integral to the Service for the Lord's Day."—Directory for Worship, *The Constitution of the Presbyterian Church (U.S.A.)*, Part II, *Book of Order* (Louisville, Ky.: Office of the General Assembly, 1989–1994), W-2.4009.

36. For documentation of the increase in frequency of celebrating the Eucharist, and strategies for moving toward weekly celebration, see Harold M. Daniels, "Weekly Eucharist Among Presbyterians," *Reformed Liturgy & Music* 19, no. 1 (1985): 18–23; and Harold M. Daniels, "Presbyterians at the Table of the Lord," *Reformed Liturgy & Music* 25, no. 2 (1991): 60–64.

9. Four Primary Liturgical Reforms

1. Walter Brueggemann, *Biblical Perspectives on Evangelism: Living in a Three-Stories Universe* (Nashville: Abingdon Press, 1993), 45.

2. In an increasingly secular age, a greater number of converts will have little or no experience in the church, be unbaptized with limited understanding of the faith. Furthermore, a growing number of them will have pursued other spiritual quests in search of meaning. Thus the way converts are formed in the faith as they prepare for Baptism has increasing urgency if the faith is to have integrity in the church's life. This has resulted in a reexamination of the ancient catechumenate, and its adaptation for our time. The catechumenate process passes through three stages. Inquiry is the first stage. Having been drawn to the Christian community, persons are guided

in deciding whether they wish to become Christians and commit themselves to the discipline of exploring the implications of Christian living. The catechumenate is the second stage, a period involving persons in the process of conversion in claiming the ways of faith. A period of candidacy for Baptism is the third stage, taking place throughout Lent. This period is a time of reflection on the implications of the Lenten lectionary readings upon their conversion. This period culminates in Baptism at the Easter Vigil, and their welcome at the Lord's Table. Following their baptism, until Pentecost, the meaning of the event of Baptism is explored, during which the newly baptized are assisted to experience the fullness of the communal life of the church, both in its life together and in its ministries of compassion in the world. The catechumenate thus engages converts over a significant period of time, guiding them into the life of discipleship. While conversion takes a lifetime, the catechumenate begins the conversion process giving promise for faithfulness in the Christian life. This process can be a vital aspect of a congregation's evangelism. In the years following the publication of the *Book of Common Worship*, Presbyterians have joined with other churches to examine the catechumenate process.

3. *Book of Common Worship*, prayer [411], pp. 410–411.
4. Directory for Worship, W-3.3605; *Book of Common Worship*, p. 413. See also p. 39.
5. For the importance of the space for Baptism, in liturgical reform, see Harold M. Daniels, "The Font: a Bath, a Womb, and a Tomb," *Reformed Liturgy & Music* 29, no. 1 (1995): 22–27; and S. Anita Stauffer, "Space for Baptism," *Reformed Liturgy & Music* 19, no. 4 (1985): 174–178. Stauffer has also prepared an excellent video, *Re-examining Baptismal Fonts: Baptismal Space for the Contemporary Church* (Collegeville, Minn.: Liturgical Press, 1991).
6. "Proposed Chapter on Baptism for a New Directory for Worship," received for study by the 196th General Assembly (1984) of the Presbyterian Church (U.S.A.), 30.203–204. See also Directory for Worship, W-2.3009, which is a revision of this text for inclusion in the Directory. An excellent commentary on the services for the reaffirmation of the baptismal covenant is Robert M. Shelton, "Services for the Renewal of Baptism," *Reformed Liturgy & Music* 19, no. 4 (1985): 215–218. Though addressing the services in the Supplemental Liturgical Resource on Baptism published prior to the *Book of Common Worship*, it is largely applicable to the *Book of Common Worship* services. The major difference is the change in terminology from "renewal of Baptism" to "reaffirmation of the baptismal covenant."
7. The commentary in Supplemental Liturgical Resource 2, *Holy Baptism and Services for the Renewal of Baptism* (Philadelphia: Westminster Press, 1985), pp. 13–23, 48–62, remains a valuable resource to use in relation to the baptismal liturgy in the *Book of Common Worship*, even though it was published prior to the adoption of the current Directory for Worship. For ecumenical possibilities in baptismal practice see Harold M. Daniels, "Baptism: A Basic Bond of Unity," *Reformed Liturgy & Music* 29, no. 2 (1995): 88–94.
8. *Book of Common Worship*, p. 61.
9. This text appears in the eucharistic prayers in the *Book of Common Worship* as follows: pp. 71, 154, 182, 195, 202, 351, 398, and 931. Other eucharistic prayers express this similarly, "Accept this our sacrifice of praise and thanksgiving as a living and holy offering of ourselves that our lives may proclaim the One crucified and risen." See pp. 230, 239, 258, 276, 320, 345, 388, 871.
10. Directory for Worship, W-2.4006.
11. B. A. Gerrish, *Grace and Gratitude: The Eucharistic Theology of John Calvin* (Minneapolis: Fortress Press, 1993), 156.
12. *Book of Common Order of the Church of Scotland* (London: Oxford University Press, 1940), p. 119. This text elaborates the mystery Calvin recognized in the Sacrament.

13. Directory for Worship, W-2.4005f.
14. Directory for Worship, W-2.4006.
15. *Book of Common Worship,* prayer [115], p. 129.
16. *Book of Common Worship,* p. 72. The same text may be found in other of the eucharistic prayers.
17. Directory for Worship, W-2.4006.
18. *Book of Common Worship,* p. 68; based on Luke 13:29.
19. Directory for Worship, W-2.4006.
20. Two valuable essays on eucharistic practice are: Horace T. Allen Jr., "Lord's Day—Lord's Supper," *Reformed Liturgy & Music* 18, no. 4 (1984): 162–166; and Marney Ault Wasserman, "The Shape of Eucharistic Thanksgiving," *Reformed Liturgy & Music* 29, no. 3 (1995): 139–145.
21. "The Second Helvetic Confession," *The Constitution of the Presbyterian Church (U.S.A.),* Part I, *Book of Confessions,* 5.226.
22. *Liturgical Year,* Supplemental Liturgical Resource 7 (Louisville, Ky.: Westminster/John Knox Press, 1992), p. 20. The commentary from *Liturgical Year* from which this quotation was taken was republished as "Liturgical Time," *Call to Worship: Liturgy, Music, Preaching & the Arts* 35, no. 1 (2001): 46–86 (see p. 47). This essay, the major portion of which was written by Peter C. Bower, is an exceptionally fine commentary on the Liturgical Year section of the BCW.
23. Ibid., p. 21. Cited in connection with this paragraph is Peter C. Bower, "Editorial Introduction," *Reformed Liturgy & Music* 16, no. 4 (1982): 146.
24. In the *Book of Common Worship,* the Triduum bears the title "the Three Days" (see pp. 118–119).
25. Since Maundy Thursday, Good Friday, and the Easter Vigil form one unified liturgy, there are no benedictions at the end of the liturgies for Maundy Thursday and Good Friday (see pp. 279 and 291 of the *Book of Common Worship*). The people simply recess until the next portion of the liturgy resumes. The blessing comes at the end of the Triduum, at the Great Vigil of Easter.
26. *Liturgical Year,* p. 38. Cited in relation to this quotation is: Brian Heldge, *A Triduum Sourcebook,* ed. Gabe Huck and Mary Ann Simcoe (Chicago: Liturgy Training Publications, 1983), pp. 77, 78.
27. Richard Rowe and his wife, Ann, are retired Presbyterian fraternal workers, having served in Cameroon, Ethiopia, and Pakistan.
28. Dr. Eva Fleischner is a retired professor of religion at Montclair State University in Upper Montclair, New Jersey. A Roman Catholic with a Jewish background, she has focused her studies primarily on the Holocaust, although her interests range over a broad spectrum of religion, including the study of Native American religion.
29. Quoted from a letter to the author, dated September 12, 2000.
30. Philip Pfatteicher in *Praying with the Church . . . ,* 33–44, has a wonderful chapter, "With All God's Creatures," recommended reading for all who pray the Daily Office. In it Pfatteicher reflects on the words from the *Te Deum* (We Praise You, O God"), *omnis terra veneratur,* "all creation worships you." Literally, it means "all the earth, all creation, every aspect of the universe, every part of God's creation, all creatures" (cf. A Canticle of Creation, and Ps. 148). Since apart from human beings the rest of creation is wordless, humans have responsibility to express in words the wordless praise of all creation. The impact of this recognition will influence how we live with the rest of creation.
31. Phos Hilaron is included in the *Book of Common Worship* as "Hymn to Christ the Light," pp. 507, 576–577. A musical setting for this translation of this ancient hymn is included in *The Presbyterian Hymnal* (no. 548), along with two paraphrases (nos. 549 and 550). See also nos. 167, 168, 169 in *The Psalter—Psalms & Canticles for Singing* (Louisville, Ky.: Westminster/John Knox Press, 1993).

32. See *Book of Common Worship,* pp. 505–513.
33. Arlo Duba, "Worship, Daily Life, and the Sacraments," *Reformed Liturgy & Music* 31, no. 1 (1997): 51.
34. In contrast, Reformed churches on the Continent have taken greater care in preserving the Psalms.
35. For guidance in beginning the discipline of daily prayer see Harold M. Daniels, "Every Day I Will Bless You," *Reformed Liturgy & Music* 33, no. 4 (1999): 3–12. An excellent overview of daily prayer, prepared for the laity, is Philip Pfatteicher, *Praying with the Church.*
36. Worship resources prepared by individual writers continue to flood the market. Often seen as a quick fix for Sunday morning, they find their way to the shelves of those preparing worship. Their quality as well as their usefulness varies widely. One may occasionally find a prayer or text that not only is creative but also reflects a solid understanding of the nature of Christian liturgy, and is therefore useful. However, the use of such prayers should be approached with critical caution. Their major weakness lies in their reflecting the piety of one person, the author. Since they express the creativity of one individual, a predominant use of such material undermines a sense of worship shared in common. Furthermore, some worship resources published by individuals are prepared with a purposeful advocating of a particular ideology or social cause. They thus lack the breadth of the church's liturgy. Another major weakness of these popular resources is that the texts are not designed for repeated use. Use of disposable texts robs the people of the opportunity to store within their minds and hearts prayers from the treasury of liturgical prayer. The prayers in the church's liturgical treasury have come within the embrace of the whole church, whether they were written by one person or are the work of many. Prayers in a church's service book do not ordinarily bear the name of the author, for this is not in keeping with the spirit of common prayer. Common prayer is the church's prayer. A church's prayer book, such as the *Book of Common Worship,* is not simply one resource among other resources on a pastor's shelf to occasionally dip into when preparing worship. A book of services invites a congregation into an ordered discipline that is foundational to all that the church is and does.

10. The Promise for Renewal

1. *Book of Common Worship,* prayer [23], p. 23.
2. *Book of Common Worship,* prayer [8], p. 19.
3. See Acts 17:28 and prayer of Augustine of Hippo, *Book of Common Worship,* prayer [2], p. 17.
4. Joan Zwagerman Curbow, "Honey in the Rock: Liturgy as Conversion," *Reformed Liturgy & Music* 33, no. 4 (1999): 18. Originally published in *Perspectives: A Journal of Reformed Thought* (September 1999), a journal of Western Theological Seminary, Holland, Michigan.
5. Ibid.
6. Ibid., 18–20.
7. Marva J. Dawn, *Reaching Out without Dumbing Down: A Theology of Worship for the Turn of the Century* (Grand Rapids: Wm. B. Eerdmans Publishing Co., 1995), 256. The Pelikan reference is to *The Vindication of Tradition* (New Haven, Conn.: Yale University Press, 1984), 65.
8. Gordon W. Lathrop, "How Awesome Is This Place! The Lutheran Book of Worship and the Encounter with God," in Ralph R. Van Loon, ed., *Encountering God . . . ,* 44.
9. Stanley Hauerwas and William H. Willimon, *Resident Aliens: Life in the Christian Colony* (Nashville: Abingdon Press, 1989), 11–12.

10. Lefferts A. Loetscher, *The Broadening Church: A Study of Theological Issues in the Presbyterian Church Since 1869* (Philadelphia: University of Pennsylvania Press, 1957), 2.

11. Fritz A. Rothschild, *Between God and Man: An Interpretation of Judaism from the Writings of Abraham Joshua Heschel* (New York: Free Press, 1959), 183. This quotation is taken from an excerpt in Rothschild's book from Heschel's *God in Search of Man: A Philosophy of Judaism* (New York: Farrar, Straus & Cudahy, 1955).

12. Douglas John Hall, *Remembered Voices: Reclaiming the Legacy of Neo-Orthodoxy* (Louisville, Ky.: Westminster/John Knox Press, 1998), 144.

13. *Book of Common Worship,* 9.

14. Ibid., 6.

15. Ibid., 6–7.

16. Bernhard W. Anderson, *Understanding the Old Testament* 3rd ed. (Englewood Cliffs, N.J.: Prentice-Hall, 1975), 55, 56.

17. Thomas Cahill, *The Gifts of the Jews: How a Tribe of Desert Nomads Changed the Way Everyone Thinks and Feels,* Hinges of History 2 (New York: Doubleday, Anchor Books, 1998), 110.

18. Aurelia Fule emphasized this in quotations from John Calvin's commentaries, in an address, "The Trinity in Theology and Worship," given at "Sisters in Santa Fe," a conference sponsored by the National Association of Presbyterian Clergywomen and the Women's Ministries Program Area of the Presbyterian Church (U.S.A.), at Plaza Resolana in Santa Fe, New Mexico, September 21–24, 2000:

> "God cannot be comprehended by us except as far as he accommodates himself to our standard" (Calvin, Com. Ezek. 9:3, 4). "For since he is himself incomprehensible, he assumes when he wishes to manifest himself to [women and] men, those works by which he may be known" (Com. Gen. 3:8). "God in his greatness can by no means be fully comprehended by our minds. . . . God accommodates to our measure what he testifies of himself" (Com. Rom. 1:19). "He accommodates himself to our capacity in addressing us" (Com. 1 Cor. 2:17).
>
> Accommodation, the recurring term, refers "to the process by which God reduces or adjusts to human capacities what he wishes to reveal of the infinite mysteries of his being. . . ." (E. Dowey, *The Knowledge of God in Calvin's Theology,* p. 3).
>
> The essence of God is unknown and inaccessible to us and all speculation is blasphemy, according to our tradition. We do have knowledge of God, however, in both creation and revelation, as we just heard from Calvin and one of his best interpreters, Professor Dowey.

19. The great Reformed theologian Karl Barth wrote voluminously, expounding every aspect of the faith. His greatest work was his *Church Dogmatics,* a whole shelf of thick volumes elaborating his theological concepts. Yet he understood the limitations of the theological task in seeking to fathom the unfathomable. Toward the end of his life, he said, "There can only be 'little' theologians." He once commented, "The angels laugh at old Karl. They laugh at him because he tries to grasp the truth about God in a book of Dogmatics. They laugh at the fact that volume follows volume, and each is thicker than the previous one. As they laugh, they say to one another, 'Look! Here he comes now with his little pushcart full of volumes of the Dogmatics!' And they laugh, too, about the men who write so much about Karl Barth instead of writing about the things he is trying to write about. Truly, the angels laugh." This delightful anecdote was shared shortly after his death in 1968. Unfortunately, I have lost the original source.

20. Calvin teaches us that what God has made known about God's self is not God's essence, but "how [God] is toward us." God "consists more in living experience than in vain and high-flown speculation." Toward us, God is known in kindness, goodness, mercy, justice, judgment, and truth. See Calvin, *Institutes* 1.10.2, pp. 97, 98.

21. Philip H. Pfatteicher, *Liturgical Spirituality* (Valley Forge, Pa.: Trinity Press, 1997), 251–252. This book is highly recommended, as it probes the spiritual depths of the liturgical heritage. Although it does not always reference the *Book of Common Worship* in every place it might, it is instructive to all who seek to understand the liturgical tradition. It unfolds the strength and majesty of the liturgy and its power to transform. In my judgment, it merits careful study by all who take the *Book of Common Worship* seriously, and by those who wish to know what the liturgical heritage is all about. It is a book to read and reread. It was reviewed in *Reformed Liturgy & Music* 32, no. 2 (1998): 116–117.

Part II. The Sources of the Book of Common Worship

1. Bard Thompson, *Liturgies of the Western Church* (Cleveland: World Publishing Co., 1961), 198.

2. Ibid., 209.

3. For more on the sign of the cross, see: Harold M. Daniels, "The Sign of the Cross," *Reformed Liturgy & Music* 21, no. 1 (1987): 39–44.

4. The church in the West came to express the concept of the Trinity using the Latin word *persona* (the mask worn by an actor), in translating the Greek word *hypostasis*. Our word *person* evolved from *persona*. However our usage of *person* as an individual, distinct and separate identity is not what those early theologians were saying when they spoke of the three *personae* of the Trinity. What they sought to convey may be better understood as three ways in which we know the one God. The word *mode*, comes closer to the meaning of *persona*. Therefore, to avoid any semblance of tritheism, careful catechesis needs to accompany our singing and speaking, in hymn and creed, of "God in three persons."

5. "The Confession of 1967," *The Constitution of the Presbyterian Church (U.S.A.)*, Part I, *Book of Confessions*, 9.27–9.30.

6. For an analysis of Solemn Intercessions see Marion J. Hatchett, *Commentary on the American Prayer Book* (New York: Seabury Press, 1980, 1995).

7. Philip Pfatteicher, *Commentary on the Lutheran Book of Worship: Lutheran Liturgy in Its Ecumenical Context* (Minneapolis: Augsburg Fortress, 1990), 253.

8. For an analysis of the Exsultet, see: ibid., 265–273.

9. Sermon XX in Newman's *Sermons on Subjects of the Day.*

10. Psalm 104:1,14c–15; BCW, pp. 728–729.

11. Gordon Lathrop and Gail Ramshaw: *An Inclusive-Language Psalter of the Christian People* (Collegeville, Minn.: Liturgical Press, 1993). See pp. 60–61 for an account of how this came to be included in the BCW.

12. See the excellent collection by Hal H. Hopson, *Psalm Refrains and Tones for the Common Lectionary* (Carol Stream, Ill.: Hope Publishing Company, 1988; revised in 1992 to be in harmony with the Revised Common Lectionary).

13. Fyodor Mikhailovich Dostoyevsky, *The Brothers Karamazov,* part II, book six, chapter 3, "From Talks and Homilies of the Elder Zosima," section (g), "Prayer, Love, and the Touching of Other Worlds." Page 319 in the edition by Richard Pevear and Larissa Volokhonsky (New York: Vintage Books, 1990).

14. Hatchett, *Commentary on the American Prayer Book,* 436.

15. Pfatteicher, *Commentary on the Lutheran Book of Worship,* 499.

For Further Reading

The *Book of Common Worship* is more than an outstanding collection of prayers. To simply use it as a resource on a shelf alongside others to draw upon when needing help to restart one's own creative juices, or to turn to find something for next Sunday, is to misunderstand the role and purpose of the *Book of Common Worship*. It is rather to be embraced as a *reforming discipline* for the church in our time. Its major contribution is in providing the *ordo*, that is, the essential shape of Christian liturgy, that has formed the community of faith from ancient times. Its texts and prayers, much of which provide us something of the cherished liturgical heritage from across time, give flesh to the *ordo*. To take the *Book of Common Worship* seriously is to embrace the discipline that it sets forth understanding that it portrays the very essence of what the church is and is to be about. In becoming liturgically informed, the role and purpose of the *Book of Common Worship* comes clearly into focus.

It is essential that ministers of Word and Sacrament, and laypersons who share with ministers in preparing and leading worship, have basic knowledge about Christian worship, and its central role in the life of the church. A knowledgeable leadership will not only be more effective in liturgical leadership, but can guide a congregation into a deeper understanding of the meaning and purpose of worship, thereby strengthening the life of faith and service of the people. Continued study in the roots, history, theology, purpose, and practice of Christian worship is just as important in congregational life as are biblical, theological, pastoral care, and missional studies. Indeed, it is crucial to seek integrity in worship, since it is the center of the church's life where the faith and life of the people are formed. Only by increasing our understanding of the meaning and purpose of Christian worship can we expect to overcome the unhealthy prejudices, resulting from ignorance and indifference, that often hinder efforts to find integrity in worship.

Furthermore, knowledge of the theology and practice of Christian worship can equip leadership with skills of discernment in embracing worship forms that strengthen the people in the faith, and in avoiding ways of worship that short circuit the essential purpose of Christian worship.

Confronted with the extensive literature on Christian worship, it is often confusing to know where to begin in becoming liturgically informed. A filter is needed to direct persons to the best resources that will help them understand the role and purpose of the *Book of Common Worship*, and to guide them in its use. The reading guide that follows is such a filter. Pursuing the levels of reading suggested can lead those who care about the church's worship to an increasingly valuable understanding of essential aspects of Christian worship. The guide is not intended to be a comprehensive reading list on worship and its varied aspects, but rather to provide foundational commentary on what the *Book of Common Worship* is all about.

A READING GUIDE IN THE FOUNDATIONS OF CHRISTIAN WORSHIP

Use of the guide that follows will be most effective if the *Book of Common Worship* is a constant companion and studied in relation to the readings.

First, study carefully:

The preface in the *Book of Common Worship* (pp. 1–13); and the section introducing the Service for the Lord's Day (pp. 33–45).

The Directory for Worship in the *Book of Order*. *The Constitution of the Presbyterian Church (U.S.A.)*, Part II, *Book of Order* (Louisville, Ky.: Office of the General Assembly, 2001)

Second, read the following:

Gordon W. Lathrop, *What Are the Essentials of Christian Worship?* in the series Open Questions in Worship (Minneapolis: Augsburg Fortress, 1994).
Peter C. Bower, ed. *Companion to the Book of Common Worship* (Louisville: Geneva Press, forthcoming).
James F. White, *Introduction to Christian Worship*, revised ed. (Nashville: Abingdon Press, 1980, 1990).

Follow these foundational readings by reading the following books, which will engage one in the study of worship at a deeper level:

Donald Saliers, *Worship as Theology: A Foretaste of Glory Divine* (Nashville: Abingdon Press, 1994).
Philip H. Pfatteicher, *Liturgical Spirituality* (Valley Forge, Pa.: Trinity Press International, 1997).
Gail Ramshaw, *Reviving Sacred Speech: The Meaning of Liturgical Language* (Akron, Ohio: OSL Publications, 1999).

William Seth Adams, *Shaped by Images: The One Who Presides* (New York: Church Hymnal Corporation, 1995).
Marva J. Dawn, *Reaching Out without Dumbing Down* (Grand Rapids: Wm. B. Eerdmans Publishing Co., 1995).

Along with these readings one will find brief essays referenced in the endnotes of this book to be highly informative. See especially the following notes for suggested readings elaborating on the four major areas of liturgical reform: *Baptism* (p. 274, notes 5, 6, and 7; p. 278, note 3); *Eucharist* (p. 272, note 8; p. 273, note 36; p. 275, note 20); *Liturgical Year* (p. 275, note 22); and *Daily Prayer* (p. 276, note 35).

With this background, other valuable readings include:

Gordon W. Lathrop, *Holy Things: A Liturgical Theology* (Minneapolis: Fortress Press, 1993), and *Holy People: A Liturgical Ecclesiology* (Minneapolis: Fortress Press, 1999).
Donald Saliers, *Worship as Spirituality*, 2nd ed. (Akron, Ohio: OSL Publications, 1996); *Worship Come to Its Senses* (Nashville: Abingdon Press, 1996); and *The Soul in Paraphrase: Prayer and the Religious Affections* (Akron, Ohio: OSL Publications, 1991).
Gail Ramshaw, *Words That Sing* (Chicago: Liturgy Training Publications, 1992).

In these readings one will be led to other resources that will provide a more thorough treatment of important aspects of the subject of worship touched on in these readings. This will include such important topics as the music of the liturgy (including psalmody), space for worship, inclusiveness in liturgical language, worship and culture, lectionary and preaching. For a more extensive bibliography on these and other liturgical topics, contact the Office of Theology and Worship of the Presbyterian Church (U.S.A.) at 100 Witherspoon Street, Louisville, KY 40202–1396 or visit their Web site at www.pcusa.org/theologyworship.

To embark on a study program such as the one outlined above, will quicken one's spiritual appetite, and help satisfy the deepest hunger for meaning in all of life's relationships. It will set one on a quest that can be a deeply satisfying experience of knowing God, of knowing who we are and are to be in relation to God, and of understanding the very essence of what the church is about, both in its life together, and in its engagement with the world. Into this journey, you, the readers of this book, are invited.

Index of Sources for the
Book of Common Worship

For a list of abbreviations, see pp. 147–151. Numbers refer to note numbers in part 2, chapters 1–10. Prayer entries can be found under the corresponding headings in part 2.

AC
  Litanies and Prayers for Various Occasions
      701
  Prayers for Use before Worship   3
ASB
  Additional Texts for the Service for the
      Lord's Day
    Prayer after Communion   124
    Prayers of the People: Concluding Col-
      lects   112, 114
  Advent   144
  Baptism of the Lord   178
  Christian Marriage: Rite I
    Exchange of Rings (or Other Symbols)
      793
    Statement on the Gift of Marriage
      "We gather in the presence of God"
  Christmas   164
  Epiphany—January 6   168
  The Funeral: A Service of Witness to the

    Resurrection   "May God in end-
      less mercy"
  The Great Litany   666
BAS
  Additional Texts for the Service for the
      Lord's Day, Prayer after Commu-
      nion   124
  Advent   144
  Ascension of the Lord   298
  Ash Wednesday   "Friends in Christ," 212
  Christmas   163
  Easter Sunday through Seventh Sunday of
      Easter   276, 282, 291
  Good Friday   "Behold the cross"
  The Great Litany   666
  The Great Vigil of Easter   "Friends in
      Christ," 254, 255, 256, 258, 262,
      264
  Lent   221, 234

BAS *(continued)*
  Maundy Thursday   "On this day," 245,
      249
  Passion/Palm Sunday   241
  Prayers at Mealtime   523
  Psalms   536, 544, 547, 549, 552, 553,
      559, 560, 561, 564, 565, 567, 568,
      569, 571, 572, 577, 584, 588, 591,
      594, 597, 600, 601, 603, 604, 606,
      608, 609, 624, 626, 627, 628, 631,
      633, 636, 641, 645, 649, 653, 654,
      657, 658
  Sacrament of Baptism, Profession of Faith
      412
  Sundays between Baptism of the Lord and
      Transfiguration of the Lord   182,
      185, 188, 195, 197, 199
  Sundays between Trinity Sunday and
      Christ the King   331, 333, 340,
      341, 345, 346, 353, 355, 358, 360,
      369, 372, 375, 381
  Trinity Sunday   325
  Vigil of the Resurrection
      Dismissal   "May God the Father"
      Prayer   519
BCO (1940)
  Christmas   161
  Easter Sunday through Seventh Sunday of
      Easter   294
  The Service for the Lord's Day—Order
      with Texts, Prayer of the Day or
      Opening Prayer   47
  Sundays between Trinity Sunday and
      Christ the King   336, 364, 379,
      388
BCO (1874)
  Prayers for Use before Worship   8, 10
  The Service for the Lord's Day—Order
      with Texts, Prayer of the Day or
      Opening Prayer   46
BCO (1940)
  Additional Texts for the Service for the
      Lord's Day
      Commemoration of Those Who Have
          Died in the Faith   104
      Prayer for Illumination   77
      Prayers of the People   96
      Prayer of Thanksgiving   129, "The
          peace of God, which passes all
          understanding"
  The Funeral: A Service of Witness to the
      Resurrection   814, 819
  Litanies and Prayers for Various Occasions
      724
  Prayer at the Close of the Day, Prayer
      507, 512, 513
  Prayers for Use before Worship   2, 8, 25

Prayers for Worship Leaders   38
Sacrament of Baptism, Laying on of Hands
    413, 414
The Service for the Lord's Day—Order
    with Texts
    Confession and Pardon   50, "Holy
        God," "Jesus, Lamb of God" and
        "Lamb of God"
    Prayer of the Day or Opening Prayer
        44, 46
    Prayer for Illumination   56
    Prayer of Thanksgiving   66
Sundays between Baptism of the Lord and
    Transfiguration of the Lord   198
Sundays between Trinity Sunday and
    Christ the King   349, 363, 377,
    378, 383
BCO (1979)
  Additional Texts for the Service for the
      Lord's Day, Prayer of Thanksgiving
      "The peace of God, which passes all
      understanding"
  Christian Marriage: Rite I, Statement on
      the Gift of Marriage   "We gather
      in the presence of God"
  Christmas   161
  The Committal   827, 834
  The Funeral: A Service of Witness to the
      Resurrection   814, 819
  Prayers for Use before Worship   12
  The Service for the Lord's Day—Order
      with Texts
      Confession and Pardon   49, "Jesus,
          Lamb of God" and "Lamb of God,"
          "Glory to God"
      Prayer of the Day or Opening Prayer
          44
      Prayer for Illumination   "Glory to
          you, O Lord"
BCO (1994)
  The Committal   834
  The Funeral: A Service of Witness to the
      Resurrection   814
  Prayer at the Close of the Day, Prayer   504
  Prayer at the Time of Death   "Depart, O
      Christian soul, in peace"
BCP
  Additional Texts for the Service for the
      Lord's Day
      Great Thanksgiving, *Baptism, Passion/
          Palm Sunday*   117, 119
      Prayer of Confession   68
      Prayer for Illumination   79
      Prayer of Thanksgiving   129, "The
          peace of God, which passes all
          understanding"
      Prayers of the People   95, 96, 97

Prayers of the People: Concluding Collects   107, 108, 111, 113
Advent   139, 142
Alternative Texts for Seasons and Festivals: Morning and Evening Prayer
Lent   488
Midday Prayer   496, 501
Ascension of the Lord   306, 307
Ash Wednesday   "Accomplish in us," "Go in peace," "Remember that you are dust," 208, 209, 210
Baptism of the Lord   175
Canticles and Ancient Hymns: Texts   18, 20, 21, 49
Christian Marriage: Rite I
Prayer   794
Statement on the Gift of Marriage "We gather in the presence of God"
Christian Marriage: Rite II
Blessing of the Couple   797
Christ the King (or Reign of Christ)   405
Christmas   161, 162
Comforting the Bereaved   802, 804, 806
The Committal   "Christ is risen from the dead," 827, 834
daily lectionary
Easter Sunday through Seventh Sunday of Easter   270, 286, 287, 294
Evening Prayer, Opening Sentences   "O God, come"
The Funeral: A Service of Witness to the Resurrection   "You only are immortal," 818, 822, 825
Good Friday   251, 252
The Great Litany   666
The Great Vigil of Easter   256, 258, 259, 262
Litanies and Prayers for Various Occasions   669, 672, 673, 675, 684, 685, 687, 688, 691, 700, 704, 722, 728, 729, 730, 731, 735, 738, 740, 741, 745, 746, 749, 751, 752, 754, 757, 758, 766, 768, 770, 774, 779, 780, 782, 790
Maundy Thursday   "The mercy of the Lord"
Passion/Palm Sunday   "Go in peace," 235, 237
Prayer at the Close of the Day
Opening Sentences   "O God, come"
Prayer   "Into your hands," 504, 506, 508, 509, 512, 513
Prayers at Mealtime   531
Prayers for Use before Worship   3, 6, 10, 11, 12
Prayer at the Time of Death   "Depart, O Christian soul, in peace," 866

Sacrament of Baptism
Laying on of Hands   "N., child of the covenant," 414
Profession of Faith   "Will you devote," 411
The Service for the Lord's Day—Order with Texts
Charge and Blessing   "Go in peace," "Go forth into the world"
Communion of the People   "The body of Christ, given for you"
Confession and Pardon   49, "The Mercy of the Lord"
Lord's Prayer   "As our Savior Christ has taught us"
Offering   "With gladness, let us present"
Prayer after Communion   63
Prayer of the Day or Opening Prayer   44
Prayer for Illumination   "Glory to you, O Lord"
A Service of Wholeness for Use with a Congregation   "N., may the God of all mercy"
Sundays between Baptism of the Lord and Transfiguration of the Lord   198
Sundays between Trinity Sunday and Christ the King   330, 349, 356, 363, 376, 377, 378, 384, 388, 391, 394, 399
Transfiguration of the Lord   202
Trinity Sunday   324
BCP (1549)
Additional Texts for the Service for the Lord's Day
Great Thanksgiving   117
Prayer for Illumination   79
Prayers of the People: Concluding Collects   113
Ash Wednesday   208
Christmas   161
Easter Sunday through Seventh Sunday of Easter   292, 294
Evening Prayer, Opening Sentences   "O God, come"
Litanies and Prayers for Various Occasions   768
Prayers for Use before Worship   6, 10, 12
The Service for the Lord's Day—Order with Texts, Prayer of the Day or Opening Prayer   44
Sundays between Baptism of the Lord and Transfiguration of the Lord   198
Sundays between Trinity Sunday and Christ the King   330, 394

BCP (1552)
  Additional Texts for the Service for the Lord's Day, Prayer of Confession 68
  Ash Wednesday   "Accomplish in us"
  The Committal   "In sure and certain hope"
  Litanies and Prayers for Various Occasions 768
  Sacrament of Baptism, Laying on of Hands 414
BCP (1662)
  Additional Texts for the Service for the Lord's Day, Prayer of Thanksgiving 129
  The Funeral: A Service of Witness to the Resurrection   822
  Litanies and Prayers for Various Occasions 768
  Sundays between Trinity Sunday and Christ the King   399
BCP (1928)
  Alternative Texts for Seasons and Festivals: Morning and Evening Prayer, Midday Prayer   496
  Christmas   165
  Comforting the Bereaved   804
  The Committal   827
  Easter Sunday through Seventh Sunday of Easter   287
  The Funeral: A Service of Witness to the Resurrection   822
  Litanies and Prayers for Various Occasions 673, 701, 728, 729, 730, 749, 752
  Prayer at the Close of the Day, Prayer   504
  Prayers for Use before Worship   3
  Psalms   550
  The Service for the Lord's Day—Order with Texts, Charge and Blessing "Go out into the world in peace"
  Sundays between Trinity Sunday and Christ the King   377, 391
BCW (1906)
  Additional Texts for the Service for the Lord's Day
    Great Thanksgiving   117
    Prayer of Confession   67
    Prayer of Thanksgiving   129, "The peace of God, which passes all understanding"
    Prayers of the People   96
  Canticles and Ancient Hymns: Texts   1, 2, 3, 5, 6, 18, 27
  Christmas   161
  The Committal   "In sure and certain hope"
  Litanies and Prayers for Various Occasions 768, 775, 776
  Maundy Thursday   "The mercy of the Lord"

  Passion/Palm Sunday   237
  Prayer at the Close of the Day, Prayer 504, 511, 512
  Prayers at Mealtime   529, 530, 531
  Prayers for Use before Worship   6, 8, 10, 25
  Sacrament of Baptism, Laying on of Hands 414
  The Service for the Lord's Day—Order with Texts
    Confession and Pardon   50, "The Mercy of the Lord"
    Prayer of the Day or Opening Prayer 44, 46, 47
    Prayer of Thanksgiving   66
  Sundays between Trinity Sunday and Christ the King   347
BCW (1932)
  Additional Texts for the Service for the Lord's Day
    Great Thanksgiving   117
    Prayer of Confession   67, 68
    Prayer of Thanksgiving   129, "The peace of God, which passes all understanding"
    Prayers of the People   96
  Canticles and Ancient Hymns: Texts   1, 2, 3, 5, 6
  Christmas   161
  The Committal   "In sure and certain hope"
  Easter Sunday through Seventh Sunday of Easter   277
  Litanies and Prayers for Various Occasions 768, 775, 776
  Maundy Thursday   "The mercy of the Lord"
  Passion/Palm Sunday   237
  Prayer at the Close of the Day, Prayer 504, 511, 512
  Prayers at Mealtime   529, 530, 531
  Prayers for Use before Worship   6, 8, 10, 25
  Sacrament of Baptism, Laying on of Hands 414
  The Service for the Lord's Day—Order with Texts
    Confession and Pardon   50, "The Mercy of the Lord"
    Prayer of the Day or Opening Prayer 44, 46, 47
    Prayer of Thanksgiving   66
  Sundays between Trinity Sunday and Christ the King   336, 347, 349, 397
BCW (1946)
  Additional Texts for the Service for the Lord's Day
    Commemoration of Those Who Have Died in the Faith   103

Great Thanksgiving   117
Prayer of Confession   67, 68
Prayer for Illumination   79
Prayer of Thanksgiving   129, "The peace of God, which passes all understanding"
Prayers of the People   96, 100
Ascension of the Lord   306
Canticles and Ancient Hymns: Texts   2, 3, 5, 6, 27
Christian Marriage: Rite I
  Exchange of Rings   "This ring I give you"
  Vows   "I, N., take you, N., to be"
Christmas   147, 161
Comforting the Bereaved   807
The Committal   "In sure and certain hope"
Easter Sunday through Seventh Sunday of Easter   266, 274, 277, 294
Epiphany—January 6   169
The Funeral: A Service of Witness to the Resurrection   808, 811, 814, 815, 829
The Great Litany   666
Litanies and Prayers for Various Occasions   768, 769, 775
Maundy Thursday   "The mercy of the Lord"
Prayer at the Close of the Day, Prayer   504, 507, 511, 512, 513
Prayers at Mealtime   529, 530, 531
Prayers for Use before Worship   2, 3, 4, 6, 7, 8
Prayers for Worship Leaders   38
Sacrament of Baptism, Laying on of Hands   413, 414
The Service for the Lord's Day—Order with Texts
  Charge and Blessing   "Go out into the world in peace"
  Confession and Pardon   49, 50, 52, "Glory to God," "Lord, have mercy," "Jesus, Lamb of God" and "Lamb of God," "The Mercy of the Lord"
  Lord's Prayer   "As our Savior Christ has taught us"
  Prayer of the Day or Opening Prayer   44, 47
  Prayer for Illumination   "Glory to you, O Lord"
  Prayer of Thanksgiving   66
Sundays between Baptism of the Lord and Transfiguration of the Lord   198
Sundays between Trinity Sunday and Christ the King   336, 349, 356, 363, 364, 367, 377, 378, 379, 380, 383, 387, 388, 390, 391, 394, 397
Trinity Sunday   323

BCW-CSI
  Prayers for Use before Worship   11
BCWP
  Additional Texts for the Service for the Lord's Day
    Affirmation of Faith   "This is the good news"
    Prayer after Communion   126
    Prayer of Confession   68
    Prayer for Illumination   73
    Prayer of Thanksgiving   "The peace of God, which passes all understanding"
    Prayers of the People   80, 81, 83, 84, 85, 87, 88, 89, 90, 96
  Christmas   157
  The Committal   827
  Good Friday   250
  Maundy Thursday   "The mercy of the Lord,"   246
  Prayer at the Close of the Day, Prayer   504, 505
  Prayers for Use before Worship   1, 4, 6
  Prayers for Worship Leaders   40, 42, 43
  The Service for the Lord's Day—Order with Texts
    Call to Worship
    Confession and Pardon   50, 51, "The Mercy of the Lord"
    Prayer of the Day or Opening Prayer   44
    Prayer for Illumination   54
BCW-PCC
  Additional Texts for the Service for the Lord's Day
    Commemoration of Those Who Have Died in the Faith   106
    Great Thanksgiving   118
    Prayer of Confession   70
    Prayers of the People   80, 82
  The Committal   827, "In sure and certain hope"
  The Funeral: A Service of Witness to the Resurrection   819, 823
  Prayer at the Close of the Day, Prayer   504
  The Service for the Lord's Day—Order with Texts, Offering   "Let us return"
BW-UCC
  Additional Texts for the Service for the Lord's Day, Prayer of Confession   69
  Christian Marriage: Rite I, Charge and Blessing   "The grace of Christ"
  The Committal   "In sure and certain hope"
  The Funeral: A Service of Witness to the Resurrection   822, 823
  Passion/Palm Sunday   236, 239
  Prayer at the Close of the Day, Prayer   504
  Prayer at the Time of Death   "Depart, O Christian soul, in peace"

BW-UCC *(continued)*
A Service of Wholeness for Use with a Congregation   "Jesus said, 'Ask'"

CB
An Alternative Service for the Sacrament of Baptism   419, 420, 421

CBW
Christian Marriage: Rite I, Prayer   795

ELLC
Canticles and Ancient Hymns: Texts   1, 2, 3, 5, 6
Passion/Palm Sunday   243

GA74
Baptism of the Lord   176
Christmas   159
Sundays between Trinity Sunday and Christ the King   397

HCY
Good Friday, Solemn Reproaches of the Cross

ICEL
Additional Texts for the Service for the Lord's Day, Great Thanksgiving 118, 120
Advent   140, 143, 146
Ascension of the Lord   297
Christ the King (or Reign of Christ)   407
Christmas   156, 160
Easter Sunday through Seventh Sunday of Easter   280, 293, 296
Epiphany—January 6   167
Evening Prayer, Service of Light, Thanksgiving for the Light   448, 450, 451
Lent   223
Sundays between Baptism of the Lord and Transfiguration of the Lord   193
Sundays between Trinity Sunday and Christ the King   339, 348, 351, 368, 371, 374, 386, 389, 400, 403
Vigil of the Resurrection, Thanksgiving for Light   517

ION
Prayer at the Close of the Day, Prayer of Confession   503
A Service of Wholeness for Use with a Congregation   "Spirit of the living God"

ISIT
Litanies and Prayers for Various Occasions 682, 716, 677

KJV
Litanies and Prayers for Various Occasions 749

LBW
Additional Texts for the Service for the Lord's Day
Commemoration of Those Who Have Died in the Faith   104, 105
Prayer after Communion   128
Prayers of the People   95
Prayers of the People: Concluding Collects   110
Advent   131, 142
Ash Wednesday   "Accomplish in us," "Remember that you are dust," 208, 209
Christmas   165
Comforting the Bereaved   804
The Committal   834
daily lectionary
Day of Pentecost   310, 316
Easter Sunday through Seventh Sunday of Easter   270, 288, 292
Evening Prayer, Service of Light
Opening Sentences   "Behold, now is the," "Jesus Christ is the light," "Jesus Christ is risen," "The people who walked," "The Spirit and the church"
Thanksgiving for the Light   448
The Funeral: A Service of Witness to the Resurrection   822
Good Friday   "Behold the cross"
The Great Litany   666
The Great Vigil of Easter   258
Lent   222, 228, 232
Litanies and Prayers for Various Occasions 685, 701, 704, 707, 722, 728, 729, 730, 731, 735, 738, 740, 741, 742, 745, 746, 749, 751, 752, 754, 770, 774, 776, 779, 780
Maundy Thursday   245
Morning Prayer, Prayers of Thanksgiving and Intercession   446
Passion/Palm Sunday   237
Prayer at the Close of the Day
Opening Sentences   "O God, come"
Prayer   "Into your hands," 509
Prayers for Use before Worship   9, 11
Psalms   534, 539, 540, 558, 563, 564, 583, 590, 596, 599, 614, 616, 621, 625, 635, 640, 644, 647, 650, 652, 660, 663
Sacrament of Baptism, Laying on of Hands 413
The Service for the Lord's Day—Order with Texts
Communion of the People   "The body of Christ, given for you"
Confession and Pardon   49, "Worthy Is Christ, the Lamb"

Prayer for Illumination "Glory to you, O Lord"

A Service of Wholeness for Use with a Congregation   856

Sundays between Baptism of the Lord and Transfiguration of the Lord   187

Sundays between Trinity Sunday and Christ the King   329, 338, 344, 354, 356, 401

Transfiguration of the Lord   201

LH

Alternative Texts for Seasons and Festivals: Morning and Evening Prayer

Advent   "Like the sun," 471

Christmas   "Today Christ is born"

Epiphany   "This is a holy day," 481

Easter   491

Midday Prayer   502

Christmas   151

Day of Pentecost   314

Easter Sunday through Seventh Sunday of Easter   268

Evening Prayer, Prayers of Thanksgiving and Intercession   464

Lent   217

Morning Prayer, Prayers of Thanksgiving and Intercession   443

Prayer at the Close of the Day

Opening Sentences   "O God, come"

Prayer   "Into your hands," 508, 514

Psalms   534, 539, 550, 552, 553, 558, 563, 564, 569, 573, 579, 581, 582, 583, 587, 588, 591, 596, 599, 602, 614, 616, 617, 620, 621, 624, 625, 635, 644, 647, 650, 652, 660, 661, 663

LHP

Litanies and Prayers for Various Occasions   784

MPE

Evening Prayer, Service of Light, Evening Psalm   456

MR

Easter Sunday through Seventh Sunday of Easter   278

Lent   229

Sundays between Baptism of the Lord and Transfiguration of the Lord   192

Sundays between Trinity Sunday and Christ the King   337, 362, 365, 373

Transfiguration of the Lord   203

NEB

Canticles and Ancient Hymns: Texts   13, 16, 18, 22, 23, 24, 27

NRSV

Canticles and Ancient Hymns: Texts   7, 8, 13, 15, 20, 22, 23, 24, 25, 26, 27, 28

NZPB

Additional Liturgical Texts for the Service for the Lord's Day   430

Additional Texts for the Service for the Lord's Day, Prayers of the People   98, 99

Alternative Texts for Seasons and Festivals: Morning and Evening Prayer, Pentecost   494

Ascension of the Lord   299

Canticles and Ancient Hymns: Texts   9, 10, 11, 12, 17, 19

Day of Pentecost   308, 309, 312, 321

Easter Sunday through Seventh Sunday of Easter   276, 284, 290, 295

The Funeral: A Service of Witness to the Resurrection   821

Lent   226, 227, 233

Morning Prayer, Prayers of Thanksgiving and Intercession   445, 447

The Service for the Lord's Day—Order with Texts

Confession and Pardon   "Hear the good news!"

Offering   57

Prayer for Illumination   "Hear what the Spirit"

Sundays between Baptism of the Lord and Transfiguration of the Lord   183, 200

Sundays between Trinity Sunday and Christ the King   330, 332, 333, 335, 340, 352, 359, 361, 370, 385

OCF

The Committal   834

The Funeral: A Service of Witness to the Resurrection   818

OS

The Committal   834

Ministry with the Sick   854

Prayer at the Time of Death   "Depart, O Christian soul, in peace," 865

OW

Litanies and Prayers for Various Occasions   722

PBCP

Additional Texts for the Service for the Lord's Day

Great Thanksgiving   117

Prayer of Confession   68

Prayer for Illumination   79

PBCP *(continued)*
Prayer of Thanksgiving   129
    Prayers of the People   96
Ash Wednesday   208
Canticles and Ancient Hymns: Texts   1, 2,
    3, 5, 6, 27
The Committal   "In sure and certain hope"
Easter Sunday through Seventh Sunday of
    Easter   294
The Great Litany   666
Litanies and Prayers for Various Occasions
    768
Maundy Thursday   "The mercy of the
    Lord"
Prayer at the Close of the Day, Prayer
    508, 512
Prayer of the Day or Opening Prayer   44
Prayers for Use before Worship   6, 10, 12
The Service for the Lord's Day—Order
    with Texts
    Confession and Pardon   "Glory to
    God," "The Mercy of the Lord"
Sundays between Baptism of the Lord and
    Transfiguration of the Lord   198
Sundays between Trinity Sunday and
    Christ the King   330, 349, 378,
    388
PCS
    Prayer at the Time of Death   865
PG
    Alternative Texts for Seasons and Festivals:
    Morning and Evening Prayer
    Christmas   478, 479
    Epiphany   "Sealed with the sign"
    Ascension of the Lord   300
    Baptism of the Lord   177
    Christmas   148, 150
    Easter Sunday through Seventh Sunday of
    Easter   267
    Epiphany—January 6   170, 171
    Good Friday   253
    Lent   213
    Passion/Palm Sunday   243
PGIS
    Evening Prayer
    Opening Sentences   "Light and peace"
    Evening Prayer, Service of Light
    Opening Sentences   "Light and peace"
    Thanksgiving for the Light   452, 453,
    454, 455
    Vigil of the Resurrection
    Dismissal   "May God the Father"
    Opening Sentences   "Light and peace"
    Psalm   118, 518
    Thanksgiving for Light   516
PH
    Passion/Palm Sunday, Procession into the
    Church

The Service for the Lord's Day—Order
    with Texts, Confession and Pardon
    "Worthy Is Christ, the Lamb"
PNW
    Litanies and Prayers for Various Occasions
    702, 727, 750
    Prayers for Use before Worship   15
PR
    Litanies and Prayers for Various Occasions
    709
PTWS
    Litanies and Prayers for Various Occasions
    670

RS
    Additional Texts for the Service for the
    Lord's Day
    Great Thanksgiving, *Christ the King
    (Or Reign of Christ), Trinity Sunday*
    119
    Prayer after Communion   125, 127
    Advent   145
    Baptism of the Lord   175
    Christ the King (or Reign of Christ)   404
    Easter Sunday through Seventh Sunday of
    Easter   268
    Good Friday   "Behold the cross," Solemn
    Reproaches of the Cross, 252
    The Great Vigil of Easter   "Rejoice, heav-
    enly powers!" "Sisters and Brothers
    in Christ," 254, 255, 263
    Sacrament of Baptism, Laying on of Hands
    413
    The Service for the Lord's Day—Order
    with Texts
    Communion of the People   "The
    body of Christ, given for you"
    Lord's Prayer   "And now, with the confi-
    dence"
    Prayer for Illumination   "Glory to you, O
    Lord"
RSV
    Canticles and Ancient Hymns: Texts   8,
    14, 15, 16, 18, 23, 25, 26
    Evening Prayer, Service of Light, Opening
    Sentences   "Jesus Christ is risen"
    Ministry with the Sick   851

SBK-92
    Advent   140, 143, 146
    Ascension of the Lord   297
    Christ the King (or Reign of Christ)   407
    Christmas   160
    Day of Pentecost   311
    Easter Sunday through Seventh Sunday of
    Easter   278, 280, 293, 296
    Epiphany—January 6   167
    Lent   229

Sundays between Baptism of the Lord and Transfiguration of the Lord   193

Sundays between Trinity Sunday and Christ the King   339, 348, 351, 368, 371, 374, 386, 389, 400, 403

Transfiguration of the Lord   203

SB-UCC

Additional Texts for the Service for the Lord's Day, Commemoration of Those Who Have Died in the Faith   102

Prayers for Use before Worship   17

The Service for the Lord's Day—Order with Texts, Prayer of the Day or Opening Prayer   48

SB-UCC (people's edition)

The Service for the Lord's Day—Order with Texts

Prayer after Communion   62

Prayer of Thanksgiving   65

SB-URC

The Service for the Lord's Day—Order with Texts, Prayer after Communion   62

SLDL

Additional Texts for the Service for the Lord's Day

Prayer after Communion   126

Prayer of Confession   68

Prayers of the People   80, 81, 83, 84, 85, 87, 88, 89, 96

Prayer of Thanksgiving   129

Maundy Thursday   "The mercy of the Lord"

Prayers for Use before Worship   1, 4, 6

Prayers for Worship Leaders   40, 42, 43

The Service for the Lord's Day—Order with Texts

Call to Worship

Confession and Pardon   50, "Jesus, Lamb of God" and "Lamb of God," "The Mercy of the Lord"

Prayer of the Day or Opening Prayer   44

Prayer for Illumination   54, "Glory to you, O Lord"

SLR-1

Additional Texts for the Service for the Lord's Day

Affirmation of Faith   "This is the good news"

Commemoration of Those Who Have Died in the Faith   102, 103, 104, 105

Great Thanksgiving, *Advent, All Saints' Day, Ascension of the Lord, Baptism, Baptism of the Lord, Christ the King (Or Reign of Christ), Christmas, Day of Pentecost, Easter, Epiphany, Funeral (or Memorial Service), Lent,*

Maundy Thursday, Ordinary Time I, Ordinary Time II, Ordinary Time III, Passion/Palm Sunday, Reaffirmation of the Baptismal Covenant, Transfiguration of the Lord, Trinity Sunday   115, 116, 117, 119, 120, 121

Prayer after Communion   123, 125, 126, 127, 128

Prayer of Confession   67, 68, 71, 72

Prayer for Illumination   73, 75, 77, 78, 79

Prayer of Thanksgiving   129, 130, "The peace of God, which passes all understanding"

Prayers of the People   80, 81, 82, 96, 100

Prayers of the People: Concluding Collects   107, 108, 109, 110, 111, 112, 113, 114

Christian Marriage

Rite I, Reading from Scripture   792

Rite II, Prayer after Communion   799

Maundy Thursday   "The mercy of the Lord"

Prayers for Use before Worship   1, 2, 3, 4, 5, 6 ,7, 8, 9, 11, 12

Prayers for Worship Leaders   38, 39, 40, 41, 42, 43

The Service for the Lord's Day—Order with Texts

Call to Worship   "Praise the Lord"

Charge and Blessing   "Go in peace," "Go forth into the world," "Go out into the world in peace,"

Communion of the People   "The gifts of God for the people of God," "The body of Christ, given for you"

Confession and Pardon   49, 50, 51, 52, "Lord, have mercy," "Holy God," "The Mercy of the Lord," "Hear the good news!," "Glory to God," "Worthy Is Christ, the Lamb"

Invitation to the Lord's Table   "Friends, this is the joyful feast"

Lord's Prayer   "Let us pray for God's rule," "And now, with the confidence"

Offering   "With gladness, let us present"

Prayer after Communion   60, 61, 62, 63

Prayer for Illumination   53, 54, 55, 56, "Glory to you, O Lord," "The Word of the Lord"

Prayer of the Day or Opening Prayer   44, 45, 47, 46, 48

Prayer of Thanksgiving   64, 66

SLR-2
An Alternative Service for the Sacrament of
Baptism
Baptism and Reaffirmation of the Bap-
tismal Covenant   422
Prayers . . . for Inclusion in the Prayers of
the People   415, 416, 417, 418
Reaffirmation—Congregation
Profession of Faith "Sisters and
brothers in Christ"
Thanksgiving for Baptism "Remem-
ber your baptism"
Reaffirmation—Growing in Faith
Call to Discipleship "The call of
Christ"
Laying on of Hands "N. and N., you
are"
Profession of Faith "The grace
bestowed"
Reaffirmation—Pastoral Counseling
Profession of Faith "In your baptism"
Reaffirmation—Public Profession of Faith
424
Presentation "N. and N. are pre-
sented"
Profession of Faith "Now, as you"
Reaffirmation—Those Uniting with a
Congregation, Profession of Faith
425, 426
Sacrament of Baptism
Laying on of Hands "N., child of
God," "N., child of the covenant,"
413
Presentation "Obeying the Word,"
"Relying on God's grace"
Profession of Faith "Do you
promise," Renunciations No. 2,
"through baptism we enter, 411
Welcome "N. and N. have been
received," "With joy"
Vigil of the Resurrection, Thanksgiving for
Our Baptism "Remember your
baptism"
SLR-3
Christian Marriage: Rite I "N., I give you
this ring," "This ring I give you"
Affirmation of the Congregation
"Will all of"
Affirmations of the Families "N., N.
[Names of family members]," "We
(I) give our"
Announcement of Marriage "Before
God," "Those whom God has
joined"
Charge and Blessing "The grace of
Christ"
Declaration of Intent "N., in your
baptism," "N., understanding that"

Exchange of Rings (or Other Symbols)
793
Prayer   794, 795
Reading from Scripture   792
Statement on the Gift of Marriage
"We gather in the presence of God"
Vows "Before God and these," "N.
and N., since it is"
Christian Marriage: Rite II
Blessing of the Couple   797
Confession of Sin   796
Great Thanksgiving   798
Prayer after Communion   799
Prayer of Thanksgiving   800
SLR-4
Canticles and Ancient Hymns: Texts   5
Comforting the Bereaved "The Lord
bless us," 801 802, 803, 804, 805,
806, 807
The Committal "Christ is risen from the
dead," "In sure and certain hope,"
826, 827, 828, 829, 830, 833, 834
The Funeral: A Service of Witness to the
Resurrection "Let us now ask,"
"May God in endless mercy," "You
only are immortal," 808, 809, 810,
811, 812, 813, 814, 815, 816, 817,
818, 819, 820, 822, 823, 824, 825
Prayer at the Close of the Day, Prayer
504, 505
Prayers at Mealtime   520
Prayer at the Time of Death "Depart, O
Christian soul, in peace," 864, 865,
866, 867, 868, 869, 870, 871
SLR-5
Additional Texts for the Service for the
Lord's Day, Prayers of the People
95
Advent   131
Alternative Texts for Seasons and Festivals:
Morning and Evening Prayer
Advent "Like the sun," "The Lord
shall come," 471, 472, 473, 474,
475, 476
Christmas "Today Christ is born,"
478, 479
Easter   490, 491, 492, 493
Epiphany   481, 482
Lent   483, 484, 485, 486, 487
Midday Prayer   496, 497, 500, 502
Pentecost   494
Ascension of the Lord   300, 301
Baptism of the Lord   177, 178
Canticles and Ancient Hymns: Texts   1, 2,
3, 4, 5, 6, 7, 10, 11, 12, 15, 18, 19,
20, 21, 22, 23, 24, 25, 27, 28, 29
Christmas   148, 151
Day of Pentecost   314, 315, 317, 318

Easter Sunday through Seventh Sunday of Easter   267, 269, 279
Epiphany—January 6   170, 171
Evening Prayer
   Prayers of Thanksgiving and Intercession   457–63, 464, 465, 466, 467, 468, 469
Evening Prayer, Service of Light
   Evening Psalm   456
   Opening Sentences   "Behold, now is the," "Jesus Christ is the light," "Jesus Christ is risen," "The people who walked," "The Spirit and the church"
   Thanksgiving for the Light   448, 449, 451, 452, 453, 454, 455
Good Friday   253
The Great Litany   666
Lent   213, 214, 216, 217
Morning Prayer
   Prayers of Thanksgiving and Intercession   "Satisfy us," 434–40, 441, 442, 443, 444, 446
Passion/Palm Sunday   243, 244
Prayer at the Close of the Day
   Prayer   504, 505, 506, 507, 508, 509, 512, 513, 514
   Prayer of Confession   503
Prayers at Mealtime   521, 522, 524, 528, 529, 530, 531, 532–33
Psalms   537, 538, 539, 540, 541, 543, 545, 546, 548, 550, 551, 552, 553, 554, 557, 558, 562, 563, 564, 566, 575, 576, 578, 579, 580, 582, 583, 585, 586, 588, 589, 592, 593, 598, 602, 603, 607, 610, 611, 613, 614, 615, 616, 617, 618, 619, 620, 621, 622, 623, 629, 630, 632, 634, 635, 637, 638, 642, 643, 646, 648, 650, 652, 655, 659, 660, 661, 662, 663, 665

SLR-6
Additional Texts for the Service for the Lord's Day, Great Thanksgiving   121
Holy Communion   "In the Lord's Supper," "The mercy of the Lord"
Ministry with the Sick   836, 837, 838, 839, 840, 841, 842, 843, 844, 845, 846, 847, 848, 849, 850, 851, 852, 854, 855
Prayer at the Time of Death   "Depart, O Christian soul, in peace," 864, 865, 866, 867, 868, 869, 870, 871, 872
Psalms   651
A Service of Wholeness for Use with a Congregation   "As you are anointed," "I anoint you," "Jesus said, 'Ask',"

"The mercy of the Lord," "N., may the God of all mercy," "N., may God deliver you," "N., may the," "Spirit of the living God," 856, 857, 858, 859, 860, 861
A Service for Wholeness for Use with an Individual   862, 863

SLR-7
Advent   133, 134, 135, 136,138, 141, 142, 144, 145, Lighting of the Advent Candles
Ascension of the Lord   298, 302, 303, 304
Ash Wednesday   "Friends in Christ," 207, 208, 210, 211, 212
Baptism of the Lord   176, 179, 180, 181
Christ the King (or Reign of Christ)   404, 405, 406, 409, 410
Christmas   153, 154, 155, 157, 158, 159, 162, 163, 165, 166
Day of Pentecost   310, 313, 314, 315, 320, 322
Easter Sunday through Seventh Sunday of Easter   266, 268, 270, 272, 273, 274, 275, 276, 282, 288, 289, 291, 292, 294
Epiphany—January 6   168, 173, 174
Good Friday   "Behold the cross," Solemn Reproaches of the Cross, 250, 251, 252
The Great Vigil of Easter   "Friends in Christ," "Rejoice, heavenly powers!," "Sisters and brothers in Christ," 254, 255, 256, 257, 258, 259, 260, 261, 262, 263, 264, 265
Lent   215, 218, 219, 220, 221, 222, 224, 225, 228, 234
Maundy Thursday   "On this day," 245, 246, 248, 249
Passion/Palm Sunday   235, 236, 237, 238, 239, 240, 241, 242
Prayers for Use before Worship   6
Sundays between Baptism of the Lord and Transfiguration of the Lord   182, 184, 185, 186, 187, 188, 189, 190, 191, 192, 194, 196, 197, 198, 199
Sundays between Trinity Sunday and Christ the King   329, 331, 333, 337, 338, 340, 341, 344, 345, 346, 350, 354, 357, 358, 360, 365, 368, 369, 372, 373, 375, 378, 381, 384, 393, 395, 396, 397, 398, 399, 401, 402
Transfiguration of the Lord   201, 202, 204, 205, 206
Trinity Sunday   324, 325, 327, 328

SP
Psalms   546, 548, 575, 613, 615, 618, 659, 662

SPJP
  Psalms   542, 605, 638
TEV
  Canticles and Ancient Hymns: Texts
TO
  Baptism of the Lord   177
  Christmas   148, 150
  Easter Sunday through Seventh Sunday of
    Easter   269
  Epiphany—January 6   170, 171
  Lent   213

UMBW
  Additional Texts for the Service for the
    Lord's Day
    Prayer after Communion   123
    Prayer of Confession   72
  Christian Marriage: Rite I
    Affirmation of the Congregation
      "Will all of"
    Affirmations of the Families   "N., N.
      [Names of family members]"
  Christmas   149
  The Committal   826
  Easter Sunday through Seventh Sunday of
    Easter   285
  Epiphany—January 6   169
  The Funeral: A Service of Witness to the
    Resurrection   809, 810, 822
  The Great Vigil of Easter   257, 261
  Litanies and Prayers for Various Occasions
    674
  The Service for the Lord's Day—Order
    with Texts
    Lord's Prayer   "And now, with the
      confidence"
    Prayer for Illumination   53
UW (leader's edition)
  Additional Texts for the Service for the
    Lord's Day
    Commemoration of Those Who Have
      Died in the Faith   101
    Prayer after Communion   124
  The Committal   827, 831, 832
  Lent   224, 225
  Ministry with the Sick   855
  Passion/Palm Sunday   238
  Prayers for Use before Worship   13
  Prayer at the Time of Death   872
  The Service for the Lord's Day—Order
    with Texts, Prayer after Commu-
    nion   60, 61
  Sundays between Baptism of the Lord and
    Transfiguration of the Lord   186,
    189, 192
  Sundays between Trinity Sunday and
    Christ the King   337, 343, 350,
    357, 362, 365, 373, 392, 393, 398

UW (people's edition)
  Prayers for Use before Worship   25

WAGP
  Additional Liturgical Texts for the Service
    for the Lord's Day   433
  Prayer at the Close of the Day, Prayer   510
WBK
  Additional Texts for the Service for the
    Lord's Day
    Affirmation of Faith   "This is the good
      news"
    Great Thanksgiving   116, *Day of Pen-
      tecost, Easter, Lent, Maundy Thurs-
      day,* Ordinary Time I, Ordinary
      Time III
    Prayer of Confession   71
    Prayers of the People   81, 82, 83, 84,
      85, 86, 87, 88, 89, 90, 91
    Prayers of the People: Concluding Col-
      lects   109
  Advent   132, 136, 137, 141
  Alternative Texts for Seasons and Festivals:
    Morning and Evening Prayer, Mid-
    day Prayer   500
  Ascension of the Lord   302, 304, 305
  Baptism of the Lord   176
  Calendar and Lectionary for Sundays and
    Festivals
  Christian Marriage
    Rite I, Prayer   795
    Rite II, Confession of Sin   796
  Christmas   152, 155, 157, 158, 159, 166
  The Committal   826, 828, 835
  Day of Pentecost   319
  Easter Sunday through Seventh Sunday of
    Easter   275, 289
  Epiphany—January 6   172
  The Funeral: A Service of Witness to the
    Resurrection   815, 816, 817
  Good Friday   250
  Lent   215
  Litanies and Prayers for Various Occasions
    667, 668, 671, 676, 680, 681, 686,
    690, 693, 694, 695, 696, 697, 698,
    699, 703, 705, 710, 712, 713, 714,
    717, 719, 720, 721, 732, 733, 734,
    736, 739, 743, 744, 747, 748, 753,
    755, 756, 759, 760, 761, 777, 778,
    781, 785, 786, 788, 789
  Maundy Thursday   246, 247
  Ministry with the Sick   837, 843, 846
  Passion/Palm Sunday   242
  Prayer at the Close of the Day, Prayer
    504, 505
  Prayer at the Time of Death   868
  Prayers for Use before Worship   1, 4
  Prayers for Worship Leaders   39, 41, 42, 43

Reaffirmation—Those Uniting with a Congregation, Profession of Faith 425
Sacrament of Baptism, Profession of Faith, Renunciations No. 3
The Service for the Lord's Day—Order with Texts
  Call to Worship
  Charge and Blessing "Go out into the world in peace"
  Confession and Pardon "Hear the good news!"
  Invitation to the Lord's Table "Friends, this is the joyful feast"
  Prayer for Illumination   54, 55, "Hear what the Spirit"

Prayer of Thanksgiving 64
Sundays between Baptism of the Lord and Transfiguration of the Lord   184, 191, 194
WBK-SH
  Maundy Thursday, Footwashing
  Prayers for Use before Worship   37
  The Service for the Lord's Day—Order with Texts, Communion of the People 59
WTL
  A Service of Wholeness for Use with a Congregation 856

Index of Subjects

Abbey of Solesmes, 264n. 13
Advisory Council on Discipleship and Worship, 53, 58
Allen, Horace T., Jr., 52, 70
American Church Service Society, 27–28
American liturgy, 83–84
American Presbyterianism
    common liturgy available to (1932), 33
    ecumenism in, post–World War II, 37–38
    roots of, 23–24
American worship, seventeenth and eighteenth
    centuries, 23–24
Anderson, Bernhard W., 137
Andrews, James, 65
Anglican tradition, 80
Apostles' Creed, 9, 71
Armed Forces Chaplains Board, adopting Presbyterian lectionary, 69
"Articles Concerning the Organization of the
    Church and Worship at Geneva"
    (Calvin and Farel), 96
Assembly Committee on Liturgy and Worship,
    53–54

Baird, Charles, 21, 24–25
Baptism, 108–11
    beliefs about, 8–9
    living out of, 110–11
    steps in, 109–11
    trivialization of practice, 108–9
Baptism, Eucharist and Ministry (Faith and
    Order), 59, 72, 86
baptismal rite, 268–69n. 12
    importance in *Book of Common Worship*,
    71–72
    preparation of, 60
Barth, Karl, 277n. 19
Benedictine monasticism, 264n. 13
Benson, Louis, 27, 28
Bethune, George Washington, 22
biblical interpretation, integrity in, 132
biblical movement, 28
biblical theology, recovery of, 46
Blake, Eugene Carson, 40
Blake-Pike proposal, merging Presbyterians,
    Methodists, and Episcopalians, 40
The Book of Alternative Services (Anglican

Church in Canada), 80
The Book of Common Order (1940), 27
  on offering of Lord's Supper, 114
  source for 1946 *Book of Common Worship*,
    36
The Book of Common Order (1994), 90
Book of Common Order (Knox), 29, 68
The Book of Common Prayer, 25
  daily lectionary from, 72
  source for 1946 *Book of Common Worship*,
    36
The Book of Common Prayer (1552), 68
*The Book of Common Prayer and Administration
    of the Sacrament . . . as Amended by the
    Westminster Divines in the Royal Com-
    mission of 1661 and in Agreement with
    the Directory for Public Worship of the
    Presbyterian Church in the U.S.A.*
    (1864), 27, 98
The Book of Common Worship (1906), 28–32
  borrowing from *Book of Common Prayer*, 31
  characteristics of, 31
  contents of, 30–31
  encouraging congregational participation,
    31
  festivals recognized in, 116–17
  music in, 76
  prepared for voluntary use, 31
  published before 1906 General Assembly,
    30–31
  sources for, 31
The Book of Common Worship (1932)
  development of and changes from 1906
    edition, 32–33
  liturgical calendar, increased attention to,
    117
  Lord's Supper not mentioned for Lord's
    Day service, 99
  music in, 76
  Psalter in, 71
The Book of Common Worship (1946), 35–37
  changes from prior edition, 36
  criticized for Episcopal influence, 36–37
  first full service of Word and Eucharist, 99
  influence of Episcopal-Presbyterian discus-
    sions, 36
  liturgical calendar, increased attention to,
    117
  music in, 76
  order of Sunday worship, 42
  sources for, 36
Book of Common Worship (1993)
  alternative texts in, 68–69
  authorship of, 146
  avoiding colloquial language in, 74
  Baptism, approach to, 108–11
  baptismal rite in, 71–72
  Baptism's formative character in, 9

blueprint for rebuilding church, 3, 6–7,
    19–20
bringing bodies into worship, 78
catholic, Reformed, and evangelical nature
    of, 79–80
challenging church to rethink understand-
    ing of worship, 19
commended for church use, 64–65
common lectionary in, 69–70
daily prayer in, 72, 120–25
Daily Prayer edition, 11
development surviving reunion and
    restructuring, 48
differences from previous resources, 67–81
discipline offered in, 125–26
ecumenical convergence in, 80–81
ecumenical impact on, 59–61
emerging from desire for church's reform
    and renewal, 5–6
first availability of, 63
forms for daily prayer, 11
four reforms embodied in, 108
gender-inclusive language in, 73–74
goals of, 19
great thanksgivings, 69
guidelines for worship leaders in preparing
    own prayers, 80
inclusive-language Psalter in, 71
incorporating earlier gender-inclusive lan-
    guage suggestions, 45
international ecumenical acclaim for,
    65–66
liturgical calendar, approach to, 70–71,
    116–19
living expression of worship of whole
    church, 7
Lord's Supper, approach to, 111–16
mission as recurring theme, 16
observing liturgical year, 14
pastoral offices in, 72–73
pew edition not available, 75–76
prayers of intercession, 69
prayers for various occasions, 73
preparing final draft, 62
preserving contributions of *Worshipbook*,
    68
priority on restoring weekly celebration of
    Lord's Supper, 112
Psalter in, 57
purpose of, 139–40
recovery of, xii
reflecting evolution of liturgical calendar,
    117
reinforcing Word and Eucharist as norma-
    tive for Lord's Day service, 100–102
reminder of Eucharist's importance, 93
restoring centrality of Scripture in liturgy,
    11

Book of Common Worship (1993) *(continued)*
    revision proceeding after updating of
        Directory of Worship, 39
    "Service of Light," 122
    Service for the Lord's Day, 10, 68–69
    software edition, 65, 76, 90
    sources of, 143–46
    strengths of, 91
    subversiveness of, 7
    testing of approach to Eucharist, 101
    theocentric focus of, 8
    title of, 67–68
    tool for reinforcing faith, 134
    triduum in, 118
    underscoring importance of music in
        liturgy, 76, 77–78
The Book of Common Worship: Provisional Ser-
    vices and Lectionary for the Christian
    Year, 41
book on forms of service, opposition to, 29, 30
The Book of Occasional Services (1999), 65
The Book of Order, xii
book of services
    Presbyterian recovery of, 21
    providing depth and direction to praying,
        xi
    providing orders and liturgical texts, xii
    reinforcing catholicity of the church, 12
    revitalizing use of directory, xii
    for voluntary use, xii
Brand, Eugene L., 84
Brenner, Scott E., 37, 41, 43–44
Briner, Lewis A., 38, 44, 70
Brown, James D., 65
Brown, Robert McAfee, 38, 41, 87
Brueggemann, Walter, 108
Bucer, Martin, 22
burning bush, symbol and tradition of, 136–37
Byrne, Patrick, 59

Cahill, Thomas, 138
called by God, 8–9
Call to Worship, 40
Calvin, John, 5, 29, 34–35, 87, 128
    eucharistic legacy of, 94–97
    The Form of Prayers According to the Custom
        of the Early Church, 13
    liturgical expectations, 134
    liturgy of, 21, 22
    sacraments as essence of the church, 95–96
Calvinistic Liturgy, Church of Strasburg, 29
catechumenate process, 273–74n. 2
catholic, 12–14
catholicity, eroding sense of, 13
Catholic lectionary, revising for Presbyterian
    use, 44
ceremonial, 78
Chalmers, Dwight, 41

children and youth services, in 1946 *Book of*
    Common Worship, 36
Christ, union with, 114–15
Christian Faith and Life curriculum, 46
Christian festivals, loss of, 116
Christian life, worship at core of, 128
Christian Marriage (1986), 57, 73
Christian Ordinances of the Netherlands Con-
    gregations, 29
church
    community of hope, 15–16
    community of memory, 14–16
    countercultural nature of, 131
    living in God's future, 15
    meaning of reform to, 6
    negative effects of quest for self-preserva-
        tion, 20
    observing liturgical year, 14
    relationship with secular culture, 6
    splintering of, 85
    threat of secularism and individualism to,
        7–8, 85, 132
Church of England, online availability of
    prayer book, 90
Church(es) of Christ Uniting, 87
Churches Uniting in Christ, 88–89
church life, discipline needed in, 4, 5
Church of Scotland, 90, 136
Church Service Society, 39–40
Church of South India, *Book of Common Wor-*
    ship, 40
COCU. *See* Consultation on Church Union
Comegys, Benjamin Bartis, 27
Commission on Worship of the Consultation
    on Church Union, 40, 271n. 17
Committee on the Book of Common Worship,
    35–36, 37, 41
Committee on Forms of Service, 28–29
common
    importance of, 67
    levels of meaning, 7
common lectionary, adoption of, 69–70
common prayer, 17–18
common worship, Protestant roots of, 22
Common Worship (Church of England), 90
communing, importance of, 96–97
Communion, comfort with infrequency of,
    97–99
compline, 122–23
Confession of 1967, 178
Confiteor, 225n. 503
congregational participation
    encouraged in *Book of Common Worship*
        (1906), 31
    increased in 1946 *Book of Common Wor-*
        ship, 36
Constantinian Christendom, 131, 132
Constitution on the Sacred Liturgy, 40

Consultation on Church Union, 40, 59, 69, 87, 89
Consultation on Common Texts, 41, 60, 69–70, 83, 89, 271n. 17
conversion, 127–31
Cook, Merrill, 65
Costen, Melva W., 62, 65
Cranmer, Thomas, 22, 34, 87
Cumberland Presbyterian Church, 38, 55
    adopting Book of Common Worship, 65
Curbow, Joan Zwagerman, 129

daily lectionary, 72
Daily Office, 120
daily office, silence in, 124
daily prayer, 11
    communal nature of, 120
    following daily cycle, 121–23
    importance in Book of Common Worship, 72
    occasions for, 124–25
    psalms and Scripture readings, 123–24
Daily Prayer (1987), 57, 64
Daniels, Harold M., 50, 65
Dawn, Marva J., 130
denominationalism, 35
Detscher, Alan, 60, 61
The Directory for the Publique Worship of God (Westminster Directory), 23
Directory of the Westminster Assembly, 38
directory for worship. See Book of Order
Directory for Worship (United Presbyterian Church, 1961), 38, 39, 99, 102
    influence on Lord's Day service in Worship-book, 42–43
    study guide for, 46
Directory for the Worship of God, 98, 99
Directory for the Worship and Work of the Church (1963), 39
Disciples of Christ, adopting Presbyterian lectionary, 69
discipleship
    actions of, 4
    response of as goal of Book of Common Worship, 19
discipline, inviting church into, 125–26
diversity, finding unity in, 89–91
"Divine Service for the Lord's Day," 98–99
Division of National Mission, 52
Dobler, David, 65
Duba, Arlo D., 50, 123, 267n. 6

Easter, 14
Ecumenical Century, 35
ecumenical movement, 28
    convergence with liturgical movement, 37, 83–85
    strengthening of, 34

ecumenism
    in baptismal rite, 71–72
    behind Book of Common Worship, 59–61
    in Book of Common Worship, 80–81
    grassroots, 84
    in lectionary, 111
    new directions in, 85–88
    reconciliation and mutual recognition as aspects of, 85–86
    three stages of, 86–87
Edward VI, 22
English church, party lines emerging within, 23
English Language Liturgical Commission, 83
English Language Liturgical Consultation, 60, 89, 271n. 17
English Reformation, 22–23
Epiphany, 223–24
Episcopalians, altering Roman Catholic lectionary for own use, 69
Episcopal influence on 1946 Book of Common Worship, 36–37
Episcopal/Lutheran Concordat, 271n. 19
Espy, George, 65
Eucharist
    add-on to preaching service, 98
    Calvin's legacy, 94–97
    changing direction in frequency of celebration, 99–100
    core of church's life, 92–93
    distorting practices and beliefs of, 93
    dramatic increase in celebration of, 102–3
    frequency determined locally, 98–99
    frequency as issue, 96–97
    fundamental to liturgy, 9–10
    loss of centrality of, 93–94
    means of grace, 95–96
    memory and hope joined, 15–16
    objective of unifying Lord's Supper and Lord's Day, 103
    possible effects of failure to restore, 104
    real presence in, 271–72n. 7
    reasons for failing to fully restore, 103–4
    recovery of as centerpiece of liturgical reform, 92–104
    reminder of church's mission, 16
    restoration of, 10
    weekly, 96–97
    Zwingli's influence on practice of, 94
eucharistic prayer, 16, 113–16, 265n. 5
Euchologion: A Book of Common Order, 27
Eutaxia, or the Presbyterian Liturgies: Historical Sketches, 21, 24, 25
evangelical feasts, 116
evening prayer, 122–23

faith
    communal nature of, 7
    maturing in, 9

faith *(continued)*
  renewal of as goal of *Book of Common Worship*, 19
Faith and Order Conference (1937), 35
Faith and Order movement, 35, 37, 59, 83, 86
Farel, Guillaume, 95, 96–97
Fife, John, 65
fixed prayer, dismissed as canned prayer, 31–32
Fleischner, Eva, 122
Flue, Aurelia, 277n. 18
The Form of Prayers According to the Custom of the Early Church (Calvin), 13
The Forme of Church Prayers (Calvin), 68
Forme of Prayers . . . (Knox), 68
Forms for Special Occasions (Johnson), 27
Formula of Agreement, between Lutherans (ELCA) and Reformed churches, 40, 87, 89, 271n. 19
Fourth World Conference on Faith and Order, 41
free prayer, 17
fundamentalism, 132
funeral service, 73
The Funeral: A Service of Witness to the Resurrection (1986), 57

Gallen, John, 267n. 6
gender-inclusive language, 45, 60–61, 73–74
General Assembly
  adopting 1644 Westminster Directory for U.S. use, 24
  desire for church's renewal, 5
General Assembly Mission Council, 54
General Liturgy and Book of Common Prayer (Hopkins), 27
Genevan Liturgy, 29
German Reformed Church, source of liturgical reform, 26
Gerrish, Brian A., 114
The Gifts of the Jews (Cahill), 138
Glory to God (Gloria in Excelsis), 8
God
  knowledge of, 137–39
  presence and call of, 136
Good Friday, 14
gospel, movement reviving social dimensions of, 28
gospel events, trivializing, 118
grace, means of, 271n. 5
Great Thanksgiving, 113
great thanksgivings, 10, 68, 69
Great Vigil of Easter, centrality and power of, 118–19
Guéranger, Prosper, 264n. 13

Hall, Charles Cuthbert, 28
Hall, Douglas John, 133
handicapping conditions, hospitality for people with, 79

Hanson, Duncan, 48–49, 53, 64–65
Hauerwas, Stanley, 131–32
"Hermann's Consultation," 29
Heschel, Abraham J., 77, 133
Hickman, Hoyt, 56
Hippolytus, 92
Hodge, Archibald Alexander, 27
Hodge, Charles, 25
Holton, David, 60, 61
Holy Baptism and Services for the Renewal of Baptism (1985), 57
Holy Communion, celebrating with people unable to attend public worship, 73
Holy Is the Lord, 78
Hoon, Paul Waitman, 84
hope, 15–16
Hopkins, Samuel H., 27
Hotchkin, John F., 86, 87
human feelings, preoccupation with, 8
hymnal, preparation of, 75
hymnbook, living encounter with God, x–xi

"Inclusive Language—Definition and Guidelines," 73
Independents, belief in total autonomy of local congregation, 23
individualism, threat to church, 7, 132
Institutes (Calvin), 95
Interim Task Force on Women (1973), 45
interior life, nurturing, 4, 5
International Consultation on English Texts, 41, 83

Jesus the Christ, God revealed in, 139
Johnson, Herrick, 27
Joint Declaration on the Doctrine of Justification (Lutherans–Roman Catholics), 87, 271n. 19
Joint Office of Worship
  Administrative Committee, 50–51, 56, 58
  assuming responsibility for developing successor to *Worshipbook,* 52–53
  funded by three churches for revision to *Worshipbook,* 55
Justin Martyr, 92–93

Kerr, Hugh Thomson, 35
Kirk, James, 50–51, 52
Kling, August J., 53
Knox, John, 23, 29, 68, 94
  liturgy of, 21, 22
koinonia (fellowship of believers), 9–12

LabOra software, 76
Lackey, Wesley D., 54
Langford, Norman, Jr., 46
Lathrop, Gordon, 6, 20, 61, 130–31
laypersons, worship training for, 19

lectionary
    complete in 1946 *Book of Common Worship,*
        36
    growing acceptance and use of, 11, 111–12
    purpose of, 43–44
    two-year, 124
Lewis, C. S., 263n. 35
Liebert, Marion, 55
liturgical calendar, 70–71, 116–19
    ecumenical consensus about, 117
    loss and recovery of, 116–17
    misunderstanding of, 118
    new appreciation of, 14
Liturgical Conference, 37, 83, 89
liturgical forms
    harmonious with Presbyterian principles,
        29
    rejection of, 23
liturgical integrity, 133–35
liturgical leadership, improving skills in, 19
liturgical movement, 82–83
    concurrent with other reforming move-
        ments, 28
    convergence with ecumenical movement,
        37, 83–85
    influence on new Directory for Worship,
        38
    origin of, 264n. 13
liturgical practice, lowest point for, 24
liturgical prayer
    bifocal nature of, 12
    suspicion of, 17
Liturgical Press, 61
liturgical reform, 13, 18
    agenda for, xii
    call to (mid-nineteenth century), 24–26
    calls for, 21–22, 29
    Eucharistic recovery as centerpiece, 92–104
    Mercersburg movement, 26
    obstacles to, 17–19
    sixteenth and seventeenth centuries, 22–23
liturgical theology, 17
liturgical training, 263n. 34
liturgical year, emphasized in 1946 *Book of
    Common Worship,* 36
The Liturgical Year (1992), 57, 118, 119
liturgy
    balancing Word and Sacrament, 22
    caution about changes in, 263n. 35
    centrality in ecumenical discussions, 84
    as conversion, 127–31
    Eucharist fundamental to, 9–10
    growing focus on shape of, 90–91
    heart of theology, 35
    importance of familiarity with, 263n. 35
    importance of music in, 77–78
    Lutherans' contribution to Presbyterian
        understanding of, 266n. 13

North American, 13–14
    recovery of, 4, 5
    singing, 76–78
    transformation effects of, 20
    treating with same seriousness as lectionary,
        19
    undertaking variations in, 135
Liturgy of the Palatinate, 29
liturgy of repentance and forgiveness, 73
Liturgy of St. Basil, 187n. 119
local, 12–14
Loetscher, Lefferts A., 132
Lord's Supper, 111–16
    central part of liturgy, 4–5
    earliest Christians' understanding of,
        115–16
    gratefully remembering, 113–14
    invoking, 114–15
    offering, 114
    recovery of, 112
Lucernarium, 122
Luther, Martin, 95
Lutheran Book of Worship, 72, 80, 130–31
Lutheran-Episcopal Concordat, 87
Lutheran-Reformed Declaration of Agreement,
    87
Lutherans
    altering Roman Catholic lectionary for
        own use, 69
    dialogues with other denominations, 40,
        86

MacGregor, Geddes, 3–5, 17, 261n. 1
Macleod, George F., 78–79
The Manual of Forms (Hodge), 27
The Manual for Worship, 37
marriage service, 72–73
Mary Tudor, 22
Maundy Thursday, 14
McArthur, A. Allan, 44
McKinley, Deborah, 65
megachurches, 132
Melanchthon, 34, 87
Melton, Julius, 25, 30
memorial, Jewish understanding of, 113
memory, 14–15
Mercersburg movement, 26
Methodists, adopting Roman Catholic lec-
    tionary, 69
midday prayer, 122
Miller, Samuel, 25
missa sicca, 5
mission, linked to worship, 39
missionary movement, 35
Mission Yearbook for Prayer and Study, 72
modern liturgical movement, 29
Moffatt, James, 131
morning prayer, 121–22, 219

Mudge, Lewis S., 32
music, with *Worshipbook* made clearly integral to worship, 46

Native American religion, adaptation for daily prayer, 121–22
Naughton, Michael, 61
Nevin, John Williamson, 26, 43–44
New School, attempted liturgical reform, 27
Nichols, James Hastings, 12–13, 24, 25–26
North American Academy of Liturgy, 60, 83, 89, 267n. 6
North American churches, cooperation among, 88
North American liturgy, 13–14

O Antiphons, 190n. 131
O'Connor, Maureen, 63
Oecolampadius, John, 95
Office of Worship, 58
Office of Worship and Music, 52
Order of Worship, 26
An Order of Worship with Forms of Prayer for Divine Worship (Comegys), 27
ordination rites, incorporated into separate book of occasional services, 57
ordo, 68
Overture 10, 49–50, 51, 53–54

Parker, Joel, 27
pastoral offices, 72–73
pastors, lacking adequate liturgical preparation in seminary, 17
Paul, 128
Pelikan, Jaroslav, 130
pew book, loss of, 74–76
Pfatteicher, Philip H., 139–40
phased reconciliation, third stage of ecumenism, 86
piety, 4
Pike, James, 40
popular religion, 132
posture, language of, 78–79
prayer, preserving relationship between personal and communal, 7
Prayer Book (New Zealand), 80
prayer books, usefulness of, 18
prayers, silence and, 124
prayers of intercession, 12, 68–69
prayers of the people, 12, 68–69
"Prayers on the Psalms," 29
Prayers We Have in Common, 41, 60
Praying Together, 60
praying in unison, 17–18
praying without ceasing, 123
preaching
    importance to liturgy, 22
    increasing biblical nature of, 11

prefuneral service, 73
Presbyterian Association of Musicians (PAM), 75, 269n. 18
Presbyterian Church in Canada, 88, 136
Presbyterian Church in the U.S., 38, 52, 99, 136
    adopting Directory for the Worship and Work of the Church, 39
    approval of *Book of Common Worship* (1932), 33
    defeat of including liturgical year on directory, 117
    directory for worship adopted, 28
    Division of National Mission, 55
    endorsing *Book of Common Worship* (1946), 39
Presbyterian Church (U.S.A.), 43, 55, 136
Presbyterian Church in the U.S.A., 27
    authorizing book of worship forms and services, 28–29
    calling for revision of service book (1955), 37
    permanent committee on revising *Book of Common Worship*, 35
The Presbyterian Hymnal (1990), 57, 71, 75, 78, 267n. 1
Presbyterian polity, influence of collective wisdom, 12
A Presbyterian Prayer Book for Public Worship (Comegys), 27
Presbyterian Program Planning Calendar, 117
Presbyterians
    calls for liturgical reforms (pre-twentieth century), 27–28
    choices in worship styles, 18
    involvement in liturgical societies, 89
    liturgical history of, 21
Presbyterian worship forms, 28, 30
Presbyterian Worship Planner, 76
Presbytery of the Cascades, frustrated with *Worshipbook*, 49, 51
professional academies, Presbyterian involvement in, 60
profession of faith, in baptism, 109
Protestantism
    elements basic to reformation of, 4
    losing vision of the Reformers, 3–4
    worship's loss of integrity, 5
Provisional Liturgy, 26
Psalms, 123–24
Psalter, 57
    in *Book of Common Worship*, 57, 60–61
    inclusive-language selection in *Book of Common Worship*, 71
Psalter of the Church of the Province of New Zealand (Anglican), 60–61
The Psalter—Psalms and Canticles for Singing (1993), 57, 71, 78
Puritan party, 23

Ramshaw, Gail, 61
rationalism, effect of, 24
Reaching Out without Dumbing Down (Dawn), 130
reform
    meaning of, 6
    promise of, 19–20
Reformation
    consolidating efforts of, 34–35
    objective of, 12
Reformation Day, 87
Reformed, preserving tradition of, 132–33
Reformed Church in America, 38, 88
Reformed churches
    adopting Presbyterian lectionary, 69
    characteristics of, 79–80
Reformed liturgies, 21
Reformed Liturgies, 40
Reformed Liturgy & Music, 40
Reformers
    desire to reform one church, 79
    practices denounced by, 93
    purging liturgies from medieval church, 22
renewal, 6
Resident Aliens: Life in the Christian Colony (Hauerwas and Willimon), 131–32
The Revised Common Lectionary, 11, 60, 70, 258–59
revivalism
    contributor to liturgical decline, 24
    Mercersburg movement's attack against, 26
ritualism, avoiding in forms of service, 28
Roman Catholic Church
    changes in worship post–World War II, 37
    International Commission on English in the Liturgy, 37
    liturgical reforms from Second Vatican Council, 80
Roman Catholic–Presbyterian openness, 40–41
Rowe, Richard, 121
royal and episcopal party, 23

Sacrament, theology of, 103–4
sacraments, role usurped, 24
sanctification, 4
Sanctus, 40
Savoy Conference (1661), 27
Schaff, Philip, 26
Scripture
    central book in church's life, ix–x
    emphasized in 1946 *Book of Common Worship,* 36
    readings as part of daily prayer, 124
    restoring to prominence in liturgy, 10–11
    Spirit speaking through, 4
Second Helvetic Confession of 1566, 116
Second Vatican Council, 40, 44, 80

broadening span of ecumenism, 83
Decree on Ecumenism, 87
liturgical reforms following, 48, 59, 264n. 13
new service book called for in wake of, 48
seeking to reclaim daily prayer, 120
secularism, 7–8, 132
service books
    collaboration as alternative, 89
    coordinating with Directory for Worship, 38
    disagreement over contents (seventeenth century), 23
    ecumenical convergence among, 88
    future revisions of, 88–89
    online availability of, 90
    opposition to, 23–24
    process for developing *Worshipbook* and earlier materials, 51
    product of Reformation, 22
Service for the Lord's Day, 10, 100
The Service for the Lord's Day (1984), 57, 102
Service for the Lord's Day and Lectionary for the Christian Year, 41
Services for the Ordination of Pastoral Care (1990), 57
service for wholeness, 73
service of the Word and Sacrament, as norm of Christian worship, 42–43
Shepherd, Massey, Jr., 44
Shields, Charles W., 27, 98
Smith, T. Ralston, 27
Snyder, Dorothea, 54
Societas Liturgica, 41, 60, 83, 89
Solemn Reproaches of the Cross, 201–2
spirituality, 4
St. Peter's Church (Rochester, NY), 264n. 7
Stake, Donald Wilson, 53, 64–65
Stookey, Laurence Hull, 268–69n. 12
Strassburg
    liturgical reforms of, 22
    treatment of Eucharist in, 94
Stripping of the Church, 201
Studia Liturgica, 41
Sunday school movement, 116
Supplemental Liturgical Resources, 56–58, 61–62

Taizé Community, 37
Terwilliger, Robert E., 85
Tetragrammaton, 137
thanksgiving, in baptism, 109
theological discourse, integrity in, 132
theological-liturgical link, 35
Theology and Worship Ministry Unit, 58, 62
Three Days, unity of, 118–19
Thurian, Max, 10
topical preaching, 11

transsignification, 272n. 7
transubstantiation, Calvin's dispute with, 95
trial-use resources, 56–60
Triduum, 14, 70, 118

united church, increasing hopes for (1960), 40
United Church of Canada, 136
United Church of Christ, 38, 69, 88
United Methodist Church, 50
United Presbyterian Church, 99, 117
United Presbyterian Church in North America,
    37
United Presbyterian Church in the U.S.A., 37,
    38, 52, 55, 136
    Advisory Council on Discipleship and
        Worship, 52
    overture made to prepare new book of wor-
        ship (1980), 49–50
unity in diversity, 89–91

van der Leeuw, Gerardus, 35
van Dyke, Henry, 27, 28, 30, 32–33
vernacular Mass, first, 95
Vos, Wiebe, 41

Ward, Levi A., 264n. 7
Way of Worship: A Study in Ecumenical Recovery
    (Brenner), 37
Weaver, John, 269n. 18
Weil, Louis, 40
Westminster Assembly (1643), 23
    Directory for the Publique Worship of
        God, 23, 98
    tradition of, xii
Westminster/John Knox Press, 57, 61–62
Westminster Press, 57
White, James F., 50, 56
    on ecumenism of Supplemental Liturgical
        Resources, 59
    review of Book of Common Worship, 13
Willimon, William H., 131–32
World Alliance of Reformed Churches, 88
World Conference on Faith and Order, 35, 86
World Council of Churches, 86
world missionary conference, 35
worship
    anticipating Lord's Supper, 22
    appropriate postures for, 78
    as event, 90
    expanded resources for in 1946 Book of
        Common Worship, 36
    fundamentally theocentric, 8
    importance of understanding ordering of,
        134–35

importance of vitality in, 131–32
levels of meaning, 7–8
life-giving characteristics of, 6
needing disciplined church life, 5
participation in, 17–18
possibility for distortion, 4
primary means by which faith is reinforced,
    22
sensory approach to, 78
superficial styles of, 20
as theological expression, 17
The Worshipbook—Services (1970), 41, 100
The Worshipbook—Services and Hymns (1972),
    5, 41
    approach to Eucharist as most important
        contribution of, 100, 102
    break from Elizabethan English, 42, 44–45
    combining liturgical orders and texts with
        music for services, 73–74
    contributions of, 42–47
    development of successor to approved,
        54–55
    ecumenical approach to, 88
    evangelical concerns addressed in, 80
    first American Presbyterian service book
        with liturgies for morning and evening
        prayer, 120
    great thanksgiving, 69
    issues for successor book to address, 54
    lectionary taken seriously after advent of,
        11
    litany of intercession, 69
    liturgical calendar addressed in, 70
    psalms cited in, 71
    resources for Sunday and festivals, 117
    subjects proposed for development of suc-
        cessor book, 52
    sung liturgy in, 76–77
    vulnerability because of exclusive use of
        contemporary English, 44–45
worship folders, 76, 269–70n. 19
Worship and Music Conferences, 50, 65
Worship and the Oneness of Christ's Church,
    41
worship resources, individually prepared, 276n.
    36

YHWH, 137–38

Zurich, Eucharist little regarded in, 94
Zwingli, Ulrich, 94, 95